KV-191-023

7/94

ON

COPYRIGHT

FIRST SUPPLEMENT TO THE THIRTEENTH EDITION

BY

KEVIN GARNETT, M.A.
One of Her Majesty's Counsel

SIR JOHN MUMMERY, M.A., B.C.L.
One of Her Majesty's Judges of the High Court
Bencher of Gray's Inn
An Honorary Fellow of Pembroke College, Oxford

JONATHAN RAYNER JAMES, M.A., LL.B.
One of Her Majesty's Counsel
Bencher of Lincoln's Inn

International Copyright
GILLIAN DAVIES
of Lincoln's Inn, Barrister
Member, Boards of Appeal, European Patent Office
Honorary Professor, University of Wales, Aberystwyth

ART AND
LAW LIBRARY
UNIVERSITY OF
WOLVERHAMPTON
Not to be removed

Copyright Law of the U.S.A.
DAVID NIMMER, A.B. (STANFORD), J.D. (YALE)
Of Counsel
Irell & Manella, Los Angeles, California

Taxation
STEPHEN SILMAN, M.A.
of the Middle Temple, Barrister

Industrial Designs
ROBERT SKONE JAMES, M.A.
Chartered Patent Agent
Gill Jennings & Every, London

UNIVERSITY OF WOLVERHAMPTON
LIBRARY
Acc No. 872873
CONTROL
0421509708
DATE 17. AUG. 1995
CLASS 346.
0482
SITE AL
Cop

LONDON
Sweet & Maxwell
1994

WP 0872873 9

First edition by W.A. Copinger 1870
Second edition by W.A. Copinger 1881
Third edition by W.A. Copinger 1893
Fourth edition by J.M. Easton 1904
Fifth edition by J.M. Easton 1915
Sixth edition by F.E. Skone James 1927
Seventh edition by F.E. Skone James 1936
Eighth edition by F.E. Skone James 1948
Ninth edition by F.E. & E.P. Skone James 1958
Tenth edition by E.P. Skone James 1965
Eleventh edition by E.P. Skone James 1971
    Second impression by E.P. Skone James 1977
Twelfth edition by E.P. Skone James, John F. Mummery
    and J.E. Rayner James 1980
Thirteenth edition by E.P. Skone James, John F. Mummery,
    J.E. Rayner James and K.M. Garnett 1991

Published in 1994 by
Sweet and Maxwell Limited of
South Quay Plaza, 183 Marsh Wall,
London E14 9FT
Typeset by York House Typographic Ltd.,
London W13 8NT
Printed by The Alden Press Ltd., Oxford.

No natural forests were destroyed to make this product:
only farmed timber was used and re-planted

**A CIP catalogue record for this book is
available from the British Library**

ISBN Main Work 0-421-39200-2
Supplement 0-421-50970-8

All rights reserved.
UK Statutory material in this publication
is acknowledged as Crown copyright

*No part of this publication may be reproduced or transmitted
in any form or by any means, or stored in any retrieval system of
any nature without prior written permission, except for permitted
fair dealing under the Copyright, Designs and Patents Act 1988, or
in accordance with the terms of a licence issued by the Copyright
Licensing Agency in respect of Photocopying and/or reprographic
reproduction. Application for permission for other use of copyright
material including permission to reproduce extracts in other
published works shall be made to the publishers.
Full acknowledgement of author, publisher and source
must be given.*

SWEET & MAXWELL
1994

FOREWORD

Edmund Skone James died on June 23, 1992, scarcely six months after the Thirteenth edition of *Copinger and Skone James on Copyright* was published. For over 30 years, and through five editions, he edited the book, first with his father, then on his own and latterly at the head of an editorial team. He brought to the work an encyclopedic knowledge of the subject and a painstaking attention to detail. His co-editors have lost a colleague and friend. Users of the book have been deprived of an editor of rare ability.

PREFACE

For the first time in its long history, the decision has been made to publish a Supplement to *Copinger and Skone James on Copyright*. This is a reflection of the rapid development which the law in this area is undergoing, both through the decided cases here and abroad and with the substantial changes which are in the process of being made to the Copyright, Designs and Patents Act 1988 to implement the various Community Directives affecting the law in this field. Following the decision of the House of Lords in *Pepper v. Hart*, it has also been necessary to look again at the 1988 Act in the light of the debates during the passage of the Bill through Parliament.

In relation to the changes to the 1988 Act which have been and will be called for to implement the Community Directives, the reader will find a review of the history of the Community measures starting at paragraph 1–51. The specific changes to the 1988 Act required to implement the Directive on the Legal Protection of Computer Programs have been noted up as appropriate. The Directive on Rental Right, Lending Right and Certain Related Rights should have been implemented by July 1, 1994, but the United Kingdom had missed this deadline. Consultation by the Department of Trade and Industry on the form of the implementing regulations has taken place and it is understood that draft regulations will be circulated to interested parties for comment in due course. Where possible, the likely changes which will be made to the 1988 Act have been indicated. Two further Directives remain to be implemented, namely, the Directive on Copyright and Related Rights Applicable to Satellite Broadcasting and Cable Retransmission and the Directive on the Harmonisation of the Term of Protection of Copyright and Certain Related Rights. These are required to be implemented by January 1, 1995 and July 1, 1995, respectively. As yet no proposals have been made by the United Kingdom Government as to the form of the implementing legislation. Probable areas of change have, however, been noted in the text of the Supplement. The Directive on the Legal Protection of Databases is still only in the form of a proposal, so that it has only been possible to signpost likely areas for change. The same applies to the Community proposals relating to Industrial Designs. Finally, Appendix H to this Supplement contains those Directives which have been issued in final form. Not all of the provisions of these Directives fit easily into the Anglo-American system of copyright protection, and no doubt resort to them will be required to help interpret the amending legislation.

As to the Parliamentary Debates which may now be relevant in the light of *Pepper v. Hart*, these have been noted up against the appropriate passages in the Main Work. In addition, the reader will now find in Appendix I of this Supplement a table of the complete Debates on the Bill and subsequent amending legislation, organised by reference to the individual provisions of the 1988 Act.

The loss of Edmund Skone James as the Senior Editor of *Copinger and Skone James* has already been referred to in the Foreword. For this Supplement, we are glad to welcome to the editorial team Gillian Davies, who has undertaken much of the work on the international aspects of the subject. Elsewhere, we are glad to acknowledge the help of Edward Bragiel, Amanda Michaels and Gwilym Harbottle on the sections dealing with the Copyright Tribunal, Community Law and Criminal Law respectively. We are also grateful for the work done by Julia Clark and Theresa Villiers in researching the overseas authorities. Our thanks too, to Mathew Nicklin and Jake Gavin, who have helped us with the proof reading. Finally, and this is no empty acknowledgement, we must thank the publishers for their usual patience with the Editors and their scripts.

We have been able to incorporate most of the developments which have come to our notice up to July 31, 1994. These included the decisions in *Ibcos Computers Ltd. v. Barclays Mercantile Highland Finance Ltd.* and *Panayiotou v. Sony Music Entertainment (UK) Ltd.* ("the George Michael case"), and also the *Practice Direction* of July 28, 1994 relating to *ex parte* Mareva injunctions and Anton Piller orders.

Lincoln's Inn.   Kevin Garnett
July 31, 1994   John F. Mummery
                                                  Jonathan Rayner James

HOW TO USE THIS SUPPLEMENT

This First Supplement to the Thirteenth Edition of *Copinger and Skone James on Copyright* is ordered according to the structure of the Main Work.

Together with the main Table of Contents, each Chapter of this Supplement has its own mini table of contents which correspond to those preceding each Chapter of the Main Work. There is a further table of contents for and preceding the Appendices. In each of these tables, whole sections of new material are denoted by bold type. The mini tables of contents to each Chapter have also been marked with square pointers next to those parts of the Supplement which change or add to corresponding sections or subsections of the Main Work.

Within each Chapter or Appendix, updating information is referenced to the relevant paragraph in the Main Work.

CONTENTS

APPENDICES

TABLE OF STATUTES

Isle of Man

TABLE OF STATUTORY INSTRUMENTS

TABLE OF CONVENTIONS AND AGREEMENTS

TABLE OF TREATIES

TABLE OF COMMUNITY SECONDARY LEGISLATION

TABLE OF UNITED STATES LEGISLATION

TABLE OF CASES

Table of Cases

TABLE OF EUROPEAN CASES

NATURE AND HISTORY OF COPYRIGHT

1. Nature of Copyright

Distinction between copyright and other similar rights: no copyright   **1–1**
in ideas. In *Total Information Processing Systems Limited v. Daman Limited*
[1992] F.S.R. 171 it was said that if there is only one way of expressing
an idea, then that way is not the subject of copyright, citing *Kenrick &
Co. v. Lawrence & Co.* (1890) 25 Q.B.D. 99. See also *John Richardson
Computers Ltd. v. Flanders* [1993] F.S.R. 497. In the same vein, it was said
in *Autodesk Inc v. Dyason* [1992] R.P.C. 575 at 583 (High Ct. of
Australia) citing *Lotus Development Corp v. Paperback Software International* (U.S. Dis. Ct.) (1990) 18 I.P.R. 1 at 25, that where the
expression of an idea is inseparable from its function, it forms part of
the idea and is not entitled to copyright protection. These recent cases
were concerned with the existence of copyright in computer programs, and generally such statements should be treated with caution.
The case of *Kenrick & Co.* was concerned with an artistic work,
consisting of a drawing of a hand holding a pencil in the act of
completing a cross on a voting slip (see § 2–24 in the Main Work). The
idea was not the subject of copyright and, the drawing not having been
reproduced sufficiently closely, there was no infringement. The true
position is that if the idea embodied in the plaintiff's work is
sufficiently general, the mere taking of that idea will not infringe. If,
however, the idea is worked out in some detail in the plaintiff's work
and the defendant reproduces the expression of that idea, then there
may be an infringement. See *Ibcos Computers Ltd. v. Barclays Mercantile
Highland Finance Ltd.* [1994] F.S.R. 275.

NOTE 3. A literary work now, expressly, includes preparatory design
material for a computer program. See *post*, para. 2–2.

NOTE 6. Although, *c.f. Tate v. Fulbrook* [1908] 1 K.B. 821 at 832, 833 and *Green v. Broadcasting Corp. of New Zealand* [1989] 2 All E.R. 1056 at 1058.

2. History of Copyright

1–21   **Early control of printing.** For a discussion of the prerogative and its residual status in the United Kingdom, see Monotti in [1992] 9 EIPR 305.

1–49   **Semiconductor Products.** Further amendments have been made by the Design Right (Semiconductor Topographies) (Amendment) Regulations 1991 (S.I. 1991 No. 2237), the Design Right (Semiconductor Topographies) (Amendment) Regulations 1992 (S.I. 1992 No. 400) and the Design Right (Semiconductor Topographies) (Amendment) Regulations 1993 (S.I. 1993 No. 2497). See *post*, paras. 20–208 and A-577L.

1–50   **The future.**

NOTE 96. The Court of Appeal decision has now been upheld in the House of Lords at [1992] A.C. 327. See *post*, para. 24–13 *et seq.*

3. Harmonisation of Copyright Laws in the European Union

1–51   The United Kingdom acceded to the European Economic Community (EEC) (now called the European Community (E.C.) and part of the renamed European Union (E.U.[1])) on January 1, 1973.[2] Prior to that

---

[1] The name of the European Communities, which encompassed the EEC, ECSC and Euratom, was changed to "European Union" with effect from November 1, 1993; from the same date, the EEC has changed its name to the E.C. Strictly speaking, all of the legislative measures taken by the Community have been in terms of EEC (now E.C.) law. Accordingly, references hereafter are to Community law or EEC/E.C. law, rather than to E.U. law. Readers should also bear in mind that with the entry into force of the European Economic Area (EEA) with effect from January 1, 1994, most Community law (including all of the copyright measures discussed below) extends to the EFTA countries (except Switzerland and, for the time being, Liechtenstein). See [1994] 1 C.M.L.R. 4 for a useful summary of the new (and old) terminology.

[2] For a discussion of the effect of the accession of the U.K. to the Treaty, in the light of the subsequent development of Community law, on the *exercise* of various rights enjoyed under the Copyright, Designs and Patents Act 1988 by the owner of copyright subsisting under that Act, see chapter 14 in the Main Work, and *post*, para. 14–1.

date, the Commission of the European Communities (the Commission) had not initiated any measures for the harmonisation of national laws in the field of copyright. However, in the last fifteen years the Commission has embarked on a programme of harmonisation of national copyright laws which, when fully implemented, is likely to result in far-reaching changes to the present United Kingdom copyright law, similar in impact to the changes brought about in United Kingdom legislation following the United Kingdom's participation in the work leading to the adoption of the Berne Convention for the Protection of Literary and Artistic Works (the Berne Convention) in 1886, and subsequent membership thereof.[3]

Directives for the harmonisation of national laws adopted by the Council of Ministers under Articles 100 and 100a of the Treaty of Rome are addressed to the Member States, which are obliged to modify their national laws so as to bring into force such laws, regulations and administrative provisions as may be necessary to comply with the particular directive by a certain date. Thus, existing and future Community legislation on copyright will exert a considerable influence on the future copyright law of the United Kingdom. It seems inevitable that, since the United Kingdom and Ireland are the only two countries in the European Union whose copyright laws follow the Anglo-American copyright tradition, the United Kingdom will be obliged to incorporate certain concepts of the Continental-European author's right approach to copyright into its law on the subject.

For newcomers to the field of copyright it should be explained that **1–51A** there are two basic approaches to the protection of the categories of right owners afforded protection in the United Kingdom under the Copyright, Designs and Patents Act 1988. The Continental-European approach to author's right (*le droit d'auteur*) is based on the protection of the individual author. A work is considered to be an expression of the author's personality and it follows, therefore, that only individual, natural persons may be accorded an author's right. The Anglo-American approach of *copyright* admits protection both of individuals and of corporate bodies and thus permits a wide variety of creative endeavour to benefit from copyright protection. Thus, in Continental-European countries, as a general rule legal persons, as opposed to natural persons, are not accorded authors' rights under the *droit d'auteur* system so that, for example, neither producers of films and sound recordings, nor broadcasting organisations are considered to be authors. To the extent that the beneficiaries of the Rome Convention for the Protection of Performers, Producers of Phonograms and

---

[3] See chap. 17 in the Main Work, and *post*, para. 17–9 *et. seq.* See also *Guide to the Berne Convention* (World Intellectual Property Organisation (WIPO), 1978) and Ricketson, S., *The Berne Convention for the Protection of Literary and Artistic Works: 1886–1986* (Centre for Commercial Law, Queen Mary College; Kluwer, 1987).

Broadcasting Organisations, 1961,[4] and film producers are afforded protection in *droit d'auteur* countries, they are protected by means of rights related to copyright, known as related or neighbouring rights (*droits voisins du droit d'auteur*).

A further distinction between copyright and *droit d'auteur* systems concerns the requirement, common to both, that only original works may be protected. The requirement of originality is defined differently in the various Member States. In Continental-European countries, originality requires a degree of creativity, whereas in the United Kingdom, original means only that the work emanates from the author and is not copied. The interpretation of the notion of originality has traditionally been reserved to the courts in both systems.

1–51B   The copyright harmonisation programme of the Commission thus has to steer a difficult course between these two approaches. The task is facilitated, however, by the existing common ground between the Member States in the field of copyright resulting from their common membership of the Berne Union (see *post*, para. 17–68).[5]

In the following, the history of Community interest in copyright is reviewed and attention is drawn to the likely impact of Community legislation on the United Kingdom law.

Detailed analysis of those Directives which have already been adopted, and either implemented or which are in the course of being implemented in United Kingdom law, are to be found in the relevant sections of the Main Work[6] and this Supplement.

The first call for action by the Commission in relation to copyright came from the European Parliament in a Resolution on the Preservation of the European Cultural Heritage in 1974. This asked "the Commission to propose measures to be adopted by the Council to approximate the national laws on the protection of the cultural heritage, royalties and other related intellectual property rights".[7] In

---

[4] Signed at Rome on October 26, 1961, the Convention entered into force on May 18, 1964. See § C-121 in the Main Work. The Rome Convention is not to be confused with the Rome Act revising the Berne Convention 1928. See also *Guide to the Rome Convention and the Phonograms Convention* (World Intellectual Property Organisation (WIPO), 1981).

[5] The Berne Union consists of those States which are signatories to the various Acts of the Berne Convention, which was adopted in 1886 and revised at Berlin (1908), Rome (1928), Brussels (1948), Stockholm (1967) and Paris (1971). Each revised text of the Convention is known as an Act, *e.g.* the Paris Act, etc. "The creation of a single Union, based on the principle of the assimilation of foreigner to national, with certain minimum standards of protection, and capable, by means of revision, of meeting world changes, allows recently joined countries to have international relationships with all the Union countries including those not yet bound by the most recently revised text of the Convention." WIPO, *op. cit.*, paragraph 1.7, n. 3.

[6] See § 20–208 in the Main Work.

[7] Resolution of May 13, 1974, paragraph 11: [1974] O.J. C62/6 and [1974] 5 E.C. Bull., point 2406.

response to this Resolution, the Commission put forward a series of policy documents on the subject of Community action in the cultural sector,[8] including some aspects of copyright law, and commissioned a number of comparative law studies[9] to examine various aspects of the protection of authors of literary and artistic works, producers of phonograms and performers,[10] in the EEC.

The need for a degree of harmonisation of the copyright laws of Member States came into focus during the late 1970s and the 1980s in the context of litigation which opposed the directly applicable provisions of the Treaty of Rome concerning the free movement of goods and freedom to provide services within the Community and the exclusive rights granted by national copyright laws, which were territorial in nature.[11] The need for such harmonisation became more urgent following the political decision to complete the internal market (defined by the Single European Act of July 1, 1987, as being "an area without frontiers in which the free movement of goods, persons, services and capital is ensured in accordance with the provisions of the Treaty") by January 1, 1993.[12] **1–51C**

The Green Paper. The Commission's first major step towards harmonisation came when, in 1988, it issued a consultative document, the Green Paper entitled "Copyright and the Challenge of Technology: Copyright Issues Requiring Immediate Action".[13] **1–51D**

---

[8] *Community Action in the Cultural Sector*, Commission Communication to the Council: [1977] 6 E.C. Bull. Supp. *Stronger Community Action in the Cultural Sector*, Commission Communication to the Council, 1982, COM (82) 590 final, October 16, 1982.

[9] See the following in the Cultural Studies Series: Dietz, A., *Copyright Law in the European Community: A comparative investigation of national copyright legislation with special reference to the provisions of the Treaty establishing the European Economic Community*, document COM. XII/125/76 (published in English by Sijthoff and Noordhoff, 1978). Dietz, A., *Le droit primaire des contrats d'auteur dans les Etats membres de la Communauté européenne*, document COM. SG-Culture/4/81–FR (1981); also published in German: *Das primäre Urhebervertragsrecht in der Bundesrepublik Deutschland und in den anderen Mitgliedstaaten der EG*, (Schweitzer Verlag, 1984). Gotzen, F., *Performers' Rights in the European Economic Community*, document COM. XII/52/78. Gotzen, F., *Performing Rights Contracts*, document COM. XII/47/80. Davies, G., *Piracy of Phonograms*, document COM. XII/235/80, (published for the Commission by ESC Publishing Limited, 1981; 2nd ed., 1986). Davies, G., *The Private Copying of Sound and Audiovisual Recordings*, document COM. SG-Culture/39/83 (published for the Commission by ESC Publishing Limited, 1984). See also Duchemin, W., *Copyright Protection for Photographs in the European Economic Community* (1977).

[10] See also, with particular reference to the rights of producers of phonograms and performers, Davies, G and von Rauscher auf Weeg, H.H., *Challenges to Copyright and Related Rights in the European Community* (ESC Publishing Limited, 1983).

[11] See *post*, para. 14–30 *et seq.*

[12] Art. 8A: for the text see § F-4 in the Main Work. See also the Commission's White Paper, *Completing the Internal Market*, COM. (85) 310 final.

[13] COM. (88) 172 final. [1988] 6 E.C. Bull., points 1.2.1 *et seq.*

The Green Paper suggested a minimalist approach, taking the view that many issues of copyright law did not need to be the subject of action at Community level. Since all Member States were party to the Berne Convention and to the Universal Copyright Convention, a fundamental convergence of many areas of their copyright laws had already been achieved.[14] The Community's approach, therefore, should be marked by a need to address Community problems and any temptation to engage in law reform for its own sake should be resisted.[15] The Green Paper therefore focused attention on six issues which it considered required immediate action. These were: piracy (unauthorised reproduction for commercial gain); private copying (home taping) of sound and audiovisual recordings; the distribution right, its exhaustion and rental rights; the legal protection of computer programs; legal problems relating to the operation of data bases; and the role of the Community in multilateral and bilateral external relations affecting these matters. In the Commission's view, legislative solutions to these issues would promote, at the Community level, the protection, the increased status and the stimulation of intellectual and artistic creativity, which it considered a precious asset, the source of Europe's cultural identity and of that of each individual State.[16]

1–51E   Of particular interest were the general comments of the Commission, in the introduction to the Green Paper, as to the overall objectives which the then EEC should seek to achieve in its legislative programme for copyright protection. These were described as four-fold. First, to ensure the proper functioning of the Common Market, so that creators and providers of copyright goods and services should be able to treat the Community as a single internal market. Second, to improve the competitiveness of the EEC economy in relation to its trading partners, particularly in areas such as the media and information. Third, the intellectual property of Community nationals, which represented considerable investment in terms of finance and effort, should not be misappropriated by others outside its external frontiers.[17] Fourth, in developing Community rules on copyright, due regard should be had to ensuring that copyright was not used to create monopolies of undue scope and duration, and, therefore, to the limitations to be imposed on the rights granted in the interests of third parties and the public at large.[18] The central theme of these concerns,

---

[14] *Ibid.*, paragraph 1.4.9, and see chap. 17 in the Main Work and *post*, para. 17–9 *et seq.*
[15] *Ibid.*, paragraph 1.4.10.
[16] *Ibid.*, paragraph 1.4.4.
[17] See, in respect of one possible method of challenging misappropriation of intellectual property by others outside the E.U., *"Re Unauthorised Reproduction of Sound Recordings in Indonesia"* [1988] 1 C.M.L.R. 387, concerning the use of the New Commercial Policy Instrument, Regulation 2641/84: [1984] O.J. L252/1, against illicit commercial practices.
[18] Green Paper, paragraphs 1.3.1 to 1.3.6.

that of using copyright to create a favourable environment to stimulate and protect the creativity and investment of individuals for the benefit of the EEC economy, balanced against the potential danger, inherent in copyright, of creating anti-competitive monopolies, is one that mirrors the conflicts with which the European Court of Justice has been faced with in developing its jurisprudence in the field of industrial property rights. (See § 14–47 *et seq.* in the Main Work.).

The Green Paper was a consultative document, intended to provide a basis for discussion. It was not a definitive statement of the Commission's position, nor an exhaustive study of all problems requiring attention. The views of governments and interested parties (authors, performers, the film, recording and broadcasting industries and consumers) were sought and a series of hearings held.[19] The Green Paper was generally welcomed but gave rise to criticism in some quarters for concentrating on issues, such as piracy, home taping and computer programs, said to be of more concern to industry than to authors.[20] It should be noted, however, that the legal basis for any action by the Community is restricted under the Treaty of Rome. Harmonisation of the laws of Member States may only be undertaken to the extent required for the proper functioning of the internal market (Article 3(h)). Thus, the Community may only legislate, where differences in the legal protection provided by the laws and practices of Member States represent sources of barriers to trade and distortions of competition, which impede the achievement and proper functioning of the internal market, and to prevent such differences becoming greater. It may not, therefore, harmonise legislation for the sake of it, but only to eliminate differences with the objective of introducing the single internal market and ensuring that competition in that market is not distorted (*c.f.* Arts. 3(f) and 8(a) of the Treaty of Rome).

1–51F

The differences in the level of protection afforded to related rights within the Community were very much greater than any differences in the protection of authors' rights and there was therefore a correspondingly greater need for action by the Community in the field of related rights.

---

[19] 1. Hearing on the Legal Protection of Computer Programs (October 1988). 2. Hearing on Audiovisual Home Copying (December 1988). 3. Hearing on Rental Rights and Certain Aspects of Piracy (September 1989). 4. Hearing on the Protection of Data Bases (April 1990). 5. Hearing on Moral Rights (November/December 1993).

[20] See Möller, M, "Author's Right or Copyright?" in *Copyright and the European Community* (Gotzen, F. ed. 1989); Schricker, G., "Harmonisation of Copyright in the European Economic Community" (1989) 20 IIC 466. See also on the Green Paper generally, Dreier, T. and von Lewinski, S., "The European Commission's Activities in the Field of Copyright", *Journal of the Copyright Society of the U.S.A.* 1991, 96.

1–51G   **Follow-up to the Green Paper.** In January 1991, the Commission
issued a document, entitled *Follow-up to the Green Paper*,[21] which put
forward a comprehensive working programme in the field of copyright (in the sense of author's right) and so-called neighbouring or
related rights.[22] In it, the Commission stressed the need to harmonise
copyright and related rights at a high level of protection, arguing that
such rights are fundamental to intellectual creation, their protection
ensuring the maintenance and development of creativity in the
interest of authors, cultural industries, consumers and society as a
whole. It was proposed that the following legislative action be taken by
December 31, 1991:

> (i) A decision that the Member States should adhere to the 1971
> Paris Act of the Berne Convention for the Protection of Literary
> and Artistic Works (the Berne Convention) and to the Rome
> Convention for the Protection of Performers, Producers of
> Phonograms and Broadcasting Organisations, 1961 (the Rome
> Convention).[23]

> (ii) Proposals for directives on the following subjects to be laid
> before the Council on:
>> (1) rental right, lending right and certain related rights;
>> (2) home copying of sound and audiovisual recordings;
>> (3) harmonisation of the legal protection of data bases;
>> (4) harmonisation of the term of protection for copyright and
>> certain related rights;
>> (5) harmonisation of copyright rules applicable to satellite
>> broadcasting and cable transmission.[24]

The Commission also announced its intention to study the need for
action on the following issues before the end of 1992: moral rights,
reprography, artist's resale right and the collective management of
copyright and related rights and collecting societies (see *post*, para.
1–60). By that date, the Commission also proposed to consolidate the

---

[21] *Follow-up to the Green Paper: Working Programme of the Commission in the Field of Copyright
and Neighbouring Rights*, Commission Communication to the Council, document
COM. (584) 90 final, January 17, 1991.

[22] Terms applied to the rights of the beneficiaries of the Rome Convention for the
Protection of Performers, Producers of Phonograms and Broadcasting Organisations 1961. Hereinafter, the term "related rights", also used by the Commission in
recent directives, is used.

[23] All Member States are party to the Berne Convention. However, Belgium and
Ireland are not parties to the Paris Act 1971 thereof. At the date of writing, Belgium
and Portugal have not adhered to the Rome Convention.

[24] *Follow-up to the Green Paper*, p. 39.

role of the Community in the field of bilateral and multilateral external relations and to establish an inventory of the intellectual property situation in certain non-Member States.[24a] The Commission stated that in its work it would be guided by two principles: the need to strengthen the protection of copyright and related rights, and the need for a comprehensive approach, aiming at a basic level of harmonisation, common to all Member States, of those aspects of copyright and related rights which might have implications for the creation of the internal market.

Present State of Community Legislation. To date, four legislative   **1–52** texts have been adopted by the Council of Ministers and one proposed text rejected. Those that have been adopted are the following: (1) the Directive on the legal protection of computer programs of May 14, 1991[25]; (2) the Directive on rental right and lending right and on certain rights related to copyright in the field of intellectual property, of November 19, 1992[26]; (3) the Directive on the coordination of certain rules concerning copyright and rights related to copyright applicable to satellite broadcasting and cable retransmission of September 27, 1993[27]; (4) and the Directive harmonising the term of protection of copyright and certain related rights of October 29, 1993.[28] The proposal which did not obtain the support of the Council of Ministers was that concerning the adherence of Member States to the Paris Act 1971 of the Berne Convention and the Rome Convention. It should also be noted that, in a separate, but related field, the Council of Ministers adopted a Directive on the legal protection of semi-conductor products as long ago as 1986.[28a]

Proposed Decision Concerning Adherence to the Berne and Rome   **1–53** **Conventions.** This was the first proposal for Community legislation in this field and was put forward in December 1990. A Council Decision was proposed which would have required all Member States before the end of 1992 to adhere to and comply with the Paris Act 1971 of the Berne Convention and the Rome Convention 1961. The proposal was rejected for political reasons in December 1991.

The Commission made the proposal, considering that adherence of all the Member States to the Conventions would provide a harmonised basis on which rules for copyright and related rights could be built. It would also represent a step forward in the fight against piracy of sound

---

[24a] *loc. cit.*
[25] 91/250: [1991] O.J. L122/42–46.
[26] 92/100: [1992] O.J. L346/61.
[27] 93/83: [1993] O.J. L248/15.
[28] 93/98: [1993] O.J. L290/9.
[28a] 87/54: [1986] O.J. L24/36. See § 14–46 and, as to the position in the United Kingdom, § 20–208 *et seq.* in the Main Work, and *ante*, para. 1–49.

recordings and audiovisual works. At the time, Belgium and Ireland were not parties to the Paris Act of the Berne Convention, while Belgium, Greece, the Netherlands, Portugal and Spain had not ratified the Rome Convention.[29] (In the meantime, Greece, the Netherlands and Spain have now ratified the Rome Convention, after having adopted new legislation on related rights.) Since the standard of protection, therefore, varied considerably among the Member States, the Commission's proposal aimed at eliminating the consequent distortions and at clearing the way for the internal market.

The proposal was rejected by the Council of Ministers, having been opposed by the Member States. It would have incorporated the Conventions into Community law, thus bringing them under E.C. (now E.U.) responsibility. This would have given the Commission negotiating authority on behalf of the Member States in the administrative bodies of the Conventions, at a time when there was no Community legislation on the subject-matter of the Conventions, and would have subjected the latter to surveillance by the European Court of Justice. The E.C. Member States were reluctant to relinquish responsibility on these issues to the Community and considered that other measures could be adopted to achieve the goal of copyright harmonisation and to ensure that all Member States adhered to the Conventions. The Council therefore in May 1992 adopted a Resolution instead, in which the Member States concerned undertook to adhere to the Paris Act of the Berne Convention and the Rome Convention by January 1, 1995, and to introduce national legislation to ensure effective compliance therewith.[30] Given the problem of piracy, this Resolution also invited the Commission, when negotiating agreements with third countries on behalf of the Community, to pay particular attention to encouraging such third countries to adhere to the Conventions and to comply effectively with the standards of protection provided for therein.

1–54   **Council Directive on the Legal Protection of Computer Programs.** The final text of the Directive was adopted on May 14, 1991, following a two-year legislative process[31] and the deadline for its implementation by the Member States was set at January 1, 1993, the date of the establishment of the internal market. The Directive had been foreshadowed in the Green Paper, in which the Commission had

---

[29] Belgium, Greece and the Netherlands had no legislation at that time on related rights. To date, Belgium still has no legislation on the subject and neither Belgium nor Ireland have yet adhered to the Paris Act of the Berne Convention.

[30] Council Resolution on increased protection for copyright and neighbouring rights of May 14, 1992: [1992] O.J. C138/01.

[31] The first draft of the Directive was published in January 1989: *Proposal for a Council Directive on the legal protection of computer programs*, COM. (88) 816 def–SYN 183: [1989] O.J. C91/4, submitted by the Commission on January 5, 1989.

announced its intention to submit a proposal for a Directive for the protection of computer programs within the framework of copyright and related rights. The Directive establishes that computer programs are to be protected under copyright law as literary works within the meaning of the Berne Convention,[32] thus following an international trend.[33] The aim was to secure clear and effective copyright protection for computer programs in all Member States, to remove differences in protection which had negative effects on the functioning of the common market and to avoid any such differences arising in the future by harmonising such issues as the beneficiaries and subject-matter of protection, the exclusive rights on which protected persons should be able to rely in order to authorise or prohibit certain acts, and the duration of protection.

By specifying that computer programs were to be protected as literary works within the meaning of the Berne Convention, the Directive effectively achieved an equally important aim for the Member States: that of integrating programs into an established system of international protection, bringing with it the advantages of certain minimum standards of protection and national treatment for Community software in the Contracting States of the Berne Convention.

On the question of authorship, the Directive defines the author of a computer program as the natural person or group of natural persons having created the program or, where the legislation of the Member State permits, the legal person designated as the right holder by that legislation. The restricted acts include reproduction, translation, adaptation, arrangement and any form of distribution to the public, including rental.[34]

During the legislative process, the draft Directive gave rise to considerable controversy.[35] It opposed the interests of the major manufacturers of computer software, on the one hand, and companies specialising in developing computer products compatible with those of the market leaders and software users, on the other hand. The major manufacturers sought a high level of copyright protection, whereas the developers wanted to be able to analyse existing programs by means of reverse engineering and software users were concerned that

---

[32] The Directive, 1(1).
[33] See chap. 17 in the Main Work, and *post*, para. 17–9A.
[34] The Directive, Art. 4.
[35] See, *inter alia*, Cornish, W.R., "Interoperable Systems and Copyright" [1989] 11 EIPR 391 and "Computer Program Copyright and the Berne Convention" [1990] 4 EIPR 129; Lake, W.T. *et al.*, "Seeking Compatibility or Avoiding Development Costs? A Reply on Software Copyright in the E.C." [1989] 12 EIPR 431; Colombe, M. and Meyer, C., "Interoperability Still Threatened by E.C. Software Directive: A Status Report" [1990] 9 EIPR 325; Miller, C.G., "The Proposal for an E.C. Council Directive on the Legal Protection of Computer Programs" [1990] 10 EIPR 347; Dreier, T., "The Council Directive of 14 May 1991 on the Legal Protection of Computer Programs" [1991] 9 EIPR 319.

the protection afforded would hinder the use and maintenance of software. The final text is a compromise which permits exceptions to the restricted acts in certain limited circumstances, *inter alia*, where necessary for the use of the computer program by the lawful acquirer in accordance with its intended purpose, including error correction, and to make it possible to connect all components of a computer system, including those of different manufacturers, so that they can work together.[36]

The Directive has been implemented in the United Kingdom by the Copyright (Computer Programs) Regulations 1992, which entered into force on January 1, 1993.[37]

1–55 **Directive on Rental Right and Lending Right and on Certain Rights Related to Copyright in the Field of Intellectual Property.** This Directive, first proposed in December 1990 and adopted on November 19, 1992, deals with two major topics which were already addressed in the Green Paper, the threat of piracy, and rental and lending of, *inter alia*, books, films and sound recordings.[38] However, it goes much further by providing for a harmonised legal framework for the protection of performers, producers of phonograms and broadcasting organisations throughout what is now the European Union.

One of the major areas where differences have existed hitherto between Member States is in the nature and level of protection afforded to performers, producers of phonograms and broadcasting organisations. In the United Kingdom and Ireland, producers of phonograms and broadcasting organisations have been protected under the copyright law, while performers have enjoyed related rights protection. In the other Member States, the situation has varied widely; some countries afford a high level of protection under related rights legislation to these categories of right owners while others afford them little or no specific protection. Likewise, the term of protection for related rights varies between 20 and 50 years[39] and, as already mentioned, not all Member States have adhered to the Rome Convention of which related rights owners are the beneficiaries.

The aim of the Directive, therefore, is two-fold: to eliminate the differences which exist between the various Member States as regards the legal protection afforded to authors and owners of related rights with respect to rental and lending rights by providing a harmonised level of legal protection for all right owners; and to strengthen the

---

[36] The Directive, Arts. 5 and 6.
[37] For a detailed analysis of the Directive and of its implementation in U.K. law, see *infra*.
[38] See chapters 2 and 4 of the Green Paper.
[39] See *post*, para. 1–57, particularly n. 68. On the Directive see also Reinbothe, J. and von Lewinski, S., *The E.C. Directive and Lending Rights and on Piracy* (Sweet & Maxwell, 1993).

position of right owners in the fight against piracy by establishing a minimum standard of rights of fixation, reproduction, distribution, broadcasting and communication to the public for owners of related rights.

As regards rental and lending, exclusive rights to authorise or prohibit rental and lending are granted to authors, performers, film and phonogram producers in respect of their works, performances, films and sound recordings.[40] However, Member States are free to derogate from the exclusive right in respect of public lending, provided that authors at least obtain a remuneration for such lending.[41] The Directive also seeks to protect authors and performers from signing away their rights by providing that, where they have transferred or assigned their rental right in a film or sound recording, they retain an inalienable right to obtain an equitable remuneration for the rental.[42]

Chapter II of the Directive on related rights affords the basic rights of the Rome Convention in relation to rights of fixation,[43] reproduction,[44] broadcasting and communication to the public.[45] In addition, it provides for an exclusive distribution right which is without prejudice to the rental and lending right and which may only be exhausted within the Community where the first sale in the Community is made by the right holder or with his consent.[46] The Directive also introduces related rights to authorise or prohibit reproduction and distribution for film producers with respect to their films.

Member States are obliged to legislate to implement the Directive not later than July 1, 1994.[47] (*Note*: The United Kingdom has missed this deadline. A consultative document has been issued to be followed, it is expected, by draft-regulations for comment.)

The majority of the rights provided for in the Directive are already   **1–55A**
provided for by United Kingdom law, but a number of changes to United Kingdom legislation will be needed to comply with it. For example, there is no provision at present in the United Kingdom for remuneration to be paid to authors for public lending of printed music and works of art. Under the Directive the principal director of a film must be treated as an author in addition to the producer, who is considered the author under the present United Kingdom law; likewise, rental rights are to be granted not only to producers of films and phonograms and to authors of computer programs (as in the

---

[40] The Directive, Art. 2.
[41] *Ibid.*, Art. 5.
[42] *Ibid.*, Art. 4.
[43] *Ibid.*, Art. 6.
[44] *Ibid.*, Art. 7.
[45] *Ibid.*, Art. 8.
[46] *Ibid.*, Art. 9.
[47] *Ibid.*, Art. 15.

present United Kingdom law), but to all authors and also to performers. Under the Directive, performers are given a statutory right to share in remuneration paid for the broadcasting and public performance of phonograms to producers, who now share such remuneration with performers in the United Kingdom on a voluntary basis. Under the present United Kingdom law, producers alone have a right to authorise or prohibit broadcasting and communication to the public of phonograms. However, according to a long-standing arrangement with the performers, represented by the Musicians' Union and Actors' Equity, the revenue derived from these rights is shared with performers.

1–56   **Directive on the Coordination of Certain Rules Concerning Copyright and Rights Related to Copyright Applicable to Satellite Broadcasting and Cable Retransmission.** This Directive was adopted on September 27, 1993, having first been proposed by the Commission to the Council in October 1991. Member States have until January 1, 1995, to bring their laws into line with it.[48] The principal feature of the Directive is that, in the case of communication to the public by satellite, it requires the broadcaster to obtain, by agreement, the authorisation of all the copyright and related rights owners concerned in the Member State where the broadcast originates.[49] Thus, the broadcaster will be obliged to clear the rights for the whole footprint in one negotiation, so avoiding the cumulative application of several national laws to one single act of broadcasting. In such negotiations, however, the Directive provides that, in arriving at the amount of the payment to be made for the rights acquired, the parties should take account of all aspects of the broadcast, such as the actual audience, the potential audience and the language version.[50]

With regard to cable retransmission of simultaneous, unaltered and unabridged programmes, the Directive provides for compulsory, collective administration of rights.[51]

These proposals were not foreseen in the Green Paper. The problem of harmonising Community copyright and related rights legislation in the field of cable retransmission had first been addressed by the Commission in its Green Paper on the establishment of a common market in the field of broadcasting, published in 1984 and known as "Television Without Frontiers".[52] There, the Commission had proposed that, in order to eliminate obstacles to the free flow of radio and television programmes by cable throughout the European

---

[48] The Directive, Art. 14(1).
[49] *Ibid.*, Recital 14 and Arts. 2(b) and (3).
[50] *Ibid.*, Recital 17.
[51] *Ibid.*, Art. 8.
[52] "Television Without Frontiers", Commission Communication to the Council, COM. (84) 300 final, June 14, 1984.

Union, once a programme had been broadcast in one of the Member States, the exclusive rights of authors and other rights owners to authorise or prohibit cable retransmission should be replaced by a system of compulsory licences. Right owners would have had a right to receive equitable remuneration for such cable retransmission but would have been obliged to exercise the right through collecting societies. A system of compulsory arbitration in the event that the parties failed to agree was also envisaged. Thus, once a right owner had consented to the broadcasting of his work in one Member State, it could have been rebroadcast throughout the Community.

This proposal, the aim of which was to overturn the *Coditel* decisions of the European Court of Justice,[53] found almost no support. The Court had ruled that the owner of a copyright work could rely on his right to prohibit transmission of the work without his authority in one Member State, even where the work had been lawfully broadcast in another Member State with the consent of the right owner in that State.[54] As a result of the strong opposition to the copyright chapter manifested during the consultation process, it was dropped from the final Directive, "Television Without Frontiers", as adopted in October 1989.[55]

The Commission subsequently returned to the subject in 1990 in its Communication on Audiovisual Policy[56] and in a discussion paper "Broadcasting and Copyright in the Internal Market".[57] The first draft of the Directive followed in October 1991.[58]

The Directive provides for a common minimum standard of protec-   **1–56A**
tion to be afforded to authors and owners of related rights in all the Member States in order to remove existing obstacles to cross-border broadcasting by satellite (whether by direct satellite or communications satellite) and cable retransmission caused by the differences between national laws. According to its preamble, the Directive sets out to harmonise legislation so as to ensure a high level of protection of authors, performers, phonogram producers and broadcasting organisations and to prevent a broadcasting organisation taking advantage of differences in levels of protection by relocating their activities.[59] As regards protection for the beneficiaries of related rights, the Directive provides for it to be aligned with the rights accorded to them under the

---

[53] Case 62/79, *Coditel S.A. v. Ciné–Vog Films S.A.* [1980] E.C.R. 881, [1981] 2 C.M.L.R. 362; and Case 262/81, *Coditel S.A. v. Ciné–Vog Films S.A. (No. 2)* [1982] E.C.R. 3381, [1983] 1 C.M.L.R. 49.
[54] See § 14–60 in the Main Work.
[55] Directive 89/552, on the coordination of certain provisions laid down by law, regulation or administrative action in Member States concerning the pursuit of television broadcasting activities: [1989] O.J. L298/23.
[56] COM. (90) 78 final, February 21, 1990.
[57] SEC. (90) 2194, November 8, 1990.
[58] [1991] O.J. C255/3.
[59] The Directive, Recital 24.

Directive on rental right and lending right and certain rights related to copyright in the field of intellectual property, referred to above.[60] This guarantees performers and phonogram producers remuneration for satellite broadcasting of sound recordings, but not a right to authorise or prohibit such broadcasting, rights which producers enjoy at present under the national laws of certain Member States, including the United Kingdom.[61]

The Directive guarantees authors the exclusive right to authorise satellite broadcasting and to exercise that right by agreement; owners of related rights are entitled to equitable remuneration.[62] Except in the case of cinematographic and audiovisual works, however, collective agreements may be extended in certain circumstances to right-holders not represented by the collecting society.[63] Existing agreements concerning satellite broadcasting may remain in force until January 1, 2000.

As regards retransmission by cable of broadcasts, the applicable copyright and related rights are to be observed, and authorisation obtained, on the basis of individual or collective contractual agreements between authors, holders of related rights and cable operators. Existing statutory licence systems are to be phased out by December 31, 1997.[64] However, such rights are only to be exercised through a collecting society and, where a rightholder has not transferred the management of his rights to a collecting society, the collecting society which manages rights of the same category shall be deemed to be mandated to manage his rights. If there is more than one such society, the right owner shall have a choice. In the case of failure to agree, the Directive provides for either party to seek the assistance of mediators.[65]

1–56B   Finally, the Commission is to submit a report, not later than January 1, 2000, on the application of the Directive and, if necessary, make further proposals to adapt it to developments in the audio and audiovisual sector.[66] This provision originated in an amendment of the European Parliament, which was concerned that the Directive should keep pace with developments in digital broadcasting technology. There is a concern that, in the future, digital broadcasting by satellite and cable will be used to operate new electronic delivery systems direct to consumers, becoming in fact a new means of distribution. Phonogram producers and performers argue that such

---

[60] *Ibid.*, Recital 25.
[61] Producers of phonograms enjoy the right to authorise or prohibit the satellite broadcasting of sound recordings in Portugal, Spain and the U.K.
[62] The Directive, Arts. 2 and 4.
[63] *Ibid.*, Art. 3.
[64] *Ibid.*, Art. 8.
[65] *Ibid.*, Art. 9.
[66] *Ibid.*, Art. 14(3).

electronic delivery systems will displace sales of recordings in the form of hard copies (pre-recorded discs and cassette tapes), thus undermining revenues and leading to a reduction in investment in recorded music. To enable them adequately to control this future market and preserve their reproduction and distribution rights, they seek the right to authorise communication to the public sound recordings by satellite and cable instead of a mere right to remuneration.

The United Kingdom at present grants rights to holders of related rights which go beyond the minimum standards of the Directive. For example, producers of films and sound recordings are protected as authors and enjoy the right to authorise or prohibit satellite broadcasting and cable distribution. Moreover, whereas most right owners are represented by and exercise their rights through collecting societies, this is done voluntarily and they are under no obligation to do so.

Directive Harmonising the Term of Protection of Copyright and   **1–57**
Certain Related Rights. The Directive was adopted on October 29, 1993, and must be implemented by Member States by July 1, 1995.[67]

The subject of term of protection was not discussed in the Green Paper. This was surprising since the periods of protection for authors and, particularly, for holders of related rights vary widely in the Community. Minimum periods of protection are laid down in the Berne Convention (50 years after the death of the author (*post mortem auctoris*, hereinafter p.m.a.)) and the Rome Convention (20 years), but Contracting States have been free to provide longer periods of protection and some Community Member States have done so. A majority grant authors 50 years p.m.a. but France (for musical works only) and Germany grant 70 years p.m.a. and Spain 60 years p.m.a. As regards related rights, no less than six different durations apply across the Member States ranging from 20 to 50 years from publication and/ or fixation.[68]

These disparities clearly create obstacles to the free movement of goods and services and lead to distortion of competition, since the same work may at the same time be protected in one Member State and not in another. Commission action on this subject was precipitated by the European Court of Justice, which in the *Patricia* case[69] ruled that, in the absence of harmonisation of national laws, it was for the national legislature to determine the conditions of such protection, including its duration. In so far as disparities between national laws might lead to

---

[67] See Directive 93/98, Art. 13, *ante*, para. 1–51, n. 28.
[68] 50 years in Denmark (from fixation), France (from fixation), Greece (from fixation), Ireland (from publication), Netherlands (from fixation), Portugal (from publication) and the U.K. (from publication); 40 years in Spain (from publication); 30 years in Italy (from deposit); 25 years in Germany (from publication or fixation) and 20 years in Luxembourg (from fixation).
[69] Case 341/87, *EMI Electrola v. Patricia and Others* [1989] 2 C.M.L.R. 413.

restriction on intra-Community trade, those restrictions were justified under Article 36 of the Treaty of Rome as long as they were due to the disparity between the rules concerning the period of protection and this was inseparably linked to the existence of the exclusive right.

In its *Follow-up to the Green Paper*, therefore, the Commission announced its intention of drawing up a directive on this subject[70] and a proposal was put forward to the Council in March 1992.[71]

1–57A The Directive provides for a uniform period of protection for authors of 70 years p.m.a., thus harmonising upwards to the longest period of protection in any Member State. The main justification for this prolongation is stated[72] to be that, under the Berne Convention, 50 years p.m.a. had been intended to provide protection for the author and the first two generations of his descendants. Since the average lifespan in Member States has increased, 50 years was no longer sufficient to cover two generations. Moreover, due regard to established rights was a general principle of law established by the Community legal order and, therefore, harmonisation of the terms of copyright and related rights could not have the effect of reducing the protection currently enjoyed by right holders in the Community.[73] The Directive does not apply to moral rights, presumably because in some Member States, for example, France,[74] such rights are perpetual. As regards related rights, the Directive set the period of protection at 50 years after lawful publication or communication to the public. This was also the period advocated by the Commission for related rights in the Uruguay Round negotiations under the General Agreement on Tariffs and Trade (GATT) (see *post*, para. 1–61).

In order to ensure full harmonisation, the date from which each term of protection is calculated was fixed, in conformity with the Berne and Rome Conventions, at the first day of January of the year following the relevant event.[75] The relevant event so far as related rights are concerned is the performance, fixation, transmission, lawful publication or communication to the public.

The preceding Directives on copyright and related rights made provision for minimum terms of protection only, subject to further harmonisation. The Directive therefore repeals and substitutes its own rules for the provisions of those Directives as regards term.

---

[70] *Follow-up to the Green Paper, op. cit, ante,* para. 1–516, n. 21.
[71] COM. (92) 33 final–SYN. 395: [1992] O.J. C92/6.
[72] The Directive, Recital 5.
[73] The Directive, Recital 9.
[74] Law on the Intellectual Property Code (Legislative Part), No. 92–597 of July 1, 1992, as last amended by Law No. 92–1336 of December 16, 1992, Art. L. 121–1: "An author shall enjoy the right to respect for his name, his authorship and his work. This right shall attach to his person. It shall be *perpetual*, inalienable and imprescriptible. It may be transmitted *mortis causa* to the heirs of the author."
[75] The Directive, Art. 8.

It is to be noted that film producers are treated, like in the Directive on rental and related rights,[76] as owners of related rights in this Directive, being granted a period of protection of 50 years calculated from first fixation or, if published, from publication or communication to the public. The Directive provides that the 70 years p.m.a. of protection for authors of cinematographic or audiovisual works will begin with the death of the last survivor of the following persons: the director, the screen writer (*i.e.* the author of the scenario), the scriptwriter (*i.e.* the author of the dialogue), and the composer of the music. Photographs are to be protected for 70 years as works if they are original in the sense that they are the author's own intellectual creation.[77] The Directive represents a departure from the standards of the Berne Convention which provides for a minimum of 50 years p.m.a. for works and only 25 years for photographs. There is, however, also a movement towards prolonging the period of protection under the Berne Convention to 70 years p.m.a.[78]

The trend towards extending the term of protection of authors from 50 to 70 years p.m.a. has not met with unanimous approval. It has been pointed out that it is seldom the descendants of an author who benefit from copyright after his death, but rather his publisher, and that no adequate debate has taken place in recent years on the justifications for longer terms in the light of the public interest.[79]

The Directive will oblige the United Kingdom to extend the period of   **1–57B** protection to "authors" within the meaning of the Directive to 70 years p.m.a. Owners of related rights as defined by the Directive already enjoy protection for 50 years.

A problem arises for the United Kingdom, however, in that the definitions of authors and holders of related rights in the Directive differ from those in the United Kingdom law. Under the present United Kingdom law, the producers of cinematographic and audiovisual works and of sound recordings are considered to be the authors thereof. As already noted (*ante*, para. 1–55A), the rental Directive has harmonised film authorship to the extent that Member States are obliged to recognise the film director as one of the authors of the film. Member States do not appear to be precluded, however, from

---

[76] See *ante*, para. 1–55.

[77] The Directive, Art. 6.

[78] See *post*, para. 17–9A, and Memorandum of the International Bureau of WIPO on Questions concerning a possible Protocol to the Berne Convention BCP/CE/I/3, October 1991.

[79] See, for example, Ricketson, S., "The Copyright Term" (1992) 6 IIC 755; von Lewinski, S. in (1992) 6 IIC 785; Dworkin, G., "Authorship of Films and the European Commission Proposals for Harmonising the Term of Copyright" [1993] 5 EIPR 151; Davies, G., "Copyright and the Public Interest", *IIC Studies*, Vol. 14, chapter 10 (VCH Verlagsgesellschaft, 1994).

considering film producers also as authors and granting them protection for 70 years.

On the other hand, the Directive specifically provides protection for producers of phonograms for a term of 50 years and there is no freedom for Member States to grant longer periods of protection as that would defeat the object of achieving total harmonisation of the duration of protection. Thus, even if the United Kingdom continues to treat producers of phonograms as authors, they will not be able to grant them the same period of protection as other authors under United Kingdom law.

The new terms will apply to all works and other subject-matter of protection still protected in at least one Member State on July 1, 1995.

1–58   **Proposal for a Directive on the Legal Protection of Databases.** At the time of writing, one further draft Directive, that on the legal protection of databases, has been put forward by the Commission.[80] Following consultation with the European Parliament, an amended proposal was submitted by the Commission to the Council on October 4, 1993.[81] The next step is for the Council to adopt a common position on the proposal before it goes to the European Parliament for a second reading. The proposed Directive is expected to be made final in 1994 and the proposal contemplates Member States bringing measures into force to implement the Directive before January 1, 1995.[82]

The Green Paper contained a chapter on databases and in it the Commission, without reaching any firm conclusions itself on these issues, requested comments on the following questions:

(a) whether the mode of compilation within a database of works should be protected by copyright and;

(b) whether that right to protect the mode of compilation, in addition to possible contractual arrangements to that effect, should be extended to databases containing material not protected by copyright and whether this protection should be copyright or a right *sui generis*.[83]

The response indicated strong interest in the harmonisation of the protection of databases and, at a hearing held in April 1990, right owners expressed overwhelming support for protection of databases by means of copyright. There was no support for a *sui generis* or related rights approach.

---

[80] Original proposal: [1992] O.J. C156/4.
[81] COM (93) 464 final—SYN 393: [1993] O.J. C308/1.
[82] The Directive, Art. 16.
[83] The Green Paper, *op. cit., ante*, para. 1–510, n. 13, p. 216.

In its *Follow-up to the Green Paper*, therefore, the Commission concluded that a uniform and stable legal environment for the creation of databases within the Community should be established without further delay, given the economic importance of the sector and the risk of distortions arising within the internal market.[84] The Commission recognised also the danger that, without such a uniform legal environment, investment in modern information storage and retrieval systems would not take place within the Community.

The databases protected under the proposed Directive are collections **1–58A** or compilations of data, works or other materials, arranged, stored and accessed by electronic means or analogous processes. Also protected are the materials necessary for the operation of the database, other than a computer program, such as its thesaurus, index or system for obtaining or presenting information.[85] The draft Directive adopts a two-tier approach to the protection of such databases. Copyright protection will apply if the database is original, in the sense that it is a collection of works or materials which, by reason of their selection or arrangement constitute the author's own intellectual creation.[86] No other criteria are to be applied, aesthetic or qualitative criteria being expressly excluded.[87] In such cases, the database will be considered a collection within the meaning of Article 2(5) of the Berne Convention. However, the Commission, recognising that many databases are unlikely to meet this requirement of originality, have sought to safeguard also the position of makers of such databases against misappropriation by providing for a so-called *right to prevent unauthorised extraction* from a database, to protect against unauthorised extraction or re-utilisation of the contents of a database for commercial purposes.[88]

The copyright in existing works incorporated into the database is not affected by the Directive, the owners of copyright therein retaining their exclusive rights.[89] Moral rights remain outside the scope of the Directive also, this aspect of protection being left to national laws.[90]

The author of a database protected by copyright is defined as being the natural person or group of natural persons who created the database, or, where national legislation permits, the legal person designated as the right holder by that legislation. Where a database is created by an employee, the copyright therein belongs to the employer unless otherwise provided by contract.[91]

---

[84] *Follow-up to the Green Paper*, p. 20.
[85] See the proposed Directive, Recital 13.
[86] *Ibid.*, Art. 2(3).
[87] *Ibid.*, Recital 15.
[88] *Ibid.*, Art. 10.
[89] *Ibid.*, Art. 2(4).
[90] *Ibid.*, Recital 22.
[91] *Ibid.*, Art. 3.

The duration of copyright protection of databases is to be that afforded to literary works, *i.e.* 70 years p.m.a. Substantial changes to the contents of the database will give rise to a new period of protection. The right to prevent unauthorised extraction will last for 15 years from January 1 of the year following the date the database is first made available to the public, and from any substantial change to the database.[92]

The usual exceptions to copyright protection permitted by the Berne Convention, including private, personal use, use for non-profit making purposes, and the reproduction of insubstantial parts of databases, are foreseen.[93]

In the interests of competition, a compulsory licence is introduced, however, to use for commercial purposes any publicly available database, including those of public bodies, which is the sole possible source of a given work or material, provided that the commercial purpose for requiring the licence is not for reasons such as economy of time, effort or financial investment.[94] The author or maker of the database is thus obliged to licence use thereof, subject to arbitration in the case of failure to agree on terms.

The beneficiaries of the right to prevent unauthorised extraction from a database are the makers of databases, who are nationals of, or have their habitual residence in, a Member State.[95] Databases protected by copyright will benefit from the international framework of protection of the Berne Convention. As regards the extension of the right to prevent unauthorised extraction to databases produced in third countries, the Directive provides for the conclusion by the Council of bilateral and multilateral agreements on the subject. The term of any such extended protection shall not exceed 15 years.[96]

1–58B   While the objective of the draft Directive to provide a harmonised system of protection for databases has been generally welcomed, certain of its provisions have been the subject of controversy.[97] Perhaps the most difficult question is the proposal that a database shall be protected by copyright if it is *original*, in the sense that it is a collection of works or materials which, by reason of their *selection or arrangement*, constitutes the author's own intellectual creation (Art. 2(3)). Although originality is a common requirement for copyright

---

[92] *Ibid.*, Art. 9.
[93] *Ibid.*, Art. 6.
[94] *Ibid.*, Art. 11(1).
[95] *Ibid.*, Art. 13(1).
[96] *Ibid.*, Art. 13(3).
[97] See, *inter alia*, Pattison, M., "The European Commission's Proposal on the Protection of Computer Databases" [1992] 4 EIPR 113; Hughes, J. and Weightman, E., "E.C. Database Protection: Fine Tuning the Commission's Proposal" [1992] 5 EIPR 147; Cerina, P., "The Originality Requirement in the Protection of Databases in Europe and the United States" (1993) 5 IIC 579. See also Chalton, S., "The Amended Database Directive Proposal: A Commentary and Synopsis" [1994] 3 EIPR 94.

protection of works in all Member States, the standards for originality vary.[98] In the United Kingdom, originality means only that the database is not copied and that it originates or emanates from the author, whereas under the Continental-European approach originality means something more; the work must show some creativity. Originality has been defined in Germany, for example, in relation to computer programs as requiring *a high degree of creativity* and to show *an author-based ability of selection, accumulation, arrangement and organisation which surpass the general, average ability.*[99]

The phrase *author's own intellectual creation* is the same as that used in the Directive on the protection of computer programs (Art. 1(3)) which was apparently adopted to indicate that the United Kingdom concept of originality was intended.[1] Recital 15 indicates this is also the case in this Directive, stating that *no aesthetic or qualitative criteria should be applied to determine eligibility for protection.* However, even if this is the intention, originality of content, according to the present United Kingdom concept, will not be sufficient to provide protection to a database. The author will have to show originality in the selection or arrangement of the content of the database. The selection or arrangement criteria derive from Article 2(5) of the Berne Convention relating to collections and compilations but appear to pose problems in the context of databases.

It has been pointed out that many databases are of value for the very reason that they are complete collections of the relevant materials, being comprehensive rather than selective in their contents. Likewise the arrangement requirement needs clarification, since the arrangement of material in a database is normally dictated by the computer program running the database and by the operating system being used on the computer and is not controlled by the author of the database.

It would seem, therefore, that, if the criterion of originality in the selection or arrangement is to be retained without clarification or modification as the basis for copyright protection in the final Directive, many commercially valuable databases will fall outside the protection of the copyright law and will benefit only from the new *sui generis* right to prevent unauthorised extraction from a database for a period of 15 years.

Other Proposals for Future Community Legislation. As mentioned above (see *ante*, paras. 1–51D and 1–51G), a number of other future Community initiatives in the field of copyright were forecast in the   **1–59**

---

[98] See Cerina, *op. cit., supra.*
[99] This definition of the Federal Supreme Court of May 9, 1985, was handed down prior to the adoption of the computer Directive.
[1] See Czarnota and Hart, *Legal Protection of Computer Programs in Europe: A Guide to the E.C. Directive* (Butterworths, 1991) p. 44.

1988 Green Paper and the follow-up thereto published in 1990. In its Follow-up to the Green Paper, the Commission announced that legislative action was to be taken on six issues by the end of 1991 (see *ante*, para. 1–51G). Though the Commission's timetable has slipped somewhat, action has been taken on the five issues already discussed; only one remains outstanding.[1a]

1–59A   **Home Copying of Sound and Audiovisual Recordings.** The issue which has not yet resulted in a proposal for a Directive is that of home copying of sound and audiovisual recordings.[2] This has proved to be another controversial issue and the Commission's position on the subject has shifted more than once.

In the Green Paper, the Commission pointed out that the topic of audiovisual private copying was ripe for discussion at the Community level for three principal reasons[3]:

(1) The industries most concerned claimed that private copying was causing them economic harm and had negative effects on right owners generally and sought greater protection.[4] These interests were opposed by interests favouring freedom for the public to engage in home copying, including manufacturers of blank tape and recording equipment and consumer organisations.[5]

(2) Measures had been introduced at the national level by some, but not all, Member States,[6] and by a number of trading partners among non-Member States[7] to compensate right owners, thus creating new divergencies in intellectual property law among Member States. That situation gave rise to concern that "the

---

[1a] See also *post*, para 20–64A, for the Community Proposals on Industrial Design.

[2] Home copying or private copying (sometimes called home taping) is the non-commercial copying of sound and audiovisual recordings for personal domestic use; in other words, it is the act of recording, in the home, the music from a pre-recorded record or tape, the film from a pre-recorded videocassette tape or videodisc or a radio or television programme as broadcast. For a recent, international comparative study of this practice, see Davies, G. and Hung, M., *Music and Video Private Copying: An International Survey of the Problem and the Law* (Sweet and Maxwell, 1993).

[3] COM. (88) 172 final, paragraphs 3.1.3 to 3.1.6.

[4] The main argument put forward by right owners today is that the practice of home copying is a new and widespread method of exploitation of works, which cannot be prevented but should give rise to remuneration.

[5] These interests deny that any prejudice is caused to right owners by private copying. See, for example, publication of the Home Taping Rights Campaign Office, London, 1987; Jerrard, D.G., "The Case for Digital Audio Tape: an Opportunity, not a Problem" [1987] 10 EIPR 279.

[6] The following Member States have introduced private copying legislation providing for remuneration to be paid to right owners: Denmark, France, Germany, Greece, Italy, the Netherlands, Portugal and Spain.

[7] See Davies and Hung, *op. cit.*, chapter 7.

divergencies may have significant, negative effects on the functioning of the internal market".[8]

(3) "New technical developments are increasing the ease and attractiveness of home copying of audiovisual material: high speed copying, improvements in the quality of home made copies, and now the arrival of digital audio tape (DAT) with its capacity for making perfect copies both rapidly and cheaply have raised new questions as to how copyright laws should deal with the matter." The question also arose how to secure the investment in time, effort and money needed for the creation of audiovisual works if technical developments make it possible to produce perfect, rapid and cheap copies on machines accessible to almost anyone.[9]

In its conclusions, the Commission recognised that the practice of home copying might cause losses to right holders to the extent that it could be a substitute for sales of pre-recorded material.[10] It concluded, however, that while royalty or "levy" schemes in existence should be retained where they already existed, if Member States considered such schemes the best way to remunerate right owners,[11] there was no need for action by the Commission at that time to make such schemes mandatory by harmonising existing schemes with respect to audio analogue products, taking the view that analogue products were becoming obsolete.[12] As regards video home taping, the Commission also considered that any initiative to generalise levy schemes would not be justified. It undertook to keep national legislation and technical developments under review to ensure that "appropriate action is taken if it becomes necessary".[13]

The Commission, however, did conclude that, with regard to digital audio tape, DAT, "Community measures to require a degree of technical protection would be desirable provided that they are technically feasible and properly balanced in respect of all the interests concerned."[14] Accordingly, the Commission invited comments on the desirability of technical solutions in general and, in particular, as regards digital audio recordings.[15]

The Commission also asked for the views of interested parties "as to whether it is accepted that levies should remain in those Member States which have introduced them, and could be introduced if

---

[8] The Green Paper, paragraph 3.1.5.
[9] *Ibid.*, paragraph 3.1.6.
[10] *Ibid.*, paragraph 3.12.1.
[11] *Ibid.*, paragraph 3.12.3.
[12] *Ibid.*, paragraph 3.10.22.
[13] *Ibid.*, paragraph 3.12.4.
[14] *Ibid.*, paragraph 3.10.5.
[15] *Ibid.*, paragraph 3.13.1.

Member States so wish in those countries which have not yet introduced them".[16]

1–59B Subsequently, the Commission continued to study the matter and to consult with interested parties. A hearing was held in December 1988[17] and a further meeting with interested parties took place in November 1989. During the consultations, the Commission's conclusion that there was no need to harmonise legislation on remuneration for private copying was much criticised. In its 1990 document, *Follow-up to the Green Paper*, the Commission announced that, given the need to complete the internal market, it intended to lay a proposal for a Directive before the Council on private copying in 1991. It stated also that it was favourably disposed to the general use of a technical system, known as SCMS (the serial copying management system),[18] which limits the copying capabilities of consumer DAT recording equipment, saying:

> "New technology is to be encouraged, but not where it would damage the interests of right holders and consumers. The SCMS satisfies these requirements by allowing copies to be made while at the same time limiting the practice; the user thus has the full benefit of technical progress. It also allows right holders to keep at least partial control of the exploitation of their works by preventing the making of the unlimited series of copies permitted by DAT technology."[19]

No proposal for a Directive has yet been submitted to the Council, although further consultations have taken place with Member States in the meantime and a working document was submitted to the Council in September 1992. No consensus was reached at that stage and, in 1993, the Commission, having decided that the issue required further

---

[16] *Ibid.*, paragraph 3.13.2.

[17] Record of the hearing on Audio-Visual Home Copying, Brussels, 1–2 December 1988 (Document 11/D/5069/89).

[18] SCMS operates by codes embedded into the digital information received by a DAT recorder and circuitry controlling the functions of the recorder. Based on the nature of the codes, the DAT recorder either permits unrestricted copying, or permits copying while labelling the copy with codes to restrict further copying, or prevents copying altogether. The technical standards for DAT systems, the Digital Audio Interface Standard (IEC–958) and the DAT Standard (IEC–60A124), were modified in 1991 to incorporate the system. In May 1990, the Japanese Government introduced administrative measures to implement SCMS with regard to DAT recorders. In October 1992, the U.S. adopted the Audio Home Recording Act (see *post*, para 18-41) which makes the incorporation of a technical control mechanism to prevent unauthorised serial copying of protected works in digital recording equipment and interface devices obligatory. The legislation applies not only to SCMS but to any other future system with the same functional characteristics certified by the Secretary of Commerce. See also Davies and Hung, *op. cit.*, ss. 5.1.4.3. and 5.2.3.

[19] *Follow-up to the Green Paper*, paragraph 3.4.

examination, issued a new consultation paper on the subject asking interested parties to submit their views by November 30, 1993. The document was specifically described as not representing a policy position or statement by the Commission.[20] It focused on the main policy issues under consideration by the Commission and indicated the various policy options available in relation thereto. Interested parties were invited to submit up-to-date information and data on the operation of the internal market in relation to private copying and responses to the following points or questions were requested:

- Should Community action be limited in principle to the harmonisation of the provision of a right to remuneration for private copying throughout the Community?

- Should the Community harmonise the right to make private copies?

- How should the Community provide for any exemptions from payment?

- Should the Community introduce detailed harmonisation of levy rates, percentage allocations to right holders and other causes (such as social or cultural funds) and the treatment of third country aspects?

- Should the Community harmonise on the products covered by levies—audio and audiovisual, analogue and digital media and equipment?

- Should the Community harmonise the way in which levies are applied, collected and enforced in the Member States?

- How far should the Community harmonise in relation to the application of copy limiting technology?

In view of the fact that no less than eight of the Member States have **1–59C** already introduced private copying legislation, it would be surprising if the Commission took no action to harmonise national legislation on this subject. If such harmonisation does take place, the United Kingdom would be obliged to reconsider its position and follow suit. To date, the United Kingdom has resisted the trend towards private copying legislation within the European Union, although like the Commission the United Kingdom Government has wavered on the issue. Following the recommendation of the Whitford Committee in 1977[21] that a "levy" on recording equipment, similar to that operated

---

[20] Consultation Paper on Private Copying, Directorate General XV of the European Commission 1993, paragraph 2.2.
[21] *Copyright and Designs Law*, Report of the Committee to consider the Law on Copyright and Designs; Chairman, the Hon. Mr Justice Whitford, Cmnd. 6732 (1977).

in the Federal Republic of Germany at the time, should be implemented, the United Kingdom Government in its Green Paper published in 1981,[22] invited public debate on the issue, but said that it was not convinced of the need for it.

Following this consultation, the government published a White Paper in 1986[23] in which it stated that it had decided to introduce a "levy" on blank audio tapes. This decision, which was announced in the Queen's speech[24] setting out the government's programme in June 1987, was subsequently overturned and the subject was dropped from the Copyright Bill introduced later that year and from the 1988 Act.

1–60   **Further Issues for Future Action.** In its Follow-up to the Green Paper,[25] as already noted,[26] the Commission discussed briefly the desirability of harmonisation in some other areas and announced its intention of carrying out further studies on these issues: moral rights, reprography, artist's resale right and the collective management of copyright and related rights and collecting societies.[27] To date, the Commission has not submitted any proposals on these matters to the Council.

The document also envisaged consolidation of the role of the Community as regards bilateral and multilateral external relations in the field of copyright and related rights. In the meantime, the Community, represented by the Commission, has played an active role in multilateral external relations in this field, for example, in the negotiations leading to the adoption of the TRIPS (Trade Related Aspects of Intellectual Property Rights) Agreement in the context of the Uruguay Round of GATT. The European Union (as it has now become) also claims competence to represent the views of the Member States, through the Commission, so far as concerns matters upon which the European Union has legislated are concerned, in inter-governmental meetings on the subject of copyright and related rights convened by the World Intellectual Property Organisation (WIPO), which administers the Berne and Rome Conventions.[28]

Furthermore, as a result of the establishment of the European Economic Area, which entered into force on January 1, 1994,

---

[22] *Reform of the Law Relating to Copyright, Designs and Performer's Protection: A Consultative Document,* Cmnd 8302 (1981) chapter 3, paragraph 23.

[23] *Intellectual Property and Innovation, presented to Parliament by the Secretary of State for Trade and Industry by Command of Her Majesty,* Cmnd. 9712 (1986).

[24] Queen's Speech: June 25, 1987. The Copyright Bill, without provisions for royalties for private copying, was introduced in October 1987.

[25] See *ante,* para. 1–51G, n. 21.

[26] See *ante,* para. 1–59.

[27] See *Follow-up to the Green Paper,* chapters 8.3, 8.4 and 8.5 and p. 39.

[28] The administration of the Rome Convention is tripartite and shared between WIPO, the International Labour Organisation (ILO) and the United Nations Educational, Scientific and Cultural Organisation, (UNESCO).

embracing the European Community and the Member States of the European Union on the one hand, and Austria, Finland, Iceland, Norway and Sweden and, under the conditions laid down in Article 1(2) of the Protocol Adjusting the Agreement on the European Economic Area, Liechtenstein[29] on the other, the latter have undertaken to accept the relevant *acquis communautaire*, that is, the general principles of the European Union Treaties and other legislation, including the existing and future directives on copyright and related rights, as interpreted by the Court of Justice of the European Union.[30]

In its bilateral relations, the Community (now the E.U.) has also been active in the field of copyright and related rights. For example, in the trade and co-operation agreements concluded in 1989 and 1990 between the Community and most of the countries of central and eastern Europe, the question of intellectual, industrial and commercial property was given particular attention, especially because of its implications for direct investment in those countries by Community businesses and for the transfer of technology.[31]

4. The TRIPS Agreement

The Uruguay Round of the GATT (General Agreement on Tariffs   **1–61**
and Trade) was concluded on December 15, 1993, after seven years of negotiations, and the final act was signed in Marrakesh, Morocco, on April 15, 1994. A successful outcome of the Round was the adoption of the Agreement on Trade-Related Aspects of Intellectual Property Rights, Including Trade in Counterfeit Goods (the TRIPS Agreement): see *post*, para. C–205 *et seq.*

The TRIPS Agreement is concerned, *inter alia*, with copyright and related rights. It sets standards for the 117 member States of the GATT ("Members") concerning the availability, scope and use of intellectual property rights generally, covering not only copyright and related rights but also trademarks, geographical indications, industrial designs, patents, layout-designs (topographies) of integrated circuits,

---

[29] In relation to the EEA Agreement, these countries are referred to as the "EFTA States". Liechtenstein has signed the EEA Agreement but has not yet ratified it, although it is expected to do so in due course. Switzerland, which is a Member State of the European Free Trade Association (EFTA), is not a Contracting State to the EEA Agreement and is not in a position to become a party to it, following the negative outcome of a referendum on the subject, which took place on December 6, 1992.

[30] See *Follow-up to the Green Paper*, chapter 7.5.

[31] *Ibid.*, chapter 7.6.

know-how (undisclosed information) and control of anti-competitive practices in contractual licences. It includes also provisions for the enforcement of intellectual property rights and dispute prevention and settlement measures.

According to the Agreement, GATT Members are obliged to legislate to provide the standards of protection laid down therein for the various categories of intellectual property right owners covered by the Agreement. Members are free to determine the appropriate method of implementing the provisions of the Agreement within their own legal system and practice.[32] They are obliged to accord the treatment provided for in the Agreement to the nationals of other Members[33] and to accord them treatment no less favourable than it accords to its own nationals with regard to the protection of intellectual property (national treatment).[34] As regards performers, producers of phonograms (sound recordings), and broadcasting organisations, the latter obligation only applies in respect of the rights provided under the Agreement. The Agreement also provides for most-favoured-nation treatment, according to which, subject to certain defined exceptions, any advantage, favour, privilege or immunity granted by a Member to the nationals of any other country shall be accorded immediately and unconditionally to the nationals of all other Members.[35]

1–61A   The standards of protection to be afforded in relation to copyright and related rights may be summarised as follows: Members shall comply with Articles 1–21 of, and also the Appendix to, the Paris Act 1971 of the Berne Convention,[36] with the one exception of moral rights falling outside the scope of the Agreement.[37]

Computer programs shall be protected as literary works under the Berne Convention and compilations of data or other material (databases), which by reason of the selection or arrangement of their contents constitute intellectual creations, shall be protected as such.[38] In principle, rental rights are to be provided for authors in respect of at least computer programs and cinematographic works.[39]

---

[32] The TRIPS Agreement, Art. 1(1).
[33] *Ibid.*, Art. 1(3).
[34] *Ibid.*, Art. 3. (This provision is subject to the exceptions provided for in the international, intellectual property conventions, including the Berne Convention and the Rome Convention.)
[35] *Ibid.*, Art. 4.
[36] See *post*, para. 17–9A.
[37] The TRIPS Agreement, Art. 9.
[38] *Ibid.*, Art. 10.
[39] *Ibid.*, Art. 11.

Terms of protection calculated on a basis other than the life of a natural person, shall be no less than fifty years from authorised publication, or in the absence of publication, from making.[40] Limitations shall not conflict with a normal exploitation of the work or unreasonably prejudice the legitimate interests of the right holder.[41]

Performers, producers of phonograms (sound recordings) and broadcasting organisations are specifically protected. Performers shall have the following rights: the possibility of preventing the unauthorised fixation of their unfixed performance and the reproduction of such fixation as well as the unauthorised broadcasting and communication of their live performances. Producers of phonograms shall enjoy the right to authorise or prohibit reproduction and rental of phonograms. Other right holders in phonograms may also enjoy a rental right therein under national law. The term of protection of performers and producers shall be not less than fifty years computed from the end of the year in which the fixation was made or the performance took place.

Broadcasting organisations shall have the right to prohibit the fixation, the reproduction of fixations, and the rebroadcasting by wireless means of broadcasts, as well as the communication to the public of television broadcasts of the same. The term of protection shall be twenty years from the end of the calendar year in which the broadcast took place.[42]

As regards enforcement, the members are obliged to ensure procedures to permit effective action against any act of infringement of intellectual property, including remedies to prevent infringements, which are expeditious and constitute a deterrent to further infringements.[43] Such procedures shall be fair and equitable, simple, cheap and timely.[44] The Agreement also lays down standards with regard to civil and administrative procedures and remedies.[45] **1–61B**

The Agreement provides for a dispute settlement procedure under the GATT.[46] This aspect of the agreement is of particular importance in view of the fact that there is no such procedure under the Berne Convention. The fact that under the Berne Convention there are no sanctions whatsoever should a member State thereof be in breach of its obligations thereunder was an important reason for the GATT TRIPS

---

[40] *Ibid.*, Art. 12. (This does not apply to photographic works or works of applied art.)
[41] *Ibid.*, Art. 13. (*C.f.* the Berne Convention, Art. 9(2)).
[42] *Ibid.*, Art. 14.
[43] *Ibid.*, Art. 41(1).
[44] *Ibid.*, Art. 41(2).
[45] *Ibid.*, ss.2–5, Arts. 42–61.
[46] *Ibid.*, Art. 64.

negotiations.[47] Under the TRIPS Agreement, should a dispute arise regarding the obligations of a Member, there will be the possibility of taking action under the GATT Understanding on Rules and Procedures Governing the Settlement of Disputes.

Transitional arrangements are provided for to give Members time to bring their legislation into line with the Agreement. In particular, the least-developed country Members are not obliged to apply the provisions of the Agreement with regard, *inter alia*, to copyright and related rights for a period of 10 years, which may be extended on motivated request.[48]

Finally, the Agreement establishes a Council for Trade-Related Aspects of Intellectual Property Rights to monitor the operation of the Agreement and, in particular, Members' compliance with their obligations thereunder.[49]

---

[47] It should be noted, however, that under the auspices of WIPO a Committee of Experts on the Settlement of Intellectual Property Disputes Between States has held five sessions to discuss a draft Treaty and Regulations on the subject. The aim of the Treaty, to be administered by WIPO. would be to establish procedures for the amicable settlement of disputes. A sixth session was held in February 1994. A Diplomatic Conference for the conclusion of the Treaty is under preparation and, according to the WIPO programme, is expected to take place in the biennium 1994/1995. For a report of the fifth Committee of Experts and the draft Treaty and Regulations, see *Copyright*, 1993, 121.

[48] The TRIPS Agreement, Arts. 65 and 66.

[49] *Ibid.*, Art. 68.

SUBJECT MATTER OF COPYRIGHT PROTECTION

1. Introduction

For a table listing the Parliamentary debates on these and other **2–1** provisions of the 1988 Act, see *post*, Appendix I.

2. Literary Works

Statutory definition. The statutory definition of "literary work" has **2–2** been amended with effect from January 1, 1993, by the Copyright (Computer Programs) Regulations 1992[1] (see *post*, para. B–279) specifically to include preparatory design material for a computer program: see *post*, para. A–6. The Regulations are intended to implement the provisions of Directive 91/250: [1991] O.J. L122/42 (see *post*, para. H–14 *et seq.*) on the legal protection of computer programs. For the full history behind the Regulations see *ante*, para. 1–51 *et seq.*

---

[1] (S.I. 1992 No. 3233).

It is not thought that the amendment makes any substantive change to the law. Preparatory design materials for a computer program, for example in the form of preliminary workings, would, presumably prior to this amendment, have been capable of protection as literary works. Design materials such as flow charts would presumably have been capable of protection as artistic works. The Directive requires Member States to accord protection to computer programs as literary works within the meaning of the Berne Convention, and specifies that the term "computer programs" is to include their preparatory design material. The Recitals to the Directive indicate, however, that such protection of preparatory design material is mandatory only where the nature of the preparatory work is such that a computer program can result from it at a later stage (see Recital 7; *post*, para. H–14.)

By regulation 12(1), the amendments of the 1988 Act made by the Regulations are stated to apply to computer programs created before, as well as on or after, January 1, 1993 (see *post*, para. B–279). On a literal reading this provision would not appear to apply to preparatory design material for a computer program, which itself will not usually have the necessary characteristics of a computer program (see § 2–9 in the Main Work) and is, by the amendment to section 3 (1) of the 1988 Act, given the status of a separate category of literary work. Such a reading of regulation 12(1) would result in the Regulations providing no transitional provisions in respect of such works. Clearly such works created on or after January 1, 1993 are capable of protection independently of any computer program created from them.

However, the position of such works created before that date, in so far as they were not protected under the 1988 Act, would be unclear. It is difficult to see any justification for such a distinction, in the application of the Regulations, between computer programs and preparatory design materials. Given that the approach in the Directive was that the term "computer program" should include their preparatory design material (Art. 1(1); see *post*, para H–16), and that the only derogation permitted in respect of computer programs (as so defined) created before January 1, 1993, is in relation to acts concluded and rights acquired before that date (Art. 9(2), see *post*, para. H–24), it seems clear that regulation 12(1) should be read as applying also to preparatory design material for a computer program.

2–4 **Written, spoken or sung.** The sentence beginning "It had been suggested that under the 1956 Act" should continue: "a literary work was required to be expressed in some form of notation".

For a discussion on the problems in connection with copyright in spoken words, see Phillips in [1989] 7 EIPR 231.

The last sentence of § 2–4 in the Main Work is supported by the discussion in *Hansard*, H.L. Vol. 490, cols. 828–829.

NOTE 9. **Add**: And see the discussion at the Report stage in *Hansard*, H.L. Vol. 493, cols. 1058–1059.

The work must take some permanent form.   **2–5**

NOTE 10. **Add**: See also *Express Newspapers Plc v. News (UK) Plc* [1991] F.S.R. 36, *per* Browne-Wilkinson V.-C. at 41–42. It is to be noted that in this case it was held to be arguable that there could be no copyright in a newspaper story which could be infringed by another newspaper reproducing that story in different words, since such a conclusion would be contrary to the common practice of newspapers in picking up stories from other papers and would confer a monopoly over the story which would be against the public interest. The position is not analogous to that of the novelist, who is entitled to a copyright in the plot in his novel, in addition to that in the actual words used (see *Kelly v. Cinema Houses Ltd.* [1928–35] Mac.C.C. 362 at 367, and § 8–130 in the Main Work).

NOTE 11. **Add**: This subsection was deliberately drafted in the widest terms, so that any recording of the work will give rise to copyright subsistence. See the debate in *Hansard*, H.L. Vol. 490, cols. 834, 835. This would include being recorded on computer: *Hansard*, the debates of House of Commons Standing Committee E in 1988, col. 23.

NOTE 12. After the first sentence. **Add:** *Walter v. Lane* remains good law; see § 3–26 in the Main Work and *post*, para. 2–10, n.64.

By whom noted.   **2–6**

NOTE 13. **Add**: This clause was added by a Government amendment specifically to allow the possibility that the recorder of a speech may have a separate copyright to that of the author of the speech, depending upon whether the former expended sufficient skill and effort to merit copyright: see *Hansard*, H.L. Vol. 495, cols. 610, 611.

NOTE 15. **Add**: See the discussion in *Hansard*, H.L. Vol. 495, cols. 610, 611.

"Literary work."   **2–7**

NOTE 16. **Add**: See also *RTE v. Magill TV Guide Ltd.* [1990] F.S.R. 561 (High Ct. of Ireland).

NOTE 17. **Add**: Two sentences did not, on their own, afford sufficient information, instruction or literary enjoyment to qualify as a literary work: *Noah v. Shuba* [1991] F.S.R. 14 at 32, 33.

NOTE 22. **Add**: In *Microsense Systems Ltd v. Control Systems Technology Ltd.* noted at [1992] I.P.D. 15006 it was held arguable (Aldous J.) that copyright subsisted in a list of three letter mnemonics, being the language code for communication with a pelican crossing controller. The list was the result of a development process involving the design of the controller itself. In *Anacon Corporation Ltd. v. Environmental Research Technology Ltd.* (Jacob J., April 21, 1994; unreported), copyright was held to subsist in an electronic circuit diagram as a literary work (as well as an artistic work). The diagram, which showed a large amount of writing and symbols and was a list of components together with information as to how they were interconnected, consisted of notation to be read by someone, as opposed to being appreciated simply by the eye.

NOTE 25. **Add**: This appears to have been the basis for the finding that copyright subsisted in a news story assembled by a journalist and consisting of quotations of the exact words used by the person interviewed by the journalist.

2–8   **Compilations.** First sentence. **Add**: see Monotti in [1993] 5 EIPR 156, arguing that the word "compilation" in the 1988 Act no longer includes a compilation including artistic material.

Second sentence. **Add**: a series of book-keeping forms consisting, individually and collectively, of a number of lines, columns and boxes, and a few words which were either headings or directions to facilitate the use of the forms: *Kalamazoo (Aus.) Pty. Ltd. v. Compact Business Systems Pty. Ltd.* [1990] 1 Qd. R. 231 (Sup. Ct. of Queensland).

If copyright subsists in individual works reproduced in a compilation, and these are reproduced by the defendant, then this individual copyright may be infringed: see *Longman Group Ltd. v. Carrington Technical Institute Board of Governors* [1991] 2 N.Z.L.R. 574; (1990) 20 I.P.R. 264 (High Ct. of New Zealand); and *post*, para. 8–31.

NOTE 31. **Add**: There may be copyright in the written schedule of programmes, but there is no copyright in a compilation of the programmes as they are broadcast during the day in accordance with the schedule: *FWS Joint Sports Claimants v. Copyright Board* (1991) 22 I.P.R. 429; (1991) 81 D.L.R. 412 (Fed. Ct. App. Canada).

See also *RTE v. Magill TV Guide Ltd.* [1990] F.S.R. 561 (High Ct. of Ireland).

For a full discussion of TV listings cases in the United Kingdom, Australia, New Zealand and Europe, see Watts and Durie in [1992] 4 Ent. L.R. 133.

NOTE 35. **Add**: *Fax Directories (Pty.) Ltd. v. S.A. Fax Listings c.c.* (1990) 2 S.A.L.R. 164 (Durban and Coast Local Division of Sup. Ct. of South Africa) (fax directory).

NOTE 55. **Add**: In *Total Information Processing Systems Ltd. v. Daman Ltd.* [1992] F.S.R. 171 it was held (Judge Baker Q.C.) that the mere linking of three computer programs did not produce a compilation in which copyright subsisted. A distinct copyright in a compilation of computer programs may subsist, however, provided it is sufficiently original: see *Ibcos Computers Ltd. v. Barclays Mercantile Highland Finance Ltd.* [1994] F.S.R. 275 at 290.

Computer programs. **2–9**

NOTE 57. **Add**: See now, as to the express inclusion of preparatory design material for a computer program, *ante*, para. 2–2.

Recitals 13 and 14 of the Directive (91/250; see *post*, para. H–14) make it clear that what the Directive seeks to protect is the expression of the computer program, not the ideas and principles underlying it. This is provided for expressly in Article 1(2) (see *post*, para. H–16). It has been suggested that where the expression of an idea is inseparable from its function, it forms part of the idea and is not entitled to copyright protection. See *Total Information Processing Systems Ltd. v. Daman Ltd.* [1992] F.S.R. 171 at 181, citing *Kenrick & Company v. Lawrence & Company* (1980) 25 Q.B.D. 99, and see *Autodesk Inc. v. Dyason* [1992] R.P.C. 575 at 583 (High Ct. Australia), citing *Lotus Development Corporation v. Paperback Software International* (1990) 740 F.Supp. 37 (Massachusetts Dist. Ct.), also reported at (1990) 18 I.P.R. 1 at 25; see also *Computer Associates International Inc. v. Altai Inc.* (1992) 23 I.P.R. 385 (U.S.C.A.). However, this statement in *Total Information Processing Systems Ltd.*, and the accompanying reliance on American authorities, were disapproved by Jacob J. in *Ibcos Computers Ltd. v. Barclays Mercantile Highland Finance Ltd.* [1994] F.S.R. 275 at 290–292.

NOTE 59. **Add**: See further, on the definition of computer program introduced into the Australian Copyright Act 1968 by the 1984 Act, *Autodesk Inc. v. Dyason (No. 1)* (1992) 104 A.L.R. 563; [1992] R.P.C. 575 (High Ct. Australia) (copyright may subsist under such Act in a set of instructions (if original) whether they are expressed in written form or are stored in a non-sensate form such as electrical impulses on disk, ROM or EPROM).

Copyright can subsist in the overall structure of a computer program, being a form of literary expression: *Computer Aided Systems (U.K.) Ltd. v. Bolwell* noted at [1990] I.P.D. 13051, following *Whelan Associates Inc. v. Jaslow Dental Laboratory Inc.* [1987] F.S.R. 1 (but as to this latter case see *Computer Associates International Inc. v. Altai Inc.* (1992) 23 I.P.R. 385 (U.S.C.A.)). It has been suggested that copyright does not subsist in the specification in high language of fields and records of the program by itself: *Total Information Processing Systems Ltd. v. Daman Ltd.* [1992] F.S.R. 171 at 181. However, such a suggestion was disapproved by Jacob J. in *Ibcos Computers Ltd. v. Barclays Mercantile Highland Finance Ltd.* [1994] F.S.R. 275 at 296, holding that copyright can subsist in the source code version of a computer program. Nor does copyright subsist in the screen display as a literary work; the screen display is the product of the program, not the program itself: *John Richardson Computers Ltd. v. Flanders* [1993] F.S.R. 497 at 527. The visual displays of computer video games programs have, however, been accorded protection as films under the South African Copyright Act: *Nintendo Co. Ltd. v. Golden China TV Game Centre* (October 1993; unreported); noted at [1994] 1 Ent. L.R. E–8.

2–10   Works refused protection as literary works.

Note 60. **Add**: See also *Kinnor (Pty) Ltd. v. Finkel T/A Harfin Agencies* noted at [1990] 5 Ent. L.R. E–84, where it was held (S.A. Supreme Court) that the word "Le Pacer" was an invented word and incapable of enjoying copyright protection.

Note 64. **Add**: See also *Noah v. Shuba* [1991] F.S.R. 14, in which the passage, "Follow clinic procedure for aftercare. If proper procedures are followed, no risk of viral infections can occur", was held incapable of constituting a work for the purposes of section 43 of the 1956 Act.

Note 70. **Add**: But see *Bookmakers' Afternoon Greyhound Services Ltd. v. Wilfred Gilbert (Staffordshire) Ltd.* (Aldous J., May 6, 1994) noted at [1994] I.P.D. 17082, in which copyright was held to subsist in a race programme and race card for greyhound racing, and in a formula which had been worked out to produce dividend forecasts at the end of each day's racing, but not in the dividend forecasts themselves.

3. Dramatic Works

2–11   Statutory definition.

For a table listing the Parliamentary debates on these and other provisions of the 1988 Act, see *post*, Appendix I.

Note 78. **Add**: But there is no copyright in a sports game, even though it is intended to follow a pre-set plan; it is not a choreographic work: *FWS Joint Sports Claimants v. Copyright Board* (1991) 22 I.P.R. 429 (Fed. Ct. App. Canada), citing *Tate v. Fulbrook* [1908] 1 K.B. 821 and *Green v. Broadcasting Corporation of New Zealand* [1989] R.P.C. 700.

2–12   Dramatic and musical works.

Note 79a. **Add**: See also the discussion in *Hansard*, H.L. Vol. 490, col. 830.

Importance of distinction between literary and dramatic and   **2–13**
musical works.

NOTE 80. **Add**: A further distinction has been introduced with the amendment of the definition of adaptation as regards computer programs (see *post*, para. 8–126 *et seq*.).

What constitutes a dramatic work.   **2–14**

NOTE 85. **Add**: Thus a screen play is a dramatic work: *Hansard*, H.L. Vol. 490, col. 837. See also *Hansard*, H.L. Vol. 490, col. 830.

NOTE 85. **Add**: Note that in *Hutton v. Canadian Broadcasting Corporation* (1989) 29 C.P.R. (3d) 398 (High Ct. Canada), noted at [1990] Ent. L.R. E–80, the Court found that there was sufficient dramatic incident and seminal storyline in the concept of a television series entitled "Star Chart" to qualify it as a dramatic work. The New Zealand High Court, however, has held that news and current affairs programmes comprising video clips, interviews and discussion lacked the choreography required to constitute them as dramatic works: *Television New Zealand Ltd. v. Newsmonitor Services Ltd.*, November 1993, unreported; noted at [1994] 1 Ent. L.R. E–6.

NOTE 85. **Add**: See also *FWS Joint Sports Claimants v. Copyright Board* (1991) 22 I.P.R. 429; (1991) 81 D.L.R. 412 (Fed. Ct. App. Canada). See as to copyright in a "format": Lane and McD. Bridge in [1990] 3 Ent. L.R. 96 and [1990] 4 Ent. L.R. 131; Freedman and Harris in [1990] 6 Ent. L.R. 209; Martino and Miskin in [1991] 2 Ent. L.R. 31; Smith in [1991] 3 Ent. L.R. 63 and in (1991) 141 N.L.J. 1265, 1305. There was an attempt to introduce legislation on this topic in the Broadcasting Bill 1990: [1990] Ent. L.R. E–71.

4. Musical Works

Statutory definition.   **2–17**

For a table listing the Parliamentary debates on these and other provisions of the 1988 Act, see *post*, Appendix I.

NOTE 93. **Add**: The words "exclusive of any words or action intended to be sung, spoken or performed with the music" were introduced to avoid any doubt about the distinction between the music itself, and works to be sung or performed with music, and words instructing a musician how to play, which are not to form part of the music. See *Hansard*, H.L. Vol. 490, col. 837.

5. Artistic Works

2–20   Statutory definition. For a table listing the Parliamentary debates on these and other provisions of the 1988 Act, see *post*, Appendix I.

2–21   Graphic works, etc. "Drawing" does not require production by means of a pen or pencil but denotes that the work is a product of an artist who represents his ideas by line or delineation in colour. Thus, labels made by cutting out various parts and sticking on the appropriate background were artistic works, namely a "drawing": *Ornstin Ltd. v. Quality Plastics* noted at [1990] I.P.D. 13027 (Aldous J.). Such a work would also appear to be a collage: see the text at note 17 in the Main Work.

"Diagram" would include a circuit diagram or flow chart. However, a flow chart will now also qualify as a literary work where it constitutes preparatory design material for a computer program: see the notes *ante*, para. 2–2.

NOTE 8. **Add**: See the cases cited at note 15, *infra*.

NOTE 10. **Add**: It was considered that the definition of "photograph" was such that it embraced holograms: *Hansard*, H.L. Vol. 495, col. 1065.

NOTE 15. **Add**: In *Talk of the Town Pty. Ltd. v. Hagstrom* (1990) 19 I.P.R. 649 (Fed. Ct. of Australia) it was held that a mould or die of the ordinary kind (for making extruded PVC sections) was not an engraving, not following *Wham-o Manufacturing Co. v. Lincoln Industries Ltd.* In *Greenfield Products Pty. Ltd. v. Rover-Scott Bonnar Ltd.* (1990) 95 A.L.R. 275 (Fed. Ct. of Australia) (discussed by Ricketson in [1990] EIPR 421) it was held that moulds for machine parts were neither engravings nor sculptures. An engraving meant cutting, marking or otherwise working a surface which was typically flat (but see, as to the statement that the surface is typically flat, *Talk of the Town Pty. Ltd. v. Hagstrom* (1990) 19 I.P.R. 649 at 655 (Fed. Ct. of Australia)).

NOTE 17. **Add**: No definition of a collage was considered necessary: *Hansard*, H.L. Vol. 495, col. 1067.

2–22   Artistic quality.

NOTE 18. **Add**: These words were deliberately retained, so as to avoid any doubt that artistry was not a requirement for protection as an artistic work: see *Hansard*, H.L. Vol. 490, cols. 839, 840.

Protected works.

Note 25. **Add**: In *AUVI Pte Ltd. v. Seah Siew Tee and Chai Foh Min (T/AS A. V. Electronics (Sabah) Trading Co.)* (1991) 24 I.P.R. 41, the High Court of Singapore held that copyright was capable of subsisting in a logo consisting of four letters in a stylised form. Compare *Kinnor (Pty) Ltd. v. Finkel T/A Harfin Agencies* noted at [1990] 5 Ent. L.R. E-84, where the South African Supreme Court held that a representation of the Le Pacer logo (with the loop of the "P" being elongated for the full length of the word) was too insubstantial to constitute an artistic work. For a review of the protection afforded to trade marks by the law of copyright, see Lyons in [1990] 1 EIPR 21.

Note 26. **Add**: *Frank & Hirsch (Pty.) Ltd. v. A. Roopanand Brothers (Pty.) Ltd.* [1993] EIPR D-241 (South African Appeal Court held copyright capable of subsisting in TDK cassette wrappers).

Note 35. **Add**: As to the requirements of a "drawing", see *Ornstin Ltd. v. Quality Plastics* noted at [1990] I.P.D. 13027 (Aldous J.).

Note 38. **Add**: In *Stephenson, Blake & Co. v. Grant, Legros & Co. Ltd.* (1916) 33 R.P.C. 406, designs for founts of printing type were held to be capable of protection under the 1911 Act. See also *Masson, Seeley & Co. Ltd. v. Embosotype Manufacturing Co.* (1924) 41 R.P.C. 160 (catalogue of type). For a case where copyright was held to subsist under the 1911 Act in the stylised representation of a single letter, see *Millar & Lang, Ltd. v. Polak* [1908] 1 Ch. 433. This last case has been followed by the Federal Court of Australia in *Roland Corporation v. Lorenzo & Sons (Pty.) Ltd.* (1991) 22 I.P.R. 245 (copyright held capable of subsisting in logo devices although merely depictions of single letters).

Note 39. **Add**: See *Hansard*, H.L. Vol. 490, col. 844; H.L. Vol. 493, col. 1068.

Drawings not ideas protected.

Note 41. **Add**: See also Nicholls L.J. in *Entec (Pollution Control) Ltd. v. Abacus Mouldings* [1992] F.S.R. 332 at 348 (drawings for a septic tank comprising little pencil sketches or diagrams of commonplace shapes with dimensions written on them; copying of dimensions by reverse engineering arguably not an infringement of anything protected by copyright). See also *Mirage Studios v. Counter-Feat Clothing Company Ltd.* [1991] F.S.R. 145 where Browne-Wilkinson V.-C. considered it to be an open question whether the similarities in the graphic reproduction of the defendants' product to those in the plaintiffs' product were not reproductions of a concept (of the humanoid turtle of an aggressive nature) which would not give rise to claim in copyright (at 154).

2–25   Works of architecture.

Note 45. **Add**: The word "fixed" was intended to distinguish protected structures from those which were not intended to be protected, such as moveable engineering structures (*e.g.* a ship): *Hansard*, H.L. Vol. 493, col. 1071.

The definition was deliberately wide, and includes such structures designed by engineers, rather than by architects, such as a bridge: *Hansard*, H.L. Vol. 493, col. 1071. The addition of the words "and a part of a building or fixed structure" were introduced to ensure that there was no doubt that an extension to a building would be included: *Hansard*, H.L. Vol. 493, col. 1069.

2–27   Works of artistic craftsmanship.

Note 56. **Add**: This category of works, for which no satisfactory definition could be given, was considered to give protection to works of genuine artistry, such as pottery, embroidery and other forms of craftsmanship, which might not otherwise be protected as artistic works: *Hansard*, H.L. Vol. 490, col. 847.

In *J.L. & J.E. Walter Enterprises (Pyt) Ltd. v. Kearns* [1991] S.A. 612 (High Ct. Zimbabwe) noted at [1990] 4 Ent. L.R. E-61, copyright was held to subsist in a range of pottery, as works of artistic craftsmanship, in view of the aesthetic qualities of the pottery. In *Bress Designs (Pty) Ltd. v. G.Y. Lounge Suite Mfgs (Pty) Ltd.* (1991) 2 S.A.L.R. 455 (Witwatersrand Local Division of Sup. Ct. of South Africa), a lounge suite was denied protection as a work of artistic craftsmanship since it was bought and sold for the purpose of seating. It was held that to qualify, the main purpose must be aesthetic rather than utilitarian, judged objectively.

In *Shelley Films Ltd. v. Rex Features Ltd.* [1994] E.M.L.R. 134 it was held to be arguable (on an interlocutory application) that a film set recreating a historical scene and consisting of numerous components artistically arranged was a work of artistic craftsmanship.

6. Sound Recordings

2–28   Statutory definition. For a table listing the Parliamentary debates on these and other provisions of the 1988 Act, see *post*, Appendix I.

Last sentence. **Add**: See *Hansard*, H.L. Vol. 490, col. 855, where it was accepted that there was a very great overlap between the two paragraphs.

7. Films

Statutory definition. 2–30

For a table listing the Parliamentary debates on these and other provisions of the 1988 Act, see *post*, Appendix I.

Note 78. **Add**: Under a similar definition in the South African Copyright Act it has been held that the visual displays of computer video games programs are capable of copyright protection as films: *Nintendo Co. Ltd. v. Golden China TV Game Centre* (October 1993; unreported); noted at [1994] 1 Ent. L.R. E-8.

8. Broadcasts

For a table listing the Parliamentary debates on these and other provisions of the 1988 Act, see *post*, Appendix I. 2–31

9. Cable Programmes

Statutory definition. 2–34

For a table listing the Parliamentary debates on these and other provisions of the 1988 Act, see *post*, Appendix I.

Note 96. **Add**: Thus an electronic mailbox system would not seem to fall within the definition, irrespective of whether it is excepted under section 7(2)(a): *Hansard*, H.L. Vol. 495, col. 616.

Excepted services. 2–35

Note 98. **Add**: The definition (*cf.* the words "or so far as it is not" at the end of section 7(1)), and the exception in section 7(2)(a), were intended to ensure that elements in an interactive service (*e.g.* Prestel) in which sound, images or other information are conveyed to the user are within the definition of a cable programme service, whilst those elements that are genuinely interactive (the placing of an order or the inputting of data), are not: *Hansard*, H.L. Vol. 138, cols. 113, 114. See further, *Hansard*, H.L. Vol. 501, cols. 204–206.

NOTE 99. **Add**: The exception provided for in section 7(2)(c) was intended to ensure that a system which is entirely domestic, *i.e.* comprising equipment in the private home which is not linked to any outside cable system, is not a cable programme service: *Hansard*, H.L. Vol. 490, col. 867.

10. Typographical Arrangements of Published Editions

2–37 **Statutory definition.**

For a table listing the Parliamentary debates on these and other provisions of the 1988 Act, see *post*, Appendix I.

NOTE 5. **Add**: The definition deliberately does not include typographical arrangements of artistic works. Typographical arrangement implies the layout of words or symbols on the printed page, in which the publisher makes a contribution. Where artistic works are included in a book, the publisher merely reproduces the work. In such a case the protection of the copy of the artistic work rests solely on the copyright in the original work. See *Hansard*, H.L. Vol. 490, cols. 870, 871.

11. Subject Matter Not Protected on Grounds of Public Policy

2–39 **Basis for courts' refusal to protect subject matter.** At end of first paragraph. **Add**: In *Express Newspapers Plc v. News (U.K.) Plc* ([1991] F.S.R. 36), the plaintiff, who had obtained summary judgment against the defendant for infringement of the plaintiff's copyright in an interview, was denied leave to defend a counterclaim brought against it by the defendant for infringement of the defendant's copyright in a different interview, on the basis that the defence which the plaintiff sought to put forward was the mirror image of the defence which the defendant had put forward and which had failed. The court applied the general principle of law that it is not possible to approbate and reprobate. In this case the principle was applied in favour of the protection of the copyright claimed, but the principle would be equally applicable, were the facts to merit its application, to the non-protection of copyright.

CHAPTER 3

CONDITIONS FOR SUBSISTENCE OF COPYRIGHT

1. Introduction

The Scheme of the 1988 Act compared to that of the 1956 Act. For a   **3–1**
table listing the Parliamentary debates on these and other provisions of
the 1988 Act, see *post*, Appendix I.

2. Qualifying Conditions For All Works

A. *By reference to the author*

3–5   **British citizen, etc.**

NOTE 20. **Add**: It may be necessary (see § 3–8 in the Main Work) to consider the status of the author at a time prior to January 1, 1983, when the British Nationality Act 1981 came into force. A person who after that date does not qualify as a British subject under the British Nationality Act 1981 (which, by virtue of s.51(2) of that Act governs the meaning of the term British subject in the 1988 Act) may nevertheless be treated as having been a British subject under the Copyright Act 1956, by virtue of section 51(1) of the British Nationality Act 1981, which equates the term British subject in an enactment passed before January 1, 1983, with Commonwealth citizen (as that term is defined in the British Nationality Act 1981): see *Milltronics Ltd. v. Hycontrol Ltd.* [1990] F.S.R. 273., C.A.

NOTE 24. **Add**: The list of countries in Schedule 3 to the British Nationality Act 1981 has been extended to include Pakistan (British Nationality (Pakistan) Order 1989[1]), and Namibia (British Nationality (Namibia) Order 1990.[2])

3–6   **Domicile.** For a fuller discussion on domicile, see *Dicey and Morris on The Conflict of Laws* (12th ed., Sweet & Maxwell, 1993) chapter 7, sections 1 and 2.

3–7   **Residence.** For a fuller discussion on residence, see *Dicey and Morris on The Conflict of Laws* (12th ed., Sweet & Maxwell, 1993) chapter 7, section 3.

3–8   **Material time.**

NOTE 33. **Add**: For a case decided under the 1988 Act but which had to consider the status of the author (a Canadian citizen) under the

---

[1] (S.I. 1989 No. 1331).
[2] (S.I. 1990 No. 1502).

1956 Act, see *Milltronics Ltd. v. Hycontrol Ltd.* [1990] F.S.R. 273, C.A.

B. *By reference to the place of first publication*

Publication: generally.   **3–12**

NOTE 56. **Add**: The definition provided in C.D.P.A. 1988, s.18 (2) of
the expression "issue of copies to the public" as the act of putting into
circulation copies not previously put into circulation applies equally
here: C.D.P.A. 1988, s.179.

NOTE 57. The reference to n.69 should be to n.68.

Publication: sound recordings and films. Pre-penultimate sentence.   **3–15**
Delete: "to the public". **Add**: The question is then whether such issue
of copies by the letting of copies on hire to exhibitors is issue "to the
public".

When copies of a work are issued to the public. After first sentence.   **3–16**
Add: Issue to the public means the putting into circulation of copies
not previously put into circulation (C.D.P.A. 1988, s.18 (2) and s.179).

C. *Existing works*

Subsistence of copyright in existing works.   **3–21**

NOTE 26. **Add**: See, as to preparatory design material for a computer
program created before August 1, 1989 (and therefore before January
1, 1993) in which copyright did not subsist before the amendment of
section 3(1) of the 1988 Act to include such works, the notes to *ante*,
para. 2–2.

NOTE 30. **Add**: For a case decided under the 1988 Act but which had
to consider the status of the author (a Canadian citizen) under the
1956 Act, see *Milltronics Ltd. v. Hycontrol Ltd.* [1990] F.S.R. 273, C.A.

Existing works: special provisions. See as to the specific transitional   **3–22**
provisions in respect of preparatory design material for a computer
program, the notes to *ante*, para. 2–2.

3–23 **Foreign existing works.**

NOTE 42. The Copyright Order 1989[3] has been revoked and replaced by the Copyright (Application to Other Countries) Order 1993[4]: *post,* para. D–22.

3. Literary, Dramatic, Musical and Artistic Works: Originality

A. *Introduction*

3–25 **Statutory provision.**

For a table listing the Parliamentary debates on these and other provisions of the 1988 Act, see *post,* Appendix I.

3–26 **Relevance of pre-1911 decisions.**

NOTE 64. **Add**: The correct reference for *Sands McDougall Proprietary Ltd. v. Robinson* is (1917) 23 C.L.R. 49.

B. *Originality of expression, not of content*

3–28 **Meaning of "original": expenditure of independent skill or labour.** It should be noted that the sole criterion set out in Directive 91/250 (see *post,* para. H-14 *et seq.* and *ante,* para. 2–2) for protection of a computer program is that it should be original. This is stated to mean that it is the author's own intellectual creation (Art. 1(3); *post,* para. H–16). Since that is the meaning given to "original" in the 1988 Act, no amendment was required in this respect to the 1988 Act by the Copyright (Computer Programs) Regulations in order to give effect to the Directive.

---

[3] (S.I. 1989 No. 1293).
[4] (S.I. 1993 No. 942).

Mere copy.

NOTE 72. **Substitute**: See n. 71 *ante*. **Add**: The quality of the alteration or embellishment may be more important than the quantity, and the visual impact of the alteration or embellishment on the work as a whole is more important than its technical significance: *Ornstin Ltd. v. Quality Plastics* noted at [1990] I.P.D. 13027 (Aldous J.). Mere change of scale may not be regarded as visually significant: *per* Knox J. in *Drayton Controls (Engineering) Ltd. v. Honeywell Control Systems Ltd.* [1992] F.S.R. 245 at 260.

NOTE 74. **Add**: And see, *per* Lord Oliver, in *Interlego A.G. v. Tyco Industries Inc.* [1989] A.C. 217 at 263 D/E.

Photographs.

NOTE 78. **Add**: "The question whether one photograph is a copy of another of the same subject matter will have to be decided by the usual test—is it original? Has it involved skill and effort on the part of the photographer? Or has he merely taken the work of another without any creative effort on his own part, as would clearly be the case of a photograph of a photograph?". *Hansard*, H.L. Vol. 493, col. 1073; see also *Hansard*, H.L. Vol. 495, col. 612. A different approach to originality in photographs is taken in many continental systems, (*e.g.* Belgium, France, Greece, the Netherlands, Germany, Italy and Spain), which distinguish between photographic works involving the intellectual creation of their author and other "mere" photographic works (see, for a discussion of the history of protection of photographs under the Berne Convention Ricketson, S., *The Berne Convention for the Protection of Literary and Artistic Works: 1886–1986* (Kluwer, 1987) paragraphs. 6.33–6.43). This distinction has been recognised in the Directive harmonizing the term of protection of copyright and certain related rights (Recital 17 and Art. 6; see *post*, paras. H–62 and H–69). It remains to be seen whether the changes which will be required to United Kingdom legislation in order to implement this Directive will introduce such a distinction into the law in the United Kingdom (see *ante*, para. 1–57A).

Degree of independent skill and labour required.

NOTE 79. **Add**: But see *Waylite Diaries CC v. First National Bank Ltd.* [1993] (2) S.A. 128; noted at [1992] 5 Ent. L.R. E-77 (Witwatersrand Div. High Ct. S.A.), in which it was held that a diary devised specifically for bank managers containing a few variations from standard diaries and using different coloured inks for different pages had insufficient originality to distinguish the diary from the merely commonplace. *Cf. Artifakts Design Group Ltd. v. N.P. Rigg Ltd.* [1993] 1 N.Z.L.R. 196; noted at [1993] EIPR D-136, in which the New Zealand High Court held that copyright subsisted in the original artwork (as artistic works) for the covers and other parts of corporate diaries.

C. *Kinds of skill and labour*

3–33   Use of existing subject-matter.

NOTE 87. **Add**: In *Macmillan Publishers Ltd. v. Thomas Reed Publications Ltd.* [1992] F.S.R. 455 (Mummery J.) it was held that nautical charts derived from Admiralty charts were original, in that sufficient work and skill had been expended in the creation of the simplified form of the charts, showing the outline of the coast and geographical features; see also § 3–35, Note 99, in the Main Work.

NOTE 89. **Add**: In *L.A. Gear Inc. v. Hi-Tec Sports plc* [1992] F.S.R. 121, C.A., a case in which an application was made under Ord. 14 in respect of infringement of drawings of shoes on which the evidence as to preliminary drawings was vague and the defendant argued that the final version was arguably not original, Nourse L.J. stated (at 136):

> "If, in the course of producing a finished drawing, the author produces one or more preliminary versions, the finished product does not cease to be his original work simply because he adapts it with minor variations, or even if he simply copies it, from an earlier version. Each drawing has been made by him, each is his original work."

Whilst the rejection of the defendant's argument in that case is understandable, it is nevertheless suggested that the statement should be confined to a case where a design has been produced as a continuous process spanning a short period. Otherwise the possibility is raised of the term of copyright being artificially extended by repeated redrawings, something which is to be guarded against: *per* Lord Oliver in *Interlego A.G. v. Tyco Industries Inc.* [1989] A.C. 217 at 263 E. However, see *Macmillan Publishers Ltd. v. Thomas Reed Publications Ltd.* [1992] F.S.R. 455 (Mummery J.) (also a case in which an application was made under Ord. 14) in which the argument as to lack of possible originality of later versions was rejected on the evidence as to the copyright subsisting in the earliest version (at 464).

NOTE 90. **Add**: In *Drayton Controls (Engineering) Ltd. v. Honeywell Control Systems Ltd.* [1992] F.S.R. 245 (*per* Knox J. at 259) it was emphasized that the Privy Council in *Interlego A.G. v. Tyco Industries Inc.* [1989] A.C. 217 had rejected as a single test for deciding whether or not a drawing was original, how far skill and labour had gone into the creation of the drawing. A distinction must be made between what is visually significant, where skill and labour employed are highly relevant, and work which is not visually significant, where skill and labour involved is not relevant.

(i) Change of medium

Change of medium. 3–34

NOTE 94. **Add**: For a general discussion of the position of the translator, see Vaver in [1994] EIPR 159.

NOTE 96. **Add**: In *Interlego A.G. v. Tyco Industries Inc.* [1989] A.C. 217 the opinion expressed by Whitford J. in *L.B. (Plastics) Ltd. v. Swish Products Ltd.* [1979] R.P.C. 551 at 568–569, that a drawing of a three-dimensional prototype would qualify as an original work, appears to have been accepted as correct (at 263A).

(ii) Selection and arrangement

Compilations. Note the propsal for a Directive (COM(93) 464 3–35 Final-SYN 393; [1993] O.J. C308/1) on the legal protection of databases, that is collections or complilations of data, works or other materials, arranged, stored and accessed by electronic means or analogous processes. These are to be protected by coypright if they are original, and originality is to assessed solely by reference to whether their selection or arrangement constituted the author's own intellectual creation (Art. 2(3), and see *ante*, para. 1–58 *et seq.*).

NOTE 3. **Add**: In *Total Information Processing Systems Ltd. v. Daman Ltd.* [1992] F.S.R. 171 it was held (Judge Baker Q.C.) that the mere linking of three computer programs did not produce a compilation in which copyright subsisted, but to the extent that this case sought to lay down a general principle to such effect, it was disapproved in *Ibcos Computers Ltd. v. Barclays Mercantile Highland Finance Ltd.* [1994] F.S.R. 275 at 290, by Jacob J., holding that a distinct copyright may subsist in a compilation of computer programs, if the compilation is sufficiently original.

NOTE 99. **Add**: In *Macmillan Publishers Ltd. v. Thomas Reed Publications Ltd.* [1992] F.S.R. 455 (Mummery J.) it was held that nautical charts derived from Admiralty charts were original, in that sufficient work and skill had been expended in the selection of information, such as depth soundings, geographical features, buoys and others; see also *ante*, para. 3–33, Note 87.
　In *Express Newspapers plc v. News (U.K.) Ltd.* [1990] F.S.R. 359 at 366, Browne-Wilkinson V.-C. accepted that the reporter's conduct of an

interview lasting over eight and a half hours and the selection of quotations from the interview involved sufficient skill and judgment for the reporter to acquire copyright in the quotations appearing in his report of the interview. This decision was followed by the High Court of New Zealand in concluding that scripts for news and current affairs programmes which included interviews were literary works in which copyright subsisted: *Television New Zealand Ltd. v. Newsmonitor Services Ltd.*, November 15, 1993, noted at [1994] 1 Ent. L.R. E-6.

But see *Waylite Diaries CC v. First National Bank Ltd.* [1993] (2) S.A. 128; noted at [1992] 5 Ent. L.R. E-77 (Witwatersrand Div. High Ct. S.A.), in which it was held that a diary devised specifically for bank managers containing a few variations from standard diaries and using different coloured inks for different pages had insufficient originality to distinguish the diary from the merely commonplace. *Cf. Artifakts Design Group Ltd. v. N.P. Rigg Ltd.* [1993] 1 N.Z.L.R. 196; [1993] EIPR D-136, noted at *ante*, para. 3–32.

3–36   Trade catalogues; football pools.

NOTE 9. *Warwick Film Productions Ltd. v. Eisinger* is reported at [1969] 1 Ch. 508. See also *Bookmakers' Afternoon Greyhound Services Ltd. v. Wilfred Gilbert (Staffordshire) Ltd.* (Aldous J., May 6, 1994) noted at [1994] I.P.D. 17082, in which copyright was held to subsist both in a race programme, on the basis that its preparation involved considerable skill, labour and judgment, and in the race card which reproduced that information with the addition of more information, on the basis that this involved sufficient further work for it to be original.

3–39   New arrangement of music.

NOTE 15. **Add**: In *Grignon v. Roussel* (1991) 38 C.P.R. (3rd) 4 (Can.), noted at [1992] 2 Ent. L.R. E-18, the court accepted that near variations of, or additions to, a musical work such as could be made by a fairly good musician, could not be the subject of copyright. What was required for originality was inventive genius, not mere technical skill or change. In pop music slight variations in the use of rhythm, harmony, accent and tempo may achieve originality.

4. Particular Requirements as to Form: Various Works

A. *Literary, dramatic and musical works*

3–49   Recording in writing or otherwise. See as to copyright in spoken words: Phillips in [1989] EIPR 231 and § 2–4 in the Main Work.

B. *Sound recordings and films*

Sound recordings and films: copies of previous sound recordings   **3–51**
or films.

NOTE 49. **Add**: An amendment seeking to introduce the requirement
of originality as regards sound recordings, films, broadcasts and cable
programmes and typographical arrangements of published editions
was opposed, on the basis that lack of originality in content for such
works was irrelevant, and all that was required was to exclude
copyright to the extent the work was taken from an existing work: see
Hansard, H.L. Vol. 493, col. 1057. See also the debate in *Hansard*, H.L.
Vol. 493, cols. 1073, 1074 as to how this provision came to be worded as
it is.

C. *Broadcasts and cable programmes*

Broadcasts and cable programmes.   **3–52**

NOTE 54. The Copyright Order 1989[5] has been revoked and replaced
by the Copyright (Application to Other Countries) Order 1993[6]: see
post, para. D-22.

Repeat broadcasts and cable programmes.   **3–53**

NOTE 55. **Add**: See *ante*, para. 3–49, note 49. The reason for the
different wording is explained in *Hansard*, H.L. SCE, col. 50.

Typographical arrangements.   **3–54**

NOTE 62. The reference to s.8(1)(c) should be to s.8(1).

---

[5] (S.I. 1989 No. 1293).
[6] (S.I. 1993 No. 942).

D. *Typographical arrangements*

3–55   **Copies of previous typographical arrangements.**

NOTE 65. **Add**: See *ante*, para. 3–49, note 49.

5. Copyrights Belonging to the Crown, Parliament and Certain International Organisations

3–56   **Subsistence of Crown and Parliamentary copyright.** For a table listing the Parliamentary debates on these and other provisions of the 1988 Act, see *post*, Appendix I.

CHAPTER 4

THE FIRST OWNER OF COPYRIGHT

Contents

2. Literary, Dramatic, Musical and Artistic Works

A. *Authorship*

Meaning of author. Note that in relation to the categories of work under consideration, and save for computer-generated works (see § 4–14 in the Main Work), the "author" must be a natural person: see, for example, section 12(1) of the 1988 Act and *Fax Directories (Pty) Ltd. v. SA Fax Listings CC* [1990] 2 S.A.L.R. 164 (Durban and Coast Local Division of Sup. Ct. of South Africa). **4–6**

"Author" of collective or composite work. Note that under the proposed E.C. Directive on the legal protection of databases (93/C 308/1), **4–7**

the author of a database is to be taken to be the natural person or group of natural persons who created the database, or where the legislation of the Member States permits, the legal person designated as the rightholder by such legislation. The provisions relating to authorship and ownership as presently drafted do not appear to require any changes to United Kingdom law; although, note that a separate *sui generis* right is proposed. See, generally, *ante*, para. 1–58 *et seq.*

4–11 **"Author" of photographs: the 1988 Act.** Last sentence. Note that in the course of the passage of the Copyright Bill, an amendment which would have had the effect of making the photographer the author in all circumstances was resisted, it being pointed out on behalf of the Government that:

> "In certain cases someone other than the person who operates the camera will make a substantial creative contribution to the final image—perhaps in the darkroom, perhaps in composing the picture through the viewfinder without actually pressing the button—and it would not be right to deny him a copyright in it on the grounds that he was not the actual photographer." (*Hansard*, H.L. Vol. 490, col. 883.)

For an article on ownership of copyright in photographs, see Gendreau in [1993] 6 EIPR 207.

4–14 **"Author" of computer programs and computer-generated works: the 1988 Act.** The provisions of the 1988 Act as originally enacted are consistent with the relevant provisions of the computer software Directive (see *ante*, para. 1–54 and *post*, para H–14 *et seq.*), and therefore no amendments were made to the 1988 Act in this area by the Copyright (Computer Program) Regulations 1992. The Directive provides:

(1) the author of a computer program shall be the natural person or group of natural persons who has created the program or, where the legislation of the Member State permits, the legal person designated as the rightholder by that legislation. Where collective works are recognised by the legislation of a Member State, the person considered by the legislation of the Member State to have created the work shall be deemed to be its author. (Art. 2(1));

(2) in respect of a computer program created by a group of natural persons jointly, the exclusive rights shall be owned jointly;

(3) where a computer program is created by an employee in the execution of his duties or following the instructions given by his

employer, the employer exclusively shall be entitled to exercise all economic rights in a program so created, unless otherwise provided by contract. (Art. 2(3)).

In a short debate on the implementing Regulations, it was confirmed on behalf of the Government that they were intended to give full effect to the Directive: *Hansard*, H.L. Vol. 541, cols. 514–516.

See *ante*, para. 4–7 regarding the proposal for the E.C. Directive on the legal protection of databases.

B. *Commissioned Artistic Works*

Commissioned photographs. In *Apple Corps Ltd v. Cooper* [1993] **4–21** F.S.R. 286 the following principles in relation to commissioned photographs were stated:

(1) The vesting of the copyright in the commissioner of a photograph takes place at the moment the film is first exposed.

(2) At this moment, for copyright to vest all the elements referred to in section 4(3) of the 1956 Act must have existed.

(3) These elements are:
   (a) The commissioner must have commissioned the taking of the photograph before the film was exposed;
   (b) The commissioner must have paid or agreed to pay for it before this moment;
   (c) The negative must have been taken in pursuance of that commission.

(4) (a) "Commission" is another word for "order".
   (b) Where sufficient of the circumstances in which the request for taking the photograph are known and it is an ordinary case, the court will readily imply that a sitter has to pay for the taking of the photograph (analysing *Boucas v. Cooke* [1903] 2 K.B. 227).
   (c) In the informal circumstances which often accompany the taking of a photograph, a bare request may be enough to raise the question whether an obligation to pay should be implied.
   (d) A commissioning does not itself imply an obligation to pay, but it does connote it.

(5) An agreement to pay requires a consensus between the commissioner and the photographer. Thus a mere intention to pay by the commissioner, and not expressed to the photographer, is not sufficient. Neither is the mere expectation of payment by the photographer, without any promise to pay, sufficient.

(6) The payment or agreement to pay is the quid pro quo for the photographer losing his copyright.

(7) The requirement of subsection 4(3) is satisfied if the commissioner paid or agreed to pay for the *taking* of the photograph, rather than the photograph once it had been taken. That is, the word "it" in subsection 4(3) refers to "the taking of a photograph" not to "a photograph".

For a case on industry practice in the music industry, see *Planet Earth Reproductions Inc. v. Rolands* (1990) 73 O.R. 2d 505 (Sup. Ct. of Ontario).

C. *The work of employees*

(1) Works made for publication in a newspaper, magazine or similar periodical

4-30   The 1956 Act. In the equivalent provisions of the Australian Copyright Act, a "newspaper" was held to be a publication containing a narrative of recent events and occurrences, published regularly at short intervals from time to time. See *D.C.T. v. Rotary Offset Press Pty. Ltd.* (1971) 45 A.L.J.R. 418 applied in *De Garis v. Nevill Jefress Pidler Pty Ltd.* (1990) 18 I.P.R. 292 (Fed. Ct. of Australia). Further, supplementary advertising material and "fliers" inserted in Sunday newspapers were held to be part of the newspaper: see *John Fairfax & Sons Ltd. v. D.C.T.* (1988) 15 N.S.W.L.R. 620 (Sup. Ct. of New South Wales), followed in *De Garis v. Neville Jefress Pidler Pty. Ltd., supra.*

The retained copyright includes the right to prevent photocopying of the journalist's work and its use in a press clippings service: see *De Garis v. Neville Jefress Pidler Pty. Ltd.* (1990) 18 I.P.R. 292 (Fed. Ct. of Australia). Again, copying for the purposes of a press clippings service does not constitute publication or reproduction for the purposes of publication in a newspaper: *ibid.*

(ii) Works made by employees generally

4-41   What is a "contract of service"?

NOTE 3: **Add**: *Hall (Inspector of Taxes) v. Lorimer* [1994] 1 W.L.R. 209 (freelance vision mixer: no contract of service); *R v. Lord Chancellor's Department, ex p. Nangle* [1991] I.C.R. 743 (civil servant holding clerical position: employed under contract of service); *Hawkley v. The Queen* (1990) 30 C.P.R. (3d) 534, [1990] 71 D.L.R. 632 (Fed Ct. of Canada) (prisoner, required to be gainfully employed).

Course of employment. After sentence ending " . . . incurred." **Add**:   **4–45**
Similarly, where a consultant epidemiologist wrote, at home in the
evenings and at weekends but not at the instigation or direction of his
employers, a guide on hygiene in relation to skin piercing activities.
See *Noah v. Shuba* [1991] F.S.R. 14. Because the presumption of
ownership contained in section 20(2) of the 1956 Act applied, the
burden of proof was on the defendant to show that the plaintiff had
made the work in the course of his employment.

Agreement to the contrary. See, generally, *Noah v. Shuba* [1991] F.S.R.   **4–48**
14.

Second sentence. **Delete**, and **substitute**: The agreement must have
been made before the work came into existence: *Noah v. Shuba* [1991]
F.S.R. 14. Such a term may, for example, be implied as a result of a
longstanding practice adopted by an employer whereby the employee
retained the copyright: *ibid*. No doubt it may also be part of an oral
agreement.

Final sentence. Much will, however, depend on the circumstances.
The question will turn on whether it is to be implied that the publisher
is to be entitled to exploit, on an exclusive basis, all the rights included
within the copyright or only some of them; for example, book
publication rights. See § 15–14 *et seq.* in the Main Work.

3. First Owner in Relation to Other Works

B. *Films*

The 1988 Act. Note that E.C. Directive 92/100 on Rental and Lending   **4–55**
Rights (see *ante*, para. 1–55 *et seq.* and *post*, para. H–26 *et seq.*), which is
required to be implemented by July 1, 1994, will require the 1988 Act
to be amended so that the principal director of a film be treated as one
of its authors for the purpose of the rental right (the Directive, Art.
2(2)). Member States are, however, to have freedom to introduce a
presumption that, where a contract for the production of a film is
concluded by an author with a film producer, the author is to be
presumed to have transferred his rental right (Art. 2(6)), subject to an
unwaivable right to equitable remuneration. Member States are free to
designate others as co-authors (Art. 2(3)). The provisions of Article
2(2) do not have to be applied to films created before July 1, 1994 (Art.
13(4)) and Member States may determine a date, being no later than
July 1, 1997, from which Article 2(2) is to apply (Art. 13(5)).

(Implementation of the Directive by the United Kingdom will not now occur by the required date.)

These provisions of Directive 92/100 regarding authorship of films have been repeated, in almost identical terms, in Directive 93/83 relating to satellite broadcasting and cable retransmission (Art. 2(5), *post*, para. H–47 and see generally *ante*, para. 1–56) and in Directive 93/98 harmonizing the term of copyright protection (Art. 2(1), *post*, para. H–62 and see, generally, *ante*, para. 1–57). Both Directives also provide for the same freedom for Member States to determine that these provisions should not apply to films created before July 1, 1994, and that the date from which they should apply should be no later than July 1, 1997. (See Directive 93/83, Art. 7(1), *post* para. H–53 and Directive 93/98, Arts. 10(4) and (5), *post*, para. H–73.)

After first sentence of § 4–55 in the Main Work. **Add**: Having regard to the definition of "author" in section 9(1) of the Act, these words should be construed bearing in mind that they are intended to define the persons who created the film: see *Beggars Banquet Records Ltd. v. Carlton Television* [1993] E.M.L.R. 349.

NOTE 43: *Adventure Film Productions SA v. Tully* is now reported at [1993] E.M.L.R. 376.

NOTE 44: Note, however, that the provision of finance is only one factor to be considered. A person who merely provides finance, such as a bank, as opposed to the person who is directly responsible for paying the production costs, will not normally be the author: *Beggars Banquet Records Ltd. v. Carlton Television* [1993] E.M.L.R. 349. See also *Century Communications Ltd. v. Mayfair Entertainment U.K. Ltd.* [1993] E.M.L.R. 335, where the maker of the film was held to be the person who initiated the project, organised the activity necessary for the film to be made and paid for it. The local company whose help had necessarily been invoked to help shoot the film in mainland China was not the maker.

4. Ownership in Other Circumstances

A. *Equitable ownership*

4–67 In *Cableship Ltd. v. Williams* noted at [1991] I.P.D. 14205 it was apparently held that an equitable owner was entitled to the remedies available under the 1988 Act against the bare legal owner. Again, in *Ibcos Computers Ltd. v. Barclays Mercantile Highland Finance Ltd.* [1994] F.S.R. 275 where it may have been arguable that the plaintiff was only the equitable owner and the defendant, against whom infringement was alleged, was the legal owner, no point was taken.

NOTES 67 and 70. See also *John Richardson Computers Ltd. v. Flanders* [1993] F.S.R. 497.

NOTE 69: **Add**: *Ibcos Computers Ltd. v. Barclays Mercantile Highland Finance Ltd.* [1994] F.S.R. 275.

B. *Ownership by Partnership*

Again, in *Ibcos Computers Ltd. v. Barclays Mercantile Highland Finance Ltd.*   **4–68** [1994] F.S.R. 275 it was held that a computer program which had been modified for the purposes of a partnership (in fact a "quasi-partnership" carried on through a limited company), and which formed the very foundation of the venture, belonged to the partnership (or company). This result was "absolutely necessary" (distinguishing *Miles v. Clark* [1953] 1 W.L.R. 537), for otherwise the partnership business could have been severely damaged, for example, if the person who would otherwise have been the owner of the copyright had left (presumably revoking any licence; see *post*, para. 5–43) or if the partnership was unable to bring infringement proceedings against third parties. This conclusion applied not only to the modifications of the program made for the purposes of the partnership but also to the original program which had been brought to the partnership.

5. Ownership of Copyright and Physical Materials

Power of governments to publish or withold letters. Note also section   **4–73** 48 of the 1988 Act which provides for the copying and publication of materials communicated to the Crown. See § 10–54 of the Main Work.

CHAPTER 5

TRANSMISSION OF AND DEALINGS IN COPYRIGHT

Contents   *Para.*

1. Introduction

5–1 **Distinction between title to copyright and to physical material.** Final
sentence. **Add**: Like other personal property, copyright may be

charged or mortgaged. For a discussion of some of the problems relating to mortgages of films, see Henry in [1992] 4 Ent. L.R. 115.

2. Transmission by Operation of Law

A. *Death*

For a table listing the Parliamentary debates on these and other   **5–2**
provisions of the 1988 Act, see *post*, Appendix I.

C. *Bankruptcy*

NOTE 23. See also sections 283 and 306 of the Insolvency Act 1986.   **5–5**

D. *Execution*

NOTE 25. As to whether copyright is subject to seizure by a writ of *fi.*   **5–6**
fa., see *Planet Earth Reproductions Inc. v. Rolands* (1990) 73 O.R. (2d)
505, 20 I.P.R. 431 (Sup. Ct. of Ontario). Note that the Canadian
Statute permitted execution against choses in action or any interest in
or in respect of goods, chattels or personal property. *C.f. Re Baldwin*
(1858) 2 De G. & J. 230.

3. Assignment

B. *Varieties of Assignments*

Partial assignment. Note that the normal term of copyright is to be   **5–9**
extended to 70 years after the death of the author (see *post*. para.
6–5A). It remains to be seen whether, when implementing the E.C.
Directive, the United Kingdom will introduce provisions aimed at
regulating the position between authors and their assigns in respect of
the extended term. Provisions of this kind were contained in the
Copyright Act 1911 (s.24; see § A–601 in the Main Work), by which
the term of copyright was also extended. If no such provision is made,

difficult questions of construction may arise as to whether assignments of copyright carry the extended term.

5–11   **Examples.**

NOTE 49. In *Greenfield Products Pty. Ltd v. Rover-Scott Bonnar Ltd* [1990] A.I.P.C. 90–667 an assignment of copyright was implied even though not mentioned. *Savory Ltd. v. World of Golf Ltd.* [1914] 2 Ch. 566 was followed.

5–15/   **Time.** Note, however, that under the 1988 Act the sale and distribu-
5–16   tion of such copies will usually amount to the issue of copies to the public within the meaning of section 18 (see § 8–92 *et seq.* in the Main Work). Whether such acts are unlicensed, and therefore an infringement, will no doubt turn upon the proper construction of the assignment.

5–20   **Particular purpose.** Second paragraph. During the passage of the 1988 Act through Parliament it was stated that the use of the word "things" in section 90 was intended to make it clear that copyright could be subdivided into subsidiary rights, such as hardback rights, paperback rights or book club rights, thus enabling a grantee of such rights to sue for infringement of copyright. See *Hansard*, H.L. Vol. 493, col. 1342; H.L. Vol. 495, cols. 667 and 668.

4. Licences

A. *General*

5–43   **Position of licensee.** See, generally, *post*, para. 8–144 *et. seq.*
    After sentence ending " . . . custom". **Add**: The existence and scope of a licence to do an act which would otherwise be an infringement of copyright may be inferred from all the circumstances of the case: *Noah v. Shuba* [1991] F.S.R. 14 at 28, 29.
    Sentence beginning "As it was put by Tindal C.J. . . . ." The quotation starts at: "a dispensation . . . " The quotation is from *Thomas v. Sorrell*, Vaughan Rep. 351 and is cited by Tindal C.J. in *Muskett v. Hill*.
    In *Ibcos Computers Ltd. v. Barclays Mercantile Highlands Finance Ltd.* [1994] F.S.R. 275, the defendant was held to be estopped from revoking his licence to use software which had become embedded in an improved version, developed by the plaintiff with his co-operation

over several years. The effect of the licence being revocable would have been to leave the plaintiff's business at his mercy.

Fourth line on page 123, after the word "assignable". **Add**: If the licence contains a prohibition against assignment, either in absolute terms or without consent, of the benefit of the licence, a purported assignment of contractual rights (including accrued causes of action) is ineffective to vest the benefit of the licence in the assignee. If the position were otherwise, the law would defeat the legitimate commercial reason for inserting the prohibition, namely, to ensure the original parties to the licence are not brought into direct contractual relations with third parties. See *Linden Gardens Trust Ltd. v. Lenesta Sludge Disposals Ltd.* [1994] 1 A.C. 85.

B. *Exclusive licences*

Right of exclusive licensee to sue under the 1911 Act. Last sentence   **5–44**
on page 123. The end of the sentence should read " . . . and has been much debated since the 1911 Act was passed."

Under the 1988 Act.   **Add**: An exclusive licence to sell licensed copies   **5–46**
of the plaintiff's work is not by itself sufficient to make the licensee an exclusive licensee within the meaning of the 1988 Act (see, for example, *Avel Pty. Ltd. v. Multicoin Amusements Pty. Ltd* (1990) 18 I.P.R. 443 (High Ct. of Australia), distinguished in *Broderbund Software Inc. v. Computermate Products (Australia) Pty. Ltd.* (1991) 22 I.P.R. 215 (Fed. Ct. of Australia). If, however, such a licence could be construed as an exclusive licence to put into circulation copies of the plaintiff's works which have not been previously put into circulation, that would probably be sufficient to make the licensee an exclusive licensee within the meaning of the Act. See § 8–92 *et seq.* in the Main Work.

5. Transitional Provisions

A. *General Principles*

During the passage of the 1988 Act through Parliament, it was stated   **5–54**
that the general principles underlying Schedule 1 included those that existing copyright owners should not suddenly find themselves with a right substantially less valuable than they enjoyed before and that those already exploiting or dealing with existing works should not suddenly find themselves unable to continue. See *Hansard,* H.L. Vol. 491, Col. 582.

CHAPTER 6

DURATION OF COPYRIGHT

1. Introduction

6–5 **The 1988 Act.** For a table listing the Parliamentary debates on these and other provisions of the 1988 Act, see *post*, Appendix I.

6–5A **Council Directive 93/98/EEC.** The position described at § 6–5 in the Main Work remains the current position. However, on October 29, 1993, the Council of the European Communities adopted Directive 93/98 harmonizing the term of protection of copyright and certain related rights: [1993] O.J. L290/9. The text of the Directive is set out at *post*, para. H–62 *et seq.* Member States have until the July 1, 1995, to introduce the provisions necessary to implement this Directive.
   The Directive is intended to achieve harmonization in the laws of the Member States of:

   (1) the period of copyright protection for authors to a period of 70 years after the death of the author;

   (2) the period of related rights protection to a period of 50 years;

   (3) the manner of calculation of the period of protection;

   (4) the protection afforded to the works of non-Community nationals.

Amending legislation will not be required in the United Kingdom to provide for (2), (3) and (4) above, where the position in the United Kingdom already accords with the requirements of the Directive. Amending legislation will, however, be required to provide for (1) above, and this will have to deal with a number of subsidiary matters raised by the Directive, in particular as to the application of the extended term to existing works. No draft of such legislation has as yet been produced.

The works which are to benefit from the extension of the term of protection of copyright are those which are treated as literary or artistic works under the Berne Convention; that is, all those works which are, under the 1988 Act, literary, dramatic, musical, or artistic works or films and which are protected in any Member State on January 1, 1995.

Whether a work is protected in a particular Member State on January 1, 1995, will, of course, in the first instance be a matter for the law of that State. Most Member States, as is permissable under the Berne Convention, apply comparison of terms to the works of foreign nationals. Thus, where the author of the work is a national of State B, State A's law would normally apply comparison of terms to that work, with the effect that the work enjoys in State A only the term of protection which the work enjoys in State B.

Where State A accords a term of protection to its nationals for such works which extends beyond January 1, 1995, then such works of its nationals will benefit under the Directive from the extended term throughout the territories of all Member States. But where State B accords to its nationals a shorter term of protection for such works which expires before January 1, 1995, then if State A is permitted to apply comparison of terms to the works of the nationals of State B, such works will not benefit from the extended term under the Directive.

It is to be noted that the effect of the decision of the Court of Justice in Joined Cases 92 & 326/92, *Phil Collins v. Imtrat HandelsGmbH* and *Verwaltungesellschaft mbH v. EMI Electrola GmbH* [1993] 3 C.M.L.R. 773, on what is now Article 6 of the Treaty (see *post*, para. F–3A), is thought to be that in such a situation State A may not apply comparison of terms based solely on nationality. The result in the situation discussed above would then be that the work of the national of State B will then enjoy the extended term accorded under the law of State A, and thus will benefit under the Directive from the extended term throughout all the territories of the Member States. For an article on the effect of this decision in relation to the Directive, see Dworkin and Sterling in [1994] EIPR 187.

The extended term of protection in relation to photographs is stated to be required to apply only to photographs which are original "in the sense that they are the author's own intellectual creation". The protection to be afforded to other photographs is a matter for individual Member States. (See further, as to this distinction, *ante*, para. 3–31, Note 78.)

As regards films, the amending legislation will have to take into account the definition of "authors" under the Directive (Art. 2(1); and see *post*, para. H–65), which follows that provided for in the rental Directive (Directive 92/100: [1992] O.J. L346/61; see *ante*, para. 1–55 *et seq.*), namely that it is to include the director. The United Kingdom is free to determine the date as from which this provision shall apply, provided that it is no later than July 1, 1997 (Art. 10(5); see *post*, para. H–73).

For a general history of the Directive and further discussion of its terms in the context of harmonization, see *ante* para. 1–51 *et seq.* For a discussion on the Directive (prior to its final form) see Silvestro in [1993] 3 Ent. L.R. 73.

2. Literary, Dramatic, Musical and Artistic Works

6–6   General position: new works.

NOTE 17. **Add**: In relation to such works which are the subject of copyright protection in one of the Member States on January 1, 1995, the 1988 Act will have to be amended to extend the period of protection of such works to 70 years from the end of the calendar year in which the author died: Directive 93/98, Articles 1(1) and 10(2) (see *ante*, para. 1–57 and *post*, paras. H–64 and H–73).

NOTE 20. **Add**: Whether the work has been published or otherwise publicly exploited will equally remain irrelevant to the extended term of 70 years: Directive 93/98, Article 1(1) (see *ante*, para. 6–5A and *post*, para. H–64).

6–7   General position: existing works.

NOTE 27. **Add**: The general principles underlying the schedule were stated to be that existing copyright should not be lost; that existing works not in copyright should not suddenly acquire it; that existing copyright owners should not suddenly find themselves with a right substantially less valuable than they already enjoyed and that others already exploiting or dealing with existing works should not suddenly find themselves unable to continue: *Hansard*, H.L. Vol. 491, col. 582.

Although this statement of principles would not have prevented the extension of the rights of owners of copyright in existing works which enjoyed protection at commencement (August 1, 1989), the approach taken in the schedule to the 1988 Act is, generally speaking, to preserve the position as to duration of rights which existed under the previous applicable legislation. That is not the approach adopted in Directive 93/98 which requires the extended term to be given to works which enjoy protection as at January 1, 1995, in any Member State (see Art. 10(2), *post*, para. H–73). How the provisions of Schedule 1 will be affected when the legislation is introduced to implement the Directive in the United Kingdom, remains to be seen.

On the other hand, one of the principles stated above was that existing works not in copyright should not suddenly acquire it. An exception to this has already been discussed in the case of foreign existing works which may qualify for copyright protection in the United Kingdom after commencement by virtue of an Order made under section 159 of the 1988 Act (see §§ 3–23 and 3–24 in the Main Work). It appears that the Directive introduces a further exception, in that it is to suffice for a work to be entitled to the extended term of copyright that it remains protected by copyright on January 1, 1995, in one Member State. This could result in a work in which copyright in the United Kingdom has expired prior to that date, but in which copyright in another Member State continues to subsist at that date, being entitled in the United Kingdom, as from January 1, 1995, to a fresh term of copyright of up to a further 20 years. In such a case the Directive is expressed to be without prejudice to any acts of exploitation performed before such date and to the protection of acquired rights of third parties (see Art. 10(3), *post*, para. H–73). Again it remains to be seen how the amending legislation will make provision for such matters (but see § 3–23 in the Main Work, and the Copyright (Application to Other Countries) Order 1993,[1] paragraphs 7(1) and (2), *post*, para. D-28).

It also remains to be seen whether when implementing the Directive the United Kingdom will introduce provisions aimed at regulating the position between authors and their assigns in respect of the extended term. Provisions of this kind were contained in the Copyright Act 1911 (s.24; see § A–601 in the Main Work), by which the term of copyright was also extended.

Photographs.   6–8

NOTE 41. **Add**: Whether a photograph which is the subject of protection in any Member State on January 1, 1995, will benefit from the extension of the term of copyright protection in the United Kingdom to 70 years from the end of the calendar year in which the author died, will depend on how the 1988 Act is amended to implement Directive 93/98. Under the Directive, only a photograph which is "original in the sense that it is the author's own intellectual creation" is required to benefit from the extension: see Articles 1(1) and 6, and the explanation given in Recital 17 (*post*, paras. H–63 and H–64). The Directive leaves the extent of protection to be accorded to

---

[1] (S.I. 1993 No. 1293).

other photographs to Member States (Art. 6). Whether the amending legislation will seek to introduce such a distinction into the 1988 Act, or will apply the extended term to all photographs without making such a distinction, remains to be seen.

NOTES 44, 46 and 47. **Add**: These transitional provisions, which were aimed at maintaining the shorter period of protection accorded under the legislation in force when the photographs were taken, would appear to be inconsistent with the requirement of Directive 93/98 that the period of copyright is to be extended to 70 years from the end of the calendar year in which the author died in respect of all works protected in any Member State on January 1, 1995 (subject to the point made *supra*, Note 41).

6–9   Posthumous works.

NOTES 52 and 53. **Add**: How these provisions will be affected by the amendment of the 1988 Act to implement Directive 93/98 remains to be seen: see *ante*, para. 6–6.

6–10   Works of unknown authorship.

NOTE 61. **Add**: This is to be extended to 70 years when Directive 93/98 is implemented: see Article 1(3), *post*, para. H–64.

NOTE 62. **Add**: Availability to the public was intended to include, but to be wider than, publication: *Hansard*, H.L. Vol. 490, col. 1158; H.C. SCE, cols. 116–120.

NOTE 63. **Add**: This will remain the same when Directive 93/98 is implemented: see Article 1(3), *post*, para. H–64.

NOTE 64. **Add**: See *Hansard*, H.L. Vol. 493, cols. 1083, 1084.

6–11   Computer-generated works.

NOTE 75. **Add**: The period will be extended to 70 years when Directive 93/98 is implemented, since although the Directive is primarily aimed at works which have a natural person as their author, in respect of works which do not have such an author, such as computer-generated works, a fixed period of 70 years from the end of the year of their creation is to be applied: see Articles 1(6) and 8, *post*, paras. H–64 and H–71.

3. Sound Recordings and Films

General position: new works.   **6–12**

E.C. Directive 93/98 on harmonizing the term of protection of copyright and certain related rights (see *ante*, para. 6–5A and *post*, para. H–62 *et seq.*), makes a distinction between films and sound recordings, see also *ante*, para. 1–57. Films are treated similarly to other works covered by the Berne Convention and are to enjoy copyright protection for a period of 70 years after the end of the calendar year in which the last of a number of designated persons died. Those designated persons are (irrespective of whether they are designated as the author or co-author of the film): the principal director, the author of the screenplay, the author of the dialogue and the composer of music specifically created for use in the film (see Art. 2(2), *post*, para. H–65).

So far as the rights of the producer of a film are concerned, however, the Directive provides that these are to be treated, as are the rights of producers of phonograms and performers, as related rights, the duration of which under the Directive is to be harmonised to 50 years; see also *ante*, para. 1–57B.

Thus, the producer's rights in a film are to expire 50 years from the end of the year in which the film was first published or communicated to the public (see Art. 3(3), *post*, para. H–66). In the case of sound recordings, the 50 years is to run from the end of the calendar year in which the sound recording is first fixed, and if the sound recording is lawfully published or communicated to the public within this period then the rights are to expire 50 years from the end of the calendar year in which such event first happened (see Art. 3(2), *post*, para. H–66).

Existing published sound recordings.   **6–16**

NOTE 97. **Add**: These provisions will not require amendment, as they conform to the requirements of Directive 93/98: see *ante*, para. 6–12.

Existing published films.   **6–17**

NOTE 1. **Add**: These provisions will require amendment as regards any film protected by copyright in any Member State on January 1, 1995, and which is therefore entitled to the extended term of 70 years after the death of the last of a number of specified persons, so as to accord with Directive 93/98 (see Arts. 2(2) and 10(2), *post*, paras. H–65 and H–73 and *ante*, para. 6–12).

6–18   Existing unpublished works.

Notes 6 and 7. **Add**: This will remain the case as regards sound
recordings, but as regards films which remain protected by copyright
in any Member State on January 1, 1995, this is subject to the
transitional provisions which will be required to implement Directive
93/98 (see Arts. 2(2) and 10(2), *post*, paras. H–65 and H–73 and see *ante*
para. 6–12).

4. Broadcasts and Cable Programmes

6–19   General position.

Note 8. **Add**: Directive 93/98 requires broadcasting organisations to
be accorded copyright protection in their broadcasts for a period of 50
years from the end of the calendar year in which they are first
transmitted (see Art. 3(4), *post*, para. H–66). The position as regards
the duration of copyright in broadcasts will not therefore require any
amendment when the Directive is implemented.

6–20   Repeat broadcasts and cable programmes.

Note 10. **Add**: The rationale of this provision is that a repeat
broadcast is not made from a recording of the first broadcast. It will be
made from a recording made at the same time as or even before the
first broadcast. For copyright protection to be adequate, each repeat
must be given its own copyright, albeit for an abbreviated time: see
Hansard, H.L. Vol. 490, col. 1163.

5. Typographical Arrangements of Published Editions

6–21   Typographical arrangements.

Notes 14 and 15. **Add**: Such works are not literary or artistic works
within the meaning of Article 2 of the Berne Convention, and the term
of their protection is unaffected by Directive 93/98.

CHAPTER 7

WORKS OF JOINT AUTHORSHIP AND OWNERSHIP

1. Definition

NOTE 3. The decision to adopt the same formulation as in the 1911 Act   **7–1**
was deliberate: see *Hansard*, H.L. Vol. 493, col. 1085. In the course of
the debate it was said by the Government spokesman that the question
is not whether the contributions are separable or can ultimately be
distinguished, but whether they are distinct in the work itself.

NOTE 5. *Adventure Film Productions Ltd. v. Tulley* is now reported at
[1993] E.M.L.R. 376. For a case under the 1988 Act, see *Beggars
Banquet Records Ltd. v. Carlton Television* [1993] E.M.L.R. 349.

A drummer's contribution to a composition is capable of making him a   **7–2**
joint author: see *Stuart v. Barrett* (1992) noted at [1992] 8 EIPR D-162.

NOTE 8. **Add**: *Bartos v. Scott* (1993) 26 I.P.R. 27

6. Term of Copyright in Joint Works

Note that in respect of computer generated works, works the subject of   **7–10**
Crown and Parliamentary copyrights, sound recordings, broadcasts,

cable programmes and typographical arrangements of published editions, the term of copyright is defined under the 1988 Act without reference to the life of any author. The fact that the work may be a work of joint authorship does not therefore affect the term. See sections 12 to 15 of the 1988 Act and chapter 6 of the Main Work. The position under the 1988 Act is the same in respect of films but will be changed (see *infra*).

The effect of implementation of the Directive 93/98 harmonising the term of protection of copyright and certain related rights (see *ante*, para. 1–57 *et seq.* and *post*, para. H-62 *et seq.*), will be to extend the term of copyright in literary, dramatic, musical and artistic works to 70 years from the end of the calendar year in which the author died. See *ante*, para. 6–5A *et seq.* for a detailed discussion of the changes which will be required to the 1988 Act, where it is also pointed out that the term of copyright in films will also now be 70 years after the end of the year in which the last of certain designated persons dies. In dealing with works of joint authorship, the Directive adopts the same system as the Berne Convention (Art. 7 *bis*; see § C–11 in the Main Work) and the 1988 Act, namely that the term is to be calculated by reference to the death of the last surviving author (see Art. 1(2)). The Directive does not specify what is to happen where copyright subsists only because one or more, but not all, the authors satisfy the qualifying provisions. The Directive is required to be implemented by July 1, 1995.

7. Term of Copyright: Identity of Authors Unknown or Only Partly Known

7–11 See *ante*, para. 7–10 as to the extension generally of the term of copyright. The Directive (Art. 1(3)) specifies that in the case of anonymous or pseudonymous works the term of protection is to run for 70 years after the work is lawfully made available to the public, except that if the author discloses his identity before the end of this period, the normal term of life and 70 years is to apply. The Directive does not specify what is to happen in the case of works of joint authorship where the identity of one or more of its authors is not known.

CHAPTER 8

INFRINGEMENT OF COPYRIGHT: PRIMARY INFRINGEMENT

1. Introduction

The 1988 Act. For a table listing the Parliamentary debates on these   **8–3**
and other provisions of the 1988 Act, see *post*, Appendix I.

Licence and consent: permitted acts. Since the absence of licence is   **8–6**
an ingredient of the tort, the onus of proof in establishing this fact rests
on the plaintiff: see *Avel Pty. Ltd. v. Multicoin Amusements Pty. Ltd.*
(1990) 97 A.L.R. 19, (1990) 18 I.P.R. 443 (High Ct. of Australia) and

Mateffy Perl Nagy Pty. Ltd. v. Devefli Pty. Ltd. [1993] R.P.C. 493 (Fed. Ct. of Australia).

2. Infringement by Copying

A. *Copying in relation to all works*

(i) General principles

8–8 **Form, not idea, protected.** See also *ante*, para. 1–1, and in particular *Ibcos Computers Ltd. v. Barclays Mercantile Highland Finance Ltd.* [1994] F.S.R. 275.

8–12 **Proof of copying.** See also § 11–92 in the Main Work and *post*, para. 11–92.

Second sentence. This is particularly so in the case of copying of computer source code, which will usually contain many such matters: see, for example, *Ibcos Computers Ltd. v. Barclays Mercantile Highland Finance Ltd.* [1994] F.S.R. 275. Unless explained, such similarities will usually be sufficient to establish that the whole of the plaintiff's work has been copied, not just the similar parts: see, for example, *Fax Directories (Pty.) Ltd. v. SA Fax Listings CC* [1990] S.A.L.R. 164 (Sup. Ct. of S.A.(D)). In carrying out this comparative exercise, the unimportant parts of the two works may be examined for unexplained similarities as well as the important parts: *Billhöfer Maschinenfabrik GmbH v. Dixon & Co. Ltd.* [1990] F.S.R. 105 and *Ibcos Computers Ltd. v. Barclays Mercantile Highland Finance Ltd.* [1994] F.S.R. 275.

8–13 NOTE 73. **Add**: *Ibcos Computers Ltd. v. Barclays Mercantile Highland Finance Ltd.* [1994] F.S.R. 275.

8–14 **Indirect copying.** Where part of a computer program had been copied indirectly by using an oscilloscope to discover a series of digits in the plaintiff's computer program, this was held to be an infringement: see *Autodesk Inc. v. Dyason* [1992] R.P.C. 575 (High Ct. of Australia).

NOTE 78: The reference should be to s.16(3)(b).

8–17 **Subconscious copying.** The possibility of subconscious copying was apparently accepted in *John Richardson Computers Ltd. v. Flanders* [1993]

F.S.R. 497 and was assumed in *EMI Music Publishing Ltd. v. Evangelos Papathanassiou* [1993] E.M.L.R. 306. See also *Bright Tunes v. Harrisongs* 420 F. Supp. 177 (S.D.N.Y. 1976).

Reproduction in computers and in other transient forms. No change **8–19** to the provisions of the 1988 Act dealing with reproduction was required to implement the computer software Directive (see *ante*, para. 1–54 and *post*, para. H–14 *et seq.*), Article 4 of which provides that one of the exclusive rights of the owner of the copyright in a computer program is to include the right to do [*sic*] or to authorise the permanent or temporary reproduction of a computer program by any means and in any form, in part or in whole, and that in so far as the loading, displaying, running, transmission or storage of the computer program necessitates such reproduction, such acts shall be subject to the authorisation of the copyright owner. Note, however, that certain new permitted acts have been introduced following the amendment of the 1988 Act. These are dealt with at *post*, para. 10–59A *et seq.*

NOTE 4. The decision of the Canadian Federal Court of Appeal in *Apple Computers Inc. v. Mackintosh Computers Ltd.* was affirmed on appeal: (1990) 71 D.L.R. 95.

(ii) Colourable imitation and substantial part

Suggested test of "copy". In *Ibcos Computers Ltd. v. Barclays Mercantile* **8–22** *Highland Finance Ltd.* [1994] F.S.R. 275, the matter was stated to be one of degree, a good guide being whether there has been an over-borrowing of the skill, labour and judgment which went into the copyright work.

Quality not quantity taken the test. It is the similarities between the **8–27** works which matter, not the differences: *Entec (Pollution Control) Ltd. v. Abacus Mouldings* [1992] F.S.R. 332.

Second sentence. Such statements should be treated with caution, **8–28** however, since they only serve as a guide. The taking of a substantial part must still be proved. See *Ibcos Computers Ltd. v. Barclays Mercantile Highland Finance Ltd.* [1994] F.S.R. 275.

B. *Copying in relation to literary works*

Compilations. Note that under the proposal for the E.C. Directive on **8–31** the legal protection of databases (93/C 308/1), stated in the proposed text to be implemented by January 1, 1995, the copyright owner is to have, in respect of (a) the selection or arrangement of the contents of the database and (b) the electronic material used to create or operate the database, the exclusive right to reproduce it, translate it, adapt it, arrange it, issue copies of it to the public (including by way of rental) or perform it in public.

It does not appear that any change will be required to United Kingdom law to implement this part of the proposal. Note, however, that a separate *sui generis* right is also proposed, whereby, subject to various limitations, the owner of the rights in a database will be entitled for a 15 year term to prevent extraction or re-utilisation of all or part of the material in the database for commercial purposes. It is not clear to what extent the new *sui generis* right will give greater protection than that already afforded to databases by United Kingdom copyright law. See, generally, *ante*, para. 1–58 *et seq.*

8–37   **Directories.** For another example of such copying, see *Fax Directories (Pty) Ltd. v. S.A. Fax Listings* [1990] 2 S.A.L.R. 164; (1992) S.A. 64 (D) (Sup. Ct. of S.A.).

In *Waterlow Directories Ltd v. Reed Information Services Ltd.* [1992] F.S.R. 409 the differences between *Morris v. Wright* (1870) L.R. 5, Ch. 279, *Kelly v. Morris* (1866) 1 Eq. 697 and *Morris v. Ashbee* (1868) L.R. 7, Eq. 34 were analysed as follows. In the latter two cases, the defendant had reproduced a substantial part of the plaintiff's work. In *Morris v. Wright*, the defendant intended, at the date of the hearing, only to use the plaintiff's work as a reference to request information. There had been no reproduction of the plaintiff's work and therefore no infringement. It seems therefore that the information in a directory may be used to compile another directory, provided reproduction does not take place. The case where names and addresses from the plaintiff's directory are reproduced in the form of envelopes and letters was left open. It is thought, however, that this would constitute an infringement.

NOTE 57.   The statement in *Kelly v. Morris* (1866) 1 Eq. 697 at 701, that a person cannot take "one word" of the information previously published in a directory without independently working the matter out for himself is too wide. Only copying of a substantial part is prohibited. It is clear that a person may not copy entries from a directory and use that information to compile his own directory: see *Waterlow Directories Ltd. v. Reed Information Services Ltd* [1992] F.S.R. 409.

NOTE 59.   *Waterlow Directories Ltd. v. Reed Information Services Ltd.* is now reported at [1992] F.S.R. 409.

8–38   **Other compilations.** Although in *Total Information Processing Systems Ltd. v. Daman Ltd.* [1992] F.S.R. 171 it was observed that it is unlikely that a table of the contents of a book could be described as a substantial part of the book, it was pointed out in *Ibcos Computers Ltd. v. Barclays Mercantile Highland Finance Ltd.* [1994] F.S.R. 275 that in each case it must be a matter of degree. The work involved in arranging topics in various headings and subdivisions might well mean that it amounted to a substantial part of the work as a whole. In the same way, the data division of a computer program might be a substantial part of the program: *ibid.*

So also, where copyright subsists in a compilation of separate computer programs (see *ante*, para. 2–8), that copyright will be infringed if a substantial part of the compilation is reproduced, even though some programs have been combined into one and further programs added. See *Ibcos Computers Ltd. v. Barclays Mercantile Highland Finance Ltd.* [1994] F.S.R. 275.

Parodies and burlesques.   **8–45**

NOTE 82. See also *A.G.L. Sydney Ltd. v. Shortland County Council* [1990] A.I.P.C. 90–661 (Fed. Ct. of Australia) (parody of advertisement by advertisement).

Computer programs. Note that Article 4 of the computer software   **8–46** Directive (see *ante*, para. 1–54 and *post*, para. H–19) provides that one of the exclusive rights of the owner of the copyright in a computer program shall include the right to do [*sic*] or to authorise the permanent or temporary reproduction of a computer program by any means and in any form, in part or in whole. In so far as loading, display, running, transmission or storage of the computer program necessitates such reproduction, such acts shall be subject to authorisation by the right holder. No change to the 1988 Act was required to implement this part of the Directive.

Note also that in respect of a computer program the restricted act of making an adaptation under section 21 has been widened to include making an arrangement or altered version of the program. See *post*, para. 8–126. Sections 17 and 21 are not, however, apparently mutually exclusive: see section 21(5).

Note also the new series of permitted acts in relation to computer programs which have been introduced by amendment. See *post*, para. 10–59A *et seq.*

NOTE 85. The decision in *Apple Computers Inc. v. Mackintosh Computers Ltd.* was affirmed on appeal: (1990) 71 D.L.R. 95.

NOTE 87. Note the amendment now made to the definition of adaptation in relation to a computer program, considered at *post*, para. 8–126.

At end of paragraph. In defined circumstances, the making of backup copies is now expressly a permitted act: see *post*, para. 10–59B.

8–47   Note the provisions of the computer software Directive, (see *ante*, para. 1–*54*) in particular Article 1(2) (see *post*, para H–16), which provides that: "Ideas and principles which underlie any element of a computer program, including those which underlie its interfaces, are not protected by copyright under this Directive." No corresponding amendment was made to the 1988 Act when the Directive was implemented, and presumably the 1988 Act must be taken to reflect this position accurately, a view confirmed when the Regulations amending the 1988 Act were debated in the House of Lords: *Hansard*, H.L. Vol. 541, cols. 514–516.)

In accordance with the usual principles:

(1) The copyright in a computer program will be infringed if a substantial part has been reproduced in the defendant's program, notwithstanding that the defendant has added a substantial amount of new and original material.

(2) It is not necessary to examine every part of the source code of the defendant's program to establish reproduction of a substantial part. A comparison of samples will be sufficient if they are representative.

See *Ibcos Computers Ltd. v. Barclays Mercantile Highland Finance Ltd.* [1994] F.S.R. 275 and *Accounting Systems 2000 (Developments) Pty. Ltd. v. C.C.H. Australia Limited* (1993) 114 A.L.R. 355 (Fed. Ct. of Australia).

First sentence of § 8–47. The fact that two devices produce the same output in response to a challenge, *i.e.* perform the same function, does not necessarily mean that there is any similarity between the computer program within, was confirmed in *John Richardson Computers Ltd. v. Flanders* [1993] F.S.R. 497; *Autodesk Inc v. Dyason* [1992] R.P.C. 575 (High Ct. of Australia) and *News Datacom Ltd., British Sky Broadcasting Ltd. v. Lyons*, noted at [1994] 4 EIPR D–76.

Third sentence. In a decision of the Australian High Court, a computer program which included a 127-bit "look-up table", by reference to which the program processed information, was held to be infringed by a device which reproduced the look-up table in a 127-bit series stored within an EPROM. The EPROM contained a set of digits which was identical with the digits produced by the look-up table when read as the computer program read it: see *Autodesk Inc v. Dyason* [1992] R.P.C. 575 (High Ct. of Australia). The fact that the work had been copied indirectly by using an oscilloscope to discover the series of numbers made no difference. It is not clear that an English court would reach the same decision on the facts. What had been taken from the plaintiff's work was a randomly generated series of numbers which, it seems, would not by itself have qualified for copyright protection. (See, for example, *John Richardson Computers Ltd. v. Flanders*

[1993] F.S.R. 497). For criticism of the decision, see Lahore in [1992] 12 EIPR 428 and Prescott in [1992] 6 EIPR 191. See also the doubts expressed about the decision in *Autodesk Inc v. Dyason (No. 2)* [1993] R.P.C. 259 and the more recent decisions in the United States, *infra*.

NOTES 91 and 92. Note that *Whelan* has not been followed in the United States. See *Computer Associates International Inc. v. Altai Inc.* 23 U.S.P.Q. 2d. 1241 (2nd Cir. 1992); *Atari Games Corp. v. Nintendo of America, Inc.* 975 F. 2d 832 (Fed. Cir. 1992); *Sega Enterprises Ltd. v. Accolade Inc.* (1992) 977 F. 2d. 1510; *Apple Computers Inc. v. Microsoft Corp.* 24 I.P.R. 225 (U.S. Dis. Ct.); and see *infra*. But note the caution against over-reliance on United States authorities expressed in *Ibcos Computers Ltd. v. Barclays Mercantile Highland Finance Ltd.* [1994] F.S.R. 275.

The question of what amounts to an infringement of one computer program by another, where the structure rather than the text is alleged to have been copied, arose for the decision of an English court for the first time in *John Richardson Computers Ltd. v. Flanders* [1993] F.S.R. 497 (although, see also *M.S. Associates v. Power* [1988] F.S.R. 242, where the issue arose on an interlocutory application). It was held that there could be such structural copying although it is a difficult issue, both in principle and in practice, to decide whether such copying has occurred. This general conclusion was confirmed in *Ibcos Computers Ltd. v. Barclays Mercantile Highland Finance Ltd.* [1994] F.S.R. 275.

In the *Richardson* case the facts were that the plaintiff company had developed a program designed to produce labels for medicines. The defendant had assisted in this and subsequently wrote a competing program which was alleged to infringe. The two programs were written in different computer languages. It was not alleged that the plaintiff's program had merely been translated, but rather that the general scheme had been taken, together with the detail of certain idiosyncratic routines. The plaintiff relied on such cases as *Rees v. Melville* [1911–16] Mac.C.C. 168, *Harman Pictures N.V. v. Osborne* [1967] 1 W.L.R. 723 and *Nichols v. Universal Pictures Corporation* (1930) 45 F. 2d 119. It was held that the correct approach was, following *Ladbroke (Football) Ltd v. William Hill (Football) Ltd.* [1964] 1 W.L.R. 273, to decide whether the plaintiff's program as a whole was entitled to copyright and then to decide whether any similarities between the two programs which were attributable to copying amounted to a substantial part of the plaintiff's program.

The difficulty remained of evaluating what constituted a substantial part. It was said that this evaluation should be undertaken bearing in mind that: (a) copyright protects only the expression of ideas and not the ideas themselves; and (b) the parts of the plaintiff's work which lacked originality were not entitled to protection in themselves, when robbed of any collocation. Controversially, it was held that in dealing with this issue, a similar approach should be adopted to that taken in the United States cases of *Computer Associates International Inc. v. Altai*

Inc. 23 U.S.P.Q. 2d 1241 (2nd Cr. 1992) and *Sega Enterprises Ltd. v. Accolade Inc.* (1992) 977 F. 2d 1510 (not following the earlier decision in *Whelan Associates Inc. v. Jaslow Dental Laboratory Inc.* [1987] F.S.R. 1), where an "abstraction" test had been used, stemming from the decision in *Nichols v. Universal Pictures Corporation* (1930) 45 F. 2d 119 (see *post*, para. 18–45). *Nichols* concerned the infringement of copyright in the structure of a play by a film, and it was pointed out in *Nichols* that a work such as a play has layers of decreasing complexity, as more and more detail is left out. As this process continues, there will come a point at which the "layer" is no longer protected, since it consists only of ideas and not their expression. With this in mind, the United States Court of Appeals in *Computer Associates* said that:

> "Initially, in a manner that resembles reverse engineering on a theoretical plane, a court should dissect the allegedly copied program's structure and isolate each level of abstraction contained within it. This process begins with the code and ends with the articulation of the program's ultimate function. Along the way, it is necessary essentially to retrace and map each of the designer's steps—in the opposite order to that in which they were taken during the program's creation. As an anatomical guide to this procedure, the following description is helpful:
> 'At the lowest level of abstraction, a computer program may be thought of in its entirety as a set of individual instructions organised into a hierarchy of modules. At a higher level of abstraction, the instructions in the lowest level modules may be replaced conceptually by the functions of those modules. At progressively higher levels of abstraction, the functions of the higher-level modules conceptually replaces the implementations of those modules until finally, one is left with nothing but the ultimate function of the program . . . A program has structure at every level of abstraction at which it is viewed. At low levels of abstraction, a program's structure may be quite complex; at the highest level it is trivial.'"

In the *Richardson* case it was therefore held that the test involves discovering the program's "abstraction levels". These abstractions must be filtered to disclose a "core" of protectable material. The process of filtration requires exclusion from consideration:

– elements dictated by efficiency, that is, those elements which result from the expression of an idea where there is only one way to express the idea;

– elements dictated by external factors, that is, elements which result from the description of the same facts, which can only be described in a particular way;

– elements taken from the public domain (or presumably those elements in which the plaintiff does not own the copyright).

A comparison must then be made between what is left of the abstractions made from the plaintiff's work with the defendant's program.

The test can be criticised on a number of grounds. Most importantly, as was pointed out in *Ibcos Computers Ltd. v. Barclays Mercantile Highland Finance Ltd.* [1994] F.S.R. 275, the United States law of copyright is not the same as the United Kingdom law. Section 102 of the United States Code specifically denies copyright protection to "any idea, procedure, process, system, method of operation, concept, principle, or discovery, regardless of the form in which it is described, explained, illustrated, or embodied" (see § E–16 in the Main Work). Although this may find an echo in decisions under the United Kingdom Copyright Acts (see §§ 1–1 and 8–8 in the Main Work) and now the computer software Directive (see *ante*, paras. 2–9 and *supra*) the fact is that the courts of the United States have traditionally been more reluctant to afford copyright protection where concepts of idea and function are involved. The position under the law of the United Kingdom as stated in *Ibcos* is that if the idea embodied in the plaintiff's work is sufficiently general, the mere taking of the idea will not infringe. If, however, the idea is worked out in detail in the plaintiff's work and the defendant reproduces the expression of that idea, he will infringe (see *ante*, para. 1–1). There is, however, no protection for the choice of design features (such as the number of security levels) which, although of interest to the user, do not require skill, labour or judgment on the part of the programmer. The conclusion reached in *Ibcos* was that in each case it is a question of degree, and a good guide is to consider whether there has been "an overborrowing of the skill, labour and judgment which went into the copyright work" (see also § 8–22 in the Main Work). In the end, this will be a matter for the court's value judgment, helped, especially in this field, by expert evidence.

The test propounded in *Richardson* can also be criticised because it appears to ignore the fact that, in general, copyright may subsist in a collection of non-copyright material if skill and labour has gone into its compilation.

Even if the test put forward in *Richardson* is the correct one, it is easier to propound than to apply (as was recognised in that case) and indeed the test does not appear to have been directly applied in the case itself. The plaintiff in the event did not rely on a comparison of the respective source codes or any abstractions from them and the case appears to have been decided on the basis of a comparison of the two programs in operation. This comparison appears to have formed the basis of both establishing the similarities in the programs and whether they were the result of copying, despite it being acknowledged that similarities in the external operation of the programs could at best only support an inference of copying. Certain similarities in the operation of the two programs were rejected as amounting to evidence of copying on the grounds that such operations of the plaintiff's program lacked originality or consisted merely of similarity of an idea rather than its expression. In other instances, where similarities were said to support the inference of copying, the items in question were held not to amount to a substantial part of the plaintiff's program. Finally certain features were held to be the result of the copying of a substantial part, although the amount of infringement was minimal.

The approach can be criticised, since it comes close to saying that copying can be established by setting up a case based on inference, relying on similarities in the operation of the two programs rather than in the programs themselves, coupled with the opportunity of copying. Unless the defendant can prove that he did not copy (which in *Richardson* he was unable to do, despite being acquitted of any deliberate copying), he will be liable.

In *Ibcos*, although there was a finding of structural copying within individual programs, the judgment contains little analysis of what it consisted of. In addition to a finding of copying of a compilation copyright (see *ante*, para. 8–38,), there was clear evidence of textual copying since numerous mistakes and idiosyncrasies had been reproduced. It was held that the amount taken was substantial.

See also Carr, H. and Arnold, R., *Computer Software: Legal Protection in the U.K.* (Sweet & Maxwell, 2nd ed., 1992).

D. *Copying in relation to musical works*

8–51   Fourth sentence. For a case where expert evidence was used, see *Grignon v. Roussel* (1991) 38 C.P.R. (3d) 4 (Fed. Ct. of Canada). Ultimately, however, the question remains one for the court.

NOTE 9. **Add**: *EMI Music Publishing Ltd. v. Evangelos Papathanassiou* [1993] E.M.L.R. 306: objective similarity between two works was not established simply because both works included a four note sequence, described as a "musical commonplace".

E. *Copying in relation to artistic works*

NOTE 22. **Add**: *Mono Pumps (N.Z.) v. Amalgamated Pumps* [1992] 1 N.Z.L.R. 728.

8–54   General principles.

NOTE 24. **Add**: *Mirage Studios v. Counter-Feat Clothing Co. Ltd* [1991] F.S.R. 145 (held; arguable that copyright in drawings for humanoid turtle figures had been infringed by figures which reproduced the concept but not the actual lines of the plaintiff's figures).

NOTES 25 and 26. How much of an artistic work is substantial cannot be defined by inches or measurement: see *Alan Nuttall v. Equipashop Ltd.* noted at [1992] I.P.D. 15097.

The test is: have the essential features and substance of a plaintiff's **8–55** work been adopted? See *Drayton Controls (Engineering) Ltd v. Honeywell Control Systems Ltd.* [1992] F.S.R. 245 following *Merchant Adventurers Ltd v. M. Grew & Co. Ltd.* [1973] R.P.C. 1.

NOTE 30. Thus the more simple and more commonplace the drawing, the more clearly must the alleged infringement adhere to it if liability is to be established: see *Collier Constructions Pty. Ltd. v. Foskett Pty. Ltd.* (1991) 20 I.P.R. 666 (Fed. Ct. of Australia); *Dixon Investments Pty. Ltd. v. Hall* (1990) 18 I.P.R. 481 (Fed. Ct. of Australia).

Infringement by reproduction 8–57

NOTE 34. See also *Ancher, Mortlock Murray & Woolley Pty. Ltd. v. Hooker Homes Pty. Ltd.* [1971] 2 N.S.W.L.R. 278 (Sup. Ct. of New Zealand).

NOTE 41. See also *A.G.L. Sydney Ltd. v. Shortland County Council* [1990] A.I.P.C. 90–661 (Fed. Ct. of Australia) (parody of advertisement by advertisement).

Substantial part. For a discussion of the principles of infringement **8–60** and substantiality, see *Ainsworth Nominees Pty. Ltd. v. Andclar Pty. Ltd.* (1988) 12 I.P.R. 551, [1989] A.I.P.C. 90–550, *Dixon Investments Pty. Ltd. v. Hall* (1990) 18 I.P.R. 490 (Fed. Ct. of Australia).

NOTE 46. In relation to a manufacturing drawing, reproduction of a substantial part means reproduction of the dimensions and spatial arrangements which are important for the purposes of manufacturing the article: see *Entec (Pollution Control) Ltd v. Abacus Mouldings* [1992] F.S.R. 332 (at first instance).

NOTE 47. So where the drawings relied on were little sketches of commonplace shapes and what was important and crucial were the dimensions written on them, it was distinctly arguable that a defendant who had copied the three-dimensional article made in accordance with the drawings had not copied a substantial part of what was visually significant. See *Entec (Pollution Control) Ltd v. Abacus Mouldings* [1992] F.S.R. 332. In that case, the drawings were so simple that the figures and dimensions which accompanied them might well have been calculated without any accompanying drawings at all.

Note 49. **Add**: *Monsoon Ltd. v. India Imports of Rhode Island Ltd.* [1993] F.S.R. 486.

8–67   **Functional objects.** Note that the Court of Appeal in *British Leyland Motor Corp. v. Armstrong Patents Co. Ltd.* [1986] A.C. 577 rejected the argument that copyright protection in three-dimensional reproductions of functional objects was unlawful under Article 30 of the Treaty of Rome: see *Entec (Pollution Control) Ltd v. Abacus Mouldings* [1992] F.S.R. 332.

8–73   **Infringement of plan by sketch.** Thus the copyright in the floor plans for a house, which included the room divisions, windows, entrances and various fittings, was not infringed by the reproduction of the outline only in an advertisement comparing overall sizes. See *Collier Constructions Pty. Ltd. v. Foskett Pty. Ltd.* (1991) 20 I.P.R. 666 (Fed. Ct. of Aus.). See also *Dixon Investments Pty. Ltd. v. Hall* (1990) 18 I.P.R. 481 (Fed. Ct. of Australia) and the cases cited there.

F. *Copying in relation to other works*

(i) Sound recordings

8–76   **The 1988 Act.** Note that the Directive on rental and lending rights 92/100 (see *ante* para. 1–55 and *post*, H–26 *et seq.*) requires Member States to provide for producers of sound recordings to have the exclusive right to authorise or prohibit the direct or indirect reproduction of such recordings (Art. 7(1)). No change is envisaged as being required to the 1988 Act.

As to "sampling", see *Grand Upright Music Ltd v. Warner Bros. Records Inc.* 91 Civ. 7648 U.S. Dist. See also Tackaberry in [1990] Ent. L.R. 87 (for Canadian Authorities) and Bently and Sherman in [1992] Ent. L.R. 158.

(ii) Films

8–80   **The 1988 Act.** Note that the Directive on rental and lending rights 92/100 (see *ante*, para. 1–55 and *post*, H–26 *et seq.*) requires Member States to provide for the producers of films to have the exclusive right to authorise or prohibit the direct or indirect reproduction of their films (Art. 7(1)). No change is anticipated to this part of the 1988 Act but see *ante*, para. 4–55 as to changes in the authorship provisions that will be required.

(iii) Broadcasts

The 1988 Act. Note that the Directive on rental and lending rights   **8–84**
92/100 (see *ante*, para. 1–55 and *post*, H–26 *et seq.*) requires Member
States to provide for broadcasters to have the exclusive right to
authorise or prohibit the "fixation" of their broadcasts or the direct or
indirect reproduction of such fixations (Art. 7(1)). No change is
anticipated to this part of the 1988 Act.

3. Infringement by the Issue of Copies to the Public

The 1988 Act. An amendment has been made to section 18 of   **8–92**
the 1988 Act by the Copyright (Computer Programs) Regulations
1992[1] to implement the Computer Software Directive (see *ante*, para.
1–54 and *post*, paras. A–21, B–279 and H–14 *et seq.*). Subsection 18(2)
has been amended and a new subsection (3) added, to read as follows:

> "(2) References in this Part to the issue to the public of copies of a
> work are except where the work is a computer program to the act
> of putting into circulation copies not previously put into circula-
> tion, in the United Kingdom or elsewhere, and not to—
>> (a) any subsequent distribution, sale, hiring or loan of those
>> copies, or
>> (b) any subsequent importation of those copies into the United
>> Kingdom;
> except that in relation to sound recordings and films the restricted
> act of issuing copies to the public includes any rental of copies to
> the public.
>
> (3) References in this Part to the issue to the public of copies of a
> work where the work is a computer program are to the act of
> putting into circulation copies of that program not previously put
> into circulation in the United Kingdom or any other member
> State, by or with the consent of the copyright owner, and not to—
>> (a) any subsequent distribution, sale, hiring or loan of those
>> copies, or
>> (b) any subsequent importation of those copies into the United
>> Kingdom;
> except that the restricted act of issuing copies to the public
> includes any rental of copies to the public."

---

[1] (S.I. 1992 No. 3233).

The provisions, as amended, apply to computer programs when-ever made (see reg. 12(1)), although note the existing provisions of Schedule 1, paragraph 14(2), of the 1988 Act.

The effect of the amendments seems to be as follows. Before amendment, if copies of a computer program had been put into circulation in, for example, the United States, there would have been no infringement by subsequently putting those copies into circulation in the United Kingdom. Following amendment, such an act will be an infringement. The computer software Directive, which these amend-ments were intended to implement, provides, *inter alia*, that the exclusive rights of the owner of the copyright in a computer program shall include the right to do [*sic*] or to authorise any form of distribution to the public, including rental, of the original computer program or of copies thereof, but that the first sale in the Community of a copy of a program by the rights owner or with his consent shall exhaust the distribution right within the Community of that copy, with the exception of the right to control further rental: see Article 4(c), *post*, para. H–19. Thus in respect of that copy, subject to the principle of exhaustion within the Community, any distribution of the program whether in the form of legitimate or infringing copies requires the copyright owner's consent.

8–93   The 1956 Act.

NOTE 80. **Substitute**: n. 75, p. 21.

8–95   The 1988 and 1956 Acts compared. Fourth sentence. Confirmed in *The British Phonographic Industry Ltd. v. Mechanical-Copyright Protection Society Ltd. (No. 2)* [1993] E.M.L.R. 86 at 98, note 9.

8–96   The Parliamentary debates on these provisions shed light on some of the problems referred to in the Main Work. (For a table listing the Parliamentary debates in full, see *post*, Appendix I). It seems clear that it was not the intention to make the mere act of distribution an infringement (see, for example, *Hansard*, H.L. Vol. 490, col. 1196). Further, the word "subsequent" was introduced into subsection (2)(b) to remove what was seen as an ambiguity in relation to imported copies (see *Hansard*, H.L. Vol. 140, col. 270; H.L. Vol. 501, cols. 214, 215). The amendment was intended to make clear that:

(1) Where there had been no prior issue to the public abroad, the importation of articles in bulk, for example, to a publisher, should not prevent the first issue thereafter being an infringement.

(2) Where issue to the public had taken place abroad and the articles were subsequently imported into the United Kingdom, there could be no infringement under section 18 (although there might be infringement by importation or sale with knowledge, etc.).

It therefore appears that it was not the intention to make the mere act of importation an infringing act under section 18.

The "rental" right. The definition of "rental" was amended during   **8–98** the passage of the Bill through Parliament with the example referred to in the Main Work (the provision of video cassette recordings of films by hotel owners to guests) specifically in mind. It was considered that in reality the guests paid for this service in the basic room charge and so the copyright owner should have a right to remuneration (see *Hansard*, H.C. Vol. 138, col. 128; H.L. Vol. 501, col. 215).

Note that separate provision is now made in respect of computer programs by the new subsection 18(3) added by the Copyright (Computer Programs) Regulations 1992 (see *ante*, para. 8–92).

Further amendment will, however, be required to the 1988 Act as a result of the Directive on rental and lending right 92/100 (see *ante*, para. 1–55 and *post*, para. H–26 *et seq.*), which was due to be implemented by July 1, 1994. The Directive requires that the exclusive right to authorise or prohibit rental and lending is to belong to:

(1) The author in respect of the original and copies of his work;

(2) The producer of sound recordings in respect of such recordings;

(3) The "producer" of a film in respect of the original and copies of such films.

For these purposes, the Directive defines "rental" as meaning the making available for use, for a limited period of time and for direct or indirect economic or commercial advantage (Art. 1(2)). "Lending" is defined as meaning the making available for use, for a limited period of time and not for direct or indirect economic or commercial advantage, when it is made through establishments which are accessible to the public (Art. 1(3)). Thus, in general, and subject to the exceptions referred to below, the copyright in all literary, dramatic, musical and artistic works will include the rental and lending right and not just, as at present, computer programs, films and sound recordings. Note also the provisions of Article 2(2), referred to at *ante*, para. 4–55 which will require amendment to the 1988 Act to widen the definition of author in relation to a film, to include, at least, the principal director.

Exceptions are to be provided in respect of rental and lending in relation to buildings and works of applied art (Art. 2(3)) and Member

States will be allowed to derogate from the exclusive rights in respect of public lending, provided that at least authors obtain reasonable remuneration for such lending. In the United Kingdom, the Public Lending Right Scheme 1982 (see § 12–12 in the Main Work and *post*, para. 12–12 *et seq.*) already provides for the public library lending of books. Lending by a library authority of computer programs, sound recordings and films is treated as rental within the meaning of section 18, whether or not a charge is made and so is already subject to the exclusive control of the copyright owner. See section 8 of the Public Libraries and Museums Act 1964, as amended by Schedule 7, paragraph 8 of the 1988 Act. It is understood that no fundamental change is envisaged to the Public Lending Right Scheme, although consideration will be given to bringing computer programs, films and sound recordings within the scheme, together with other works, such as printed music and works of art.

Member States may also exempt certain categories of establishment from payment of reasonable remuneration (Art. 5(3)) and it is understood that lending by libraries in the educational sector, and perhaps others, is likely to be excepted.

4. Infringement by Performance, Showing or Playing of the Work in Public

8–103   The person liable for the infringement.

NOTE 15. Followed in *Canadian Performing Right Society Ltd. v. Ford Hotel* [1935] 2 D.L.R. 391 and *Performing Right Society Ltd. v. Gillette* [1943] 1 All E.R. 413. **Add**: *Messager v. British Broadcasting Co. Ltd.* [1929] A.C. 151.

8–112   "In public".

NOTE 57. **Add**: *Canadian Admiral Corporation Ltd. v. Rediffusion Inc.* [1954] Ex. C.R. 382.

The playing of a sound recording by means of a videocassette in the presence of 11 employees, the general public being unable to see or hear it, was held to be "in public", the purpose of the playing of the videocassette being to impart information to the employees: *Australasian Performing Rights Association v. Commonwealth Bank of Australia* (1992) 111 A.L.R. 671 (Fed. Ct. of Australia).

8–114   Note that in *Australasian Performing Right Association Ltd. v. Telstra Corp. Ltd.* [1994] R.P.C. 229, the transmission of signals to a mobile telephone user was held not to amount to a transmission "to the public". The transmission was intended to facilitate a private communication (see also *post*, para. 8–118).

5. Infringement by Broadcasting or Inclusion in Cable Programme Service

The 1988 Act. Note that the Directive on satellite broadcasting and   **8–118** cable retransmission 93/83 (see *ante*, para. 1–56 and *post*, para. H–44 *et seq.*), due to be implemented by January 1, 1995, requires Member States to confer on authors of copyright works the exclusive right to authorise the communication to the public of the work by satellite. (The rights of producers of sound recordings and broadcasting organisations are to be protected, for this purpose, in accordance with the rights conferred by Articles 6, 7 and 8 of the Directive on rental and lending rights 92/100 (see *ante*, para. 1–55 and *post*, para. H–27 *et seq.*). Broadly, the communication to the public is for this purpose to be taken to occur at the place where the signals are transmitted to the satellite, that is, at the "up-leg" (Art. 1(2)(a)), and only at that place. More specifically, the communication is to be treated as taking place where the signals intended for reception are introduced into an uninterrupted chain of communication leading to the satellite and down towards the earth. Prima facie, therefore, the broadcast and, if unlicensed, the act of infringement, will take place in the Member State where the signal originated and not in the State where the signal is received. Where the signal originates in a non-Community state not providing equivalent protection, but transmission in fact occurs from an up-link station situated within a Member State, the communication is to be taken as having taken place from that Member State. Where no such link station is used, but a broadcasting organisation established within a Member State has commissioned the communication, the communication will be deemed to have taken place in that Member State and the organisation will be liable for any infringement (Art. 1(2)(d)(ii); and see *post*, para. H–47.

The Directive enables Member States to introduce a degree of blanket control through collecting societies although it is not certain to what extent the United Kingdom will introduce such measures. Thus Article 3(2) provides that a Member State may provide that a collective agreement between a collecting society and a broadcasting organisation concerning particular categories of works may be extended to rightholders of the same category who are not represented by the collecting society, provided that the communication to the public by satellite "simulcasts" a terrestrial broadcast by the same broadcaster. The unrepresented rightholder is, however, to have the right to have his works excluded from the collective agreement and to exercise his rights individually or collectively outside the scope of the collecting society's agreement (Art. 3(2)). These provisions are also not to apply to cinematographic works and works created by any analogous process (Art. 3(3)).

As to cable re-transmission, the Directive requires that the consent of the right holder is required for simultaneous retransmission by cable of programmes from other Member States (Art. 9(1)). Generally, this corresponds to the existing position under United Kingdom law (see § 10–123 in the Main Work), but the Directive requires that the cable retransmission right is only exercised through a collecting society. Provisions are to be implemented to enable mediation where no agreement on terms can be reached.

Third sentence. Note that under the Australian Copyright Act 1968, which as amended defines broadcast to mean "transmit by wireless telegraphy to the public", the transmission of signals to a person as part of a mobile telephone network was held not to amount to broadcasting. The transmission was intended to facilitate a private conversation and was not therefore "to the public". See *Australasian Performing Right Association v. Telstra Corp. Ltd.* (1993) 118 A.L.R. 683 (Fed. Ct. of Australia).

6. Infringement by Making an Adaptation

8–126   **Meaning of adaptation.** A separate definition of adaptation in relation to a computer program has now been inserted by amendment to the 1988 Act made by the Copyright (Computer Programs) Regulations 1992 brought into force to implement the computer software Directive (see *ante*, para. 1–54 and *post*, para. H–14 *et seq.*). Section 21(3) now provides:

> "(3) In this Part 'adaptation'—
> . . .
>
> (ab) in relation to a computer program, means an arrangement or altered version of the program or a translation of it."

The only definition of adaptation in the original definition which was in any sense appropriate to a computer program was "a translation", which was further defined in respect of a computer program to include a version of the program in which it was converted into or out of a computer language or code or into a different computer language or code, otherwise than incidentally in the course of running the program: see section 21(4). This section has now been amended by the

Regulations by the deletion of the words "otherwise than incidentally in the course of running the program" (see below). The amendment therefore adds to the definition of "adaptation", in respect of a computer program, an arrangement or altered version of the program. It is questionable whether an "arrangement" or "altered version" of a computer program, not amounting to a translation, in which sequences of commands or routines are re-arranged, would not have constituted a reproduction within the meaning of section 17 of the 1988 Act. (In this context note section 21(5), which provides that no inference shall be drawn from section 21 as to what does or does not amount to copying of a work).

The Directive provides that one of the exclusive rights of the owner of the copyright in a computer program is to include the right to do or to authorise the translation, adaptation, arrangement or any other alteration of the computer program and the reproduction of the results thereof (Art. 4(b).

Translation. See also as to translations, Vaver in [1994] EIPR 159.   **8–128**

"Translation" of a computer program. As noted above, the definition   **8–129** of translation in respect of a computer program has now been amended by the Copyright (Computer Programs) Regulations 1992 to delete the words "otherwise than incidentally in the course of running the program". This amendment has been made to give effect to Article 4 of the computer software Directive which provides that one of the exclusive rights of the owner of the copyright in a computer program is the right to do or to authorise the permanent or temporary reproduction of a computer program by any means and in any form, and that in so far as the loading, displaying, running, transmission or storage of the computer program necessitates such reproduction, such acts are to be subject to the authorisation of the copyright owner.

7. Infringement by Authorisation

Note 61. **Add**: *Georges de Tervagne v. Town of Beloeil*, noted at [1993]   **8–137**
E.I.P.R. D–279 (Fed. Ct. of Canada).

Note 68. *C.f. Brintons Ltd. v. Feltex Furnishings of New Zealand Ltd.*   **8–138**
[1991] 2 N.Z.L.R. 677 (High Ct. of N.Z.), where it was held that a person who merely authorised another to make an article could not be liable for infringement unless he knew that the article was a copy of another work. The decision was apparently based on the premise that "there can only be copying if the infringer knows he is copying". *Sed quaere.*

8–139   **Examples of "authorisation".** For a case concerning a company director see *Australasian Performing Rights Assn. Ltd. v. Jain* (1990) 18 I.P.R. 663 (Fed. Ct. Australia).

NOTE 69. See also *Georges de Tervagne v. Town of Beloeil* (Fed. Ct. of Canada) noted at [1993] Ent. L.R. E–107.

8–140   So, too, a seller of a computer program ordinarily authorises the purchaser to use it. See *Ibcos Computers Ltd. v. Barclays Mercantile Highland Finance Ltd.* [1994] F.S.R. 275.

8–142   **Other matters.** In *Century Communications Ltd v. Mayfair Entertainment UK Ltd.* [1993] E.M.L.R. 335, a defendant had been given informal consent to distribute a film and consequently had authorised its public performance by third party exhibitors. The plaintiff subsequently revoked the consent and sued for infringement. Held, in respect of acts of public performance subsequent to revocation of the consent, but authorised beforehand, there was no infringement by authorisation.

8. Licence and Non-derogation from Grant

8–144   **Introduction.** It will be for the plaintiff to establish the absence of a licence: see *Computermate Products (Aust.) Pty. Ltd. v. Ozi-Soft Pty. Ltd.* (1988) 83 A.L.R. 492; *Avel Pty. Ltd. v. Multicoin Amusements Pty. Ltd.* (1990) 97 A.L.R. 19 (High Ct. of Australia) and *Devefi Pty. Ltd. v. Mateffy Pearl Nagy Pty. Ltd.* [1993] R.P.C. 493 (Fed. Ct. of Australia).

8–146   **Formalities.** For an example of an informal licence, see *Century Communications Ltd v. Mayfair Entertainment UK Ltd.* [1993] E.M.L.R. 335, noted at *ante*, para. 8–142.

8–147   **Implied licences.** Second sentence. **Delete:** " . . . its terms." **Substitute:** " . . . its existence and extent." See *Noah v. Shuba* [1991] F.S.R. 14; see also *De Garis v. Neville Jeffress Pidler Pty. Ltd.* (1990) 18 I.P.R. 292 (Fed. Ct. of Australia), confirming the position on the onus of proof.

NOTE 3. **Add:** *Noah v. Shuba* [1991] F.S.R. 14. See also the cases cited at *ante*, para. 8–144.

NOTE 6. See *De Garis v. Neville Jeffress Pidler Pty. Ltd* (1990) 18 I.P.R. 292 (Fed. Ct. of Australia) (no licence from journalists to use published work in commercial press clippings service, there being no business efficacy requirement). Where the use complained of is common practice, this will not necessarily mean a licence is implied: *ibid.*, applying *Maxwell v. Somerton* (1874) 30 L.T. 11.

The licensee. The right to transfer the right or licence to use sketch   **8–148** plans may be implied, but obviously no licence will pass to an assignee where the contract expressly prohibits assignment. See *Linden Gardens Trust Ltd. v. Lenesta Sludge Disposals Ltd.* [1994] 1 A.C. 85. See also *Devefi Pty. Ltd. v. Mateffy Pearl Nagi Pty. Ltd.* [1993] R.P.C. 493 (Fed. Ct. Australia) (contract for complex professional services—no right to assign benefit without express provision) and *Beck v. Montana Constructions Pty. Ltd.* [1964–65] N.S.W.R. 229.

NOTE 53. The page reference to *Bowden Bros.* should be 386.

NOTE 54. **Delete**: n.51. **Substitute**: n.53.

Other examples of implied licences. Add (at end): Held arguable   **8–158** that purchasers of computer hardware had an implied licence to use diagnostic software to repair it: *Digital Equipment Corp. v. L.C.E. Computer Maintenance Ltd.* noted at [1992] I.P.D. 15121.

   Add (at end): There is no implied licence to reproduce part of a directory when compiling a rival directory: see *Waterlow Directories Ltd. v. Reed Information Services Ltd.* [1992] F.S.R. 409.

Non-derogation from grant: the right to repair. It was held arguable   **8–161** that the purchasers of computer hardware had the right to use diagnostic software to repair it in *Digital Equipment Corp. v. L.C.E. Computer Maintenance Ltd.* noted at [1992] I.P.D. 15121.

NOTE 67. In *Flogates Ltd. v. Refco Ltd.*, noted at [1994] I.P.D. 10072, it was confirmed that the "spare part" doctrine continues to apply even after the passing of the 1988 Act (reliance also being placed on paragraph 19(1) of Schedule 1 to the Act). In the same case it was held arguable that the doctrine was applicable to parts of a machine which needed to be replaced regularly ("mere consumables") and whose replacement could not be described as "repair". The question may turn on whether the enforcement of the copyright would potentially render the machine unfit for the purpose for which it was bought.

CHAPTER 9

SECONDARY OR INDIRECT INFRINGEMENT OF COPYRIGHT

2. Dealings in Infringing Copies

A. *Introduction*

9–3   **The 1988 Act.** For a table listing the Parliamentary debates on these and other provisions of the 1988 Act, see post, Appendix I.

B. *Infringing copy*

9–4   Second sentence. Following the amendments made to the 1988 Act by the Copyright (Computer Programs) Regulations 1992 (see *ante*, para. 1–54 and *post*, para. B–279), this definition of an infringing article must now be read subject to the new subsection 27(3A) which provides that a copy of a computer program which has previously been sold in any other Member State, by or with the consent of the copyright owner, is not an infringing copy for the purposes of subsection (3). This amendment was no doubt intended to give effect to Article 4 of the computer software Directive (see *post*, para. H–14 *et seq.*) which provides that one of the exclusive rights of the owner of the copyright in a computer program is to include the right to do or to authorise any form of distribution to the public, including the rental, of the original computer program or of copies thereof, but that the first sale in the Community of a copy of a program by the copyright owner or with his consent shall exhaust the distribution right within the Community of that copy (except in relation to further rental; see *ante*, para. 8–92).

It is not clear that this amendment adds anything to the effect of subsection 25(5), which already provides that nothing in subsection (3) shall be construed as applying to an article which may lawfully be imported into the United Kingdom by virtue of an enforceable Community Right within the meaning of section 2(1) of the European Communities Act 1972. (See § 9–7 in the Main Work.)

The European Communities Act 1972.   **9–7**

NOTE 18. The bare fact that an article has been sold in a Community territory, and the owner has not prevented it, will not be enough to raise a defence in the absence of any evidence supporting the inference that the copyright owner knew that the sale was taking place and could have prevented it and so must be taken to have authorised it: see *EMI Records Ltd. v. The C.D. Specialists Ltd.* [1992] F.S.R. 70. See also *supra*, para. 9–4.

E. *Infringement by possession*

The expression "possession in the course of a business" must be given   **9–12** some limited interpretation, for otherwise a party's solicitor might be liable if he came into possession of an infringing article while acting for a client. This would be absurd. See *L.A. Gear Inc. v. Hi-Tec Sports plc.* [1992] F.S.R. 121. This view is supported by a statement made by the Government when resisting an amendment to section 24. It was said that a person who was merely looking after an article for a friend would have "custody or control" of it, but that the friend would have "possession" of it. *Hansard, H.L.* Vol. 490, col. 1216. (Note, however, that the words "in the course of a business" were subsequently added to the infringing act of possession.)

The expression "in the course of a business" is not limited to a course of doing business in the article: see *L.A. Gear Inc. v. Hi-Tec Sports plc.* [1992] F.S.R. 121.

F. *Infringement by sale*

9–14   Articles which were concealed from view at a trade exhibition and were produced only to those who asked to see them, but were not for sale although a brochure and price list referring to them were openly available, were neither offered for sale nor exposed for sale and were arguably not exhibited in public. See *L.A. Gear Inc. v. Hi-Tec Sports plc.* [1992] F.S.R. 121.

H. *Infringement by importation*

9–16   Import means "bring into". Thus cargo which is brought into country B when in transit from countries A to C, is imported into B. The position may be different if the cargo comes into the country involuntarily, for example, as a result of a hijack or bad weather. See *Mattel Inc. v. Tonka Corp.* [1992] F.S.R. 28 (High Court Hong Kong). Importation into England occurs when the goods are physically received in the country and become subject to the English Court's jurisdiction. See *L.A. Gear Inc. v. Hi-Tec Sports plc.* [1992] F.S.R. 121.

I. *Knowledge*

9–18   **Necessity to prove knowledge.** The provisions as to knowledge in the 1988 Act should not be construed in accordance with the provisions of the 1956 Act and such cases as *Van Dusen v. Kritz* [1936] 2 K.B. 176 and *Hoover plc v. George Hulme (Stockport) Ltd.* [1982] F.S.R. 565. The words "has reason to believe" should be construed in accordance with their ordinary meaning and proper construction and effect, although in doing so the same result may be arrived at as under the 1956 Act: see *L.A. Gear Inc. v. Hi-Tec Sports plc.* [1992] F.S.R. 121. Thus:

(1) "reason to believe" involves a concept of knowledge of facts from which a reasonable man would arrive at the relevant belief. The test is thus an objective one.

(2) Facts from which a reasonable man might suspect the relevant conclusion cannot be enough.

(3) The section connotes the allowance of a period of time to enable the reasonable man to evaluate the facts and to convert them into a reasonable belief.

Further, mere knowledge of disputed allegations of fact, the truth of which is not known to the defendant, is not enough for these purposes.

See *Hutchinson Personal Communications Ltd. v. Hook Advertising Ltd.*, noted at [1994] I.P.D. 17073.

These principles, particularly (1) and (2) above, are consistent with what was said during the Parliamentary debates on this and related provisions of the 1988 Act (for a full table of the debates, see *post*, Appendix I). Thus, it is clear that it was the intention that the requirement of guilty knowledge be relaxed (see also the White Paper (Intellectual Property and Innovation, Cmnd. 9712, paragraph 12.12). It was stated that the intention was to make liable a person who turned a blind eye to the facts, whether they would be obvious to a reasonable person or not, and also a neglectful person. It was not, however, the intention to make liable a person who had "grounds to suspect" but failed to appreciate the significance of the facts.

In *L.A. Gear Inc. v. Hi-Tec Sports plc.* [1992] F.S.R. 121, Staughton L.J. indicated that even if a defendant might not have the necessary knowledge at the date of the issue of the writ, this might still justify the claim for an injunction (if not other remedies) if he subsequently acquired this knowledge and demonstrated an intention to deal in the goods. *Sed quaere.* The plaintiff would have had no cause for action at the date of the writ nor any justification for seeking a *quia timet* injunction.

In *Monsoon Ltd. v. India Imports of Rhode Island Ltd.* [1993] F.S.R. 486,   **9–22** 21 days was considered a reasonable time, given that inquiries needed to be made abroad.

3. Providing the Means of Making Infringing Copies

Second paragraph. It was made clear during the debates on this   **9–24** provision of the Bill that it was intended to apply only to articles which are specific to a particular work. An amendment to alter the wording from "an article specifically designed. . .for making copies of that work", to "an article designed for making copies of that class of works" was successfully resisted. See *Hansard* H.L. Vol. 490, col. 1217 and the report of the debates of House of Commons Standing Committee E in 1988, col. 166. As to the meaning of the word possession, see *ante*, para. 9–12.

Chapter 10

Permitted Acts

Contents   *Para.*

1. Introduction

10–2 For a table listing the Parliamentary debates on these and other provisions of the 1988 Act, see *post*, Appendix I.

NOTE 15, and the sentence ending ". . .express contractual term." For confirmation that this was the purpose of this provision in section 28(1), see the report of the debates of House of Commons Standing Committee E in 1988, col. 178 and *Hansard*, H.L. Vol. 501, col. 228.

2. General Provisions

A. *Research and private study*

10–4 **The 1988 Act.** In the equivalent Australian provision, "research" was held to have the ordinary dictionary meaning, namely, the "diligent and systematic inquiry or investigation into a subject in order to discover facts or principles." (See *De Garis v. Neville Jeffress Pidler Pty. Ltd.* (1990) 18 I.P.R. 292 (Fed. Ct. of Australia).) Thus, the taking of copies of articles from newspapers, as part of a press clippings service by which photocopies were provided to subscribers in return for a fee, was not done for research.

In the same case, "study" was held to have the ordinary dictionary meaning, namely: (1) The application of the mind to the acquisition of knowledge, as by reading, investigation or reflection. (2) The cultivation of a particular branch of learning, science, or art [as in the study of law]. (3) A particular course of effort to acquire knowledge [as in the pursuance of medical studies] (4) A thorough examination and analysis of a particular subject.

10–7 **"Fair Dealing".** The 1988 Act has been amended by the Copyright (Computer Programs) Regulations 1992 to make further provision in section 29 as to what does not amount to fair dealing. See generally, *ante*, para. 1–54 and *post*, para. B–279). A new subsection (4) has been inserted as follows:

"(4) It is not fair dealing—
   (a) to convert a computer program expressed in a low level language into a version expressed in a higher level language, or

(b) incidentally in the course of so converting the program, to copy it,
(these acts being permitted if done in accordance with section 50B (decompilation))."

The new decompilation right is considered at *post*, para. 10–59A.
Where the defendant prepared competing educational course materials using the plaintiff's copyright works, this was not fair dealing. See *The Longman Group Ltd. v. Carrington Technical Institute Board of Governors* [1991] 2 N.Z.L.R. 574; (1990) 20 I.P.R. 264 (High Ct. of N.Z.)

NOTE 31. **Add**: *The Longman Group Limited v. Carrington Technical Institute Board of Governors* [1991] 2 N.Z.L.R. 574; (1990) 20 I.P.R. 264 (High Ct. of N.Z.); *De Garis v. Neville Jeffress Pidler Pty. Ltd.* [1990] 18 I.P.R. 292 (Fed. Ct. of Australia); *Television New Zealand Ltd. v. Newsmonitor Services Ltd.* noted at [1993] Ent. L.R. E-6 (High Ct. of N.Z.).

B. *Criticism, review and news reporting*

"Fair dealing". *B.B.C. v. British Sky Broadcasting Ltd.* is now reported **10–10**
sub nom. B.B.C. v. British Satellite Broadcasting Ltd. at [1992] Ch. 141.
In *Time Warner Entertainment Co. LP v. Channel Four Television Corp. plc* [1994] E.M.L.R. 1, the issue arose as to what amounted to fair dealing with a film for purposes of criticism or review. The film, *A Clockwork Orange*, had been withdrawn from public exhibition in the United Kingdom for almost twenty years, although it continued to be exhibited abroad. The defendant proposed to broadcast a half–hour programme about the film using twelve clips, representing about 8 per cent. of the film and occupying about 40 per cent. of the programme. On an application for an interlocutory injunction, the Court of Appeal held, perhaps surprisingly, that a defence of fair dealing was clearly established so that there was no serious issue to go to trial. As to the various matters raised by the plaintiff:

(1) It was held that the fact that a defendant had obtained a copy of the work in question in a clandestine manner would seldom make subsequent dealing unfair where the work was already in the public domain. (Compare the position where the work was unpublished: see § 10–10, note 52, in the Main Work). It was said that the "mischief at which the Act is aimed is to prevent copyright owners of works which they have put in the public domain from picking and choosing as to who may review

their works, when they may do so, and what clips they may use."
(See also *Chatterton v. Cave* (1878) 3 App. Cas. 483 at 492: "Books
are published with an expectation, if not a desire, that they will
be criticised in reviews."

(2) It was not necessary that the parts of the work used be
representative of the work as a whole. Criticism of a single aspect
of the work was capable of constituting fair dealing.

(3) Fair criticism of a film might require showing clips for a
substantial part of the programme.

(4) The defence of fair dealing might apply even where the criticism
was not of the work or another work but, as here, of the decision
to withdraw the work from public exhibition. This conclusion
seems contrary to the express wording of the Act but was
justified on the basis that in the particular case such criticism was
inseparable from criticism of the work.

NOTE 46. So where a broadcaster took excerpts from another's sports
programmes, each excerpt consisting of about 30 seconds from a
broadcast lasting 90 minutes, and repeated each excerpt three or four
times in each news report and each report three or four times over a
24-hour period, this was fair in the context of reporting World Cup
football, even though it was the highlights which had been taken. See
British Broadcasting Corporation v. British Satellite Broadcasting Ltd. [1992]
Ch. 141.

NOTE 48 **Delete**: reference to n.61, *ante*. **Substitute**: Thus, the dealing
must be for the purposes referred to in the section and not some other
oblique motive. See *Beloff v. Pressdram Ltd.* [1973] R.P.C. 765 and
Johnstone v. Bernard Jones Publications Ltd. [1938] Ch. 599 at 607. Where
one television broadcaster of sports news used short extracts from
another's sports programmes, the fact that the former was in competition with the latter and wished to make its programmes attractive to
viewers did not amount to an oblique motive. See *British Broadcasting
Corporation v. British Satellite Broadcasting Ltd.* [1992] Ch. 141.

NOTE 52. See also *Commonwealth v. John Fairfax & Sons Ltd.* (1980) 147
C.L.R. 39 (High Ct. of Australia) and *Wiggington v. Brisbane TV Ltd.*
(1992) 25 I.P.R. 58 (Sup. Ct. of Queensland).

10–11 **"Criticism or review"**. In both *De Garis v. Neville Jeffress Pidler Pty. Ltd.*
(1990) 18 I.P.R. 292 (Fed. Ct. of Australia) and *Wiggington v. Brisbane
TV Ltd.* (1992) 25 I.P.R. 58 (Sup. Ct. of Queensland), "criticism" was
given its dictionary definition of: (1) The act or art of analysing and
judging the quality of a literary or artistic work, etc. [as in literary
criticism]; (2) The act of passing judgement as to the merits of

something . . . (4) A critical comment, article or essay, a critique. In the same case "review" was given its dictionary definition of: a critical article or report, as in a periodical, on some literary work, commonly some work of recent appearance; a critique.

End of paragraph. For copying to be justified as being for research or private study, there must be a request for supply not just a supply generated by a librarian or teacher: *ibid.*

Reporting current events   10–13

Note 65 *B.B.C. v. British Sky Broadcasting Ltd.* is now reported *sub nom.* *B.B.C. v. British Satellite Broadcasting Ltd.* at [1992] Ch. 141.

C. *Incidental Inclusion of Copyright Material*

As to the special provision made for musical works, etc., during the   **10–16** debates on this provision of the Bill the distinction was made between the following examples:

(1) An outside broadcast or film made of a sporting event, during which musical works played over the public address system might be picked up: no infringement, even if the film of the event was subsequently edited, leaving in the recording of the musical works; and

(2) the playing of music on a radio as part of the background in a television drama, or the inclusion of specially written music in the soundtrack of a film: not incidental inclusion, because the producer had a choice as to whether or not to include the work.

See *Hansard*, H.L. Vol. 491, cols. 123, 124 and the report of the debates of the House of Commons Standing Committee E in 1988, cols. 218–220. The fact that special provision was made for musical works, etc., appears to have been the result of lobbying by the music industry, whereas other groups did not appear to see any grounds for concern, presumably because non-musical works are unlikely to be used in this way to the same extent: *ibid.*

3. Education

B. *Anthologies for educational use*

The 1988 Act. Final sentence. The purpose of subsection 33(4) was to   **10–23** make sure that the exception provided by section 33 can be made use of by the Open University and similar organisations, where use of publications would take place mostly in the home of the student rather than on the premises of the institution itself. See *Hansard*, H.L. Vol. 493, col. 1166.

5. Public Administration

D. *Material communicated to the Crown*

10–54   **The 1988 Act.** For the purposes of this provision, the "Crown" is now to include a health service body as defined in the National Health Service and Community Care Act 1990 and a National Health Service Trust established under that Act or the National Health Service (Scotland) Act 1978. The reference to "public business" is to be construed accordingly. See the National Health Service and Community Care Act 1990, section 60, Schedule 8, paragraph 3 and see *post*, para. A–51.

Penultimate sentence. The purpose of subsection 48(2) is to enable any person, body or company which submits evidence to a government body to be sure that the evidence or submission will not be unfairly used but will be used in connection with a purpose for which it was originally intended. Thus, a person providing material to a Government body or department which is looking into some matter, can reasonably anticipate that the material will be published. The Crown should not be limited in using the evidence in a report: see *Hansard*, H.L. Vol 495, cols. 642, 643.

F. *Acts done under Statutory Authority*

10–58   Clause 50(1) was amended during the passage of the Bill through Parliament to make it clear that no exemption from copyright control was being given to some whole class of activity which is authorised by Act of Parliament, for example, broadcasting by independent television authorised by the Broadcasting Acts. See *Hansard*, H.L. Vol. 495, Col. 643.

5/1. Permitted Acts in Relation to Computer Programs

10–59A   A new series of permitted acts has been introduced by amendment to the 1988 Act to implement the computer software Directive (see *ante*, para. 1–54 and *post*, para. H–14 *et seq.*). The new permitted acts are broadly as follows:

(1) The making of back up copies by a "lawful user" of a computer program (see *infra*, para. 10–59B).

(2) In certain limited conditions, the decompilation of a computer program, that is, its conversion into a higher level language, as part of the creation of another independent computer program (see *post*, para. 10–59C).

(3) The copying or adaptation of a program where a lawful user needs to do so, in particular where he needs to do so to correct errors (see *post*, para. 10–59D).

In conjunction with these new permitted acts, a new section 296A has also been introduced, striking down certain contractual terms which would have the effect of nullifying the new permitted acts. Section 296A provides that where a person has the use of a computer program under an agreement, any term or condition under the agreement shall be void in so far as it purports to prohibit or restrict:

(a) the making of any back up copy of the program which it is necessary for him to have for the purposes of the agreed use;

(b) where the conditions for the decompilation right are met, the decompiling of the program; or

(c) the use of any device or means, to observe, study or test the functioning of the program in order to understand the ideas and principles which underlie any element of the program.

The amendments are not, however, to affect any agreement or any term or condition of an agreement where the agreement, term or condition was entered into before January 1, 1993: see paragraph 12(2) of the Copyright (Computer Programs) Regulations 1992, *post*, para. B–279.

A. *Back up copies*

The right to make back up copies of computer programs was debated **10–59B** during the passage of the 1988 Act through Parliament but no provision was, however, made. The making of back up copies was therefore an infringement unless the copyright owner had consented to such use (see § 8–46 in the Main Work). In practice, of course, the purchaser of a legitimate computer program was often granted the express right to make back up copies. The computer software Directive, however, while not expressly providing a right to make back up copies, provides that the copyright owner may not in the absence of contractual stipulation prevent acts which are necessary for the use of the program by its lawful acquirer in accordance with its intended purpose and further that the making of a back up copy by a person having a right to use the computer program may not be prevented by contract in so far as it is necessary for that use (see Art. 5(2)). A new section 50A of the 1988 Act, as inserted by the Copyright (Computer Programs) Regulations 1992, therefore provides as follows:

> "(1) It is not an infringement of copyright for a lawful user of a copy of a computer program to make any back up copy of it which it is necessary for him to have for the purposes of his lawful use.
>
> (2) For the purposes of this section and sections 50B and 50C a person is a lawful user of a computer program if (whether under a licence to do any act restricted by the copyright in the program or otherwise), he has a right to use the program.
>
> (3) Where an act is permitted under this section, it is irrelevant whether or not there exists any term or condition in an agreement which purports to prohibit or restrict the act (such terms being, by virtue of section 296A, void)."

10–59C   As already noted, (see *ante*, para. 10–59A), section 296A provides that where a person has the use of a computer program under an agreement, any term or condition in the agreement shall be void in so far as it purports to prohibit or restrict the making of any back up copy of the program which it is necessary for him to have for the purposes of the agreed use. This section does not, however, affect any agreement or any term or condition of an agreement where the agreement, term or condition was entered into before the January 1, 1993 (see paragraph 12(2) of the Regulations, *post*, para. B–279). The Regulations apply in relation to computer programs created before January 1, 1993, as they apply to programs created after that date (see paragraph 12(1) of the Regulations).

10–59D   **Lawful user.** The section clearly contemplates a purchaser of a computer program who thereby acquires, expressly or impliedly, a licence to use the program. Where the term of the purchase contract expressly limits any licence to the purchaser alone, it seems that any other user, or any subsequent purchaser, would not be a lawful user. He would not have the right to use the program since the use of the program inevitably involves reproduction, even in a transient form (see §§ 8–19 and 8–46 in the Main Work). Where the purchase contract is silent as to any licence, the extent and scope of any licence will be a matter of implication (see § 8–147 *et seq.* in the Main Work). Note also the provisions of section 56 of the 1988 Act which permit a transferee of a work in electronic form to do anything which the transferor was permitted to do (see § 10–65 *et seq.* in the Main Work). Examples of cases where a person might have a right to use the program "otherwise" than under licence, would presumably be where that person was exercising one or more of the permitted acts in Chapter III of the 1988 Act.

Back up copy. This expression is not itself defined, but presumably **10–59E** means a copy made by the user as a reserve in case of loss of or damage to the version copied. The computer software Directive uses the same expression. The section only permits the making of a back up copy if it is "necessary" for the user to have it for the purposes of his lawful use. This follows the wording of the computer software Directive (see *ante*, para. 10–59B). While the making of a back up copy is no doubt highly desirable, it seems arguable that it will not usually be necessary. It is thought, however, that a benevolent construction will be given to this provision and that the making of back up copies as part of the ordinary and prudent use of a program will fall within the scope of the section, provided the general use being made of the program is permitted under any relevant agreement. Otherwise the section would be of virtually no application.

B. *Decompilation*

Decompilation. The new section 50B is designed to meet the "intero- **10–59F** pability" requirements of the computer software Directive. The final form of this part of the Directive was the result of intense negotiation and lobbying between the various interested parties, in particular the large manufacturers of computer products, the companies engaged in the development of compatible products and finally the actual users. The fundamental issue at stake was the extent to which designers of computer programs and computer products should be entitled to look at and study other programs to enable compatible products to be produced, particularly through knowledge of the program's inter- faces. Without such knowledge, communication between the two systems is generally impossible, and thus also the development of compatible, non-infringing products such as application programs and peripheral devices. Because of the nature of computer programs, such study inevitably involves reproducing the program at some stage, since the program will normally only be available in machine code, from which its fundamental characteristics will not be apparent. The machine code must first be converted into a more intelligible, higher level language, and this process inevitably involves copying. It is interesting to note that in the United States, the problem has been solved not by legislation but by the courts' application of the "fair use" doctrine. See *Atari Games Corp. v. Nintendo of America, Inc.* 975 F.2d 832

(Fed. Cir. 1992), *Sega Enterprises Ltd. v. Accolade, Inc.* 977 F.2d 1510 (9th Circ. 1992) and *post*, para. 18–45. Under the 1988 Act, any defence of fair dealing for the purposes of research or private study has been ruled out, in the case of decompilation, by the addition of a new subsection (4) to section 29 of the Act (see *ante*, para. 10–7).

Thus the Directive stipulates that lawful users of computer programs are entitled to obtain the necessary information so that other programs can be designed to interconnect and interact with the program. Where necessary, this could include the right to copy the program code or translate it for these limited purposes. Generally, the Directive also requires that lawful users be entitled to observe, study or test the function of a program in order to determine the ideas and principles which underlie it, if this is done in the context of permitted loading, displaying, running, transmitting or storing of the program. (This latter requirement did not require any amendment to the 1988 Act). The new section 50B therefore provides:

> "(1) It is not an infringement of copyright for a lawful user of a copy of a computer program expressed in a low level language—
>   (a) to convert it into a version expressed in a higher level language, or
>   (b) incidentally in the course of so converting the program, to copy it,
>   (that is, to "decompile" it), provided that the conditions in subsection (2) are met.
>
> (2) The conditions are that—
>   (a) it is necessary to decompile a program to obtain the information necessary to create an independent program which can be operated with the program decompiled or with another program ("the permitted objective"); and
>   (b) the information so obtained is not used for any purpose other than the permitted objective.
>
> (3) In particular, the conditions in subsection (2) are not met if the lawful user—
>   (a) has readily available to him the information necessary to achieve the permitted objective;
>   (b) does not confine the decompiling to such acts as are necessary to achieve the permitted objective;
>   (c) supplies the information obtained by the decompiling to any person to whom it is not necessary to supply it in order to achieve the permitted objective; or
>   (d) uses the information to create a program which is substantially similar in expression to the program decompiled or to do any act restricted by copyright.

(4) Where an act is permitted under this section, it is irrelevant whether or not there exists any term or condition in an agreement which purports to prohibit or restrict the act (such terms being, by virtue of section 296A void).”

As already noted (*ante*, para. 10–59A), section 296A provides that where a person has the use of a computer program under an agreement, any term or condition in the agreement shall be void in so far as it purports to prohibit or restrict, where the conditions for decompilation are met, the decompiling of the program. Nothing, however, is to affect any agreement or any term or condition of an agreement where the agreement, term or condition was entered into before January 1, 1993 (see paragraph 12(2) of the Copyright (Computer Programs) Regulations 1992, *post*, para. B–279). The provisions of the new section 50B apply in relation to computer programs created before January 1, 1993, as they apply to computer programs created on or after that date (see paragraph 12(1) of the Regulations).   **10–59G**

It will be seen that the decompilation right is limited in its scope. The following points should be noted: **10–59H**

(1) As to “lawful user”, see *ante*, para. 10–59D.

(2) Reproduction without change of language is not specifically referred to, but this will be covered by subsection 50B(1)(b), which permits incidental copying in the course of conversion to a higher level language.

(3) “Low” and “higher” level languages are not defined but no doubt machine code, assembly code and object or source code represent ascending levels of language.

(4) The conditions are not met if the information is already available. Information regarding a program’s interfaces will often be available from the manufacturer.

(5) Infringement will occur if decompilation goes beyond what is necessary to achieve its object. This reflects Article 6(1)(c) of the Directive, which provides that all acts must be confined to the parts of the original program which are necessary to achieve interoperability.

(6) Decompilation may be carried out with the object of creating a program to be operated with a program other than the one decompiled.

(7) Difficulties may arise where the conditions are not complied with since some are conditions subsequent not precedent. Thus where decompilation takes place without infringement (because the conditions are all met at the time) but, for example, the

111

decompiler subsequently supplies the information in contravention of subsection 50B(3)(c) or uses it contrary to subsection 50B(3)(d), it appears that the original decompilation will become, retrospectively, an infringement.

(8) It is clear that decompilation for the purpose of producing an infringing program is not permissible. It should be noted that in order to produce a compatible product it may be necessary to reproduce "lock and key" routines contained within the decompiled program. Neither the Directive nor the amendments to the 1988 Act deal with the question of the extent to which this is permissible (the Directive states only that ideas and principles which *underlie* interfaces are not to be protected). Under United Kingdom law the test remains, therefore, whether the part of the program reproduced in the compatible product forms a substantial part of the decompiled program. As to this see *ante*, para. 8–47 and § 8–47 in the Main Work.

(9) Subsection 50B(3)(d) might be thought to contemplate the possibility of a computer program being substantially similar in expression to another and yet not an infringing copy. However, the Directive prohibits the decompilation right being used to develop, produce or market a computer program substantially similar in its expression or for any *other* act which infringes copyright. Presumably the words "which is substantially similar in expression to" in section 50B will be interpreted as being equivalent to "which reproduces a substantial part of", so that development of a non-infringing program will not fall foul of the conditions.

C. *Other permitted acts*

10–59I Article 5(1) (*post*, para. H–20) of the computer software Directive provides that, in the absence of specific contractual provisions, authorisation by the owner to do the acts restricted by the copyright in a computer program should not be required where they are necessary for the use of the computer program by the lawful acquirer in accordance with its intended purpose, including for error correction. The new section 50C of the Act therefore provides as follows:

"(1) It is not an infringement of copyright for a lawful user of a copy of a computer program to copy or adapt it, providing that the copying or adapting—
(a) is necessary for his lawful use; and
(b) is not prohibited under any term or condition of an agreement regulating the circumstances in which his use is lawful.

(2) It may, in particular, be necessary for the lawful use of a computer program to copy it or adapt it for the purpose of correcting errors in it.

(3) This section does not apply to any copying or adapting permitted under section 50A or section 50B."

Note that unlike the right to make back up copies and the decompilation right, this use may be prohibited under the terms of any relevant contract.

The Directive also requires that a person having the right to use a copy of a computer program should be entitled, without the authorisation of the owner of the copyright, to observe, study or test the function of the program in order to determine the ideas and principles which underlie any element of the program if he does so while performing any of the acts of loading, displaying, running, transmitting or storing the program which he is entitled to do (see Art. 5(3), *post*, para. H–20). The implementation of this provision has not required any amendment to the substantive provisions of the 1988 Act, but section 296A(1)(c) does now provide that, where a person has the use of a computer program under an agreement, any term or condition in the agreement shall be void in so far as it purports to prohibit or restrict the use of any device or means to observe, study or test the functioning of the program in order to understand the ideas and principles which underlie any element of the program. This is not to affect any agreement or any term or condition of an agreement where such agreement, term or condition was entered into before January 1, 1993 (see paragraph 12(2) of the Regulations, *post*, para. B–279).

7. Works in Electronic Form

The 1988 Act. Note that a number of permitted acts in relation to   **10–65** computer programs have been added by amendment to the 1988 Act (see *ante*, para. 10–59A *et seq.*).

NOTE 31. Note that in relation to computer programs, the definition of adaptation has been amended (see *ante*, para. 8–126).

8. Miscellaneous Provisions: Literary, Dramatic Musical and Artistic Works

B. *Notes or recordings of spoken words*

The permitted uses. In the debates on this provision it was made clear   **10–78** that if the record is made for one of the defined purposes it may not be used for the other and that if, for example, it is made for the purpose of broadcasting it may be used repeatedly in broadcasts. See *Hansard*, H.L. Vol. 501, cols. 198–200.

10–79   First sentence. This provision was inserted to enable broadcasters to follow their usual practice of making copies of their original recordings for the purposes of their broadcasts. See the report of the debates of the House of Commons Standing Committee E, 1988, cols. 484, 485.

E. *Recordings of Folksongs*

10–85   **Making recordings.** Final sentence. The title "folksongs" is merely a signpost: *Hansard*, H.C. Vol. 138, col. 110.

F. *Representation of certain artistic works on display*

10–87   **The 1988 Act.** Note that the building need not be situated in a public place.

H. *Making of subsequent works by the same author*

10–93   **Comment.** In the course of the Parliamentary debates on this provision, the following statements were made about its intended effect:

(1) It would allow an author of an artistic work, for example an ornamental pattern or design applied by an architect to a building, to reproduce some part of the motif of the original design in some other work. He would be able to reproduce the earlier work, or part of it, provided he avoided repeating or imitating the main design.

(2) It would allow the painter of a group portrait to reuse sketches to reproduce individual portraits.

(3) As to whether an artist who had painted a picture of some building or scene would infringe by painting a second picture of the same building or scene, this would depend on the circumstances.

See *Hansard*, H.L. Vol. 491, col. 191; H.L. Vol. 493, col. 1187.

11. Miscellaneous Provisions: Broadcasting and Cable Programmes

A. *Incidental recording for purposes of broadcasting, etc.*

Last sentence. But see *Bishop v. Stephens* [1990] 72 D.L.R. (Sup. Ct. Canada) where such a term was not implied. **10–112**

C. *Recording for purposes of time-shifting for private purposes*

NOTE 76. Or, apparently, a more convenient place. See *Hansard*, H.L. Vol. 501, col. 267. **10–117**

F. *Reception and retransmission of broadcast in cable programme service*

The 1988 Act. See *ante*, para. 8–118 for the changes to be introduced in relation to the simultaneous retransmission by cable and microwave in one Member State of the E.C. of broadcasts from another. **10–123**

H. *Recording for Archival Purposes*

NOTE 5. The Copyright (Recording for Archives of Designated Class of Broadcasts and Cable Programmes) (Designated Bodies) (No. 2) Order 1989[1] has been revoked. See now The Copyright (Recording for Archives of Designated Class of Broadcasts and Cable Programmes) (Designated Bodies) Order 1993[2] *post*, para. B–208. Eight bodies have now been designated. **10–126**

I. *Information about programmes*

For background, see Arnold in [1991] 1 Ent. L.R. 23. **10–127**

---

[1] (S.I. 1989 No. 2510).
[2] (S.I. 1993 No. 74).

10–132   Payment

NOTE 33. For the procedure on such an application, see Rules 41A–D of the Copyright Tribunal Rules, at § B–267 in the Main Work.

   In 1992 the appropriate rate for publication of the listings of programmes broadcast by the BBC and the Independent Television Companies was determined by the Copyright Tribunal to be 0.003p per day in respect of which the listings were published multiplied by the aggregate circulations of the publications, subject to a minimum of £200 per annum. See *News Group Newspapers Ltd. v. Independent Television Publications Ltd.* [1993] R.P.C. 173. The rate was subsequently raised to 0.004p on the compromise of an appeal: see [1993] E.M.L.R. 1 at 4. It was held that the Tribunal's jurisdiction extended only to determine terms for payment for information which the broadcasters were required by statute to provide, that is, details of the dates, times and titles of the broadcasts, not for additional information (the "billings") which were in fact also provided. In reaching its decision the Tribunal emphasised that it was making a value judgement. It was not its function to value the copyrights in issue or compensate the broadcasters for loss of their monopoly. Implementing the policy of the Broadcasting Act meant ensuring that it was easy for individuals to find out what was being broadcast so that they could exercise a choice. This was best achieved by moderate payment terms. Attempts to evaluate what fee might have been reached in free negotiation were rejected as unreliable in the light of the fact that there had been no negotiations and because of the dominant monopoly position of the broadcasters. The broadcasters had considerable interest in the publication of the material and it was not shown that publication of the listings boosted circulation (such that a payment based on profits made by the publishers might be appropriate). The cost of providing the information was a useful starting point, to which there should be added something for the fact that an intellectual property right was being used.

J. Use as right of sound recordings in broadcasts and cable programme services

10–134   For a detailed account of the history of the matter, see *The Association of Independent Radio Companies Ltd. v. Phonographic Performance Ltd.* [1994] R.P.C. 181.

10–139   The copyright tribunal.

NOTE 64.   The reference to § 19–94 should be to § 15–54. For the procedure on such applications to the Copyright Tribunal, see Rules 26A–D of the Copyright Tribunal Rules, at § B–267 in the Main Work.

In *The Association of Independent Radio Companies Ltd. v. Phonographic Performance Ltd.* [1994] R.P.C. 181 the following points were established:

(1) In assessing the payment terms, the amount of needletime required is a relevant consideration but the terms do not have to be assessed wholly or partly on a usage basis.

(2) In relation to subsection 135(1)(b) (the requirement to avoid unreasonable discrimination), the Tribunal may discriminate between applicants of the same kind, provided this is done on reasonable criteria and so long as there is no unreasonable discrimination between licensees under the scheme or licence in issue and those under other schemes or licences operated by the same person.

(3) The Tribunal did not have to ignore previous orders of the Performing Right Tribunal and start with a clean sheet (*c.f.* note 76 in the Main Work). The requirement merely meant that the Tribunal was not to use the earlier orders as a basis on which to produce an up-dated determination, for example by adjusting the rates to allow for statutory modifications. The Tribunal was free to refer to such orders as an essential part of the history of the matter. Changed circumstances might mean, however, that such orders afforded little guidance. Statements made on behalf of the Government during debates on the Broadcasting Bill are to the same effect. See *Hansard*, H.L. Vol. 522, col. 841.

(4) The Tribunal was not required to eliminate from its assessment that element of value which might be attributable to the monopoly power of the licensing body, such that the payment terms should be assessed by reference to the royalties which would be negotiated in a free market in which neither those whom the licensing body represented not the broadcasters acted collectively. On the contrary, the Broadcasting Act had continued the statutory recognition of the existence of collective licensing subject to the overriding jurisdiction of the Tribunal to moderate its monopolistic effects.

(5) The Tribunal did not have jurisdiction to limit the form of the broadcasting, for example, by excluding digital audio broadcasting.

(6) It was doubted that the Tribunal had jurisdiction, when considering operating terms under section 135E, to impose a condition which would give broadcasters the right to dub recordings and keep the copies indefinitely (*c.f.* the right to make ephemeral recordings under s.68 of the 1988 Act).

The Tribunal concluded that the tariff should be as simple as possible and assessed by reference to a flat rate percentage (5 per cent.) of the broadcasters' net advertising revenue (including sponsorship), not their actual usage of the licensed material. There should be concessionary rates for low revenue broadcasters and the rate should be less for "talk" stations.

CHAPTER 11

CIVIL REMEDIES

Contents

1. Introduction

11–1   In accordance with the Supreme Court Act 1981, section 61 and Schedule 1, High Court proceedings for infringement of copyright should be instituted in the Chancery Division. If they are wrongly instituted in the Queen's Bench Division, they should be transferred to the Chancery Division. See *Apac Rowena Ltd. v. Norpol Packaging Ltd.* [1991] F.S.R. 273.

As infringement of copyright is a tort (see § 11–96 in the Main Work) the County Court has jurisdiction to hear a copyright infringement action. Jurisdiction was conceded in *P.S.M. International plc. v. Specialised Fastener Products (Southern) Ltd.* [1993] F.S.R. 113.

The Patents County Court (currently the Central London County Court—see the Patents County Court (Designation and Jurisdiction) Order 1994, S.I. No. 1609 (*post*, para. B–233)) has a special jurisdiction to hear any action relating to "designs" over which the High Court would have jurisdiction, together with any claims or matters ancillary thereto or arising therefrom. The term "designs" includes both registered designs and designs protected by the Design Right (see § 20–60 in the Main Work). See *P.S.M. International plc. v. Specialised Fastener Products (Southern) Ltd.* [1993] F.S.R. 113. In addition, the Patents County Court has jurisdiction in a copyright infringement action concerning a design document within the meaning of section 51(1) of the 1988 Act (as to which, see § 20–50 *et seq.* in the Main Work): *ibid.* The Patents County Court also has jurisdiction to entertain copyright infringement claims which are ancillary to a patent or design claim. See *McDonald v. Graham, The Times,* January 12, 1994.

2. Who May Sue

C. *Relevant date of title*

Note 9.   See also *John Richardson Computers Ltd. v. Flanders* [1993]   **11–5**
F.S.R. 497 at 516–519. (Plaintiff legal owner of some copyrights, but
equitable owner of others. The legal owner was joined as a defendant.)
   End of paragraph. **Add**: *C.f. Roland Corp. v. Lorenzo & Sons Pty. Ltd.*
(1991) 22 I.P.R. 245 (Fed. Ct. of Australia) where it was said that a
plaintiff could obtain declaratory and injunctive relief, even though he
had no title, legal or equitable, at the date of the issue of the writ. See
also *L.A. Gear Inc. v. Hi-Tec Sports plc.* [1992] F.S.R. 121, 139, *per*
Staughton L.J.
   Leave may be granted to amend proceedings to plead infringements
which have occurred after the issue of proceedings provided the
plaintiff had some other cause of action at the date of the writ. See
Banks v. C.B.S. Songs Ltd [1992] F.S.R. 278; *Vax Appliances Ltd. v. Hoover
plc* [1990] R.P.C. 656.

D. *Equitable owner*

Add: In *Tableship Ltd. v. Williams* noted at [1991] I.P.D. 14205 it was   **11–6**
apparently held that an equitable owner of copyright was entitled to
the remedies for infringement of copyright available under the 1988
Act in an action against the bare legal owner. See also *Ibcos Computers
Ltd. v. Barclays Mercantile Highland Finance Ltd.* [1994] F.S.R. 275 and
ante, para. 4–67.

3. Who May Be Sued

B.*Secondary Infringers*

Note 31.   **Add**: *Monsoon Ltd. v. India Imports of Rhode Island Ltd.* [1993]   **11–11**
F.S.R. 486. (A reasonable time should be allowed for the prospective
defendant to investigate the claim.)

C. *Joint tortfeasors*

After note 35 in the text. **Add**: The law as to what facts may establish   **11–12**
liability on the grounds that two companies have acted pursuant to a

common design was reviewed in *Unilever plc v. Gillette (UK) Ltd.* [1989] R.P.C. 583. The mere capacity of a parent company to control a subsidiary company does not make the two companies joint tortfeasors. What matters is the extent of control actually exercised by one over the other: see *Intel Corporation v. General Instrument Corporation and Ors. (No.2)* [1991] R.P.C. 235.

End of first paragraph. **Add**: The plaintiff can choose which tortfeasor to sue. He does not have to sue all of them. The defendant cannot dictate whom the plaintiff shall sue or make the choice for him. The plaintiff can also choose which joint tortfeasor to enforce a judgment against. It is permissible to join an alleged tortfeasor for the purpose of obtaining discovery against him. See *Molnycke AB v. Proctor-Gamble Ltd. (No. 6)* [1992] R.P.C. 21.

First sentence of the second paragraph. **Add**: For a defendant to be liable for procuring the importation, sale, etc., of infringing copies with knowledge by another, as part of a common design, both the defendant and that other person must have the requisite degree of knowledge. See *Mattel Inc. v. Tonka Corp.* [1992] F.S.R. 28.

End of second paragraph. **Add**: A person who only facilitates a tort will not be liable as a joint tortfeasor, whereas a person who procures a tort is so liable: see *P.L.G. Research Ltd. v. Ardon International Ltd.* [1993] F.S.R. 197, following *CBS Songs Ltd. v. Amstrad Consumer Electronics plc* [1988] R.P.C. 567 and *Belegging-En Exploitatiemaatschappij Lavender BV v. Witten Industrial Diamonds Ltd.* [1979] F.S.R. 59.

What amounts to facilitating varies from case to case. For example, selling materials for the purpose of infringing copyright to a person who is going to infringe and agreeing to indemnify him, does not by itself make the person who so sells an infringer. He must be a party with the person who infringes: *ibid*, citing *Townsend v. Hawarth* (1879) 48 L.J. Ch. 770, 773.

D. *Conspiracy*

11–13 Second sentence. **Delete**, and **substitute**: A conspiracy to injure may be established in cases where there is an agreement to damage a person by unlawful means or to effect, by means which are not in themselves unlawful, an unlawful purpose for the sole or predominant purpose of injuring the plaintiff. See *Lonhro plc v. Fayed* [1992] 1 A.C. 448; *Lonhro plc v. Fayed (No. 5)* [1993] 1 W.L.R. 1489.

End of paragraph. **Add**: A conspiracy may take the form of the alleged conspirators sponsoring or encouraging or causing a third party to inflict actual pecuniary loss on the plaintiff. Damages for injury to reputation or feelings are not recoverable in an action for conspiracy. See *Lonhro plc v. Fayed (No. 5)* [1993] 1 W.L.R. 1489.

F. *Directors of companies*

After note 46 in the text. **Add**: Leave to amend to join a director on the grounds that he is liable for the acts of a company will not be given if the facts proposed to be pleaded do not disclose a case which could succeed at trial. The fact that an application to join a director is made because it is feared that damages and costs may be irrecoverable against a corporate defendant is not, by itself, considered a mere tactical ruse, putting unfair pressure on the defendant to settle. See *PLG Research Ltd. v. Ardon International Ltd.* [1992] F.S.R. 59. **11–15**

A director of a company will not be liable for the acts of the company, unless his involvement was such as to render him liable as joint tortfeasor if the company had not existed: See *P.L.G. Research Ltd. v. Ardon International Ltd.*, [1993] F.S.R. 197.

One of several directors of a company, who did not have any knowledge of the work performed or any personal involvement in its performance, and who did not directly authorise, procure or instruct its performance, or impliedly authorise its performance, was held not liable for infringement of copyright. See *Australasian Performing Right Association Ltd. v. Valamo Pty. Ltd.* (1990) 18 I.P.R. 216 (Fed. Ct. of Australia).

4. Rights Against Persons in Possession

See *post*, para. 11–51. **11–17**

5. Right of seizure without court order

End of sub-paragraph (2). **Add**: That person need not be an "infringer". It may include a person who had an infringing copy in his possession in the course of a business, regardless of the existence of any knowledge on the part of that person that the copy is an infringing copy. Such a person can be ordered to disclose the identity of the persons to whom copies have been supplied. See *Lagenes Ltd. v. It's At (UK) Ltd.* [1991] F.S.R. 492 at 504. **11–20**

123

6. Defences

E. *Public interest*

11–30   Note that section 171(3) of the 1988 Act provides that nothing in Part 1 of the Act affects any rule of law preventing or restricting the enforcement of copyright on the grounds of public interest or otherwise.

See Davies, G., *Copyright and the Public Interest, IIC Studies*, Vol. 14, (VCH) Verlagsgesellschaft 1994. For a criticism of the public interest defence, see *Collier Construction Pty. Ltd. v. Foskett Pty. Ltd.* (1990) 19 I.P.R. 44 (Fed. Ct. of Australia).

Note 95. The word "indiscretion". **substitute**: "in the discretion".

End of paragraph. **Add**: The defence of public interest allows the publication of secret information which, in the public interest, should be known. The fact that the information may interest the public is not, however, sufficient. Once the information has been published there is no further public interest requirement for further publication: *Express Newspapers v. News (UK) Ltd.* [1991] F.S.R. 37.

7. Remedies and Procedure

A. *Introduction*

11–31   **Jurisdiction.**

Note 97. On *Tyburn Productions Ltd. v. Conan Doyle*, see Arnold in [1990] 7 EIPR 254.

Note 99. **Add**: In *L.A. Gear v. Gerald Whelan & Sons Inc. Ltd.* [1991] F.S.R. 670, it was held that the English court would have no jurisdiction to determine claims for passing off against a defendant who was not domiciled in the United Kingdom and was committing acts of passing off abroad. *C.f. An Bord Trachtala v. Waterford Foods plc* [1994] F.S.R. 316 (High Ct. of Ireland) (defendant domiciled in the jurisdiction of the Court).

B. *Interlocutory relief*

(i) Injunction

Third sentence. **Delete**, and **substitute**: The court has no jurisdiction   **11–35**
to grant an interlocutory or final injunction against the Crown or its
officers except in applications for judicial review when the power may
be exercised in limited circumstances. In the majority of cases a
declaration is the appropriate remedy: see *In re M* [1993] 3 W.L.R.
433.

After note 20 in the text. **Add**: In *Whitbread v. Calder Valley Inns*   **11–36**
(unreported) cited in *Square Moves Limited v. Moorcroft* noted at [1992]
I.P.D. 15122, Slade L.J. said:

> "It is, I think, well known that any Court should be particularly
> cautious in granting relief by way of injunction *ex parte* before the
> defendant has had a proper opportunity to put his case by
> evidence. While it has, of course, jurisdiction to do so, it would
> ordinarily grant such relief *ex parte* only if the plaintiff shows
> grave urgency or possible risk of irreparable damage or some
> other particular circumstances which would justify the grant of
> relief at this early stage. It is by no means a form of relief to which
> a plaintiff can regard himself as entitled as of right merely because
> he appears to show a strong cause of action."

Thus *ex parte* orders should only be made in exceptional circumstances. The most obvious are where, (a) the situation is one of extreme
urgency so that there is no time to warn the defendant, or (b) where
the purpose of the injunction might be frustrated if the defendant
were warned, or (c) where the defendant cannot be found. See *TRP
Ltd. v. Thorley*, C.A., (1993) noted in the *Supreme Court Practice News*,
Issue 8/93.

Ex parte orders should not be granted without giving the respondent
an opportunity to be heard, unless by giving such opportunity it is
likely that the applicant would suffer injustice and either the defendant could be compensated for any damage by the cross-undertaking
in damages or the potential injustice to the applicant outweighs the
risk of injustice to the respondent. See *In Re First Express Ltd.*, *The
Times*, October 10, 1991.

At the interlocutory stage, a defendant may be ordered to take all
practical steps to recover allegedly infringing copies of a work which
have been distributed. In respect of copies to which title has passed to
donees or purchasers, the obligation is then simply to ask for their
return. See *British Broadcasting Corporation v. Precord Ltd.* noted at
[1991] I.P.D. 15023.

11–37   **Arguable case.** The second and third sentences in the second paragraph. **Delete**, and **substitute**: The right to an interlocutory injunction does not exist in isolation, but is always incidental to and dependant on the enforcement of the substantive right which usually takes the form of a cause of action, though not invariably. The jurisdiction conferred by section 37(1) of the Supreme Court Act 1981 to grant injunctions in all cases in which it appears to the court to be just and convenient is circumscribed by judicial authority. In most cases the party seeking the injunction must show that the other party has invaded, or threatens to invade, a legal or equitable right of the former and that the latter is amenable to the jurisdiction of the court for the enforcement of the right. See *South Carolina Insurance Co. v. Assurante Maatschappij* [1987] A.C. 24; *Channel Tunnel Group Ltd. v. Balfour Beatty Construction Ltd.* [1993] A.C. 334; *Khorasandjian v. Bush* [1993] Q.B. 727.

11–38   **Decision on motion.**

NOTE 30. **Add**: *Mirage Studios v. Counter-Feat Clothing Co. Ltd.* [1991] F.S.R. 145.

End of first paragraph. **Add**: There may be cases where the plaintiff's evidence is so strong that to refuse an injunction and allow the case to go through to trial would be an unnecessary waste of time and expense and indeed do an overwhelming injustice to the plaintiff: see *Cayne v. Global and Natural Resources plc* [1984] 1 All E.R. 225 at 238. The sort of case referred to is where there would be no defence to an application for summary judgement under Order 14. The relative strength of the parties' case comes in, however, at the very last stage of the *Cyanamid* process: see *Entec (Pollution Control) Ltd. v. Abacus Mouldings* [1992] F.S.R. 332.

11–39   **Adequacy of Damages.**

NOTE 41. **Add**: *Games Workshop Ltd. v. Transworld Publishers Ltd.* [1993] F.S.R. 705; *Ciba-Geigy plc v. Parke Davis & Co. Ltd.* [1994] F.S.R. 8 at 22.

11–40   **Balance of convenience**

NOTE 47. **Add**: *Mirage Studios v. Counter-Feat Clothing Company Ltd.* [1991] F.S.R. 145 at 154.

End of paragraph. **Add**: At the outset of a character merchandising operation, it is often critical to put an immediate end to infringement:

see *Mirage Studios v. Counter-Feat Clothing Company Ltd.* [1991] F.S.R. 145.

Status quo. After note 56 in the text. **Add**: Where a defendant will   **11–41**
suffer certain damage if an injunction is granted, but the likelihood of
the plaintiff suffering damage if an injunction is not granted is very
small, this is particularly material to the question of choosing which
course of action is least likely to cause injustice. See *Management
Publications Ltd. v. Blenheim Exhibition Group plc* [1991] F.S.R. 550;
Waterlow Directories Ltd. v. Reed Information Services Ltd. [1992] F.S.R.
409.

NOTE 57. **Add**: *Stacey v. 2020 Communications plc* [1991] F.S.R. 49 at 54.

The time factor. Add: In the absence of material delay, the appropri-   **11–42**
ate status quo may be that which exists immediately before the
defendant begins the acts complained of. See *The British Diabetic
Association v. The Diabetic Society Ltd.* noted at [1992] I.P.D. 15103,
observing that the passage on status quo in *Garden Cottage Foods v. Milk
Marketing Board* [1984] A.C. 140, H.L., was *obiter*.
    It may be very difficult to identify the status quo in a rapidly
changing commercial situation; for example, at the outset of a
character merchandising operation. See *Mirage Studios v. Counter-Feat
Clothing Company Ltd.* [1991] F.S.R. 145 at 153.
    Where there is no letter before action and there is delay after the
issue of the writ before service, the date of service of the writ may be
the relevant date for deciding what represents the status quo. See
Graham v. Delderfield [1992] F.S.R. 313.

Ability to pay damages   **11–43**

NOTE 60. **Add**: *Mirage Studios v. Counter-Feat Clothing Company Ltd.*
[1991] F.S.R. 145 at 152.

Other relevant considerations. End of first paragraph. **Add**: The fact   **11–44**
that in practice the grant of an injunction would be the end of the
action is a material consideration against the grant of an injunction:
see *Management Publications Ltd. v. Blenheim Exhibitions Group plc* [1991]
F.S.R. 550.

    After note 69 in the text. **Add**: Although a defendant who chooses to
continue with a course of action after a dispute arises cannot gain any
benefit thereby, if the defendant was substantially committed to a
course of action when the dispute arose and continued along that

course, the status quo is represented by the defendant being committed to that course of action. The position is not analogous to the building cases where the defendant builder presses ahead as quickly as possible with construction after complaint is made so as to present the court with a *fait accompli*. That type of situation represents a change of course. See *Management Publications Ltd. v. Blenheim Exhibitions Group plc* [1991] F.S.R. 550.

After note 72 in the text. **Add**: Less injustice is likely to result by refusing an injunction where its grant would mean that the defendant would go out of business pending the trial so that there never would be a trial. See *Entec (Pollution) Control Ltd. v. Abacus Mouldings* [1991] F.S.R. 332, applying *Cayne v. Global Natural Resources plc* [1984] 1 All E.R. 225. But there is no inflexible rule that an injunction will never be granted in such a case. *Ibid.*

The court, in deciding whether to grant an interlocutory injunction, should take the course which carries the lower risk of injustice should it turn out to be the wrong decision. The conduct of the parties is a relevant consideration; for example, an application made by a plaintiff after a delay of one year from being informed of the defendant's intentions: *Dalgety Spillers Foods Ltd. v. Food Brokers Ltd.*, [1994] F.S.R. 504.

Where the trial may not take place until most of the period for which the plaintiff seeks an injunction has expired, it is appropriate to consider the parties' prospects of success: see *Lansing Linde v. Kerr* [1991] 1 W.L.R. 251.

NOTE 74. **Add**: *Kaye v. Robertson* [1991] F.S.R. 62 at 67.

After note 74 in the text. **Add**: At the interlocutory stage the court will not grant an injunction restraining alleged libels or trade libels, if the defendant can reasonably justify the statement. But an injunction may be granted if there is an alleged misrepresentation which can be pleaded in passing off or trade libel and the misrepresentation is not one which the defendant wishes to justify. In such a case there is no substantial infringement of the defendants' right to free speech: *Ciba-Geigy plc v. Parke Davis & Co. Ltd.* [1994] F.S.R. 8 at 21.

The mere fact that the plaintiff's claim can be framed in defamation makes no difference unless, perhaps, the court concludes that the plaintiff's principal purpose is in fact to seek damages for defamation. If, however, there is some other serious interest to be protected, such as confidentiality, infringement of trade mark or interference with commercial relations with third parties, an injunction may be granted. It is a question of balancing the rights of free speech against the right asserted by the plaintiff. See *Microdata Information Services Ltd. v. Rivendale Ltd.* [1991] F.S.R. 681.

Where neither side can point to material damage being caused by the grant or withholding of an injunction respectively, and the relative strengths of the parties' cases are not clear, a relevant consideration may be a defendant's right of freedom of speech. See *Secretary of State for the Home Department v. Central Broadcasting Ltd.* [1993] E.M.L.R. 253 (no injunction to restrain use of four minute extract from filmed interview with serial killer in an hour-long television programme).

NOTE 75. *R. v. Secretary of State for Transport, Ex p. Factortame Ltd. (No. 2)* is now reported at [1991] A.C. 603.

Cross-undertaking in damages   **11–45**

NOTE 80. **Add**: *Air Express Ltd. v. Ansett Transport Industries (Operations) Pty.* (1979) 146 C.L.R. 249 at 267 (High Ct. of Australia.)

After note 81 in the text. **Add**: The court has a discretion whether or not to enforce the undertaking in all the circumstances of the case and as to when and how to enforce it. The time at which the court will determine whether the undertaking should be enforced and, if so, how, will vary from case to case. If the injunction is discharged before the trial there are a number of possible courses of action open to the court: in straightforward cases the court can decide at once to enforce the undertaking and assess the damages immediately or direct an inquiry as to damages, covering issues of causation and quantum; it can decide forthwith not to enforce the undertaking; or it may adjourn the application for enforcement to the trial or further order. The court may adopt the last course where, for example, issues and facts relevant to enforcement cannot be finally determined before the trial has taken place: *Cheltenham & Gloucester Building Society v. Ricketts* [1993] 1 W.L.R. 1545 at 1551, 1552 and 1557. See also Practice Direction, *The Times*, August 2, 1994, and *post*, para. 11–50A, subpara. (7).

After note 82 in the text. **Add**: The fact that the injunction is made by consent makes no difference when the defendant later proceeds under the cross undertaking as in damages.

After note 83 in the text. **Add**: The cross undertaking as extended to third parties only covers loss incurred in complying with the Order, not loss incurred as a result of the Order. See *Guinness Peat Aviation (Belgium) NV v. Hispanii Lineas Aereas SA* [1992] 1 Lloyds' Rep. 190.

The ordinary principles of contract law apply both as to causation and to quantum when it is sought to enforce the cross undertaking in damages. See *Finansiera Avenida S.A. v. Shiblaq, The Times*, January 14, 1991.

Procedure. After note 86 in the text. **Add**: In accordance with the   **11–46** Supreme Court Act 1981, section 61 and Schedule 1, High Court proceedings for infringement of copyright should be instituted in the Chancery Division. If wrongly instituted in the Queen's Bench

Division, they should be transferred. See *Apac Rowena Ltd. v. Norpol Packaging Ltd.* [1991] F.S.R. 273.

After third sentence. **Add**: On any application, whether *ex parte* or *inter partes*, a party is not entitled to rely on confidential evidence which has not been or will not be revealed to the other side. See *V.N.U. Business Publications B.V. v. Ziff Davies (U.K.) Ltd.* [1992] R.P.C. 269, following *Re K* [1963] Ch. 381, C.A. and *W.E.A. Records v. Visions Channel 4* [1983] 1 W.L.R. 721, C.A. Thus a defendant against whom an *ex parte* injunction has been granted is entitled to see all the evidence on which the injunction was granted, so that he can comment on it, challenge it and adduce contrary evidence.

NOTE 90. **Add**: *The Financial Times Ltd. v. The Evening Standard Co. Ltd.* [1991] F.S.R. 7.

After note 91 in the text. **Add**: On the question of full disclosure, it is now unnecessary to go further back into the authorities than the Court of Appeal decision in *Brink's Mat Ltd. v. Elcombe* [1988] 1 W.L.R. 1350. (See *Lagenes Ltd. v. It's At (U.K.)* [1991] F.S.R. 465.) The relevant principles are summarised in the judgment of Ralph Gibson L.J. at 1356 and 1357 in the *Brink's Mat* case as follows:

(1) The applicant is under a duty to make full and fair disclosure of all the material facts.

(2) The material facts are those which are material for the judge to know in dealing with the application made. The decision on materiality is one for the court and not for the applicant or his legal advisers.

(3) The applicant must make proper inquiries before the application. The duty of disclosure extends to facts which the applicant would have known if he had made proper inquiries.

(4) The extent of inquiries which are proper and necessary depends on all the circumstances of the case. Relevant factors include the nature of the case, the nature of the order for which the application is made and the probable effect of the order on the defendant, the degree of legitimate urgency and the time available for making inquiries.

(5) If non-disclosure is established the court will ensure that the plaintiff who obtains an order without full disclosure is deprived of any advantages that he may have obtained by breach of his duty.

(6) Whether the fact which has not been disclosed is of sufficient materiality to justify or require immediate discharge of the order without examination of the merits depends on the importance of the fact to the issues which were to be decided by

the judge on the application. The innocence of the non-disclosure is an important but not decisive consideration.

(7) The injunction will not be discharged for every omission. The court has a discretion and may continue the order even after there has been proof of a material non-disclosure which justifies or requires the immediate discharge of the *ex parte* order.

The above is not an exhaustive statement of the circumstances in which the court's powers may be exercised but it is a useful starting point: see *Behbehali v. Salem* [1989] 1 W.L.R. 72.

After note 92 in the text. **Add**: See also *Apac Rowena Ltd. v. Norpol Packaging Ltd.* [1991] F.S.R. 273. An injunction obtained by a plaintiff was discharged because of gross misconduct. The misconduct consisted of instituting proceedings in the Queen's Bench Division when they should have been started in the Chancery Division and obtaining an *ex parte* injunction on wholly inadequate evidence, followed by gross delay in serving a statement of claim.

A party moving to discharge an interlocutory injunction on grounds of non-disclosure should give the other side as much notice as the circumstances will allow as to the precise grounds on which the application is made. See *EMI Records Ltd. v. V.C.D. Specialists Ltd.* [1992] F.S.R. 70.

After note 93 in the text. **Add**: It is incumbent upon a plaintiff whose position has been protected by an interlocutory injunction to proceed with due diligence so as to limit, as far as possible, the period during which the defendant's liberty is restricted without there having been any determination on the merits: See *News Group Newspapers Ltd. v. The Mirror Group Newspapers (1986) Ltd.* [1991] F.S.R. 487. A party who has obtained a Mareva injunction has an obligation to draw any subsequent change in circumstances to the attention of the court. See *The Commercial Bank of the New East v. A.B.C. & D.* [1989] 2 Lloyd's Rep. 319.

The Court of Appeal's jurisdiction under the Supreme Court Act 1981 to amend, execute and enforce its own orders enables it to vary an *ex parte* order made by it but not to discharge it. Such an application must be made to a judge of first instance. See *Ocean Software v. Kay* [1992] Q.B. 583.

After note 94 in the text. **Add**: The court may vary an injunction if there is a material change in the circumstances. The fact that the defendant has suffered some damage since the injunction beyond what might have been expected may be a material change of circumstances. The plaintiff's contempt of court in giving publicity to proceedings would also constitute a change in circumstances, as would a plaintiff's failure to comply with his duty to pursue the claim diligently in accordance with an order for a speedy trial. See *John Richardson Computers Ltd. v. Flanders* [1992] F.S.R. 391.

A court will not vary or discharge an injunction which has been made by consent based simply on a miscalculation of the practical effects. If a party elects to give an undertaking to avoid the grant of an injunction, he cannot ordinarily and in the absence of changed circumstances re-open the matter later if he concludes he could have defeated the application: *Chanel Ltd. v. F.W. Woolworth & Co. Ltd.* [1981] 1 W.L.R. 485; *Lonhro plc v. Fayed* [1994] 2 W.L.R. 209. The position is otherwise where he has retained liberty to apply: *Gantenbrink v. British Broadcasting Corporation*, noted at [1994] I.P.D. 17080.

End of last paragraph. **Add**: The form of an interlocutory injunction need not slavishly follow the form of substantive relief likely to be granted at trial if the plaintiff succeeds, so long as it is in a form appropriate to guard the interests of the parties justly. It is desirable that an injunction is expressed in words which the person restrained can readily understand, particularly if he is not present in court when it is granted. See *Khorasandrijan v. Bush* [1993] Q.B. 727.

11–47 **Costs of motions. Add**: The court may make an order for immediate taxation and payment of costs by the party responsible for bringing or conducting an interlocutory application improperly; for example, by engaging in an unnecessary or prolonged investigation of the merits. See *Apple Corps Ltd. v. Apple Computer Inc.* [1992] R.P.C. 70 at 80 and 81. It is not, however, only in cases where the court wishes to show its disapproval that such an order will be made. Other circumstances may justify it: *Kickers International S.A. v. Paul Kettle Agencies Ltd.* [1990] F.S.R. 436.

(ii) Anton Piller Orders

11–48 End of second paragraph. **Add**: The Lord Chancellor's Department has issued a Consultation Paper concerning the practical operation of Anton Piller Orders following a report by a Committee of Judges. Some of its recommendations have already been implemented (see *post*, para 11–50). Others will require statutory implementation.

The privilege against self incrimination (see §§ 11–53 and 11–54 in the Main Work) applies just as much to Anton Piller Orders as to an order for discovery. See *Tate Access Floors Inc. v. Boswell* [1991] Ch. 512.

11–50 **Conditions for making order.** End of last paragraph. **Add**: The court may discharge the order and refuse to make any fresh order in its place if, on the application, counsel has failed in his duty to lay the relevant facts before the court. If a large mass of paper is put before the court in the form of affidavits and exhibits, it is the duty of counsel to call the judge's attention to everything which is relevant to his submission in support of the application for the order. See *Intergraph Corporation v. Solid Systems CAD Services Ltd.* [1993] F.S.R. 617.

Many cases continue to be decided as to the circumstances in which Anton Piller orders should be made and the conditions on which they are made. The most important case is *Universal Thermosensors Ltd. v. Hibben* [1992] 1 W.L.R. 840 in which the Vice-Chancellor laid down general guide-lines in relation to Anton Piller orders. Further guide-lines have been set out in a *Practice Direction, The Times*, August 2, 1994. The principles are as follows:

(1) In order that the defendant may be able to take advice, the order should only be executed on a working day during office hours when a solicitor can be expected to be available to advise the defendant.

(2) If the order is to be executed at premises where it is likely that a woman may be there alone, the solicitor serving the order must be, or be accompanied by, a woman.

(3) To avoid disputes about what documents were taken and from where, the order should expressly provide that, unless seriously impracticable, a detailed list of items should be prepared at the premises before they are removed, and the defendant given an opportunity to check the list. Where the nature of the items removed under the order makes it appropriate, the applicant should be required to insure them.

(4) While such an injunction may contain provision restraining the recipient from informing others of the existence of the order, this should not last for longer than is necessary, and not more than seven days.

(5) The order should provide that, unless there is good reason to the contrary, it should not be executed at business premises save in the presence of a responsible officer or representative of the company or trader.

(6) Consideration should be given to a means of avoiding a situation whereby a senior representative of the plaintiff carries out a thorough search of all the competitor's documents.

(7) The provision that the order should be served by solicitors does not always provide an adequate safeguard. To some extent the duties of such solicitor involve protecting the defendant's interests. Usually, therefore, the order should provide that:
   (a) The order should be served by a solicitor other than a member of the firm acting for the plaintiff.
   (b) Such a solicitor should be experienced generally and have some experience in particular of the workings of Anton Piller Orders. This should preferably be dealt with in the plaintiff's evidence in support of the application for the Order.
   (c) The solicitor should prepare a written report on what took place on execution of the order.

(d) A copy of the solicitor's written report should be served on the defendant.

(e) The plaintiff should return to court within the next few days after execution of the order and present the report at an inter parties hearing, preferably to the judge who made the order.

The costs of engaging an independent solicitor will be borne by the plaintiff in the first instance, but without prejudice to the court's later decision as to who should be ultimately responsible for the costs. If in any particular case the judge does not think it appropriate to make such provision, his reasons should be expressed in the order itself.

(8) The applicant should undertake not to inform any third party of the proceedings until after the return date.

For a form of order incorporating these principles which should now be used, see *post*, para. G–14.

On an application for an Anton Piller order, the following matters ought to be drawn to the court's attention in the affidavit evidence and ought, therefore, to be the subject of routine inquiry (see *Naf Naf S.A. v. Dickens (London) Ltd.* [1993] F.S.R. 424):

(1) The nature and scale of the defendant's business and what is known about its directors, if it is a company, or others responsible for conducting the business. See *Thermax Ltd v. Schott Industrial Glass Ltd* [1981] F.S.R. 289.

(2) The type of premises from which the defendant operates. See *Systematica Ltd. v. London Computer Centre Ltd.* [1983] F.S.R. 313.

There is no objection to a provision in the order allowing the party executing it to list other items which he sees and which he reasonably believes infringe the rights of a third party. See *20th Century Fox Film Corp. v. Tryrare Ltd.* [1991] F.S.R. 58, applying *Tate Access Floors Inc. v. Boswell* [1991] Ch. 512. A party is entitled to use evidence so obtained to bring further proceedings: *ibid*.

As a matter of the law of evidence, information derived or obtained as a result of an Anton Piller order which ought never to have been obtained is admissible: see *Helliwell v. Piggott-Sims* [1980] F.S.R. 356. The court, however, has a jurisdiction *in personam* to restrain use made of the information where it would be inequitable for the plaintiff to do so: see *Lord Ashburton v. Pape* [1913] 2 Ch. 469. It is a question of balancing factors, such as the seriousness of the non-disclosure, the effect which such a prohibition would have on the court's ability to do justice in the particular case and the practicality of requiring a party not to make use of the information which he has obtained, but which could not be eliminated from his mind: see *Guess? Inc. v. Lee Seck Mon* [1987] F.S.R. 125 (C.A., Hong Kong). The latter difficulty may be overcome by restraining the defendant from making overt use of the information, *i.e.* the doing of an act which itself shows that it was based on the information obtained: see *English & American Insurance Co. Ltd. v. Herbert Smith* [1988] F.S.R. 232. See, generally, *Naf Naf S.A. v. Dickens (London) Ltd.* [1993] F.S.R. 424.

Discharge of Anton Piller orders. There have been further decisions   **11–50A**
on the circumstances in which an Anton Piller order will be discharged, mainly on the grounds of non-disclosure. The discussion of this problem at the bottom of page 335 and the top of page 336 in the Main Work should be read in the light of the following decisions:

(1) The court may discharge an Anton Piller order on the grounds of material non-disclosure and order costs to be awarded on an indemnity basis, with immediate taxation. See *Naf Naf S.A. v. Dickens (London) Ltd.* [1993] F.S.R. 424.

(2) On an application to discharge an Anton Piller Order:
   (a) The court should consider whether an injustice has been caused to the defendant: see *Lock International plc v. Beswick* [1989] 1 W.L.R. 1268 and *Lagenes Ltd v. It's At U.K. Ltd.* [1991] F.S.R. 492.
   (b) In considering that question, the court should have regard to all the evidence on the application to discharge, including the results of the execution of the order: see *W.E.A. Records Ltd. v. Visions Channel 4 Ltd.* [1983] 1 W.L.R. 721.
   (c) If the order was obtained by material non-disclosure, the fruits of the execution will not save it from being set aside.
   (d) The fact that the evidence before the judge who granted the order was not as strong as it ultimately became does not affect the position if the evidence obtained shows that the order was justified.
   See *Hoechst U.K. Ltd. v. Chemiculture* [1993] F.S.R. 270.

(3) A party applying to discharge an Anton Piller order should give good notice of the grounds on which the application is made. See *EMI Records Ltd. v. V.C.D. Specialists Ltd.* [1992] F.S.R. 70.

(4) It is always incumbent on a court to review the grant of an Anton Piller Order on the grounds of non-disclosure, even after execution and before trial: see *BUPA v. First Choice Health Ltd.* noted at [1993] 4 EIPR D-87.

(5) Although a party who obtains an order without proper disclosure will normally be deprived of any advantage gained, it will be very exceptional that he will be deprived of the protection to which he would otherwise be entitled. See *House of Fraser Holdings plc v. New* noted at [1993] I.P.D. 16016, following *Bank Mellat v. Nicpour* [1985] F.S.R. 87.

(6) If a plaintiff fails to observe any undertaking given to the court on obtaining an Anton Piller order or otherwise acts scandalously in relation to it, the court will take this into account in deciding whether or not to set aside the order or grant further relief. See *Tate Access Floors Inc. v. Boswell* [1991] Ch. 512.

(7) If the Anton Piller order is discharged, the judge should always consider whether it is appropriate that he should assess damages and direct payment by the applicant: *Practice Direction, The Times*, August 2, 1994.

11–51   Breach of order.

NOTE 37. **Add**: *Bhimji v. Chatwani* [1991] 1 W.L.R. 989.

(iii) Identity of infringers

11–52   After note 40 in the text. **Add**: The jurisdiction to order disclosure exists if two conditions are satisfied: first, the third party has become mixed up in the transactions of which discovery is required; second, the order for discovery must not offend against the "mere witness" rule which prevents a person from obtaining discovery against someone who would be compellable to give the information as a witness, either orally or on a *subpoena duces tecum*. Finding out the identity of a tortfeasor falls outside that rule. The jurisdiction is not confined to cases of identifying wrongdoers. In *C.H.C. Software Care Ltd. v. Hopkins & Wood* [1993] F.S.R. 241 an order was made to discover the names and addresses of persons to whom the defendant had sent a letter which the plaintiff alleged contained false statements. It may be exercised to discover what has happened to property and in aid of a pre-judgment or post-judgment Mareva injunction, where it is just and convenient to make the order. See *Mercantile Group (Europe) A.G. v. Aiyela* [1993] 3 W.L.R. 1116, C.A., and [1993] F.S.R. 745 (Hobhouse J.): (although, *c.f. Arab Monetary Fund v. Hashim* [1992] 2 All E.R. 911, suggesting that the *Norwich Pharmacal* jurisdiction extends only to identifying the wrongdoers and no further).

The jurisdiction to order discovery against a person who has become mixed up in the torts of others applies *a fortiori* against the wrongdoer himself (see *Norwich Pharmacal Company v. Commissioners of Customs and Excise* [1974] A.C. 137 at 175 C-D). Discovery may therefore be ordered against a defendant if there is a reasonable cause of action pleaded against him: *C.H.C. Software Care Ltd. v. Hopkins & Wood, supra*.

In *Roberts v. Jump Knitwear* [1981] F.S.R. 527 it was held that no discovery order would be made to reveal the names of innocent third parties who had been supplied with allegedly infringing articles. It is doubtful whether that decision was correct: see *Lagenes Ltd. v. It's At*

(U.K.) Ltd. [1991] F.S.R. 492. Under section 99(1) of the 1988 Act there is a right to apply for an order for delivery up and under that jurisdiction an order for delivery up may be made regardless of the existence of any knowledge of the defendant that the copy is an infringing copy. In those circumstances the court has jurisdiction to make an order against a person who has allegedly put infringing copies into circulation requiring him to disclose the identity of the persons to whom such copies have been supplied. The fact that it has not yet been established that the copies are infringing copies is not a bar to this jurisdiction. The issue will not be decided between the plaintiffs and the third party until proceedings under section 99 have been brought and determined: *ibid.*

End of paragraph. **Add**: Where a *Norwich Pharmacal* type of discovery order has been obtained, the plaintiff is not limited to using any of the resulting information obtained only in the proceedings themselves. The information may be used, for example, to pursue proceedings against third parties: see *Levi Strauss & Co. v. Barclays Trading Corporation* [1993] F.S.R. 179.

The obligation to give information extends to all information necessary to enable the plaintiff to decide whether it is worth suing the wrongdoer or not: see *Société Romanaise de la Chaussure SA v. British Shoe Corporation Ltd.* [1991] F.S.R. 1. It was held that, in principle, a defendant may be ordered to state whether the order for goods has been solicited by the manufacturer or whether the defendant has initiated the order, and to give discovery of all relevant documents. The defendant was ordered to state the grounds of its belief that it was the only customer for the goods and that the manufacturer held no other stocks. The defendant was also ordered to give discovery of all documents relevant to the grounds of belief. It was pointed out that the information was discoverable in due course in any case. It was not harmful to the defendant to order the information to be produced now, but it was harmful to the plaintiff if left to speculate in the absence of the information.

Note that the Lord Chancellor's Department has issued a Consul- **11–54**
tation Paper regarding the privilege against self-incrimination.

It was held in *Tate Access Floors Inc. v. Boswell* [1991] Ch. 512 that:

(1) The privilege against self incrimination applies in fraud actions where there is a real risk that a defendant may be prosecuted for conspiracy.

(2) It is not necessary for the defendant to claim the privilege: an order whereby a defendant may be incriminated should never be made.

(3) Such an order can, however, usually be made against a foreign corporation because there is no risk of prosecution.

The defendant is not entitled to claim privilege against self-incrimination if he is adequately protected against prejudice: see *A.T. & T. Istel v. Tully* [1992] [1993] A.C. 45. Thus, an order may be properly made whose execution is conditional upon (a) the defendant being advised of his right to claim privilege and (b) on his expressly declining the right. See *IBM United Kingdom Ltd. v. Prima Data International Ltd.* [1994] 1 W.L.R. 719.

(iv) Mareva injunctions

11–56 Many cases continue to be reported on the grant and discharge of Mareva injunctions. Reference must be made to more specialised works for a full account of this jurisdiction. A standard form of Mareva injunction has now been issued: *Practice Direction, The Times,* August 2, 1994 (see *post,* para. G–15). The following points are worth noting from recent decisions:

(1) If the plaintiff has a substantive cause of action against a defendant, the court may grant a Mareva injunction incidental to and in aid of the enforcement of that right against a person, even if the plaintiff has no cause of action against that person: *Mercantile Group (Europe) A.G. v. Aiyela* [1993] 3 W.L.R. 1116; *T.S.B. Private Bank International S.A. v. Chabra* [1992] 1 W.L.R. 231.

(2) A Mareva injunction will not be granted which interferes with the normal course of business or where the cause of action is speculative: see *Polly Peck International v. Nadir (No.2)* [1992] 2 All E.R. 769.

(3) On an *ex parte* application for a Mareva injunction there should be disclosure in the affidavit (rather than in the exhibits) of all facts necessary to enable the judge to exercise his discretion properly and fairly between the parties: see *National Bank of Sharjah v. Dellborg, The Times,* December 24, 1992.

(4) An *ex parte* Mareva injunction should not normally be granted in the course of a trial. If it is necessary to make such an application it should be made in the presence of counsel for the respondent: see *Re All Starr Video Ltd., The Times,* March 25 1993.

(5) A Mareva injunction may only be granted in support of a cause of action arising out of an actual or threatened invasion of a legal or equitable right: see *Zucker v. Tyndall Holdings* [1992] 1 W.L.R. 1127.

(6) A plaintiff is under an obligation to notify the third party of his right to vary a Mareva injunction which affects him: see *Guinness*

Peat Aviation (Belgium) N.V. v. Hispanii Lineas Aereas S.A. [1992] 1 Lloyd's Rep. 190.

(7) If a world-wide Mareva injunction is sought, it is desirable to set out the arguments for it in a skeleton argument, identifying the exceptional circumstances: see *Alg Inc. v. Uganda Airlines Corp., The Times,* July 31, 1992.

(8) If a plaintiff does not intend to notify the defendant of the order, the Court should be informed of this fact: see *Midland Motor Vessel, The Financial Times,* December 11, 1991.

For a useful discussion of the development of Mareva injunctions, see Zuckerman in (1993) 109 L.Q.R. 432. Note also the new Order 29, Rule 1A, especially sub-rule (3), which provides that answers obtained pursuant to an order for cross-examination as part of a Mareva injunction are not to be used for other purposes without consent or leave.

C. *Final relief*

(i) Declaratory judgment

Add: Contrary to the normal rule of practice, a declaration may be **11–57** granted where a judgment is obtained without a trial (*e.g.* a default judgment), when full justice cannot otherwise be done. For example, a declaration may be granted that a publishing agreement is at an end, so facilitating an author in his efforts to sell his work elsewhere. It is important that the declaration in question should not affect the rights of anyone other than the defendants or the persons claiming through them. See *Patten v. Burke Publishing Co. Ltd.* [1991] F.S.R. 483, followed in *Aitbelaid v. Nima, The Times,* July 19, 1991.

(ii) Permanent injunction

Delay in taking proceedings. After note 56 in the text. **Add**: If there **11–59** is a delay in proceeding with the action after the grant of an interlocutory injunction, the court may discharge the injunction. It is incumbent on a plaintiff whose position is protected by an inter- locutory injunction to proceed with due diligence and so limit, so far as possible, the period during which the defendant's liberty is restrained. The plaintiff cannot assume that, in the absence of complaint, the defendant is content to treat the injunction as permanent, without further steps being taken. See *Newsgroup Newspapers Ltd. v. The Mirror Group Newspapers (1986) Ltd.* [1991] F.S.R. 487.

11–60   **Actual damage need not be proved.** End of paragraph. **Add**: Since a person whose right has been infringed is normally entitled to come to court to have his rights pronounced upon and vindicated and have an injunction granted against further infringements, a *Calderbank* offer by a defendant may be inadequate if it does not make clear that he is offering an undertaking to the court. See *Colgate Palmolive Ltd.* v. *Markwell Finance Ltd.* [1990] R.P.C. 197. Circumstances may arise during the trial which show that an injunction is not necessary for the plaintiff's protection, in which case it is usual to give the plaintiff liberty to apply for an injunction should circumstances arise where it is appropriate: *ibid.*

11–61   **Where a portion only of the work is copied. Add**: Where the claim is for a permanent injunction, as distinct from an interlocutory injunction, it will not usually be appropriate to weigh the damage which the defendant will suffer by reason of the injunction (for example, through the loss of non-infringing material which he has mixed up with infringing material), against the damage which the plaintiff will suffer if the injunction is refused. See *Macmillan Publishers Ltd.* v. *Thomas Reed Publications Ltd.* [1993] F.S.R. 455 at 466 and 467.

(iii) Damages

11–65   After note 87 in the text. **Add**: The fact that the defendant could have achieved the same result without using the plaintiff's work is not relevant when assessing the plaintiff's loss.

NOTE 87. **Add**: See also *Morton Norwich Products Inc.* v. *Intercen (No. 2)* [1981] F.S.R. 337.
The following further cases on damages have been decided:

(1) *Autodesk Australia Pty. Ltd.* v. *Cheung* (1990) 17 I.P.R. 69, [1990] A.I.P.C. 90–665 discusses the principles involved in awarding damages for infringement. Damages calculated by reference to the depreciation in the value of the copyright are difficult to assess if the market was already saturated or if the defendant increased demand. The plaintiff in that case argued that the measure of damages was the equivalent licence fee. It was held that the defendant would not have taken such a licence and damages were therefore at large and assessed as if by jury, following *Fenning Film Service Ltd.* v. *Wolverhampton, etc., Cinemas Ltd.* [1914] 3 K.B. 1171.

(2) *Oliver Homes (Manufacturing)* v. *Hamilton* [1992] F.L.T. 892 was a case of infringement of copyright in plans for a "kit-houses" by

building a house from them. The damages were assessed as equal to the reasonable licence fee for use of the plans, not by reference to the loss on the sale of one of the house kits.

(3) *CAG Construction Pty. Ltd. v. Kitchen* (1991) 23 I.P.R. 284 (Sup. Ct. of Sth. Australia.) was a case of infringement of copyright in plans for a house by building the house in accordance with the plans. Damages were claimed based on the loss of profit on construction of such a house. The claim was rejected. That basis might be appropriate where the plaintiff and defendant were in competition, so that, but for the defendant's action, the plaintiff might have obtained the contract. Since the defendant could not have afforded to engage the plaintiff, the only other reasonable basis on which damages could be assessed was that of a reasonable licence fee.

(4) *Devefi Pty. Ltd. v. Mateffy Perl Nagy Pty. Ltd.* [1993] R.P.C. 193 (Fed. Ct. of Australia.) was a case in which an engineer's plans for construction of a building were used without consent. The measure of damages was the value of a licence, assessed by reference to the outstanding contractual payments due to the engineer.

(5) In *Performing Right Society Ltd. v. Hardrock Cafe Pty Ltd.* (High Ct. of Singapore) noted at [1992] 10 EIPR D-210, damages for unauthorised public performance were assessed at 3 per cent. of the gross ticket sales, that being the royalty which would have been payable if a licence had been obtained to do the infringing act.

(iv) Additional damages

NOTE 93. See *Noah v. Shuba* [1991] F.S.R. 14 at 29–31, for a summary **11–66** of the principles for awarding damages under section 17(3) of the 1956 Act, applying *Beloff v. Pressdam Ltd.* [1973] 1 All E.R. 241 and *Ravenseft v. Herbert* [1980] R.P.C. 193.

NOTE 99. See also *A.B. v. South West Water Services Ltd.* [1993] Q.B. 507 where it was held that exemplary damages were not available in claims for public nuisance or negligence.

End of second paragraph. **Add**: In *Autodesk Australia Pty. Ltd. v.* **11–67** *Cheung* (1990) 17 I.P.R. 69, [1990] A.I.P.C. 90–665, additional damages were awarded having regard to the fact that the defendant knew that the copies he was selling were infringements. There was a significant benefit to the defendant in doing so. There were difficulties in detection and the defendant was probably infringing other copyright works.

(v) Damages for conversion

11–68 After second sentence. **Add**: In *Banks v. C.B.S. Songs Ltd.* [1992] F.S.R. 278, in proceedings commenced before August 1, 1989 (the date from which conversion damages were abolished), the court refused to grant leave to amend to plead pre- and post-writ acts of conversion. The application to amend had been made by a summons issued before August 1, 1989, though it was not heard until after that date. Leave to amend was refused because proceedings in respect of causes of action proposed in the amendment would not commence until leave to amend was actually granted, *i.e.* after August 1, 1989. The Court of Appeal held that "proceedings" did not include the application for leave to amend. It meant proceedings in which the cause of action for which the claim for conversion damages was sought and prosecuted.

(vi) Account of profits

11–76 NOTE 56. For a review of the principles involved in taking an account of profits see Kirby in [1991] 10 EIPR 367 and Bently in [1991] 1 EIPR 5. See also Bently in [1990] 3 EIPR 106 on *Potton Ltd. v. Yorkclose Ltd.* [1990] F.S.R. 11.

Election between damages and an account. Before first complete sentence on page 353. **Add**: After judgment on the issue of liability, the plaintiff may be entitled to limited discovery before making an election between damages and an account of profits, provided that this is not unfair or unjust to the defendant. See *Minnesota Mining & Manufacturing Co. v. C. Jeffries Pty. Ltd.* [1993] F.S.R. 189 (Fed. Ct. of N.S.W.).

Where a party has claimed damages, he will normally be entitled to amend his claim before judgment in the action to claim an account of profits in the alternative. He will not be held to have irrevocably elected his remedy by failing to claim the alternative relief. There is nothing unfair or unjust in allowing the plaintiff to claim alternative relief by amendment. See *Thornton Hall Manufacturing Ltd. v. Shanton Apparel Ltd.* (1988) 12 I.P.R. 48 (High Ct. of N.Z.).

NOTE 64. **Add**: See also *Dart Industries Inc. v. Decor Corporation Pty. Ltd.* (1993) 26 I.P.R. 193 (High Ct. of Australia) (a patent action), where the defendant was held liable to account for the profits made from the manufacture and sale of plastic canisters where only the lids infringed. The sales were attributable to the lid, without which the canisters would have never been made.

End of first paragraph. **Add**: In *Dart Industries Inc. v. Decor Corporation Pty. Ltd.* (1993) 26 I.P.R. 193 (High Ct. of Australia) (a patent action) it was held on the facts of that case that the proportion of overhead costs which were attributable to the obtaining of the relevant profit might be deducted in arriving at a profit figure. It was pointed out that where the manufacture of a product constituted a side line of the defendant's business and made use of spare capacity, it would not be right to deduct a proportion of overhead costs since these would have been incurred in any event. Where, however, the product was an integral part of the defendant's range, such that if the product in question had not been manufactured, some alternative product would have been, it would be wrong in principle to deny the defendant deduction of a proportion of his overheads. Otherwise the defendant would be in a worse position than if he had never manufactured the infringing article. Again, if it is shown that overheads were increased by the production of the infringing article, or would have been reduced had it not been produced, it may be appropriate to attribute the difference to the infringing product.

Note 81. Note that the Trade Marks Act 1938 is prospectively **11–79** repealed by the Trade Marks Act 1994 (c.26).

(viii) Delivery up

Note 89. As to the exercise of the discretion, see *Re Elgindata (No. 2)* **11–80** [1992] 1 W.L.R. 1207.

End of first paragraph. **Add**: The court also has jurisdiction to make a mandatory order for delivery up on an interlocutory application, if there is a high degree of assurance that the plaintiff will establish his entitlement at trial and the risk of injustice, if the injunction were refused, sufficiently outweighs the risk of injustice if it were granted. See *Nottingham Building Society v. Eurodynamics Systems plc* [1993] F.S.R. 468 at 474.

(ix) Points as to costs

After first sentence. **Add**: The court has jurisdiction to order a non- **11–81** party to the proceedings to pay costs: for example, a person who has some management of the action, such as the director of an insolvent company who has caused the company to prosecute or defend proceedings improperly; a person who has maintained or financed the action; a solicitor involved in the conduct of the action; a person who has caused the action or is a party to a closely related action; or a person who is a party in group litigation where one or two actions have been selected as test actions. The courts have developed principles for the guidance of judges at first instance in the exercise of this exceptional jurisdiction. See *Aiden Shipping Co. Ltd. v. Interbulk Ltd.* [1986] 965; *Symphony Group plc v. Hodgson* [1994] Q.B. 179.

After note 90 in the text. **Add**: Since a person whose intellectual property right has been infringed is entitled to come to court and obtain an injunction against further infringements, it follows that he is entitled to his costs of obtaining the injunction, even if the damages awarded do not exceed any payment in. Care should, therefore, be taken when framing a *Calderbank* offer to see that it offers to the plaintiff all the relief to which he is likely to be entitled. See *Colgate Palmolive Ltd. v. Markwell Finance Ltd.* [1990] R.P.C. 197.

In general, there is no obligation on the recipient of a *Calderbank* offer to make a counter-offer or negotiate. Indeed his reply to that offer is privileged, if that privilege is not waived, and it is, in any case, irrelevant. What matters is the letter making the offer and that must be clear and adequate in its terms. See *C & H Engineering v. K. Kluczaik & Sons Ltd.*, *The Times*, March 26, 1992.

11–82 End of paragraph. **Add**: Where an order for the payment of the plaintiff's costs of an action is made at the conclusion of the trial, the plaintiff is entitled to immediate taxation of those costs notwithstanding that inquiries are still to be taken. See *Molnlycke A.B. v. Procter & Gamble Ltd. (No. 6)* [1993] F.S.R. 154 distinguishing *Small v. Cohen* (1992, C.A.; unreported).

8. Procedural and Related Matters

C. *Summary judgment and striking out*

11–85 First sentence and NOTE 11. **Delete**, and **substitute**: In cases where a defendant has no defence, or no plausible defence, to a claim for infringement of copyright, the plaintiff may apply by summons for summary judgment. [NOTE 12 in the Main Work]. Where an issue of fact is involved on an Order 14 application, it is up to the defendant in his evidence to demonstrate a possibility of the issue being resolved in his favour. It is not for the court to invent hypotheses on which he may succeed at trial. See *L.A. Gear Inc. v. Hi-Tec* [1992] F.S.R. 121. If the relief sought on the application for summary judgment includes an injunction, the summons should be made returnable directly before the judge in chambers, instead of the Master. See *The Supreme Court Practice*, 1993 Vol. 2, para. 852 and *Practice Direction* [1993] 1 W.L.R. 21.

On an application for summary judgment under Order 14 where the issue is whether a substantial part of the plaintiff's work has been taken, that should normally go to trial since it is a matter of fact and degree. See *Total Information Processing systems Ltd. v. Daman Ltd.* [1992] F.S.R. 171, applying *Leco Instruments U.K. Ltd. v. Land Pyrometers Ltd.* [1982] R.P.C. 133.

Where a plaintiff alleges infringement of copyright in a number of works, he is entitled to apply for summary judgment in respect of some of them, leaving the others to a trial: *Macmillan Publishers Ltd. v. Thomas Reed Publications Ltd.* [1993] F.S.R. 455.

Where on an application under Order 14, a plaintiff succeeds in establishing that there is no triable issue that part of the defendant's work infringes, it will not normally be correct to deny the plaintiff a permanent injunction against that part because the defendant argues that such an injunction may not be granted after a full trial: *Macmillan Publishers Ltd. v. Thomas Reed Publications Ltd.* [1993] F.S.R. 455, applying *Mawman v. Tegg* (1826) 2 Russ. 385.

NOTE 13. *Express Newspapers plc v. News (U.K.) Ltd.* is also reported at [1991] F.S.R. 36. The principle that a party may not approbate and reprobate applies only to attitudes adopted in litigation. See *Compaq Computer Corp. v. Dell Computer Corp* [1992] F.S.R. 93.

End of first paragraph. **Add**: On an application for summary judgment the question for the court is: "Is there a fair or reasonable probability of the defendant having a real or bona fide defence?" The court may conclude that a defendant who has sworn two totally inconsistent affidavits on allegedly arguable issues of fact and law has no real or bona fide defence. See *National Westminster Bank plc v. Daniel* [1993] 1 W.L.R. 1453 at 1457.

Summary judgment on a question of law may be obtained on the basis of agreed or assumed facts under Order 14A.

After note 17 in the text. **Add**: An application to strike out should, in the ordinary way, be made at the earliest opportunity and not left, for example, until after the opposite party has incurred all the costs of preparing for trial. See *Halliday v. Shoessmith* [1993] 1 W.L.R. 1.

An application to strike out is not appropriate if it involves a minute and protracted examination of documents and facts in the case to see if the plaintiff has a cause of action, unless it will obviate the need for a trial or reduce the costs of preparation. See *PSM International plc v. Specialised Fastener Products (Southern) Ltd.* [1993] F.S.R. 113.

E. *Proof of copying*

See also § 8–12 in the Main Work and *ante*, para. 8–12. Inferences may **11–92** properly be drawn from the surrounding circumstances and from the nature of the similarities themselves. See *John Richardson Computers Ltd. v. Flanders* [1993] F.S.R. 497 at 543.

11–93 **Similar fact evidence.** After penultimate sentence. **Add**: It does not matter in such cases that the plaintiff has not alleged that infringement of copyright has occurred in the other cases. It is sufficient to allege that copying has occurred. Depending on the circumstances, such evidence may be just as probative. See *Perrin v. Drennan* [1991] F.S.R. 81, where leave was granted to amend pleadings to allege similar facts.

11–94 **Expert evidence.** End of first paragraph. **Add**: See *Monsoon Ltd. v. India Imports of Rhode Island Ltd.* [1993] F.S.R. 486.

End of second paragraph. **Add**: A concise statement of the duties and responsibilities of an expert witness is contained in *"The Ikarian Reefer"* [1993] F.S.R. 563.

F. *Discovery and inspection*

NOTE 53. Such discovery will not be ordered solely in the hope that it will support what is otherwise an unsubstantiated allegation. See *Chater & Chater Productions Ltd. v. Rose* [1994] E.M.L.R. 217.

After note 53 in the text. **Add**: To obtain an order for inspection under Ord. 29, r. 2, a party must establish a substantial and genuine issue to be tried and that inspection is essential for the proper determination of the case. It will only be in exceptional cases, such as where a plaintiff cannot plead his genuine case, that inspection will be ordered prior to the issue being clarified in pleadings. Inspection will not usually be essential until after discovery. See *Smith Myers Communications Ltd. v. Motorola Ltd.* [1991] F.S.R. 262. In *Dun & Bradstreet Ltd. v. Typesetting Facilities Ltd.* [1992] F.S.R. 320 inspection was ordered. It was essential so that a full and proper statement of claim could be served. Doubt was expressed whether the statement in *Smith Myers Communications v. Motorola* [1991] F.S.R. 262, that inspection will only be ordered where it is essential for the case to be able to proceed, was correct.

Page 364, sixth line. Thus, where there is to be a split trial, discovery will not be ordered before liability is established merely to enable a party to form an estimate of the amount in issue or to enable information to be given to the legal aid authorities. Special circumstances must be shown. See *Baldock v. Addison, The Times,* July 7, 1994, not following *Hazeltine Corp. v. British Broadcasting Corporation* [1979] F.S.R. 523. See also *De La Rue v. Dickinson* 3 K. & J. 388; *Fennessy v. Clark* [1887] 37 Ch. D. 184; *Lea v. Saxby* 32 L.T.R. 731 and *William Gaymer & Son Ltd. v. H.P. Bulmer Ltd., The Times,* January 19, 1984.

H. *Appeals.*

Where an unsuccessful plaintiff appeals and applies for an order to   **11–96A**
continue an interlocutory injunction against a defendant, the court
will not be astute to find in favour of the plaintiff after a finding at trial
that the defendant was acting lawfully. See *Dyason v. Autodesk Inc.*
(1990) 19 I.P.R. 399 (Fed. Ct. of Australia.). Note also that where a
plaintiff has obtained a permanent injunction at trial, the court has
jurisdiction to require the plaintiff to continue a cross-undertaking in
damages pending appeal by the defendant. See *American Cyanamid Co.
v. Ethicon Ltd.* [1979] R.P.C. 215 at 275; *Minnesota Mining and
Manufacturing Co. v. Johnson & Johnson Ltd.* [1976] R.P.C. 671, C.A.

A stay of execution pending an appeal may be obtained where the
appellant can show that, without a stay, he would be ruined, and that
his appeal has sufficient prospects of success: see *Linotype-Hell Finance
Ltd. v. Baker* [1992] 4 All E.R. 887. An inquiry as to damages will not
normally be stayed pending an appeal by the defendant: see *Minnesota
Mining and Manufacturing Co. v. Rennicks (U.K.) Ltd.* noted at [1992]
I.P.D. 15116.

CHAPTER 12

LIBRARIES

2. Deposit of Books

12–7   **Effect of failure to deliver copies.** Second sentence. **Delete**: "a fine, not exceeding £5". **Substitute**: "a fine not exceeding level 1 on the standard scale".

NOTE 23. **Delete**, and **substitute**: Copyright Act 1911 s.15(6) as amended by Criminal Law Act 1977 (c. 45), s.31(5) and (6) and Criminal Justice Act 1982 (c. 48), ss.37 and 46. In relation to offences committed on or after 1 October, 1992 the figure for level 1 on the standard scale is £200: see Criminal Justice Act 1991 (c. 53), ss. 17(1) and 101(1) and Sched. 12, para. 6.

3. Deposit of Scripts

12–10   **Definitions.** Section 18 of the London Local Authorities Act 1990 (c. 13) extends the definition of "public performance" in the 1968 Act. The extended definition is confined to performances in London boroughs and takes effect in a particular borough on a date appointed by resolution of the relevant borough council: sections 3 and 18(1) of the 1990 Act. In a borough where the extension is in force, the expression "public performance" includes "any performance which is not open to the public but which is promoted for private gain": see section 18(2) of the 1990 Act. The phrase "promoted for private gain" is defined in a new section 18A of the 1968 Act which is inserted by section 18(3) of the 1990 Act.

Effect of failure to deliver copies. First Sentence. **Delete**: "a fine not   **12–11**
exceeding £5". **Substitute**: "a fine not exceeding level 1 on the
standard scale".

NOTE 35. **Delete**, and **substitute**: *Ibid.* s.11(2) as amended by Criminal
Justice Act 1982 (c. 48), ss.37 and 38. In relation to offences committed
on or after 1 October 1992 the figure for level 1 on the standard scale is
£200: see Criminal Justice Act 1991 (c. 53), ss. 17(1) and 101(1) and
Sched. 12 para. 6.

4. Public Lending Right

A. *Public Lending Right Act 1979*

Note that the Directive on rental and lending right 92/100 (see *ante*,   **12–12**
paras. 1–55 and 8–98, and *post*, para. H–27 *et seq.*) requires Member
States to grant copyright owners rights in respect of the commercial
rental and public lending of all forms of works. Some changes in the
Public Lending Right Act and the Scheme are envisaged as a result.

NOTE 41. The basic fund was increased to £4.75m by the Public
Lending Right (Increase of Limit) Order 1991[1] and to £5m by the
Public Lending Right (Increase of Limit) Order 1993.[2]

B. *The scheme*

History of the Scheme.   **12–17**

NOTE 65. **Add**: 1991 No. 2618, 1993 No. 3049.

---

[1] (S.I. 1991 No. 858)
[2] (S.I. 1993 No. 799)

CHAPTER 13

CROWN AND PARLIAMENTARY RIGHTS.
UNIVERSITIES' AND COLLEGES' RIGHTS.

Contents

Contents   *Para.*

1. Crown Rights

A. *Crown prerogative*

13–1 For a discussion of the prerogative and its residual status in the United Kingdom, see Monotti in [1992] 9 EIPR 305 (also referred to *ante*, para. 1–21).

B. *Crown Copyright*

(iii) Position under the 1956 Act

(f) *Proceedings for infringement against Crown*

13–16 NOTE 33. Note that the Semiconductor regulations have been further amended: see *post*, para. A–577L.

(g) *Proceedings to protect Crown copyright*

NOTE 17. Note that the Semiconductor regulations have been further   **13–17**
amended: see *post*, para A–577L.

(iv) Position under the 1988 Act

(a) *Generally*

Provisions of the 1988 Act. For a table listing the Parliamentary   **13–18**
debates on these and other provisions of the 1988 Act, see *post*,
Appendix I.

D. *Design Right*

Crown a qualifying person.   **13–32**

NOTE 95. Note that the Semiconductor regulations have been further
amended: see *post*, para. A–577L.

2. Parliamentary Rights.

A. *Parliamentary copyright*

(i) Provisions of the 1988 Act

Creation of Parliamentary Copyright. For a table listing the Parlia-   **13–35**
mentary debates on these and other provisions of the 1988 Act, see
post, Appendix I.

CHAPTER 14

COMMUNITY LAW

1. Introduction

The European Union. On February 7, 1992, the 12 Member States of   **14–1A**
the European Community signed the final texts of the agreement
which had been reached between them at Maastricht on December 9
and 10, 1991, and which then became the Treaty on European Union,
otherwise known as the Maastricht Treaty.

The Maastricht Treaty amends the Treaty of Rome, and renames
the EEC the E.C., reflecting the further enlargement in the aims of the
Treaty; it also amends but preserves the separate treaties establishing
the ECSC and Euratom. The Maastricht Treaty establishes a new
structure, the European Union, with separate legal powers, but within
which the three existing communities continue to operate. The
Maastricht Treaty came into force on November 1, 1993. The
European Communities Act 1972 was amended by the European
Communities (Amendment) Act 1993 (c. 32) (in force July 20, 1993) to
give domestic legal effect in the United Kingdom to the changes to the
Community treaties effected by the Maastricht Treaty.

The debate preceding the Maastricht Treaty centred largely on the
extent to which national competence in certain areas should be
transferred to the institutions of the European Union. In the resulting
compromise, the two pillars of the Maastricht Treaty, a common
foreign and security policy and co-operation in the fields of justice and
home affairs, are left as being largely inter-governmental (see Cur-
tin,"The Constitutional Structure of the Union: A Europe of Bits and
Pieces" in (1993) 30 C.M.L.Rev. 17–69, at 28 and editorial comments,
"Post-Maastricht" in (1992) 29 C.M.L.Rev. 199–203).

The main area for amendment of the Treaty of Rome was in the
section dealing with economic and monetary union. The objective to
be achieved by the Maastricht Treaty is the adoption of an economic
policy founded on close co-ordination between Member States' economic policies, conducted in accordance with the principle of an open
market economy with free competition. The Articles of the Treaty
relevant to this chapter, namely those on which the principle of free
movement of goods is based (Arts. 30 to 36 in Chapter 2 of Title I) and
the competition rules themselves (contained in Chapter 1 of Title V),
remain, in all material respects, unaltered.

For the text of the Maastricht Treaty see *Current Law Statutes*, vol. 2,
(Sweet & Maxwell 1993), 32–219.

Scope of Chapter. The scope of the chapter and the emphasis on   **14–2**
certain provisions of the Treaty remain the same, notwithstanding the
establishment of the European Union (see *supra*, para. 14–1A).

NOTE 7. See now Wyatt and Dashwood, *European Community Law*
(Sweet & Maxwell, 3rd ed., 1993); see also Green, Hartley and Usher,

The Legal Foundations of the Single European Market (O.U.P., 1991) and Collins, *European Community Law in the UK* (Butterworths, 4th ed., 1990).

2. The EEC: Its Institutions and Law

14–3 **The EEC as a separate legal order.** See *supra*, para. 14–1A, as to the establishment of the European Union.

14–6 Note 14. **Add**: Revised Rules of Procedure for the Court were introduced with effect from September 1, 1991: [1991] O.J. L176/7; [1993] 3 C.M.L.R. 745.

14–8 Note 19. See now Wyatt and Dashwood, *European Community Law* (Sweet & Maxwell, 3rd ed., 1993).

14–9 Note 21. **Add**: See also Vesterdorf, "The Court of First Instance of the E.C. after Two Full Years in Operation" in (1992) 29 C.M.L.Rev. 897 and Millett, *The Court of First Instance* (Butterworths, 1990).

Note 22. Revised Rules of Procedure for the Court of First Instance were introduced with effect from July 1, 1991: [1991] O.J. L136/1; [1993] 3 C.M.L.R. 795.

14–10 **Interpretation of the Treaty and its implementing measures.**

Note 29. **Add**: In Case C-106/89, *Marleasing S.A. v. La Commercial Internacional de Alimentacion S.A.* [1992] 1 C.M.L.R. 305, the Court stated the principle that a national court must endeavour to interpret national law as far as possible consistently with any relevant E.C. directive, whether the national law originated before or after adoption of the directive (*cf. Organon Laboratories Ltd. v. D.H.S.S.* [1990] 2 C.M.L.R. 49, C.A.).

14–12 **Add**: Reliance on a directive against a Member State may even entitle an individual to claim damages from the Member State for losses flowing from the Member State's breach of Community law: see Joined Cases C 6 & 9/90, *Francovich v. Italy* [1993] 2 C.M.L.R. 66. Moreover, where a Member State is in breach of its obligation to implement a directive, the Member State may not rely upon any applicable national limitation period, but time will not run until the directive is in force: see Case C-208/90, *Emmott v. Minister for Social*

Welfare [1991] 3 C.M.L.R. 894, applied in *Cannon v. Barnsley Metropolitan Borough Council* [1992] 2 C.M.L.R. 795; [1992] I.C.R. 698, E.A.T.

NOTE 33. **Add**: Before national courts, see also *Foster v. British Gas plc* [1991] 2 C.M.L.R. 217; [1991] 2 A.C. 306, H.L., and *Doughty v. Rolls Royce plc* [1992] 1 C.M.L.R. 1045, C.A. For a case before the European Court of Justice, see Joined Cases C 92 & 326/92, *Phil Collins v. Imtrat HandelsGmbH* and *Verwaltungsgesellschaft mbH v. EMI Electrola GmbH* [1993] 3 C.M.L.R. 773.

NOTE 35. See now Case C-271/91, *Marshall v. Southampton & S.W. Hampshire Area Health Authority* [1993] 3 C.M.L.R. 293 and *Foster v. British Gas plc* [1991] 2 C.M.L.R. 217; [1991] 2 A.C. 306, H.L.

NOTE 37. The reference is now to "Art. 7a", following renumbering as a result of amendment of the Treaty by the Maastricht Treaty. The principle is also now expressly referred to in Art. 3(c), following amendment by the Maastricht Treaty (see *post*, para. F–2).

3. Incorporation of Community Law into the Laws of the United Kingdom

Incorporation of the Treaty and implementing measures.   **14–15**

NOTE 39. As subsequently amended by the European Communities (Amendment) Act 1986 (c. 59) (to take account of the Single European Act), the European Communities (Amendment) Act 1993 (c. 32) (to take account of the Maastricht Treaty) and the European Economic Area Act 1993 (c. 51) (to take account of the Opporto Agreement on the establishment of the EEA). The European Communities Act 1972 in its amended form is printed in *Current Law Statutes*, vol. 2, (Sweet & Maxwell, 1993) 32–275.

Incorporation of the case law of the Court of Justice.   **14–16**

NOTE 43. As amended by the European Communities (Amendment) Act 1986 (c. 59) to include the Court of First Instance.

Reference to the Court of Justice: guiding principles as to when   **14–20**
reference should be made.

NOTE 54 See now Wyatt and Dashwood, *European Community Law* (Sweet & Maxwell, 3rd ed., 1993) and Brown and Jacobs, *The Court of Justice of the European Communities* (Sweet & Maxwell, 4th ed., 1994).

NOTE 58. **Add**: For a recent example where the House of Lords applied Community law and refused a reference on the basis that the matter was clear, see *R. v. London Boroughs Transport Committee ex p. Freight Transport Association Ltd.* [1992] 1 C.M.L.R. 5; [1991] 3 All E.R. 915; [1991] 1 W.L.R. 828.

NOTE 61. **Add**: See also *Entec (Pollution Control) Ltd. v. Abacus Mouldings* [1992] F.S.R. 332 (Hoffman J. and C.A.).

NOTE 65. **Add**: See also *Kirklees Borough Council v. Wickes Building Supplies Ltd.* [1992] 2 C.M.L.R. 765; [1992] 3 W.L.R. 170, H.L.

NOTE 66. **Add**: Where the decision of the Court of Justice is likely to come too late to benefit either party, a reference should be refused: *Gebhardt's Patent* [1991] R.P.C. 1.

NOTE 67. **Add**: Costs will usually follow the event: *R. v. International Board for Agricultural Produce ex p. Fish Producers Organisation Ltd.* [1993] 1 C.M.L.R. 707.

14–21 Formulation of the reference

NOTE 72. See now Atkin, *Court Forms*, Vol. 17 (1992), pp. 165 *et seq.*

4. Principal Aims of the EEC

14–23 NOTE 73. Renumbered Art. 7a as a result of the amendment of the Treaty by the Maastricht Treaty.

End of paragraph. **Add**: Since November 1, 1993, as a result of the Maastricht Treaty, the aims of the Community include establishing an economic and monetary union, and for the purpose of achieving this objective the activities of the Community have been further extended to include the fixing of exchange rates leading to the introduction of a single currency and the definition and conduct of a single monetary policy (see *ante*, para. 14–1A and Art. 3a, *post*, para. F–2A).

14–24 Free movement of goods.

At note 75 in the text. Article 8A renumbered Article 7A, as a result of the amendment of the Treaty by the Maastricht Treaty, and see also the amendment to Article 3(c) (see *post*, para. F–2) to include an express reference to the free movement of goods as one of the four pillars of the internal market.

Article 3 was amended by the Maastricht Treaty and the reference to **14–25**
Article 3(f) should now be to Article 3(g) (see *post*, para. F–2).

Rules on Competition. See *ante*, para. 14–25. **14–28**

5. The Exercise of Industrial and Commercial Property Rights and the Free Movement of Goods and Services

A. *Conflict between copyright and the aims of the EEC*

Copyright as an industrial property right. **14–30**

NOTE 88. **Add**: In Joined Cases C 92–326/92, *Phil Collins v. Imtrat HandelsGmbH* and *Verwaltungesellschaft mbH v. EMI Electrola GmbH* [1993] 3 C.M.L.R. 773, the Court of Justice, following *Musik-Vertrieb Membran v. GEMA*, applied the principles stated in that case both to copyright and to related rights (rights in performances).

The prevention of imports: conflict with the aims of the **14–38**
Community.

NOTE 7. **Add**: This was recently re-iterated by the Court of Justice in Joined Cases C 92 & 326/92, *Phil Collins v. Imtrat HandelsGmbH* and *Verwaltungesellschaft mbH v. EMI Electrola GmbH* [1993] 3 C.M.L.R. 773 at 796 [20] and 797 [22].

B. *Resolution of the conflict between industrial property and the aims of the EEC*

(i) Creation of community industrial property rights

Proposed Community Trade Mark. Delete: "proposed" in the **14–42**
heading.

Note 11. **Add**: The Council adopted a regulation creating the Community Trade Mark (CTM) on January 14, 1994 (Council Regulation (E.C.) No. 40/4: [1994] O.J. L11/1). The Regulation came into force on April 14, 1994.

(ii) Harmonisation of national industrial property rights

14–44   **Harmonisation of national laws.** Articles 100 and 100a are set out *post*, paras. F–9A and F–9B.

Note 14. The Directive is Council Directive 89/104. The date for its implementation by the Member States was December 28, 1991 (Art. 16(1)), which was extended (under Art. 16(2)) to December 31, 1992, by Council Decision EEC92/10: [1992] O.J. 1992 L6/35. The aim of the Directive is to reduce differences between the trade mark systems of the Member States which constitute barriers to trade and affect free movement of goods and services, thus impeding the attainment of the single market. The United Kingdom will implement the requirements of the Directive in the Trade Marks Act 1994 (c.26), expected to be brought into force by the end of 1994.

14–45   **Commission Green Paper on Copyright.** Both paragraphs. **Delete**, and **substitute**: Nevertheless, with the growing importance of high technology and the service industries in the economies of the industrialised Member States, the Community has become increasingly concerned to ensure that there is available through the copyright laws of the Member States effective and uniform legal protection to prevent the misappropriation of copyright works. Consequently, in 1988 the Commission published a consultative document, the Green Paper entitled *Copyright and the Challenge of Technology*, document COM. (88) 172 final: [1988] 6 E.C. Bull., points 1.2.1 *et seq.* The publication of the Green Paper was followed by a period of consultation and in January 1991, the Commission issued a document, entitled *Follow-up to the Green Paper: Working Programme of the Commission in the Field of Copyright and Neighbouring Rights*, Commission Communication to the Council, document COM. (584) 90, final, January 17, 1991. The issues discussed and proposals for action put forward in these two documents are described *ante*, para. 1–51.

14–46   **Community harmonisation measures with regard to copyright.** First two sentences. **Delete**, and **substitute**: In the meantime, the first copyright legislation resulting from the debate stimulated by the Green Paper has been adopted (see *ante*, paras. 1–51 to 1–60). To date, four legislative texts have been adopted by the Council of the European Union: (1) Directive 91/250 on the legal protection of computer programs: [1991] O.J. L122/42–46 (see *ante*, paras. 1–54 and 2–2); (2) Directive 92/100 on rental right and lending right and on certain rights related to copyright in the field of intellectual property: [1992] O.J. L346/61 (see *ante*, para. 1–55 *et seq.*); (3) Directive 98/83 on the coordination of certain rules concerning copyright and rights related to copyright applicable to satellite broadcasting and cable retransmission: [1993] O.J. L248/15 (see *ante*, para. 1–56 *et seq.*); and (4) Directive 93/98 on harmonising the term of protection of copyright and certain related rights: [1993] O.J. L290/9 (see *ante*, para. 1–57 *et. seq.*).

The copyright harmonisation programme of the European Union is not yet complete. A proposal for a directive has been put forward to the Council and the Parliament on the legal protection of databases (see *ante*, para. 1–58) and several additional issues are still being studied with a view to introducing future E.C. legislation. These are described *ante*, paras. 1–59 and 1–60.

(iii) Resolution of the conflict by the Court of Justice

Distinction between the existence or substance of industrial property rights and their exercise.   **14–50**

NOTE 26. **Add**: See also Case C-10/89, *CNL-SUCAL v. Hag GF A.G.* [1990] 1 E.C.R. 371; [1990] 3 C.M.L.R. 571. See also Case C–9/93, *IHT Internationale Heiztechnik GmbH v. Ideal-Standard GmbH*, *The Times*, July 7, 1994.

NOTES 27 and 28. **Add**: See also Case T-69/89, *Radio Telefís Eireann v. Commission* [1991] 4 C.M.L.R. 586 at 617 [71] and Joined Cases C 92 & 326/92, *Phil Collins v. Imtrat HandelsGmbH* and *Verwaltungesellschaft mbH v. EMI Electrola GmbH* [1993] 3 C.M.L.R. 773 at 797 [22] to [25].

NOTE 30. **Add**: See also Case 434/55, *Allen & Hanburys v. Generics* [1988] 1 C.M.L.R. 701 and Cases C-30/90 and 235/89 *Commission v. United Kingdom and Italy* [1992] 2 C.M.L.R. 709 at 759.

Development of concept of the specific object of an industrial property right.   **14–53**

NOTE 39. **Add**: See also Case 434/55, *Allen & Hanburys v. Generics* [1988] 1 C.M.L.R. 701 and Cases C-30/90 and 235/89, *Commission v. United Kingdom and Italy* [1992] 2 C.M.L.R. 709 at 759.

NOTE 40. **Add**: See also Case C-10/89, *CNL-SUCAL v. Hag GF A.G.* [1990] 1 E.C.R. 371; [1990] 3 C.M.L.R. 571.

Note 41. **Add**: See also Case T-69/89, *Radio Telefis Eireann v. Commission* [1991] 4 C.M.L.R. 586 and Joined Cases C-92 & 326/92, *Phil Collins v. Imtrat HandelsGmbH* and *Verwaltungesellschaft mbH v. EMI Electrola GmbH* [1993] 3 C.M.L.R. 773 at 796 [20] and 797 [22]. This latter case dealt also with related rights (rights in performances).

(iv) Specific object of Patents, Trade Marks and Copyright

(a) *Patents*

14–54 Specific object of patents.

Note 43. **Add**: The Court of Justice has reaffirmed this definition in subsequent cases: see Case 434/55, *Allen & Hanburys v. Generics* [1988] 1 C.M.L.R. 701 and Cases C-30/90 and 235/89, *Commission v. United Kingdom and Italy* [1992] 2 C.M.L.R. 709, 759.

(b) *Trade Marks*

14–55 Specific object of trade marks. Add: In Case C-10/89, *CNL-SUCAL v. Hag GF A.G.* [1990] 1 E.C.R. 371, [1990] 3 C.M.L.R. 571, the Court of Justice described the essential function of a trade mark as being to guarantee the identity of the origin of the marked product to the consumer or ultimate user by enabling him without any possibility of confusion to distinguish that product from products which have another origin.

(c) *Copyright*

14–59 Further development by the Court of Justice.

Note 55. **Add**: The Court of Justice has since stressed that the specific object of copyright is to protect both the economic and moral rights of the copyright owner: see Case T-69/89, *Radio Telefis Eirann v. Commission* [1991] 4 C.M.L.R. 586 at 617 [71] and Joined Cases C-92 & 326/92 *Phil Collins v. Imtrat HandelsGmbH* and *Verwaltungesellschaft mbH v. EMI Electrola GmbH* [1993] 3 C.M.L.R. 773 at 796 [20].

14–60 Divisibility of copyright: reproduction right and performance right.

Notes 57, 61 and 62. *Ministère Public v. Tournier* and *Lucazeau v. SACEM* are now reported at [1991] 4 C.M.L.R. 248.

C. *Limits on the application of the principle of free movement of goods and services and exhaustion of rights to the exercise of industrial property rights*

(i) Goods originating outside the EEC

NOTE 69. **Add**: For a discussion as to the application of the exhaustion   **14–67**
of rights principle to goods originating outside the European Economic Area, see Abbey in [1992] 6 E.C.L.R. 231 and Prandl in [1993] 2
E.C.L.R. 43.

(ii) Goods originating in the territory of states associated with the
EEC

Agreements between initial countries and the EEC. The word   **14–69**
"initial" in the heading to this paragraph should read "third".

NOTE 73. **Add**: Also, Tunisia, April 25, 1977; Algeria, April 26, 1977;   **14–70**
Morocco, April 27, 1976; Jordan and Syria, January 18, 1977;
Romania, July 28, 1980 and Albania, October 26, 1992. See *Encyclope-
dia of European Community Law*, Vol. B, Part III.

The EAA. On May 2, 1992, at Opporto, the 12 Member States   **14–70A**
concluded an Agreement with the EFTA countries (Austria, Finland,
Iceland, Liechtenstein, Norway, Sweden and Switzerland) setting up
the European Economic Area (the EEA). The EEA was due to come
into force on January 1, 1993, but was delayed by Switzerland
withdrawing, following a negative result on a referendum. The
Agreement was adjusted to take account of Switzerland's withdrawal
by the Protocol signed at Brussels on March 17, 1993. The EEA came
into force on January 1, 1994. The European Communities Act 1972
was amended by the European Economic Area Act 1993 (c. 51) to allow
for the implementation of the Agreement.
    It is a principal aim of the Agreement that equal conditions of
competition should prevail throughout the EEA. The Agreement
contains Articles which precisely mirror Articles 85 and 86 of the
Treaty, and also Articles which provide for the enforcement of the
competition provisions by the EFTA Surveillance Authority which is
established by the Agreement. The Contracting Parties are required to
adjust their legislation on intellectual property to bring it into line with
the principles already established in Community law of free movement
of goods and services and the exhaustion of rights as established by the
cases of the Court of Justice. See further Bellamy and Child, *Common*

Market Law of Competition (Sweet & Maxwell, 4th ed., 1993), paragraphs 2–158 to 2–168.

(iv) Exhaustion of rights: associated problems

(c) *Common origin of rights*

14–93   Common origin of rights

NOTE 12. The Court of Justice has recognised the principle of independence of national trade mark rights, allowing for assignment of such rights for one country without at the same time such rights being assigned by its owner for other countries: Case C–9/93, *IHT Internationale Heiztechnik GmbH v. Ideal-Standard GmbH*, *The Times*, July 7 1994 and see *post*, para. 14–95.

14–94   NOTE 13. See Bellamy and Child, *Common Market Law of Competition* (Sweet & Maxwell, 4th ed., 1993), paras. 8–056 and 8–057.

NOTE 14. See Bellamy and Child, *op. cit.*, paras. 8–020 and 8–023.

NOTE 15. **Add**: See also the comments on Case C–9/93, *IHT Internationale Heiztechnik GmbH v. Ideal-Standard GmbH*, *The Times*, July 7, 1994, *infra* para. 14–95.

NOTE 16. See Bellamy and Child, *op. cit.*, paras. 8–031 to 8–041.

NOTE 17. See Bellamy and Child, *op. cit.*, paras. 8–020 and 8–033.

14–95   End of paragraph. **Add**: The Court of Justice has reaffirmed the application of the exhaustion of rights principle to trade marks, to the effect that Articles 30 and 36 prevent a trade mark owner opposing the importation of products which have been put into circulation in the exporting State by him or with his consent: Case C–9/93, *IHT Internationale Heiztechnik GmbH v. Ideal-Standard GmbH The Times*, July 7, 1994. The Court further held that the position stated in *Hag II (S.A. CNL-Sucal N.V. v. Hag GF A.G. (supra)* applied to the present case, where the unitary control of the trade mark in different countries had been lost not by sequestration (as in *Hag II*) but by voluntary assignment (*ibid*, [44]–[46]). In rejecting the Commission's argument that by assigning the mark in France the owner gave implied consent to the assignee putting into circulation heating products in France, which could not then be prevented from being imported into Germany, the Court stated (at [43]):

"The consent implicit in any assignment is not the consent required for application of the doctrine of exhaustion of rights. For that, the owner of the right in the importing State must, directly or indirectly, be able to determine the products to which the trade mark may be affixed in the exporting State and to control their quality. That power is lost if, by assignment, control over the trade mark is surrendered to a third party having no economic link with the assignor."

That wording, which does not seem to be confined by the Court's reasoning to the particular case of trade marks (see also *ibid*, [57] and [58]), would appear to be equally applicable to the case of an assignment of copyright in a work for one country by the person who owns the copyright in the work in other countries.

6. The Exercise of Industrial Property Rights and the Rules on Competition

B. *Article 85(1)*

General.   14–98

Note 29 **Add**: Performing artists often contract for their services through their own service companies, which are, of course, undertakings for the purposes of Article 85(1): see *Panayiotou v. Sony Music Entertainment (UK) Ltd.* (the "George Michael Case") [1994] E.M.L.R. 229, paragraph B1 of the judgment.

Note 30. See Bellamy and Child, *Common Market Law of Competition* (Sweet & Maxwell, 4th ed., 1993).

Agreement.   14–99

Note 35. See Bellamy and Child, *op. cit.*, Appendix 33.

Note 36. See Bellamy and Child, *op. cit.*, para. 8–067.

Assignment of rights: continuing effects.   14–101

Note 40. **Add**: In *Panayiotou v. Sony Music Entertainment (UK) Ltd.* (the "George Michael Case") [1994] E.M.L.R. 229, the Court

(Parker J.) rejected the argument that an assignment of copyright in consideration of royalties created an ongoing relationship between the assignor and assignee, such that for the purposes of Article 85 the assignment was to be treated as a licence for the full period of copyright (see paragraphs C4.17 and C4.18 of the judgment).

NOTE 43. See Bellamy and Child, *Common Market Law of Competition* (Sweet & Maxwell, 4th ed., 1993), paras. 8–067 and 8–068.

14–102   **Trade between Member States.** End of paragraph. **Add**: Where an agreement is alleged to be anti-competitive in object and/or effect and contrary to Article 85(1) it is essential first to identify the relevant market for such purposes (see the Court of Justice in *Italian Flat Glass* Cases T–68/89 and T77–78/89, [1992] 5 C.M.L.R. 302 at 342, paragraph 159). Where the agreement involves artists' services, these are to be equated, for these purposes, with raw materials, and therefore, in such a case both the markets for artists' services and for the end product, (namely, pop records) have to be separately considered (*Panayiotou v. Sony Music Entertainment (UK) Ltd.* [1994] E.M.L.R. 229, paragraph B2.8 of the judgment). In that case the evidence was insufficient to show that the agreement in question (George Michael's 1988 exclusive recording agreement with Sony) had or was capable of having an appreciable effect on trade between Member States or on competition within the Community on either of the relevant markets.

NOTE 44. **Add**: For a discussion of the *de minimis* doctrine, see Laurila in [1992] 2 E.C.L.R. 97. See also Bellamy and Child, *op. cit.*, para 2–132.

NOTE 45. See also Bellamy and Child, *op. cit.*, para. 2–132. **Add**: In *Panayiotou v. Sony Music Entertainment (UK) Ltd.* [1994] E.M.L.R. 229, in which the plaintiff, George Michael, alleged that his 1988 exclusive recording agreement with Sony was void as being prohibited by Article 85(1), the Court (Parker J.) held that the assessment of the agreement in issue, for the purposes of evaluating its effect both on trade between Member States and on competition within the Common Market, required placing the agreement in its legal, economic and commercial context (paragraph B2.4 of the judgment), which required an investigation of the nature, scale and operation of the relevant market or markets. This was a matter for evidence, which in that case was insufficient to support the plaintiff's allegation (paragraphs C2.3 and C2.27 of the judgment).

14–105   **Commission's approach to licensing agreements. Add**: For example, an exclusive licensing agreement is caught by Article 85(1) where the licensee is in a dominant position in the market which is the object of the licence: *Elopak v. Tetra Pak*: [1988] O.J. L2722/27; [1990] 4 C.M.L.R. 47.

Note 58. The reference to "Registration" should be to "Regulation".   **14–106**

Note 59. See Bellamy and Child, *Common Market Law of Competition*   **14–107**
(Sweet & Maxwell, 4th ed., 1993), para. 8–084 *et seq.*

Note 66. See Bellamy and Child, *Common Market Law of Competition*   **14–108**
(Sweet & Maxwell, 4th ed., 1993), para. 8–078.

Licensing agreements: particular clauses.   **14–109**

Note 70. **Add**: See also *Moosehead/Whitbread*: [1990] O.J. L100/32;
[1991] 4 C.M.L.R. 391 (no-challenge clause in exclusive trade mark
licence).

Note 81. *Ministere Public v. Tournier* and *Lucazeau v. SACEM* (etc.) are   **14–116**
now reported at [1991] 4 C.M.L.R. 248.

Add: The Commission has indicated that it intends to take a   **14–120**
favourable position in respect of exemption or negative clearance
sought by BBC Enterprises Limited for standard copyright licensing
agreements for facilitating retransmission of television programmes
intended for general reception in the United Kingdom to subscribers
in Eire: [1993] O.J. C105/6.

General.   **14–121**

Note 97. See Bellamy and Child, *Common Market Law of Competition*
(Sweet & Maxwell, 4th ed., 1993) chap. 9 and, in particular, para.
9–064 *et seq.*

Article 86 and industrial property rights.   **14–122**

Note 6. *Magill TV Guide/ITP, BBC and RTE* is reported at [1989] 4
C.M.L.R. 749. On appeal, the Court of Justice dismissed the appeal,
holding that RTE's conduct in using its copyright in programme
listings to secure a monopoly in the derivative market of weekly
television guides went beyond what was necessary to fulfil the essential
function of the copyright and was an abuse of a dominant position:
Case T-69/89, *Radio Telefis Eirann v. Commission* [1991] II E.C.R. 485;
[1991] 4 C.M.L.R. 586. See also Case T-70/89, *BBC v. Commission*
[1991] II E.C.R. 535; [1991] 4 C.M.L.R. 669 and Case T-76/89,

Independent Television Publications Ltd. v. Commission [1991] II E.C.R. 575; [1991] 4 C.M.L.R. 745, in which the Court of Justice dismissed in similar terms appeals brought against the Commission by the other addressees of the Commission's Decision: [1989] O.J. L78/43.

14–123   NOTE 8. *Ministère Public v. Tournier* and *Lucazeau v. SACEM* (etc.) are now reported at [1991] 4 C.M.L.R. 248.

14–129   NOTE 24. **Add**: *Ministère Public v. Tournier* and *Lucazeau v. SACEM* (etc.) are now reported at [1991] 4 C.M.L.R. 248. The Commission has subsequently rejected a number of complaints by discotheque proprietors against SACEM of abuse of its dominant position by charging excess fees for the public performance of music and referred the complaints back to the French national authorities: Press Release IP (92) 977, November 27, 1992.

D. *Direct effect of prohibition in Articles 85 and 86*

14–130   **General.**

NOTE 27. **Add**: The Commission has issued a set of guidelines with the aim of securing a greater degree of uniformity in the interpretation and application of Community competition rules by the courts of Member States: Antitrust Enforcement (National Courts) Guidelines, [1992] 4 C.M.L.R. 524 (draft proposal), discussed by Goh in [1992] 3 E.C.L.R. 114; see also Van Bael in [1994] 1 E.C.L.R. 3.

14–131   **Provisional validity: prohibited agreements.**

NOTE 34. See Bellamy and Child, *Common Market Law of Competition* (Sweet & Maxwell, 4th ed., 1993), paras. 10–008 and 11–032 *et seq.*

14–134   NOTE 40. **Add**: The Court has stated that the Commission has a duty of sincere co-operation with the national courts in the enforcement of Community competition law: Case C-234/89, *Delimitis* [1992] 5 C.M.L.R. 210. As a result the Commission issued the guidelines referred to *supra*, para. 14–130.

NOTE 41. See Bellamy and Child, *Common Market Law of Competition* (Sweet & Maxwell, 4th ed., 1993), para. 10–017.

E. *Enforcement of the rules of competition by the Commission*

NOTE 47. See Bellamy and Child, *Common Market Law of Competition* (Sweet & Maxwell, 4th ed., 1993).

Powers of the Commission. **14–136**

NOTE 48. **Add**: As to the desire for uniformity in the interpretation and application of Community competition rules by the courts of Member States, see *ante*, para. 14–130.

Notification of agreements. **14–137**

NOTE 55. See Bellamy and Child, *Common Market Law of Competition* (Sweet & Maxwell, 4th ed., 1993), chap. 11 and, in particular, para. 11-005.

NOTE 59. See Bellamy and Child, *Common Market Law of Competition* **14–138** (Sweet & Maxwell, 4th ed., 1993), para. 11–023.

Investigation by the Commission. **14–139**

NOTE 63. See Bellamy and Child, *Common Market Law of Competition* (Sweet & Maxwell, 4th ed., 1993), Appendix 35.

CHAPTER 15

ARRANGEMENTS BETWEEN COPYRIGHT OWNERS AND LICENSEES

Contents

1. Publishing Agreements

A. *Formalities of publishing arrangements*

15–2   Informal agreement: dispatch of manuscript.

NOTE 3. *Malcolm v. Chancellor, Masters and Scholars of the University of Oxford* is now reported at [1994] E.M.L.R. 17. In that case it was held on the particular facts that an oral agreement had been reached on the telephone between the author and the publisher for the publication of the book at a fair royalty. The Court of Appeal, relying on the assumption underlying *Abrahams v. Herbert Reiach Limited* [1922] 1 K.B. 477, considered that the fact that the parties had not agreed on matters such as a print run, the price of the book and the format for publication did not mean that no contract existed. The Court considered that these latter matters would either be agreed later between the parties or would be decided by the publishers. See for commentary on this case: Nyman in [1991] 3 Ent. L.R. 84.

NOTE 6. **Add**: But where there is an agreement to publish, the   **15–3** wrongful rejection by the publisher of a manuscript may amount to a repudiation of the agreement: see *Tedesco v. Bosa* (1993) 10 O.R. (3d) 799, noted at [1993] 3 Ent. L.R. E-58 (Ont. Ct. Gen. Div.).

B. *Distinction between assignment and licence*

Right to royalties.   **15–7**

NOTE 24. **Add**: In *John v. James* [1991] F.S.R. 397, Nicholls J. appears to have taken it for granted that an assignee who acquires the benefit of the original publisher's rights will take subject to any burden of exploitation. Thus, it was held that the assignee took the benefit subject to any fiduciary obligation not to make a profit for himself which was not brought into account. It is implicit in Nicholls J.'s remarks that he considered that an assignee would also take the benefit subject to the ordinary burden of accounting to the writer for his contractual entitlement to royalties.

NOTE 25. **Add**: In *Law Debenture Trust Corp. plc v. Ural Caspian Oil Corp. Ltd.* [1993] 1 W.L.R. 138 at 145E, Hoffmann J. referred to Browne-Wilkinson J.'s explanation in *Swiss Bank v. Lloyds Bank* [1979] 1 Ch. 548 at 575 of *Barker v. Stickney* as a case in which the plaintiff was trying to push the principle in *De Mattos v. Gibson* too far by securing the *positive* performance of the contract. Hoffmann J. also commented ([1992] 1 W.L.R. 138 at 147C) that it was hard to believe that *Barker v. Stickney* would have been decided differently even if the principle of pure benefit and burden had been argued. In such cases the right of the covenantee to enforce his covenant depends, curiously, on the inference being able to be drawn from the transaction that the assignee was intended to assume the burden (see *Tito v. Waddell (No. 2)* [1977] Ch. 106 at 302).

Insolvency of publisher. For a general discussion on the problems   **15–8** caused to authors by the insolvency of their publishers, and possible solutions to such problems, see Columbia-ULJ Journal of Law and the Arts, Vol. 14, No. 2., 1990, 189–232.

15–15 **Presumption against assignment.**

NOTE 49. **Add**: The principle discussed in this paragraph was applied in *Gabrielle Roy Foundation v. Alain Stanke International Editions*, (Quebec Superior Court) (May 1993; unreported), noted at [1993] 6 Ent. L.R. E-109.

C. *Common forms of publishing agreements*

15–19A **Fiduciary duty.** The question which arises in the context of all publishing agreements, particularly ones where the copyright has been disposed of on royalty terms, is whether the publisher owes a fiduciary duty to the author and, if so, what is the extent of that duty. It is clear that the scope of any duty is defined by the terms of the agreement (see *Kelly v. Cooper* [1993] A.C. 205 at 215, P.C.), but difficulties may arise where the agreement is silent on the point. In *John v. James* [1991] F.S.R. 397, a dispute concerning an artist's music publishing agreement and recording agreement, it was not disputed that a publisher has a fiduciary duty to account for royalties received. The case raised questions as to the publisher's obligation in respect of sub-publishing and sub-licensing arrangements which it had entered into. The publisher had set up overseas subsidiaries through which foreign income was channelled, the effect of which was to reduce the income eventually received by the writer.

It was argued on behalf of the publisher that there was no fiduciary obligation in respect of exploitation, so that the publisher could consult his own best interest in this regard (relying on the statement by the House of Lords in *Schroeder Music Publishing Co. v. Macaulay* [1974] 1 W.L.R. 1308 that such interest might conflict with the writer's). In the absence of an express term as to exploitation, it was argued that the contractual obligation to be implied was to use reasonable diligence to publish, promote and exploit compositions accepted under the agreement and that in doing so the publisher was obliged to act honestly and not to organise the sub-publishing in a way which no reasonable publisher would have done (relying on the decision of Plowman J. in the *Schroeder* case to the effect that such a term was to be implied (unreported; but see Russell L.J. in the Court of Appeal, [1974] 1 All E.R. 171 at 179b)).

The argument that the publisher's obligations were contractual only and not fiduciary was rejected by Nicholls J. Such a result would enable a publisher either itself or through its wholly owned subsidiaries to fix for itself or its subsidiaries once and for all the rate at which it or its subsidiary should be paid for exploitation abroad; provided that the publisher honestly considered that exploitation on these terms was for the joint benefit of author and publisher, and such terms were commonly found in the publishing trade, no objection could be sustained. Rather, he held that under the agreements in question the publisher occupied a fiduciary position in respect of any exploitation.

Thus, in addition to being under a duty to exploit the copyright only in a way which it honestly considered was for the joint benefit of the parties, the publisher was under a duty not to make for itself any profit which was not brought into account when computing the writer's royalties. This result was a natural and obvious consequence of the arrangements, having regard to the following:

(1) The agreements endured for the whole life of the copyright.

(2) The compositions in question comprised all of the compositions of the writer written during the term of the agreement.

(3) The entire copyright was assigned to the publisher.

(4) The publisher was to have complete control over the method of exploitation.

(5) The exploitation was not to be for the benefit of the publisher alone, but also for the writer's benefit, *i.e.* for their joint benefit.

(6) The agreement was therefore in the nature of a joint venture, the writer needing to place trust and confidence in the publisher over the manner in which the publisher discharged its exploitation functions.

(7) It was implicit from the royalty provisions, which provided that the publisher would account for a fixed share of royalties for sales in the home market and certain overseas markets, that the publisher's pool of profit obtained from such royalties would comprise only one pool which it shared financially with the writer. It was implicit therefore that there would not be some other pool, for example, sums earned by wholly owned overseas subsidiaries, in which the writer did not share.

The publisher was therefore in breach of its fiduciary duties in that it had established overseas subsidiaries which retained 5 per cent. of sums received there. While the establishment of such subsidiaries was not objectionable in itself, they should not be used to deduct from overseas royalties a greater sum than could otherwise have been deducted had there been no subsidiary. The publisher was therefore allowed to retain royalties at the rate which would have been charged by an independent publisher. In those territories in which subsidiaries had been established, the copyrights were in fact being administered by independent administrators, not by the subsidiaries, who were merely deducting 5 per cent. of the royalties before passing them on to the parent company. The administrators themselves were charging additional commission and at a substantially lower rate.

The following principles emerge from this judgment:

(1) An allowance should be made for the work actually done (if any) by the various subsidiaries.

(2) Although a publisher has fiduciary obligations to the writer, royalties received by a publisher are not, in general, impressed with a trust in favour of the writer (following *In Re Grant Richards, Ex Parte Warwick Deeping* [1907] 2 K.B. 33).

(3) The amount of unauthorised profit made by a fiduciary is recoverable either as money had and received or as an equitable debt (following *Reading v. The King* [1949] 2 K.B. 232).

(4) The relationship between the fiduciary and claimant is that of debtor and creditor, not that of trustee and *cestui que trust* (*Lister & Co. v. Stubbs* [1890] 45 Ch. 1).

(5) The publisher's freedom to consult its own commercial interests in balancing expense and risk against the prospects of success was not inconsistent with the existence of such fiduciary duties. The object of exploitation is to maximise the pool of royalties which can be shared. The parties therefore had a joint interest in attaining that objective. The publisher would exercise its own skill and judgment in seeking to attain that object but was not free to pursue its own commercial interests in doing so, as opposed to the joint interests of publisher and author.

(6) The publisher's ability to assign its rights under the agreement is not inconsistent with such a fiduciary duty. It was said that in the same way that an assignee from the original publisher becomes subject to the burden of exploitation when it acquires the benefit of the publisher's rights, so can an assignee become subject to the fiduciary obligation (see *ante*, para. 15–7).

15–23   **Profit-sharing creates a fiduciary relationship.**

NOTE 79. **Add**: As to the creation and consequences of such a fiduciary relationship generally, see *supra*, para. 15–19A.

D. Matters to be considered in drafting publishing agreements

15–25   **Drafting of publishing agreements.** Many publishers have reached agreement with the Society of Authors and the Writers' Guild of Great Britain to provide for minimum terms and conditions when entering into agreements with their member; for a summary of such minimum terms, see [1990] 4 Ent. L.R. E-69.

Terms as to style of publication. 15–28

NOTE 93. **Add**: See also *Malcolm v. Chancellor, Masters and Scholars of the University of Oxford* [1994] E.M.L.R. 17.

Specific performance. 15–34

NOTE 12. **Add**: See also *Malcolm v. Chancellor, Masters and Scholars of the University of Oxford* [1994] E.M.L.R. 17, where the judge at first instance would not have ordered specific performance of the contract (had he found a contract to exist); the Court of Appeal (who, by a majority, held that a contract did exist) approved the judge's decision on this point, and awarded an inquiry as to damages.

Damages for failure to publish by agreed date. 15–35

NOTE 15. **Add**: See also *Malcolm v. Chancellor, Masters and Scholars of the University of Oxford* [1994] E.M.L.R. 17, where the judge at first instance would have ordered an inquiry as to damages (had he found a contract to exist) on the basis of the author's loss of the opportunity to enhance his reputation by securing the imprimatur of the Oxford University Press on his work.

Purchaser of copyright not bound to publish. End of paragraph. 15–36
Add: Further, in *Moorhead v. Paul Brennan* [1991] 20 I.P.R. 161 (Sup. Ct. of N.S.W.) the plaintiff author granted the defendant publisher an exclusive world-wide publishing contract for her book for the legal term of copyright. The publisher had an obligation to publish the work within a stated time but had no resources to publish abroad. It was held that although no term was to be implied into the contract that the publisher should himself publish abroad, a term was to be implied that the publisher would not impede or obstruct opportunities to receive royalties from persons willing to publish under licence abroad. The publisher was in breach by refusing to grant a licence to the only likely sub-publisher abroad except on unreasonable terms.

Stock in hand. 15–37

NOTE 22. **Add**: In *Gang-Nail Australia Ltd. v. Multinail Truss Systems Pty. Ltd.* (1991) 23 I.P.R. 73 (Fed. Ct. of Australia), a patent case, the licence was for an initial term of five years (subject to immediate termination for cause) with automatic renewals for successive terms of three years, subject to either party giving 30 days prior notice of its intention not to renew at the expiration of the then current term. In addition, there was a term that the licensee would not sell any of the products or similar products for a period of three years from termination. It was held that a term permitting the licensee to sell off stock following the end of the term could not be implied in the face of such provisions.

E. *Restrictions undertaken by authors*

15–39   **The Schroeder case.** For a recent case involving an exclusive recording contract for an initial term of three years renewable for a further three years which was held to be in undue restraint of trade because of the nature, extent and duration of the obligations and restrictions imposed on the artists together with the absence of any real reciprocal obligation on the recording company, see *Sunshine Records (Pty) Ltd. v. Frohling* [1990] (4) S.A. 782 (S.A. Sup. Ct. App.) noted at [1991] 4 Ent. L.R. E-57. See also *Watson v. Prager* [1991] 1 W.L.R. 726, in which Scott J. applied the principles laid down in *Schroeder*, holding that an exclusive three-year contract between a boxer and his manager was, on its terms, unreasonable and unenforceable.

An even more recent case is *Panayiotou v. Sony Music Entertainment (UK) Ltd.*, (Parker J., [1994] E.M.L.R. 229) in which the plaintiff, the pop star George Michael, alleged that his exclusive recording agreement dated January 4, 1988, with the defendant, Sony, (the 1988 Agreement) was void or unenforceable (in so far as it remained unperformed) as being in unreasonable restraint of trade. The allegation that the agreement was void was not pursued at first instance. The plaintiff further alleged that the agreement was prohibited by Article 85(1) of the Treaty of Rome, as to which see § 14–98 *et seq.*, in the Main Work and *ante*, paras. 14–98, 14–101 and 14–102.

Although the only agreement in issue was the 1988 Agreement, the background to that agreement was important. The plaintiff and one Ridgeley, who at the time were both young, unknown and inexperienced, had entered into an exclusive recording agreement dated March 25, 1982, with Melodyshire Ltd., trading as Inner Vision (the 1982 Agreement). The 1982 Agreement was for their exclusive performances for up to four singles and 10 albums. Inner Vision had a licence agreement with Sony, and the 1982 Agreement incorporated Sony's then standard artists' conditions. The plaintiff and Ridgeley performed together as the group Wham!.

In late 1983 the plaintiff and Ridgeley were in dispute with Inner Vision, claiming that the 1982 Agreement was unenforceable as being in restraint of trade. Inner Vision commenced proceedings, which in due course were compromised by the plaintiff and Ridgeley entering into a recording agreement dated March 22, 1984, with Sony (the 1984 Agreement) on Sony's then standard form of recording contract, including an option to acquire the exclusive recording services of each artist if they ceased to perform together as a group.

The plaintiff and Ridgeley subsequently ceased to perform together as a group, and in 1986 Sony exercised its option against the plaintiff, thereby acquiring the exclusive right to his performances as a solo artist. Sony took delivery of the plaintiff's first solo album, *Faith*, which was very successful.

The plaintiff then renegotiated the terms of his recording agreement with Sony, and entered into the 1988 Agreement, whereupon the 1984 Agreement ceased to have effect. The plaintiff was obliged to deliver three albums in the initial period of the 1988 Agreement. *Faith* was treated as the first, and the plaintiff delivered *Listen Without Prejudice* as the second in July 1990. Further variations were negotiated and agreed to the 1988 Agreement. Before delivery of the third album, the present dispute arose and the plaintiff commenced proceedings in October 1992.

The material terms of the 1988 Agreement were:

– it covered the plaintiff's worldwide performing services for the production of records;

– it was for an initial contract period and five further contract periods at Sony's option;

– each contract period continued until after delivery of a minimum commitment for that period;

– the agreement was for an overall maximum term of 15 years;

– the total minimum commitment, assuming that all options were exercised, was sufficient for eight albums;

– Sony could reject product on the ground that it was not of the artistic or commercial quality of prior recorded performances;

– Sony was entitled to copyright in the master recordings throughout the world for the full period of copyright;

– the plaintiff was not entitled to perform for recording purposes any composition contained in a master recording before the later of three years after expiry of the agreement or five years from release of the master recording of the composition;

– Sony's obligation to exploit the product of the plaintiff's services was limited to the release of no less than three and no more than four single play records;

– Sony was free to assign its copyrights and, indirectly, its contractual rights under the agreement.

The terms of the 1988 Agreement were held to contain restraints of trade, as understood for the purposes of the common law doctrine, which were not dispensed from the necessity of justification, so that, apart from arguments based on public policy, the restraint of trade doctrine was applicable to the 1988 Agreement and its provisions required to be justified by reference to the test in *Nordenfelt v. Maxim Nordenfelt Guns and Ammunition Company Ltd.* [1894] A.C. 535 (see p. 143 of the judgment).

However, the judge then went on to hold that the 1988 Agreement had to be considered as a renegotiation of the 1984 Agreement, which was itself a compromise of proceedings which raised the issue of the enforceability of the 1982 Agreement. The plaintiff had expressly not sought to assert the unenforceability of the 1984 Agreement in the current proceedings. The court concluded that the 1984 Agreement had to be treated for the purposes of the current proceedings as an enforceable agreement. In these circumstances the court accepted Sony's argument that reasons of public policy relating to the compromise of disputes precluded the plaintiff from alleging that the 1988 Agreement was in restraint of trade. For that reason, the plaintiff's claim failed (see p. 150 of the judgment).

The judge then proceeded to consider whether, on the basis that the restraint of trade doctrine did apply to the 1988 Agreement, its terms were justified. His conclusion, after considering each of the relevant terms and the evidence before him, was that the restrictions contained were reasonably necessary for the protection of the legitimate interests of Sony and were commensurate with the benefits secured to the plaintiff under the agreement (see p. 201 of the judgment).

15–40   A contract is in restraint of trade if by it an artist can effectively be prevented from reaching the public over a prolonged period. It makes no difference that meanwhile the artist has a living wage. See *Silvertone Records Ltd. v. Mountfield* [1993] E.M.L.R. 152 and *Provident Financial Group plc v. Hayward* [1989] 3 All E.R. 298.

15–42   In *Silvertone Records Ltd. v. Mountfield* [1993] E.M.L.R. 152 the following terms of an exclusive recording agreement were held to be unfair:

(1) the term of the agreement which made it possible to sterilise the artist's output for seven years;

(2) a re-recording restraint of 10 years;

(3) the record company's unrestricted right to authorise the use of the artist's records to endorse products;

(4) the right to withhold advances in the event of a breach of any kind;

(5) the unequal power to terminate the agreement;

(6) the record company's right to decide on all aspects of the recording process and the denial of any artistic control to the artists;

(7) the record company's unlimited right of assignment, given the degree of co-operation required.

Note 35. **Add**: Such agreements often contain a string of option clauses enabling the publisher or record company to prolong the agreement. If the total possible length of the agreement is such as to make it unfair, the publisher or record company will not be able to save the agreement by arguing that some of the option clauses can be severed: see *Silvertone Records Ltd. v. Mountfield* [1993] E.M.L.R. 152.

Note 35. **Add**: A publisher is entitled to a reasonable period to obtain a proper reward for taking on a new writer, with all the incidental costs involved: *John v. James* [1991] F.S.R. 397 at 451. In that case, six years was considered too long, even in respect of unknown artists. In the case of the recording agreement, a five-year tie was held to be reasonable in respect of unknown artists, given the expense involved in breaking a new artist and the low success rate (*ibid.*, at 452).

Note 40. **Add**: See also *John v. James* [1991] F.S.R. 397, where it was   **14–53** held that an experienced and successful publisher assumed a dominating influence over young inexperienced writers. Even after a short acquaintance they were apprehensive of the publisher and anxious to have him as their publisher, trusting and relying on him that the terms of the contract proposed were reasonable. The publisher took charge of the arrangement and failed to explain the terms of the agreement. The agreement was liable to be set aside even though the publisher had acted in good faith and had made no conscious attempt to obtain an unfair bargain (see *ibid.*, at 451; similar considerations applied to the recording agreement: *ibid.*, at 453).

Note 38. *Zang Tumb Tuum Records Ltd. v. Johnson* is now reported at [1993] E.M.L.R. 61. See also *Silvertone Records Ltd. v. Mountfield* [1993] E.M.L.R. 152.

Note 42. **Add**: Severance of objectionable clauses is not permissible   **15–44** where it is the whole agreement which is objectionable, and the court will not strike out clauses so as to change the nature of the contract: *Silvertone Records Ltd. v. Mountfield* [1993] E.M.L.R. 152.

F. *Resale Price Maintenance and EEC rules on competition*

Price maintenance agreements: present law   **15–48**

Note 67. **Add**: Whether the Net Book Agreement remains justified in the present circumstances has been doubted; see the comments of the Monopolies and Mergers Commission in its report on the proposed merger between certain book clubs: *Book Club Associates—Leisure Circle* Cm. 277, 1988. The agreement was held by the Commission to contravene Article 85(1) in so far as it covered trade in books between the United Kingdom and Ireland, and not to be eligible for exemption under Article 85(3): *Re The Application of the Publishers Association* [1989] O.J. L22/12; [1989] 4 C.M.L.R. 825. The appeal against this decision was dismissed by the European Court of First Instance: *Re The Net Book Agreements: Publishers Association v. E.C. Commission* [1992] 5 C.M.L.R. 120; for a commentary on this decision see, Walker in [1992] 6 Ent. L.R. 215. See also *Chatto & Windus Ltd. v. Pentos plc* (Saville J., October 1990; unreported) noted at [1990] Ent. L.R. E-101/102, where an interlocutory injunction was granted to restrain the sale of net books at a discount. The Director General of Fair Trading has decided to re-examine the Net Book Agreement, by applying to the Court for leave to have its decision reconsidered on the basis of prima facie evidence of a material change in circumstances: OFT Press Release, November 23, 1993.

2. Control of Licences by the Copyright Tribunal

A. *Introduction*

15–50   **Organisations controlling the exercise of copyright.** End of paragraph: **Add**: Organisations equivalent to those in the United Kingdom exist also outside Europe, particularly in the English-speaking world: for example, in the United States, Canada and Australia.

B. *The Copyright Tribunal*

15–55   **The Copyright Tribunal.**

Note 85. The qualifications for appointment as chairman or deputy chairman of the Copyright Tribunal have now been amended to require that:

(a) he has a seven-year general qualification, within the meaning of section 71 of the Courts and Legal Services Act 1990;

(b) he is an advocate or solicitor in Scotland of at least seven years standing;

(c) he is a member of the Bar of Northern Ireland or Solicitor of the Supreme Court of Northern Ireland of at least seven years standing; or

(d) he has held judicial office.

See Courts and Legal Services Act 1990 (c. 41), section 71(2), Schedule 10, paragraph 73, *post*, para. A-148.

Procedure before Copyright Tribunal   15–58

NOTE 3. **Add**: Rule 50A of the Copyright Tribunal (Amendment) Rules 1991, which provided that notice of an intention to exercise the right conferred by the 1988 Act, section 135C (to use sound recordings in a broadcast or cable service) or by the Broadcasting Act 1990, Schedule 17, paragraph 4 (to reproduce and publish information about television programmes) could be effected by service on the Secretary of the Tribunal, has been revoked by The Copyright Tribunal (Amendment) Rules 1992.[1]

NOTE 6. Orders requiring one party to pay a proportion of the costs of the other were made by the Copyright Tribunal in *The Performing Right Society Ltd. v. British Entertainment and Dancing Association* noted at [1991] I.P.D. 14178; *British Amusement Catering Trades Association v. Phonographic Performance Ltd.* [1992] R.P.C. 149; and *The British Phonographic Industry Ltd. v. Mechanical-Copyright Protection Society Ltd.* [1993] E.M.L.R. 139.

NOTE 11. **Add**: An appeal under section 152 on a point of law was made to the High Court in *The Performing Right Society Ltd. v. British Entertainment and Dancing Association* [1993] E.M.L.R. 325.

Factors the Copyright Tribunal is required to take into account in all proceedings.   15–60
While the Copyright Tribunal must not take into account irrelevant circumstances or act irrationally (see *The British Phonographic Industry Ltd. v. Mechanical-Copyright Protection Society Ltd.* [1993] E.M.L.R. 86 at 97; and *The Performing Right Society Ltd. v. British Entertainment and Dancing Association* [1993] E.M.L.R. 325 at 330) it has a very wide discretion and what considerations are relevant will vary according to the facts of each case. Since August 1, 1989, the Copyright Tribunal has adjudicated on the following references and applications with respect to licensing schemes and licensing bodies: *The Performing Rights Society Ltd. v. British Entertainment and Dancing Association* noted at [1991] I.P.D. 14178 (licensing scheme relating to the performance of musical works in discotheques); *British Amusement Catering Trades Association v. Phonographic Performance Ltd.* [1992] R.P.C. 149 (licensing scheme relating to the performance of sound recordings on juke boxes); *Working Men's Club and Institute Union Ltd. v. The Performing Right Society Ltd.* (licensing scheme relating to the

---

[1] (S.I. 1992 No. 467).

performance of musical works in working men's clubs); *The British Phonographic Industry Ltd. v. Mechanical-Copyright Protection Society Ltd.* [1993] E.M.L.R. 86 (judgment) and 139 (Final Decision and Order) (licensing scheme relating to the reproduction of musical works on records); *The Association of Independent Radio Companies Ltd. v. Phonographic Performance Ltd. (British Broadcasting Corporation Intervening)* [1994] R.P.C. 143 (application to settle the terms relating to the right to include sound recordings in broadcasts under section 135(c)—see also *ante*, para. 10–139).

These cases show that in assessing what payment should be made for a particular type of use, matters which have been considered include the nature and extent of the use involved; the value of the licence to the licensee; the weight to be attached to previously negotiated agreements between the parties; the weight to be attached to the terms of other schemes or licences in the United Kingdom alleged to be comparable (see s.129 and note that during the passage of the Bill through Parliament an amendment requiring the Tribunal to look specifically at data from other Member States of the EEC was resisted on the grounds that there was nothing in what became section 129 to preclude it from considering comparisons from anywhere in the world if they were relevant (*Hansard*, Reports of Standing Committee E, 1988, col. 432)); the weight to be attached to the terms of other schemes or licences in operation in other parts of the world and alleged to be comparable (*ibid.*); the appropriateness of relating payment for a licence to the revenue or profits of the licensee and the relevance of profits of the licensee to the level of the licence fee to be set; the incidental benefit derived by the licensor from the public exploitation of its copyright works by the licensee; the need for simplicity and practicality in the method of charge and other conditions under a licensing scheme or licence; the importance of ensuring that the terms of a licence scheme are such as to operate fairly as between the different licensees taking licences under it (see s. 129); and even guidelines laid down for similar Tribunals in other jurisdictions.

See also *News Group Newspapers Ltd. v. Independent Television Publications Ltd.* [1993] R.P.C. 173 (application to settle the terms of payment for the use as of right of information relating to the programmes included in a television programme service under the specific jurisdiction conferred by the Broadcasting Act 1990, Schedule 17, paragraphs 5 and 6 (see § 10–127 *et seq.* in the Main Work and *ante*, para. 10–132) where the Copyright Tribunal, being similarly directed to make such order as was reasonable in all the circumstances, took account of the particular considerations relevant to such specific jurisdiction). See also *Singapore Broadcasting Corporation v. The Performing Right Society Ltd.* [1991] F.S.R. 573 (a decision of the Copyright Tribunal of Singapore in relation to a licensing scheme in respect of the broadcasting of musical works in Singapore) where such tribunal was under the Singapore Copyright Act 1987 also directed to set such charges and conditions as it considered reasonable in the circumstances in relation to the applicant; *APRA's reference*, (1992) 25 I.P.R. 257 (a reference to the Australian Copyright Tribunal under s.154 of the Australian Copyright Act 1968 in relation to a licensing scheme relating to the public performance of recorded musical and literary works to accompany dancing); *MCM Networking Pty. Ltd.'s application* (1992) 25 I.P.R. 597 (applications to the Australian Copyright Tribunal under s.157(3)(b) of the Australian Copyright Act 1968 in relation to licences from record companies to reproduce their sound recordings for radio programmes produced and syndicated by the applicant).

NOTE 14. For the reference to s.25(6), **substitute**: s.25(5).

Particular Factors: **15–64**

(iii) As to the statements in this section relating to section 134 of the 1988 Act, (dealing with particular factors relevant to licences in respect of works included in re-transmissions), the purposes of section 134 were explained by the Minister in the following terms:

> "[The Clause] . . . is intended, first, to ensure that if copyright owners license inclusion of their material in a foreign broadcast or cable programme service on terms which cover retransmission of that broadcast or service in the United Kingdom, any tribunal award that they may obtain in the U.K. in respect of royalties due from U.K. cable operators or broadcasters for retransmitting the foreign broadcast are abated to the extent that this retransmission was allowed for in the terms of the initial licence. The intention is to avert double payment to rights owners in respect of what is essentially a single transmission (or chain of transmissions) reaching the same audience. This policy is unchanged from the 1956 Act, where it is implemented by Section 28.
>
> The second objective is to ensure that, when broadcasts or cable programme services are retransmitted within the intended reception area of the broadcast or service (and this applied particularly to "in-area" retransmissions abroad of U.K. satellite broadcasts), and rights owners obtain payment from the cable operator for the retransmission under local law, tribunal decisions on licences in respect of the original broadcast shall take this into account.
>
> The third objective is to ensure that when broadcasts or cable programme services are retransmitted beyond or outside the intended reception area of the broadcast or service, the broadcaster or provider of the cable programme service which is retransmitted cannot be made to pay royalties in respect of the retransmission. It is up to the rights owners concerned to use any rights available in the country or area of the retransmission to reach an agreement with those responsible for it. If such rights do not exist it should not fall to the broadcaster to reimburse copyright owners for that fact." (*Hansard*, H.L. Vol. 491, cols. 524, 525.)

NOTES 32 and 33. **Add**: The Cable and Broadcasting Act 1984 and subs. 134(4) of the 1988 Act were repealed by s.203(3) of and Sched. 21 to the Broadcasting Act 1990 (c. 42) to the extent provided by the Broadcasting Act 1990 (Commencement No. 1 and Transitional Provisions) Order 1990[2] (See § B-25 in the Main Work).

C. *Control by the Copyright Tribunal of licensing schemes and licensing bodies*

15–67   **Licensing Body.** Third line. **Delete**: the word "of". **Substitute**: "or".

(i) References and applications with respect to licensing schemes

15–68   **References and applications involving licensing schemes.** End of last sentence. **Add**: the words "or claiming to have been unreasonably excluded from it."

15–69   **Jurisdiction over licensing schemes.** The distinction is explained by the fact that works referred to in section 117(a) come within the Berne Convention so that the United Kingdom would be in breach of its obligations if the Tribunal had power to adjudicate a licensing scheme operated by an individual author or film maker (as opposed to a licensing body) in regard to his own productions. (See *Hansard*, H.L. Vol. 491, col. 489).

15–72   **Order confirming or varying the scheme.** Such a final Order under sections 118 or 119 which is for an indefinite period (under subss. 118(4) or 119(4)) can only be reviewed under section 120 (see §15–75 in the Main Work) on a further reference under that section. See *The Working Men's Club and Institute Union Ltd. v. The Performing Right Society Ltd.* [1992] R.P.C. 227, in which nine months after the Tribunal's Order varying the tariff in question an unsuccessful attempt was made, by agreement, to substitute a revised version of the tariff; there being no application to vary the substance of the Order but only its style and presentation and no attempt to invoke section 120.

NOTE 55. **Add**: There is no presumption that a referred scheme should either be confirmed or varied: *The British Phonographic Industry*

---

[2] (S.I. 1990 No. 2347).

Ltd. v. Mechanical Copyright Protection Society Ltd. [1993] E.M.L.R. 86 at 99.

Date from which Order takes effect. End of paragraph. **Add**: The   **15–74**
Tribunal has no power to award interest: see *The Association of Independent Radio Companies Ltd. v. Phonographic Performance Ltd., (British Broadcasting Corporation intervening)* [1994] R.P.C. 143 in which it was held that the provisions of subsection 135D(2) (which are similar to the provisions of subs. 123(3) in that they provide for backdating and the making of any necessary payments by way of adjustment but are silent as to interest) impliedly excluded a power to award interest.

Application for individual licence where scheme exists.   **15–76**

NOTE 73. **Add**: On the passage of the legislation through Parliament and in speaking to an amendment to substitute the word "excluded" for the word "excepted" in what is now subsection 121(3) the Minister stated:

> "The point to bear in mind is that the word 'cases' does not refer to 'works' which may be outside a licensing scheme but types of licensing situations which may not be covered by it. For example, where a scheme covers the use of the licensing body's repertoire in village halls but not in church halls. Substituting the word 'excluded' for the word 'excepted' should help to bring out the fact that we are dealing with cases where a particular class of potential licensee has been prevented from having access to the works in question under the terms of the scheme. This exclusion is unreasonable.
>
> Thus it might be held that the circumstances in which church halls required a licence to use music or records were sufficiently similar to those in which village halls might do so for it to be unreasonable not to treat them in the same way." (*Hansard*, H.L. Vol. 493, col. 1375.)

Further reference. Last sentence. **Delete**, and **substitute**: On an   **15–78**
application for review the Tribunal is empowered to confirm or vary its previous Order as the Tribunal may determine to be reasonable having regard to the terms applicable in accordance with the licensing scheme, or, as the case may be, reasonable in the circumstances (see subs. 122(3)).

NOTE 79. **Add**: The Tribunal's jurisdiction is not limited to cases where there has been a material change in circumstances. An amendment to the Bill which would have had this effect was resisted, it being said on behalf of the Government that there may be other cases in which an early return to the Tribunal might be appropriate, such as where it turned out that it had been misled inadvertently, or deliberately, about the facts. (*Hansard*, H.L. Vol. 491, col. 496.).

(ii) References and applications with respect to licensing bodies.

15–81   **Reference of an expiring licence.**

NOTE 99.   The reference should be to C.D.P.A. 1988, s.126(4) and not s.126(3).

NOTE 1.   The reference should be to C.D.P.A. 1988, s.126(5) and not s.126(4).

15–83   **Date from which Order takes effect.** End of paragraph. **Add**: The provisions for backdating and the making of further payments by way of adjustment impliedly exclude any power on the part of the Tribunal to award interest. See *The Association of Independent Radio Companies Ltd. v. Phonographic Performance Ltd., (British Broadcasting Corporation intervening)* [1994] R.P.C. 143 at 190–191 (dealing with similar provisions contained in subs. 135D(2)).

15–85   **Further reference.** Last sentence. **Delete**, and **substitute**: On an application for review the Tribunal is directed to confirm or vary its previous Order as the Tribunal may determine to be reasonable in the circumstances.

NOTE 14.   **Delete** the reference to § 15–81.

(iii) Implied indemnity in certain licensing schemes and licenses

15–87   **Conditions for availability of indemnity.**

NOTE 21.   The reference should be to C.D.P.A. 1988, s. 136(5)(b) and not s.136(5)(a).

15–90   **Settling royalty in respect of rental right.**

NOTE 40.   The reference to § 15–65, n. 38 should be a reference to § 15–65, n. 36.

Granting consent on behalf of a performer to the making of a   **15–93**
recording from a previous recording of a performance. Consent on
behalf of performers to the making of a recording from a previous
recording of their performance was given by the Tribunal under
section 190 in *Ex Parte Sianel Cymru* [1993] E.M.L.R. 251 where the
applicant (the Welsh Fourth Television Channel Authority) wished to
make an animated version of *Under Milk Wood* and re-record the
original 1954 BBC radio production onto the soundtrack. (The
copyright owner of that recording had no objection to the proposed
re-recording.) The cast of the radio production had included
members of a school. The applicant had managed to ascertain the
identity of some of the school children but not all. The applicant
applied to the Tribunal under subsection 190(1)(a) for consent on
behalf of those performers whose identity or whereabouts could not be
ascertained and also for consent on behalf of the personal representatives of one deceased performer whose identity was known but the
identity of whose personal representatives could not be ascertained.
The Order of the Tribunal giving consent included an express liberty
for the performers and the personal representatives of the deceased
performer to apply to the Tribunal for payment.

E. *Procedure before the Copyright Tribunal*

Provisions governing procedure.   **15–94**

NOTE 73. **Add**: The Copyright Tribunal (Amendment) Rules 1991
have been amended by The Copyright Tribunal (Amendment) Rules
1992[3] which revoke rule 50A of the 1991 Rules (see *post*, para. 15–95).

Secretary and service of documents.   **15–95**

NOTE 82. The address of the office of the Secretary of the Copyright
Tribunal is now: Hazlitt House, 45 Southampton Buildings, London
WC2A 1AR.

NOTE 85. **Add**: By rule 50A of The Copyright Tribunal Amendment
Rules 1991 (see para. B–267 in the Main Work) notice of an intention
to exercise the right conferred by C.D.P.A. 1988, s.135C (to use sound
recordings in a broadcast or cable service) or by the Broadcasting Act
1990, Sched.17, paragraph 4 (to reproduce and publish information
about television programmes) could be effected by service on the

---

[3] (S.I. 1992 No. 467).

Secretary of the Tribunal. Rule 50A has, however, now been revoked by the Copyright Tribunal (Amendment) Rules 1992.

15–102 **Directions. Add**: The Tribunal will usually require each party to submit, before the hearing, a full draft of the tariff for which it contends, or alternatively the detailed amendments sought to an existing tariff. See *British Amusement Catering Trades Association v. Phonographic Performance Ltd.* [1992] R.P.C. 149 at 159.

15–105 **Costs.**

NOTES 67 to 69. Orders providing that one party should pay a proportion of the costs of the other were made by the Tribunal in *The Performing Right Society Ltd. v. British Entertainment and Dancing Association* noted at [1991] I.P.D. 14178 (PRS ordered to pay 60 per cent. of BEDA's costs down to the date of a "Calderbank" letter and 100 per cent. thereafter); *British Amusement Catering Trades Association v. Phonographic Performance Ltd.* [1992] R.P.C. 149; and *The British Phonographic Industry Ltd. v. Mechanical-Copyright Protection Society Ltd.* [1993] E.M.L.R. 139 (where regard was again had to a "Calderbank" letter).

15–106 **Appeal.**

NOTE 70. **Add**: See as to appeal on a point of law, *The Performing Right Society Ltd. v. British Entertainment and Dancing Association* [1993] E.M.L.R. 325.

F. *Other controls over copyright licensing*

15–109 **Certification of licensing schemes.**

NOTE 4. **Add**: The Copyright (Certification of Licensing Scheme for Educational Recording of Broadcasts and Cable Programmes) (Educational Recording Agency Limited) Order 1990[4] (referred to in note 4 as The Copyright (Certification of Licensing Scheme for Educational Recording of Broadcasts)) has been amended by The Copyright (Certification of Licensing Scheme for Educational Recording of Broadcasts and Cable Programmes) (Educational Recording Agency Limited) (Amendment) Order 1992,[5] and further amended by The

---

[4] (S.I. 1990 No. 879).
[5] (S.I. 1992 No. 211).

Copyright (Certification of Licensing Scheme for Educational Record-ing of Broadcasts and Cable Programmes) (Educational Recording Agency Limited) (Amendment) Order 1993,[6] and yet further amended by The Copyright (Certification of Licensing Scheme for Educational Recording of Broadcasts, and Cable Programmes) (Edu-cational Recording Agency Limited) (Amendment) Order 1994.[7] The Copyright (Certification of Licensing Scheme for Educational Record-ing of Broadcasts) (Open University Educational Enterprises Limited) Order 1990[8] has been revoked and replaced by The Copyright (Certification of Licensing Scheme for Educational Recording of Broadcasts) (Open University Educational Enterprises Limited) Order 1993.[9]

---

[6] (S.I. 1993 No. 193).
[7] (S.I. 1994 No. 247).
[8] (S.I. 1990 No. 2008).
[9] (S.I. 1993 No. 2755).

CHAPTER 16

INCOME TAX, CAPITAL GAINS TAX, INHERITANCE TAX AND STAMP DUTY

2. Income Tax

16–4 **B. Sums received by an author**

NOTE 4. **Add**: See also *Vaughan (HM Inspector of Taxes) v. Archie Parnell & Alfred Zeitlin Ltd* [1940] 23 T.C. 505.

16–6 **C. Basis of taxation.** The preceding year basis of taxation is to be abolished with effect from the 1996–97 tax year and replaced by a simplified system for assessing personal tax. The relevant legislation is contained in the Finance Act 1994.

16–9 **F. Top-slicing: Other circumstances.** A relief similar to that discussed in the main text is available for painters, sculptors and other artists. It applies to sums obtained from the sale of a painting, sculpture or other work of art or by way of commission or fee for the creation of a work of art: I.C.T.A. 1988, s. 538.

16–10 **G. Post-cessation receipts. Add**: Where an author who has permanently discontinued his profession transfers the right to receive sums to which the post-cessation receipts provisions apply, the author is taxable on the amount or value of the consideration received for the transfer or (if the transfer is not at arm's length) on the value of the right transferred: I.C.T.A. 1988, s. 106.

H. The foreign element

16–11

Note 33. **Add**: The reason why copyright royalties paid to a non-resident author are not subject to deduction of tax under I.C.T.A. 1988, s.536 appears to be that the source of the royalties is not the copyright itself but the author's profession: see, *e.g. Billam v. Griffith* [1941] 23 T.C. 757 and the cases cited in n.29, *ante*. On the same principle it can be argued that I.C.T.A. 1988, s.536 does not apply to copyright royalties paid to a non-resident author who has discontinued his profession because the receipts fall outside the scope of U.K. income tax (see n.36, *post*) and I.C.T.A. 1988, s.536 is concerned with the machinery for collecting tax and does not itself impose a charge to tax: see *Rye & Eyre v. IRC* [1935] A.C. 274. It is understood that the Revenue regard I.C.T.A. 1988, s.536 as applying in these circumstances.

I. Residence. Delete: (b). The rule that a person (other than an individual working full-time abroad) who has available accommodation in the United Kingdom will be resident for any year in which he visits the United Kingdom has been by abolished by statute: I.C.T.A. 1988, section 336(3) as amended by Finance Act 1993, section 208. 16–14

Note 43. There is now a revised version of IR20 dated December 1993.

L. Anti-avoidance provisions. For the position where a retired author transfers the right to post-cessation receipts to a third party, see *ante*, para. 16–10. In such a case the third party will not be taxable. 16–18

M. The payer

16–21

Note 69. Add: In *Rye & Eyre v. CIR* [1935] A.C. 274 a firm of solicitors who paid an advance of royalties to a non-resident on behalf of a client were held to be persons "by or through whom" the payment was made.

N. Films, tapes or discs. The rule that expenditure on the production or acquisition of a film, tape or disc is treated as revenue rather than capital expenditure has been extended to films, tapes and discs certified by the Secretary of State under Schedule 1 to the Films Act 1985 as "qualifying" for the purpose of the Capital Allowances Act 1990, (c. 1) section 68. However in the case of a qualifying film, tape or disc, an election can be made to treat the expenditure as capital expenditure eligible for capital allowances: *ibid.*, section 68(9) as amended by the Finance (No. 2) Act 1992, section 69. The conditions for certification as a qualifying film, tape or disc are the same as for the 16–23 old Eady levy (the box-office levy redistributed to makers of so-called British qualifying films).

In the case of qualifying films the Finance (No. 2) Act 1992 has introduced a new method of writing off production costs for tax purposes. Broadly, expenditure of a revenue nature incurred on the production or acquisition of a qualifying film by a person who carries on a trade which includes the exploitation of films may be written off for tax purposes as it is incurred—subject to an annual ceiling of one third of total cost of producing or acquiring the film: Finance (No. 2) Act 1992, section 42. This method is an alternative to the existing methods of writing off production costs, namely the income matching method and the cost recovery method. A finance lessor is regarded as a person whose trade includes the exploitation of films: see *Barclays Mercantile Industrial Finance Ltd v. Melluish* [1990] S.T.C. 314.

The Finance (No 2) Act 1992 also gives tax relief for expenditure incurred with a view to enabling a decision to be taken as to whether or not to make a film (s.41). To qualify for relief the person incurring the expenditure must carry on a trade which includes the exploitation of films and the film, if completed, must be a qualifying film. (If the film is not completed it must be reasonably likely that, if it were completed, it would be a qualifying film.) The total amount of expenditure qualifying for relief under section 41 may not exceed 20 per cent. of the budgeted total expenditure on the film. Neither Finance (No 2) Act 1992, section 41 nor section 42 applies where an election has been made to treat production costs as capital.

On January 11, 1993, the Revenue published a Statement of Practice dealing with the tax treatment of expenditure on films and certain similar assets (SP 1/93).

NOTES 75 and 76. **Delete**: F.A. 1982, s.72. **Substitute**: Capital Allowances Act 1990, s.68.

3. Capital Gains Tax

16–24   **A. Introduction**

NOTE 77. **Delete**: C.G.T.A. 1979, s. 18(1). **Substitute**: Taxation of Chargeable Gains Act ("T.C.G.A.") 1992 (c. 12), s.9(1).

NOTE 78. **Delete**: C.G.T.A. 1979, s. 19(2). **Substitute**: T.C.G.A. 1992, s.21(2).

NOTE 79. **Delete**: C.G.T.A. 1979, ss.19(1) and 144(c). **Substitute**: T.C.G.A. 1992, ss.21(1) and 237(c) respectively.

Note 80. **Delete**: [C.G.T.A. 1979] s.2(1). **Substitute**: T.C.G.A. 1992, s.2(1).

Note 81. **Delete**: C.G.T.A. 1979 ss.14(1)(2). **Substitute**: T.C.G.A. 1992 ss.12(1)(2).

Note 82. **Delete**: [C.G.T.A. 1979] s.18(4)(hb). **Substitute**: T.C.G.A. 1992 s.275(j).

Note 83. **Delete**: [C.G.T.A. 1979] s.31(1). **Substitute**: T.C.G.A. 1992, s.37(1). **16–25**

B. Sales   16–26

Note 86. **Delete**: C.G.T.A. 1979, s.31(3). **Substitute**: T.C.G.A. 1992, s.37(3).

Note 87. **Delete**: [C.G.T.A. 1979] s.29A(1)(b). **Substitute**: T.C.G.A. 1992, s.17(1)(b).

Note 88. **Delete**: [C.G.T.A. 1979] ss.29a(1)(A) and 62. **Substitute**: T.C.G.A. 1992, ss.17(1)(a) and 18 respectively.

C. Gifts   16–27

Note 89. **Delete**: [C.G.T.A. 1979] ss.126 and 147A. **Substitute**: T.C.G.A. 1992 ss.165 and 260 respectively.

Note 90. **Delete**: Finance Act 1981, s.79. **Substitute**: T.C.G.A. 1992, s.168.

D. Acquisition cost   16–29

Note 95. **Delete**: Finance Act 1988, s.87. **Substitute**: T.C.G.A. 1992, s.35. **Add**: Expenditure incurred by an owner of copyright is allowable for capital gains tax purposes if wholly and exclusively incurred for the purpose of enhancing the value of copyright being expenditure reflected in the state or nature of the copyright at the time of disposal, as is any expenditure wholly and exclusively incurred in establishing, preserving or defending title to, or to a right over copyright (*ibid.* s.38(1)(b).

Notes 96 and 98. **Delete**: C.G.T.A. 1979, s.32(1)(a). **Substitute**: T.C.G.A. 1992, s.38(1)(a).

NOTE 99. **Delete**: [C.G.T.A. 1979] s.33(1). **Substitute**: T.C.G.A. 1992, s.39(1).

NOTE 1. **Delete**: [C.G.T.A. 1979] ss.49(1)(a) and 153. **Substitute**: T.C.G.A. 1992, ss.62(1)(a) and 274 respectively.

NOTE 2. **Delete**: [C.G.T.A. 1979] s.38. **Substitute**: T.C.G.A. 1992, s.46.

16–30 **E. Capital sums derived from assets**

NOTE 3. **Delete**: [C.G.T.A. 1979] s.20. **Substitute**: T.C.G.A. 1992, s.22.

NOTES 10 and 11. **Delete**: C.G.T.A. 1979, s.19(5). **Substitute**: T.C.G.A. 1992, s.51(2).

5. Stamp Duty

16–36 **B. Agreements and licenses**

NOTE 35. **Add**: In *Leather Cloth Co. v. American Leather Cloth Co.* [1865] 11 H.L.C. 523 (a case concerning trademarks) it was assumed though not decided that the word "property" was aptly used with reference to copyright. See also C.D.P.A. 1988, s.90 which states in terms that copyright is transmissible as personal or moveable property.

NOTE 36. **Add**: In practice *ad valorem* duty is not charged on a revocable licence.

16–38 **D. Foreign copyright.** The statement in the Main Work that an assignment of foreign copyright executed outside the United Kingdom is subject to *ad valorem* duty if it relates to anything done or to be done in the United Kingdom should be read subject to the qualification that an instrument executed abroad does not require stamping until it is brought into the United Kingdom: see Stamp Act 1891, section 15 which provides that in the case of an instrument executed abroad, it may be stamped without penalty until the expiration of thirty days after it is first received in the United Kingdom.

CHAPTER 17

INTERNATIONAL COPYRIGHT AND THE PROTECTION OF WORKS ORIGINATING OUTSIDE THE UNITED KINGDOM

193

1. International Copyright

B. *The Berne Convention and its Revisions*

(i) History

17–9 **Paris Act.** Last sentence. **Delete**, and **substitute**: What follows, therefore, in para. 17–10 *et seq. post* is concerned mainly with an examination of the substantive provisions of the Paris Act, which are basically the same as those of the Stockholm Convention.

17–9A **Possible New Protocol to the Berne Convention.** In the course of the 1980s, a consensus developed that there was a need for new international regulations concerning the application of the Berne Convention. There were two main reasons for this. The first was the need to update the level of protection afforded by the Convention to deal with the technical developments which had emerged since the adoption of the Paris Act 1971. Secondly, the shortcomings of the Convention with respect to standards of protection and the lack of any mechanism therein for enforcing the obligations of member States or for the settlement of disputes between them were brought into focus in the context of the GATT Multilateral Trade Negotiations (the Uruguay Round). The deliberations of the GATT Working Group on Trade-Related Aspects of Intellectual Property (TRIPS) resulted, in December 1993, in agreement on the text of a new international instrument which, following the successful outcome of the Uruguay Round, was formally adopted at Marrakesh in April 1994. The TRIPS Agreement contains enforceable, copyright treaty obligations, which include the requirements of the Berne Convention and impose additional standards of protection exceeding those of the Berne Convention (see *ante*, para. 1–61 *et seq.*).

A new substantive revision of the Berne Convention has been ruled out at this stage. A formal revision would require unanimity among the member States. Such unanimity is perceived to be politically impossible in view of the widely differing standards and objects of protection in the 105 member States. Thus any new instrument such as the suggested possible Protocol to the Convention would be an independent multilateral treaty and is likely to take the form of a special agreement under Article 20 of the Convention.

Work on a possible Protocol to the Convention began in 1991. According to the relevant WIPO programme items for 1990–91 and

1992–93,[1] the purpose of the Protocol would be to clarify the existing or establish new international standards where, under the present text of the Berne Convention, doubts may exist as to the extent to which the Convention applies. It was considered that such clarification was required because governments interpret their obligations under the Convention differently. Discrepancies had arisen in respect of certain subject-matters of protection (*e.g.* computer programs, sound recordings, computer generated works); certain rights (*e.g.* rental right, public lending right, right of distribution of copies of any kind of works, right of display); the applicability of the conventional minima (no formalities, term of protection, etc.); and the obligation of granting national treatment (without reciprocity) to foreigners. The desirability of covering the rights of producers of sound recordings in the protocol was also to be examined.

Following two sessions of the Committee of Experts responsible for the preparation of the possible Protocol, held in 1991 and 1992 respectively,[2] its terms of reference were modified,[3] due mainly to the fact that agreement could not be reached on the inclusion of the protection of producers of sound recordings in the possible Protocol. According to the modified terms of reference, the issues agreed to be discussed in connection with the possible Protocol were the following: (1) computer programs, (2) data bases, (3) rental right, (4) non-voluntary licences for the sound recording of musical works, (5) non-voluntary licences for primary broadcasting and satellite communication, (6) distribution right, including importation right, (7) duration of the protection of photographic works, (8) communication to the public by satellite broadcasting, (9) enforcement of rights, and (10) national treatment. A separate Committee of Experts on a Possible Instrument for the Protection of the Rights of Performers and Producers of Phonograms (sound recordings) was established to discuss all questions concerning the effective international protection of the rights of performers and producers of sound recordings.

A third session of the Committee of Experts on the possible Protocol to the Berne Convention and a first session of the Committee of Experts on the possible Instrument were held in 1993. Further sessions will be convened in 1994.

The nature of the relationship, if any, between the possible Protocol and the possible Instrument, when and if adopted, and between the

---

[1] Programmes adopted by the Assembly and Conference of Representatives of the Berne Union, October 1989 and October 1991 (see WIPO documents AB/XX/2, item PRG. 02(2) and AB/XX/20, paragraphs 152 and 199, for the 1990–1991 biennium, and document AB/XXII/22, paragraph 197, for the 1992–93 biennium).

[2] For the reports of these sessions, see *Copyright* 1992: First Session at 30 and Second Session at 66 and 93.

[3] The terms of reference of the Committee of experts were modified by the Assembly and the Conference of Representatives of the Berne Union in September 1992 (see WIPO document B/A/XIII/2, paragraph 22).

latter and the Rome Convention for the Protection of Performers, Producers of Phonograms and Broadcasting Organisations 1961, and the Convention for the Protection of Producers of Phonograms Against Unauthorised Duplication of Their Phonograms 1971, are matters yet to be considered.

(ii) Substantive provisions of Paris Act

17–47   **Convention not to limit wider protection. Add**: The various Directives adopted by the European Union on the subject of copyright and the proposed possible Protocol to the Berne Convention (see *ante*, para. 1–51 *et seq.* and para. 17–9A) are examples of such special agreements.

(vi) Entry into force of Stockholm Convention

17–66   **State of ratifications or accessions.** First two paragraphs. **Delete**, and **substitute**: The only countries which adhered to the substantive provisions of the Stockholm Convention and the Protocol are Chad, the former East Germany (German Democratic Republic), Mauritania, Pakistan, Romania and Senegal. Notwithstanding that this was more than five countries, the substantive provisions never entered into force in view of the declarations made by Pakistan and Mauritania.[71]

On the other hand, the administrative provisions of the Stockholm Convention did come into force, the following countries having adhered thereto: Australia, Austria, Belgium, Canada, Chad, Denmark, Fiji, Finland, the former East Germany (German Democratic Republic), the former West Germany (Federal Republic of Germany), Ireland, Israel, Liechstenstein, Morocco, Pakistan, Romania, Senegal, Spain, Sweden, Switzerland and the United Kingdom. The United Kingdom ratified the Paris Act with effect from January 2, 1990.

(vii) Entry into force of Paris Act

17–67   **Ratification or accession.** The reference in the Main Work to the Director General in this section is to the Director General of the World Intellectual Property Organisation (WIPO).

Penultimate paragraph on page 574. **Delete**, and **substitute**: The following countries have now ratified or acceded to the whole of the Paris Act, including the Appendix: Albania, Australia, Austria, Barbados, Benin, Bolivia, Brazil, Bulgaria, Burkina Faso, Cameroon, Central African Republic, Chile, China, Colombia, Congo, Costa Rica, Côte d'Ivoire (Ivory Coast), Croatia, Cyprus, Czech Republic, Denmark, Ecuador, Egypt, El Salvador, Finland, France, Gabon, Gambia,

Germany, Ghana, Greece, Guinea, Guinea-Bissau, Holy See, Honduras, Hungary, India, Italy, Jamaica, Japan, Kenya, Lesotho, Liberia, Libya, Luxembourg, Malawi, Malaysia, Mali, Mauritania, Mauritius, Mexico, Monaco, Morocco, Namibia, Netherlands (for the Kingdom in Europe only), Niger, Nigeria, Paraguay, Peru, Portugal, Rwanda, Saint Lucia, Senegal, Slovak Republic, Slovenia, Spain, Suriname, Sweden, Switzerland, Togo, Trinidad and Tobago, Tunisia, United Kingdom, United States of America, Uruguay, Venezuela, Zaire and Zambia.

Second line on page 575. **Add**: Articles 22 to 38 of the Paris Act apply also to the Netherlands Antilles and Aruba.

First two full paragraphs on page 575. **Delete**, and **substitute**: Bahamas, Bulgaria, Egypt, India, Lesotho, Liberia, Libya, Malta, Mauritius, Romania, Saint Lucia, South Africa, Thailand, Tunisia and Venezuela have made declarations that they do not consider themselves bound by Article 33(1). Cameroon, Congo, India, Mexico and Uruguay have made notifications under Article 38(1) of the Paris Act. However, Cameroon, Congo, India, Mexico and Uruguay later ratified the Paris Act. Japan and Thailand have made declarations under Article 30(2)(a) of the Paris Act as to retaining the benefit of previous reservations. Portugal has made a declaration under Article 14 *bis* (2)(c). India has made a declaration under Article 14 *bis* (3).

The United Kingdom, Germany and Norway made declarations under Article VI(1)(ii) of the Appendix. The United Kingdom and Germany later ratified Articles 1 to 21 of the Paris Act. China, Egypt, Guinea, India, Lesotho, Liberia, Malaysia, Mauritius, Mexico, Tunisia and Suriname have availed themselves of the faculties in Articles II and III of the Appendix. The relevant declarations are effective until October 10, 1994. Cyprus has made a declaration under Article V(1)(a)(ii) of the Appendix.

(viii) Present Members of the Copyright Union

Countries forming the Copyright Union. As of January 31, 1994,[73] **17–68** the following countries form the Copyright Union: Albania, Argentina, Australia, Austria, Bahamas, Barbados, Belgium, Benin, Bolivia, Bosnia and Herzegovina, Brazil, Bulgaria, Burkina Faso, Cameroon, Canada, Central African Republic, Chad, Chile, China, Colombia, Congo, Costa Rica, Côte d'Ivoire (Ivory Coast), Croatia, Cyprus, Czech Republic, Denmark, Ecuador, Egypt, El Salvador, Fiji, Finland, France (including overseas territories and the territorial entity of Mayotte), Gabon, Gambia, Germany, Ghana, Greece, Guinea, Guinea-Bissau, Holy See, Honduras, Hungary, Iceland, India, Ireland, Israel, Italy, Jamaica, Japan, Kenya, Lebanon, Lesotho, Liberia, Libya, Liechtenstein, Luxembourg, Madagascar, Malawi, Malaysia, Mali, Malta, Mauritania, Mauritius, Mexico, Monaco, Morocco, Namibia, Netherlands, New Zealand, Niger, Nigeria, Norway, Pakistan, Paraguay, Peru,

Philippines, Poland, Portugal, Romania, Rwanda, Saint Lucia, Senegal, Slovak Republic, Slovenia, South Africa, Spain, Sri Lanka, Suriname, Sweden, Switzerland, Thailand, The former Yugoslav Republic of Macedonia, Togo, Trinidad and Tobago, Tunisia, Turkey, United Kingdom,[73a] United States of America (including the territories of American Samoa, Guam, the Northern Mariana Islands, Puerto Rico and the U.S. Virgin Islands), Uruguay, Venezuela, Yugoslavia, Zaire, Zambia and Zimbabwe.

NOTE 73. Second sentence. **Delete**, and **substitute**: The Treaty of Union of August 31, 1990 (BGBL, 1990, Part II, 885 *et seq.*) between the former Federal Republic of Germany and the former German Democratic Republic, which effected the reunification of Germany, provided that, in the case of copyright, the law of the former Federal Republic of Germany (*i.e.* the Copyright Law of September 9, 1965, as amended), was to apply in the territory of the former German Democratic Republic with effect from October 3, 1990.

Add: NOTE 73a. The United Kingdom has not to date extended the application of the Paris Act of the Berne Convention to any of its dependent territories.

C. *The Universal Copyright Convention and its Revision*

(iii) Entry into force of 1971 Convention

17–74   **Ratification or accession.** Third paragraph. **Delete**, and **substitute**: The following countries have now ratified or acceded to the 1971 Convention: Algeria, Australia, Austria, Bahamas, Bangladesh, Barbados, Bolivia, Bosnia and Herzegovina, Brazil, Bulgaria, Cameroon, China, Colombia, Costa Rica, Croatia, Cyprus, Czech Republic, Denmark, Dominican Republic, Ecuador, El Salvador, Finland, France, Germany, Guinea, Holy See, Hungary, India, Italy, Japan, Kenya, Korea (Republic of), Mexico, Monaco, Morocco, Netherlands, Niger, Norway, Panama, Peru, Poland, Portugal, Rwanda, Saint Vincent and the Grenadines, Senegal, Slovakia, Slovenia, Spain, Sri Lanka, Sweden, Switzerland, Trinidad and Tobago, Tunisia, United Kingdom, United States of America, Uruguay and Yugoslavia.

(iv) Parties to the Universal Copyright Convention

17–75   **Convention Countries.**[81] **Delete** section, and **substitute**: As of January 31, 1994, the following countries are parties to the Universal Copyright Convention: Algeria, Andorra, Argentina, Australia, Austria, Bahamas, Bangladesh, Barbados, Belgium, Belize, Bolivia, Bosnia and Herzegovina, Brazil, Bulgaria, Cambodia, Cameroon, Canada, Chile, China, Colombia, Costa Rica, Croatia, Cuba, Cyprus, Czech Republic, Denmark, Dominican Republic, Ecuador, El Salvador, Fiji, Finland, France, Germany,[81] Ghana, Greece, Guatemala, Guinea, Haiti, Holy See, Hungary, Iceland, India, Ireland, Israel, Italy, Japan, Kazakhstan, Kenya, Korea (Republic of), Laos, Lebanon, Liberia, Liechtenstein, Luxembourg, Malawi, Malta, Mauritius, Mexico, Monaco, Morocco, Netherlands, New Zealand, Nicaragua, Niger, Nigeria, Norway, Pakistan, Panama, Paraguay, Peru, Philippines, Poland, Portugal, Russian Federation, Rwanda, Saint Vincent and the Grenadines, Senegal, Slovakia, Slovenia, Spain, Sri Lanka, Sweden, Switzerland, Tajikistan, Trinidad and Tobago, Tunisia, United Kingdom[82] (extended to British Virgin Islands, Gibraltar, Hong Kong, Isle of Man and Saint Helena), United States of America (extended to American Samoa, Guam, the Northern Mariana Islands, Puerto Rico, the U.S. Virgin Islands), Ukraine, Uruguay, Venezuela, Yugoslavia and Zambia.

2. Protection of Works of Foreign Origin: Application of the Act

A. *General*

(iii) Position under the 1956 Act

(ii) Taiwan. The Copyright (Taiwan) Order 1990, made under **17–104** section 32 of the Copyright Act 1956 as extended to Hong Kong, provides that Parts I and II of the 1988 Act shall apply to Taiwan.

(iv) Position under the 1988 Act

Note that the heading should be numbered (iv) not D. **17–107**

Order in Council under section 159 of the 1988 Act **17–112**

(a) Generally. The Order in Council referred to,[4] has been revoked and replaced by the Copyright (Application to Other Countries)

---

[4] (S.I. 1989 No. 1293).

Order 1993,[5] *post*, para. D-23, which has itself been amended by the Copyright (Application to Other Countries) (Amendment) Order 1994.[6] References in the text to the 1989 Order should now be read as references to the 1993 Order.

A further order, the Copyright (Application to the Isle of Man) Order 1992[7] (see *post*, para. D–50) has been made under Section 159, applying sections 153 to 156 of the 1988 Act (qualification provisions) to the Isle of Man. For the position previously in relation to the Isle of Man, see § 17–147 in the Main Work.

(g) Revocation of previous Orders. As noted above, the 1989 Order, together with subsequent amending Orders, has now been replaced by the 1993 Order.

3. Protection of Works Originating in the British Commonwealth: Extension of the Act

C. *Position under the 1956 Act*

17–131   Extension Orders under the 1956 Act.

NOTE 14: The Copyright (Isle of Man) Order 1986 has now been revoked by the Copyright (Isle of Man) (Revocation) Order 1992[8] (see *post*, para. D–50) with effect from July 1, 1992. For the position now, see *ante*, para. 17–112.

D. *Position under the 1988 Act*

17–147   (iii) Isle of Man. Legislation (the Copyright Act 1991) having now been enacted in the Isle of Man equivalent to Part I of the 1988 Act, the Order in Council previously in force extending the provisions of the 1956 Act to the Isle of Man (see § 17–131 in the Main Work) has been revoked by the Copyright (Isle of Man) (Revocation) Order 1992[9] (see

---

[5] (S.I. 1993 No. 942).
[6] (S.I. 1994 No. 263).
[7] (S.I. 1992 No. 1313).
[8] (S.I. 1992 No. 1306).
[9] (S.I. 1992 No. 1306).

post, para. D–50). Instead, an order has been made pursuant to section 159. (see *ante*, para. 17–112).

(iv) Hong Kong and other dependent territories. For an article on the position in Hong Kong, see Rowlinson in [1993] EIPR 126. As to proposals for reform of Hong Kong's copyright law, see [1994] EIPR D–144.   **17–148**

COPYRIGHT LAW OF THE UNITED STATES OF AMERICA AND GENERAL TABLE OF COPYRIGHT LAWS OF COMMONWEALTH AND FOREIGN COUNTRIES

1. Copyright Law of the United States of America

A. *General*

18–2   **Copyright Act of 1909. Add**: Courts continue on occasion to construe provisions of the 1909 Act: see, *e.g. Frank Music Corp. v. Metro-Goldwyn-Mayer Inc.*, 886 F.2d 1545 (9th Cir. 1989), *cert. denied*, 494 U.S. 1017 (1990). With increasing frequency, courts fail to discriminate between decisions handed down under the old law, and apply doctrines developed under the 1909 Act to cases arising under the 1976 Act: see, *e.g. Kleier Advertising, Inc. v. Premier Pontiac, Inc.*, 921 F.2d 1036 (10th Cir. 1990) (following *Frank Music*); *Computer Associates Intern., Inc. v. Altai, Inc.*, 982 F.2d 693 (2d Cir. 1992) (reaching same conclusion as *Frank Music* and *Kleier Advertising*).

B. *Law before 1978*

(i) Domestic works

Term of copyright   **18–8**

NOTE 17. **Add**: U.S. courts continue to reach results different from
that in *Campbell Connelly*. See *Corcovado Music Corp. v. Hollis Music, Inc.*,
981 F.2d 679 (2d Cir. 1993). It is worth considering the decision in
Corcovado, given how parochially American is the opinion by the
Second Circuit, normally one of the U.S.'s outstanding copyright
tribunals. The case construed a grant from Brazilian composer
Antonio Carlos Jobim to a Brazilian music publisher. The contract,
written in Portuguese and specifying that it was to be construed under
Brazilian law, granted copyright ownership worldwide, without
specifying terms for domestic copyright law outside of Brazil.

Because U.S. courts had developed a doctrine under the 1909 Act
that grants of copyright are to be limited to the initial 28-year term,
absent explicit invocation of the word "renewal" or its equivalent (*e.g.*
"perpetual"), and because the Brazilian contract at issue in *Corcovado*
not surprisingly failed to contain such a provision geared solely to the
U.S., the argument arose that the grant was to be limited to 28 years in
the U.S. notwithstanding the apparent intent of the parties in Brazil
and the fact that elsewhere in the world the grant would endure for the
full term of copyright. Ignoring international copyright concerns, the
Second Circuit accepted that argument. For a criticism of its ruling, see
2 *Nimmer on Copyright* § 9.06[A][2]. On renewal copyright generally, see
post, para. 18–42.

Fair use.   **18–20**

NOTE 45. **Add**: Ferment continues in the U.S. over *Williams & Wilkins*.
In *Basic Books, Inc. v. Kinko's Graphics Corp.*, 758 F. Supp. 1522
(S.D.N.Y. 1991), the Court held infringing the ongoing activities of
"copy shops," which generate such materials as customized readings
for college courses selectively drawn from a variety of copyrighted
sources. In *American Geophysical Union v. Texaco Inc.*, 802 F. Supp. 1
(S.D.N.Y. 1992), the Court ruled that Texaco's library facility committed infringement by reproducing single copies of scholarly articles for
the benefit of the oil company's research scientists. The upshot of these
decisions has been a flood of applications to the Copyright Clearance
Center, a collective rights society that licenses reproduction rights in a
vast body of literature. See generally, 3 *Nimmer on Copyright*
§13.05[E][4][d].

(ii) Works of foreign origin

18–26 **Proclamations. Add**: People's Republic of China, Hungary, Indonesia, Singapore, Thailand and Ukraine.

C. *Law after 1978*

(i) Copyright Act of 1976

18–39 **Relevance of prior law.**

NOTE 74. **Add**: See the discussion at *ante*, para. 18–2.

18–41 **Subjects of copyright.** After the word "originality" in last sentence of first paragraph. **Add**: The parameters for "originality" are quite elastic, but not infinitely so. In *Feist Publications, Inc. v. Rural Telephone Service Co.*, 499 U.S. 340 (1991), the Supreme Court ruled that the "white pages" of a telephone book, simply listing all the names and phone numbers of a community in alphabetical order, are so banal as to be bereft of originality. That ruling rejects previous doctrine, primarily in the Seventh Circuit Court of Appeals, which had accorded copyright protection to an industrious collection representing no more than the "sweat of the brow".

After first paragraph. **Add**: At the end of 1990, Congress added an additional category of protection: architectural works. See the Architectural Works Copyright Protection Act, Public Law 101–650, 104 Stat. 5089, December 1, 1990 (see *post*, para. E–24). This provision was added belatedly to bring the United States more fully into compliance with the Berne Convention. See H.R. Rep. No. 101–735, 101st Cong., 2d Sess. 4 (1990). See generally, 1 *Nimmer on Copyright* § 2.20.

The question arises, given that Congress claimed upon accession to the Berne Convention in 1989 that United States law complied with all treaty requirements, why was further refinement required in 1990? The answer is that in 1989, Congress adopted an approach to Berne adherence that it labelled "minimalist". See H.R. Rep. No. 100–609, 100th Cong., 2d Sess. 20 (1988). Congress contemplated that there would be future fine-tuning, beyond the few matters absolutely required in 1989 to eliminate matters of wholesale incompatibility. This architectural amendment is one such example. Limited moral rights protection, also added in 1990, is another (see *post*, para. 18–50). In addition, prospective elimination of the renewal formality in 1992 fits into this process (see *post*, para. 18–42), as does elimination of the juke-box compulsory licence in 1993 (see *post*, para. 18–45).

At end. **Add**: In the interim since publication of the Main Work, one additional published decision has issued.

Another *sui generis* form of copyright protection — or more accurately, a compromise among competing interests — is set forth in the Audio Home Recording Act of 1992, Public Law 102–563, 102 Stat. 4248 (October 28, 1992). Like the predecessor semiconductor chip provision, this law is tacked onto the end of the Copyright Act and creates self-contained entitlements and exemptions in sections 1001 to 1010 (1992). See *post*, para. E–100 and generally, 2 *Nimmer on Copyright* chapter 8B. Produced as a compromise among hardware manufacturers, songwriters, and record companies, the law creates an exemption from copyright infringement for home audio taping undertaken for noncommercial purposes: See S. Rep. No. 102–294, 102d Cong., 2d Sess. 40 (1992). Concomitantly, the law places an obligation on all who manufacture and distribute digital audio recorders and blank tape to remit a small percentage of the purchase price of each to a general fund, which in turn is divided among composers, performers, record companies, and other interested copyright parties. See generally, 2 *Nimmer on Copyright* § 8B.02[B].

Term of copyright and termination of grants. After second para-   **18–42**
graph. **Add**: The discussion in the Main Work remains completely applicable to works for which renewals were due through the end of 1991. Works coming due for renewal in 1992 and thereafter, *i.e.* works that first obtained statutory copyright on or after January 1, 1964, are now governed by a new scheme, instituted by the Copyright Renewal Act of 1992, Public Law 102–307, 106 Stat. 264 (June 26, 1992). That amendment introduced the innovation that renewal registration following expiration of the initial 28-year term would no longer be a condition for continued copyright subsistence: see section 304(a)(3)(B) (1992), *post*, para. E–34. It is, however, prospective only: see Public Law 102–307, 106 Stat. 264, § 102(g)(1). Accordingly, it does not upset, for example, the ruling that Vittorio De Sica's classic movie, *The Bicycle Thief*, entered the United States public domain because of the hyper-technical defect that the party who timely filed a renewal certificate in 1976 was a mere licensee, and hence not the appropriate party to file: *International Film Exchange, Ltd. v. Corinth Films, Inc.*, 621 F. Supp. 631 (S.D.N.Y. 1985). The upshot is that for works published before 1964, failure to renew after 28 years dooms continued copyright subsistence. For works first published in 1964 and thereafter, that danger is inapplicable. See generally, 2 *Nimmer on Copyright* § 9.05[B][2].

Note that U.S. duration provisions are approaching Berne Convention norms, although areas of discontinuity remain. See Nimmer, *Nation, Duration, Violation, Harmonization: An International Copyright Proposal to the United States*, 55 L. & Contemp. Probs. 211 (1992).

On the subject of renewal, it is also necessary at least to mention the Supreme Court's landmark decision in *Stewart v. Abend*, 495 O.S. 207

(1990), rejecting the approach previously followed in *Rohauer v. Killiam Shows, Inc.*, 551 F.2d 484 (2d Cir. 1977), *cert. denied*, 431 U.S. 949 (1977). In brief, *Abend* rules that when a motion picture is made under licence from the copyright owner of a literary work, and ownership of the renewal term of the book subsequently reverts to a party other than the original licensor, continued exploitation of the motion picture may infringe the copyright in the book. See Nimmer, "Refracting the Window's Light: *Stewart v. Abend* in Myth and in Fact", (1991) 39 J. Copr. Soc'y, 18.

18–43 **Ownership and assignment.** First sentence. **Add**: There is continuing uncertainty as to who qualifies as "joint authors", when two or more authors collaborate in creating a work. Recent cases have recognized as a joint author only one who contributes material that, standing alone, would qualify as copyrightable. That approach excludes, for example, one who masterminds the idea of a work but leaves its composition to another. See *Andrien v. Southern Ocean County Chamber of Commerce*, 927 F.2d 132 (3d Cir. 1991); *Ashton-Tate Corp. v. Ross*, 916 F.2d 516 (9th Cir. 1990). Many commentators quarrel with that interpretation: see Spyke, "The Joint Work Dilemma: The Copyrightable Contribution Requirement and Co-Ownership Principles", (1993) 40 J. Copr. Soc'y, 463; 1 *Nimmer on Copyright* § 6.07.

18–44 **Notice and registration.** End of paragraph. **Add**: Courts continue to place undue emphasis on the formality of registration, notwithstanding the supposed loosening of formalities upon accession to the Berne Convention. For example, one appellate panel ruled that the scope of injunction, and all other relief, must be limited to works for which registration has been secured. That ruling would require a copyright owner who continually produces new works that are routinely infringed to file a new suit every day. The entire Court of Appeals subsequently vacated the ruling on procedural grounds. See *Cable News Network, Inc. v. Video Monitoring Services of America, Inc.*, 940 F.2d 1471 (11th Cir. 1991), *vac'd en banc*, 949 F.2d 378 (11th Cir. 1991). A bill is, however, passing through Congress to greatly limit the effect of registration.

18–45 **Rights.** Before note 30 in the text. **Add**: The juke-box compulsory licence was instituted in 1978. Previously, a complete exemption from both infringement liability and licensing obligations shielded juke-box operators. In 1989, as part of the process of adhering to the Berne Convention, Congress supplemented the juke-box compulsory licence with a scheme encouraging voluntary licensing among the affected parties. That alternative worked so well that in 1993, Congress eliminated the compulsory licence altogether. At present, therefore, music owners and juke-box operators either reach an agreement as to the appropriate licence fee or else jointly agree to arbitrate their disputes. See 2 *Nimmer on Copyright* § 8.17[C].

After note 24 in the text. **Add**: One contentious area within the fair use doctrine that has been extensively litigated is reverse engineering. Whereas a novel can be read and its unprotected ideas extracted without copying its protected expression, software's unprotected aspects cannot be understood without detailed examination, which may necessarily entail copying its expression. See *MAI Systems Corp. v. Peak Computer, Inc.*, 991 F.2d 511 (9th Cir. 1993), *cert dismissed*, 114 S. Ct. 671 (1994) (simply loading computer program into computer's central processing unit infringes, in the absence of any applicable defense). On that basis, several appellate courts have now clarified an issue on which the lower courts previously disagreed, ruling that when no alternative means of access is available to an entity lawfully in possession of its rival's copyrightable software, it may engage in reverse engineering in order to examine the unprotected elements contained therein. See *Atari Games Corp. v. Nintendo of America Inc.*, 975 F.2d 832 (Fed. Cir. 1992); *Sega Enterprises Ltd. v. Accolade, Inc.*, 977 F.2d 1510 (9th Cir. 1992). Of course, that shield is not broad enough to protect subsequent development of a commercial product that itself appropriates the program's protectable expression.

Even greater disputes have riven the courts on the proper standard to apply in determining infringement of two similar but non-identical computer programs. The Third Circuit several years ago promulgated a wide test, whereby almost any similarity could be deemed infringing: see *Whelan Associates v. Jaslow Dental Laboratory*, 797 F.2d 1222 (3d Cir. 1986), *cert. denied*, 479 U.S. 1031 (1987). In recent years, that standard has been disapproved by courts applying a more discriminating standard. In brief, this "successive filtering method" examines the plaintiff's work, filtering out from protection ideas, expressions constrained by function, and other unprotectible elements. The remaining "golden kernel" is then compared against the allegedly infringing work to determine whether liability should follow. See *Computer Associates Intern., Inc. v. Altai, Inc.*, 982 F.2d 693 (2d Cir. 1992); *Sega Enterprises Ltd. v. Accolade, Inc.*, 977 F.2d 1510 (9th Cir. 1992), citing 3 *Nimmer on Copyright* § 13.03[F].

End of paragraph. **Add**: In terms of remedy, injunctions are often, even routinely, granted in copyright infringement actions. Nonetheless, particularly in the context of news footage, the potential for injunction may infringe the media's First Amendment rights. The matter has been litigated in the context of the famous footage of the beating of Rodney King. The Supreme Court has approved in dictum withholding the remedy of injunction in appropriate cases. *Campbell v. Acuff–Rose*, 114 S. Ct. 1164, 1171 (1994).

(ii) The Berne Convention Implementation Act of 1988

18–49   **International provisions. Add**: International trade issues have recently dominated consideration of copyright protection. United States accession to the North American Free Trade Agreement has prompted Congress to amend the law in order to rescue from the public domain certain films of Mexican and Canadian origin that lost protection since January 1, 1978, because of defective copyright notice. See section 104A (1993), *post*, para. E–8. It remains to be seen what action Congress will take in response to the inclusion of Trade Related Aspects of Intellectual Property (TRIPS), a protocol to the General Agreement on Tariffs and Trade (GATT).

18–50   **Retroactivity and moral rights. Add**: The process predicted in the Main Work has come to pass to a limited extent. In 1990, Congress legislated moral rights protection, supplanting previous state law on the subject. See the Visual Artists Rights Act 1990, Public Law 101–650, 104 Stat. 5089 (December 1, 1990), section 106A (1990), *post*, para E–10. The 1990 protection is, however, extremely limited. It applies only to paintings, drawings, sculpture, and other works of fine art, and thus accords no moral rights to the vast bulk of literature, motion pictures, and technical works that copyright law protects. See section 101 (definition of "work of visual art") (1990), *post*, para. E–4. In addition, even when applicable, it protects the integrity and attribution rights of such works only insofar as they are exploited in museums, galleries, and the like. See generally, 2 *Nimmer on Copyright* § 8B.06. Thus, reproducing in a book an artist's painting, which has been grossly cropped or which lacks the artist's name, does not violate the highly circumscribed right granted by this 1990 amendment. See section 106A(c)(3), *post*, para. E–10.

2. General Table of Copyright Laws of Commonwealth and Foreign Countries[65]

The following completely replaces the Table of Copyright Laws included in the Main Work.

Country	Date of Principal Law	Period of Protection	Convention or other protection for United Kingdom works		
			Berne[66] [67]	UNESCO[68]	Other
Afghanistan	1950	20 years from registration			None–local registration
Albania	1947	Life of the author and limited rights thereafter	Paris A		None
Algeria	1973	25 years from beginning of calendar year following author's death.		Paris*	

---

[65] In many cases the principal law has been amended or additional laws have been passed. Some countries have different terms for different works and different terms for foreign works. In some cases the period of protection of moral rights is unlimited in duration. This Table is intended, therefore, as a general guide only and more detailed information can be obtained from *Copyright Laws and Treaties of the World*, published by UNESCO.

[66] For the purposes of this Table, countries which have ratified or acceded to the entire Paris revision of the Berne Convention, including the Appendix, are indicated thus "Paris A." Those countries which have declared that their ratification or accession does not apply to Arts. 1–21 and such Appendix are indicated thus "Paris B". Those countries which have given notification under Art. 38(1) are indicated thus "Paris C": unless they have later ratified the Paris Act. Those countries which have made a declaration under Art. 6(1)(ii) of such Appendix are indicated thus "Paris D". Countries which have availed themselves of the faculties in Arts. II and III of such Appendix are indicated thus "Paris E". Those countries which have made a declaration under Art. 5 of such Appendix are indicated thus "Paris F". Those countries which have made a declaration under Art. 14 *bis*(3) are indicated thus "Paris G". Those countries which have made a declaration under Art. 14 *bis*(2)(*c*) are indicated thus "Paris H".

[67] The substantive provisions of the Stockholm revision did not and cannot now come into force. However, previous conventions remain in force in relations with countries of the Union which do not ratify or accede to the Paris Act. In the case of countries which have ratified or acceded to the whole of the Paris Act and the Appendix, no reference is made to Stockholm or earlier revisions. Those countries which declared that their ratification or accession did not apply to Arts. 1–21 of the Stockholm revision and the Protocol Regarding Developing Countries, or ratified or acceded to the entire Stockholm revision, the substantive provisions of which have not come into force, are indicated thus "Stockholm B". Countries, other than those indicated as Paris A or Paris B, which have given notification under Art. 38(2) of the Stockholm revision are indicated thus "Stockholm C". For the position as to declarations as to the Protocol and other declarations see §§ 17–65 in the Main Work, and paras. 17–66 and 17–67 *ante*.

[68] Countries which have ratified or acceded to the 1971 Convention are indicated thus "Paris"; others thus "Geneva." Countries which have availed themselves of the exceptions in favour of developing countries are indicated thus "Paris*"[68].

Country	Date of Principal Law	Period of Protection	Convention or other protection for United Kingdom works		
			Berne	UNESCO	Other
Andorra	1971	50 years from death of author		Geneva	
Angola	1990	50 years from end of calendar year in which author died			
Antigua and Barbuda	1911	50 years from death of author			
Argentina	1933	50 years from death of author	Paris B Brussels	Geneva	
Australia	1968	50 years from end of calendar year in which author died	Paris A	Paris	
Austria	1936	70 years from death of author	Paris A	Paris	
Bahamas	1956	50 years from end of calendar year in which author died	Paris B Brussels	Paris	
Bahrein	1993	50 years from death of author			
Bangladesh	1962	50 years from January 1, following the death of the author			
Barbados	1982	Life of the author and 50 calendar years immediately following year of his death	Paris A	Paris	
Belgium	1886	50 years from death of author	Stockholm B, C Brussels	Geneva	
Belize	1956	50 years from death of author		Geneva	
Benin	1984	50 calendar years after end of year of author's death	Paris A		
Bolivia	1992	50 calendar years from end of year of author's death	Paris A	Paris	
Bosnia and Herzogovina	Uncertain	Uncertain	Paris A, F	Paris	
Botswana	1965	50 years from death of author			
Brazil	1973	60 years from January 1 of year following death of author	Paris A	Paris	
Bulgaria	1993	50 years from January 1, following death of author	Paris A	Paris	
Burkina Faso	1983	50 years from end of calendar year in which author died	Paris A		
Burundi	1978	50 years from end of calendar year in which author died			Uncertain
Cambodia	1934	Uncertain		Geneva	
Cameroon	1990	50 years from end of calendar year in which author died	Paris A	Paris	
Canada	1989	50 years from death of author	Stockholm B Rome	Geneva	

Country	Date of Principal Law	Period of Protection	Convention or other protection for United Kingdom works		
			Berne	UNESCO	Other
Central African Republic (Empire)	1985	50 calendar years after end of year of author's death	Paris A		
Chad	Uncertain	Uncertain	Stockholm B Brussels		
Chile	1992	50 years from death of author	Paris A	Geneva	Local registration required
China	1990	50 years from December 31 of year of author's death	Paris A, E	Paris*	
Colombia	1982	80 years from death of author	Paris A	Paris	
Congo	1982	50 years from December 31 of year of author's death	Paris A		
Costa Rica	1982	50 years from December 31 of year of author's death	Paris A	Paris	
Cote d'Ivoire	1978	99 years from end of calendar year in which author died	Paris A		
Croatia	Uncertain	Uncertain	Paris A, F	Paris	
Cuba	1977	25 years from January 1 of year following author's death		Geneva	
Cyprus	1976	50 years from December 31 of the year of the author's death	Paris A, F	Paris	
Czech Republic	1965	50 years from December 31 of the year of the author's death	Paris A	Paris	
Denmark	1961	50 years from end of calendar year in which author died	Paris A	Paris	
Dominican Republic	1986	50 years from death of author		Paris	
Ecuador	1976	50 years from death of author	Paris A	Paris	
Egypt	1954	50 years from death of author	Paris A, E		
El Salvador	1993	50 years from death of author	Paris A	Paris	
Estonia	1992	50 years from January 1, of year following death of author			
Ethiopia	1960	The life of the author and limited rights thereafter			None
Fiji	1956	50 years from death of author	Stockholm B Brussels	Geneva	
Finland	1961	50 years from end of year in which author died	Paris A	Paris	

Country	Date of Principal Law	Period of Protection	Convention or other protection for United Kingdom works		
			Berne	UNESCO	Other
France	1992	50 (70 for musical works) years from December 31 of the year of the author's death	Paris A	Paris	
Gabon	1987	50 years from end of calendar year in which author died	Paris A		
Gambia	Uncertain	Uncertain	Paris A		
Germany[69]	1965	70 years from end of calendar year in which author died	Paris A, D	Paris	
Ghana	1985	50 years from death of author	Paris A	Geneva	
Greece	1993	70 years from end of the year of the author's death	Paris A	Geneva	
Grenada	1956	50 years from death of author			
Guatemala	1954	50 years from death of author		Geneva	
Guinea	1980	80 calendar years from end of year of author's death and thereafter domain public payant	Paris A, E	Paris	
Guinea-Bissau	Uncertain	Uncertain	Paris A		
Guyana	1956	50 years from death of author			
Haiti	1968	Life of author and 25 years		Geneva	
Holy See	1960	The end of the 50th calendar year from the death of author	Paris A	Paris	
Honduras	1919	10, 15 or 20 years from issue of patent according to importance of work	Paris A		
Hungary	1969	50 years from death of author	Paris A	Paris	
Iceland	1972	50 years after year of author's death	Rome, Paris B, F	Geneva	
India	1957	60 years from January 1, following death of author	Paris A, E, G	Paris	
Indonesia	1982	50 years from death of author			Protection under local law
Iran	1970	30 years from death of author			Uncertain
Iraq	1971	25 years from death of author or 50 years from publication whichever is longer			Protection under local law

---

[69] See *ante*, para. 17–68, n.73, as to the copyright position as a result of the unification of West and East Germany on October 3, 1990.

Country	Date of Principal Law	Period of Protection	Convention or other protection for United Kingdom works		
			Berne	UNESCO	Other
Ireland	1963	50 years from December 31, of year of the author's death	Stockholm B Brussels	Geneva	
Israel	1911	70 years from January 1, following the death of the author or publication	Stockholm B Brussels	Geneva	
Italy	1941	The end of the 50th calendar year from the death of the author	Paris A	Paris	
Jamaica	1911	50 years from death of author	Paris A, E,		
Japan	1970	50 years from end of year of author's death	Paris A	Paris	
Jordan	1992	30 years from death of author			None
Kazakhstan	Uncertain	Uncertain		Geneva	
Kenya	1966	50 years from end of year in which author dies	Paris A	Paris	
Korea (Republic of)	1986	50 years from January 1, following death of author		Paris*	
Laos	Uncertain	Uncertain		Geneva	
Latvia	1993	50 years from end of year in which author died			
Lebanon	1924	50 years from death of author	Rome	Geneva	
Lesotho	1989	50 years after end of year in which author dies	Paris A, E		
Liberia	1972	25 years after death of author	Paris A, E	Geneva	
Libya	1968	25 years from death of author or 50 years from first publication whichever is the longer	Paris A		
Liechtenstein	1928	50 years from death of author	Stockholm B Brussels	Geneva	
Luxembourg	1972	50 years from January 1, following the death of author	Paris A	Geneva	
Former Yugoslav Republic of Macedonia	Uncertain	Uncertain	Paris A, F		
Madagascar	1957	50 years from end of year in which author died	Brussels		
Malawi	1989	End of 50th calendar year after year in which author died	Paris A	Geneva	
Malaysia	1987	50 years from death of author	Paris A, E		Protection under local law
Mali	1977	50 years from death of author	Paris A		

Country	Date of Principal Law	Period of Protection	Convention or other protection for United Kingdom works		
			Berne	UNESCO	Other
Malta	1967	25 years after end of year in which author dies	Paris B, Rome	Geneva	
Mauritania	Uncertain	Uncertain	Paris A		
Mauritius	1986	50 years after end of year in which author dies	Paris A, E	Geneva	
Mexico	1956	50 years from death of author	Paris A, E	Paris*	
Monaco	1948	50 years from death of author	Paris A	Paris	
Morocco	1970	50 years from the end of the year in which author died	Paris A	Paris	
Myanmar (Burma)	1911	50 years from death of author			
Namibia	Uncertain	Uncertain	Paris A		
Nepal	1966	50 years from death of author			None–local registration
Netherlands	1912	50 years from January 1, of year after death of author	Paris A	Paris	
New Zealand	1962	50 years from the end of calendar year in which author died	Rome	Geneva	
Nicaragua	1904	Life of the author with limited rights thereafter		Geneva	
Niger	1993	50 years after end of year in which author died	Paris A	Paris	
Nigeria	1988	70 years from the end of the calendar year in which author died	Paris A	Geneva	
Norway	1961	50 years from end of the year of death of author	Paris B, D Brussels	Paris	
Pakistan	1962	50 years from January 1, following the death of the author	Stockholm B Rome	Geneva	
Panama	1916	80 years from death of author		Paris	
Paraguay	1985	50 years from death of author	Paris A	Geneva	
Peru	1961	50 years from January 1, following the death of the author	Paris A	Paris	
Philippines	1972	50 years from January 1, following the death of author	Paris B Brussels	Geneva	
Poland	1952	25 years from death of author	Paris B Rome	Paris	
Portugal	1985	50 years from death of author	Paris A, H	Paris	

Country	Date of Principal Law	Period of Protection	Convention or other protection for United Kingdom works		
			Berne	UNESCO	Other
Romania	1956	The life of the author and limited rights thereafter	Stockholm B Rome		
Russian Federation	1993	50 years from January 1, of year following death of author		Geneva	
Rwanda	1983	50 years from the death of the author	Paris A	Paris	
Saint Lucia	1956	50 years from death of author	Paris A		
Saint Vincent and Grenadines	1989	50 years from end of year in which author died			
San Marino	1991	50 years from end of year in which author died			
Saudi Arabia	1989	50 years from death of author			Protection under local law
Senegal	1973	50 calendar years from end of year of author's death	Paris A	Paris	
Seychelles	1982	25 years from end of year in which author died			
Sierra Leone	1965	50 years from the end of the calendar year in which the author died			Protection under local law
Singapore	1987	50 years after expiration of calendar year in which author died			Uncertain
Slovakia	1965[70]	50 years from December 31 of year of author's death	Paris A	Paris	
Slovenia	Uncertain	Uncertain	Paris A, F	Paris	
South Africa	1978	50 years from the end of the year in which the author died	Paris B, Brussels		
Spain	1987	60 years from January 1, following the death of the author	Paris A	Paris	
Sri Lanka	1979	50 years from end of calendar year in which author died	Paris B Rome	Paris	
Sudan	1974	25 years from death of author			Uncertain
Suriname	Uncertain	Uncertain	Paris A		
Sweden	1960	End of 50th year after year in which author died	Paris A	Paris	

---

[70] The Copyright Law No. 35 of 1965 of the former Czechoslovakia.

Country	Date of Principal Law	Period of Protection	Convention or other protection for United Kingdom works		
			Berne	UNESCO	Other
Switzerland	1992	70 years from death of author	Paris A	Paris	
Syria	1924	50 years from death of author			None—local deposit
Taiwan	1993	50 years from death of author			
Tajikstan	Uncertain	Uncertain		Geneva	
Tanzania	1966	25 years from death of author		Geneva	Protection under local law
Thailand	1978	50 years from end of calendar year in which author died	Paris B Berlin		
Togo	1991	50 years from end of year in which author died			
Tonga	1985	50 years from end of calendar year in which author died			Protection under local law
Trinidad and Tobago	1985	50 years following calendar year of author's death	Paris A	Paris	
Tunisia	1966	50 years from death of author	Paris A, E	Paris*	
Turkey	1951	50 years from death of author	Brussels Paris F		
Uganda	1964	50 years from end of year in which author dies			Protection under local law
Ukraine	Uncertain	Uncertain		Geneva	
United States of America	1976	For works created on or after January 1, 1978, life of the author and 50 years expiring at end of calendar year	Paris A	Paris	
United Arab Emirates	1992	25 years from death of author			
Uruguay	1937	40 years from death of author	Paris A	Paris	
Venezuela	1993	60 years from January 1, of year after death of author	Paris A	Geneva	
Yugoslavia	1978	50 years from January 1 following death of author	Paris A, F,	Paris	
Zaire	1986	50 calendar years following year of author's death	Paris A		
Zambia	1965	25 years from death of author	Paris A	Geneva	
Zimbabwe	1967	50 years from death of author	Paris B Rome		

CHAPTER 19

CRIMINAL PROCEEDINGS

1. Criminal Proceedings for Infringement of Copyright

B. *Section 107 of the 1988 Act*

(i) Prohibited acts

19–2   For a table listing the Parliamentary debates on these and other provisions of the 1988 Act, see *post*, Appendix 1.

Add: The High Court will not restrain a properly commenced private prosecution for infringement of copyright pending the outcome of civil proceedings which have been brought by the defendant against the prosecutor after the commencement of that prosecution and in which substantially the same issue arise: see *Thames & Hudson Limited v. Design and Artists Copyright Society Limited* (Evans-Lombe J., *The Times*, August 10, 1994). Section 107 is not confined to offences committed by "pirates". Accordingly, it is not vexatious to bring private criminal proceedings against a defendant who has previously been in a commercial relationship with the prosecutor: *ibid.*

(ii) The meaning of "infringing copy"

19–5   Under section 107(1)(d)(i) the prosecution must prove that the making of the copy constituted an infringement of the copyright: see *Holmes v. DPP* [1990] C.O.D. 150, D.C.

NOTE 15.   Note the amendment made to section 27(3) of the 1988 Act by paragraph 6 of the Copyright (Computer Programs) Regulations 1992 (see *post*, para. A–30).

(iii) Proof

19–7   As to what evidence is required to prove the subsistence of copyright and that a particular copy is an infringing copy, see *Musa v. Le Maitre* [1987] F.S.R. 272 (a case on the 1956 Act).

(iv) Penalties

Add: When sentencing, the court will regard the counterfeiting of **19–8**
video films as a serious offence. To make and distribute pirate copies
of films is in effect to steal from the true owner of the copyright the
property for which he had to expend money in order to possess it: see
R. v. Carter [1993] F.S.R. 303.

(vi) Search warrants

Fourth line. **Delete**, and **substitute**: "under the provisions relating to **19–14**
the making for sale or hire, importation or distribution"

C. *Other offences*

Delete: The whole of this paragraph from "Whenever a conspiracy **19–17**
. . .", and notes 57 to 59, and **substitute**: By virtue of section 12 of the
Criminal Justice Act 1987 (c. 38), a charge of conspiracy to defraud at
common law may be brought in respect of things done on or after July
20, 1987, even though the agreed course of conduct which forms the
basis of the charge will necessarily amount to or involve the commission of a substantive offence if carried out in accordance with the
parties' intentions. To this extent *R. v. Ayres* [1984] A.C. 447 and *R. v.
Lloyd* [1985] Q.B. 829 can no longer be regarded as good law. For the
elements of the common law offence, see *Scott v. Metropolitan Police
Commissioner* [1975] A.C. 819 and *Wai Yu-tsang v. The Queen* [1992]
1 A.C. 269.[60] *R. v. Lloyd* nevertheless remains good law in relation to
the elements of the offence of conspiracy to steal.

Note 60. First sentence. **Delete**. Second sentence. **Add**: see also para.
11–13, *ante*.

2. Seizure of Imported Copies

A. *Notice procedure*

Note 64. Note the amendment made to section 27(3) of the 1988 Act **19–18**
by paragraph 6 of the Copyright (Computer Programs) Regulations
1992 (see *post*, para. A–30).

3. Infringement of Performers' Rights

B. *Criminal liability*

(iv) Order for delivery up

19–29   Third sentence. **Delete**, and substitute: The person to whom an illicit recording is delivered up under such an order must retain it pending the making of a disposal order[90] or the decision not to make such an order.[91]

RELATED FORMS OF PROTECTION—1
INDUSTRIAL DESIGNS

Contents   *Para.*

1. Interrelation of Copyright, Registered Design and Design Right protection

B. *Position after the 1988 Act*

20–4   **The 1988 Act.** In debate it was made clear that the purpose of section 51 of the 1988 Act was to take industrial designs out of copyright law and keep truly artistic works in copyright: see *Hansard* H.L. Vol 491, cols. 185, 186. For a table listing the Parliamentary debates on these and other provisions of the 1988 Act, see *post*, Appendix 1.

2. Artistic Works Created before August 1, 1989

B. *Artistic works created after June 1, 1957 and before October 25, 1968*

(ii) Corresponding design registered

20–12   **"Corresponding Design".** The meaning of corresponding design is also discussed at *post*, para. 20–33A.

C. *Artistic works created on or after October 25, 1968 and before August 1, 1989*

20–33   **Extent of protection where corresponding design applied industrially.** Last paragraph. **Delete**, and **substitute**: Where articles had been sold after their incorporation into a larger article, the articles themselves had still been "sold". See *Greenfield Products Pty. Ltd v. Rover Scott Bounar Ltd.* [1990] A.I.P.C. 90–667 (Fed Ct. of Australia).

20–33A   **Corresponding design not registrable.** But where the design was not registrable, being excluded by the rules,[65] or by the definition of "design",[66] then the amended section 10 did not apply and the design would have enjoyed the full Copyright Act term. See *Entec (Pollution Control) Ltd v. Abacus Mouldings* [1992] F.S.R. 332 following *British*

Leyland Motor Corporation v. Armstrong Patents Company Ltd. [1986] R.P.C. 279, C.A., where a design for a septic tank was held not registrable and thus unaffected by either section 10 of the 1956 Act or paragraph 19 of the first Schedule to the 1988 Act.

The corresponding design may also not be registrable if the article to which it is applied does not fall within the definition of "article" under the Registered Designs Act 1949. In that Act (s. 44(1)) "article" means "any article of manufacture and includes any part of an article if that part is made and sold separately". If it is not suggested that part of an article was ever intended to be sold separately from the rest of the article then the part of the article would not be an article as defined and would not therefore be caught by section 10 of the 1956 Act. (See *Drayton Controls (Engineering) Ltd v. Honeywell Control Systems Limited* [1992] F.S.R. 245.)

The definition of a corresponding design contained in section 10(7) is aimed only at designs which, in relation to an artistic work when applied to an article, result in a reproduction of the self-same work. (*Drayton Controls v. Honeywell, ibid.,* following *Sifam Electrical Instrument v. Sangamo Weston* [1973] R.P.C. 899.) Thus in relation to the artistic work for the drawings of a valve, the definition of a corresponding design comprehends only designs which when applied to an article would result in a reproduction of the drawings for the valve. A design consisting of the shape of a bezel of the valve would not so result if applied to an article: *ibid.*

No transitional provisions.   **20–35**

NOTE 70. **Amend** to read: Para. 8(1), Sched. 7, Copyright Act 1956.

D. *Position after August 1, 1989*

Section 52 of the 1988 Act. The effect of section 52 on existing   **20–37** drawings was considered in *Drayton Controls (Engineering) Limited v. Honeywell Control Systems Limited* [1992] F.S.R. 245.

Artistic works to which section 10 of the 1956 Act applied   **20–40**

NOTE 3. See also *Drayton Controls (Engineering) Limited v. Honeywell Control Systems Limited* [1992] F.S.R. 245.

E. *Design documents and models*

Application of section 51. Under paragraph 19(1) of Schedule 1 to   **20–41** the 1988 Act, the date on which licences are available as of right is August 1, 1994.

In respect of the three-dimensional reproduction of two-dimensional drawings, the law enunciated in *L.B. Plastics Ltd v. Swish Products Ltd.* [1979] R.P.C. 551, and followed in *British Leyland Motor Corporation v. Armstrong Patents Company Ltd.* [1986] A.C. 577, will still apply for a period of 10 years from August 1, 1989. That is, it is an infringement of copyright to make a three-dimensional copy of an object by measuring the plaintiff's three-dimensional product which had been made from the plaintiff's manufacturing drawing. The change in the law which Lord Scarman looked forward to in *British Leyland* is not yet in force. See *Entec (Pollution Control) Ltd. v. Abacus Mouldings* [1992] F.S.R. 332.

3. Position under Part I of Works Created on or after August 1, 1989

A. *Artistic Works*

20–43   **Introduction.** For a table listing the Parliamentary debates on these and other provisions of the 1988 Act, see *post*, Appendix I.

B. *Design documents and models other than for artistic works and typefaces*

20–53   **Design.** It has been held arguable that body casts for an actor, consisting of pieces of latex foam, baked in moulds, hand painted with hairs individually inserted, were "surface decoration". See *Shelley Films Ltd. v. Rex Features Ltd.* [1994] E.M.L.R. 134. As to the meaning of "design", also see Christie in [1989] 7 EIPR 253, and Dworkin and Taylor in [1990] 1 EIPR 33.

4. Design Right

A. *Introduction*

20–63   In debate it was pointed out that there was no need for an express provision overriding the judgement in the *British Leyland* case to provide that design right cannot be denied on the sole ground of dealing with a replacement part. Design right expressly goes to the design of articles; it contains express and prominent provisions for exceptions which will avoid monopolies; and it includes provisions for dealing with abuses. See *Hansard*, H.L. Vol. 491, col. 1113.

For a table listing the Parliamentary debates on these and other provisions of the 1988 Act, see *post*, Appendix I.

European Community Regulation. After issuing a Green Paper (The **20–64A** Green Paper on the Legal Protection Of Industrial Design— III/F.5131/91) in June 1991, the European Commission received comments from interested parties. The E.C. Commission has now issued a Proposal for a Council Regulation on the Community Design (COM. 93) 342 final – SYN 463: [1994] O.J. C37/20). This proposes the creation of a Community Registered Design and an unregistered Community Design Right. The unregistered right has some similarities with design right under Part III of the 1988 Act. It will come into existence automatically and will give the owner protection against unauthorised reproduction. The right will only last for three years.

Under the current proposal, to enjoy automatic design right protection a design must be novel and have "individual character". The requirement for "individual character" is new and requires a new positive test in contrast to the "commonplace" exclusion under Part III of the 1988 Act.

The proposal excludes designs which are a realisation of a technical function leaving no freedom as regards arbitrary features of appearance and also excludes designs which are dictated in order to permit a product incorporating the design or to which it is applied to be assembled or connected with another product. A derogation from this latter exclusion is permitted in the case of certain modular systems.

If implemented it would be possible for the Community Design Right to exist alongside a national United Kingdom design right under Part III of the 1988 Act. This leads to the possibility of up to four different design rights and design registrations subsisting simultaneously in a design with different requirements for subsistence and different terms. It is to be hoped that some harmonisation will be undertaken to avoid a potential minefield of confusion before the Regulation is enacted. It is not known when the Regulation will come into effect.

Simultaneously, the European Commission issued a proposal for a Directive on the approximation of the legislations of the Member States on the legal protection of design (COM. (93) 344 final – SYN464: [1993] O.J. C345/14). The definition of design is substantially the same as under the proposed Council Regulation and many of the other Articles mirror Articles in the proposed Regulation. If implemented in its current form, some amendment of the Registered Designs Act will be necessary, particularly to reflect the requirement for "individual character", the removal of the need for eye appeal, the proposal for a one year grace period, and the removal of the limitation to "local" novelty.

C. *Conditions for subsistence*

(i) Definition of "design"

20–68   Design right is not restricted to visible features; that is, features which are visible to the naked eye. Features which are not visible to the naked eye because they are internal, concealed features in the finished product or because they are too small to be seen, are covered by design right. See *Hansard*, H.C. Vol. 138, col. 69.

20–70   **Kits**. This provision was included to make absolutely sure that design rights cannot be evaded simply by making and selling kits rather than selling complete and assembled articles. See *Hansard*, H.C., SCE col. 592.

(ii) Excluded designs

(b) *Must-fit exclusion*

20–73   The reason this and the must-match exclusions appear in the 1988 Act is to prevent design right conferring a monopoly. The problem is that where one article has to fit another, it must of necessity be a copy of the design of that other article to some extent. That is of particular application to spare parts used to repair equipment of all kinds. Because of the need to fit (and hence the need to copy), design right without these provisions could completely shut competitors out. In committee it was stated that this was very firmly not what the Government wanted. Accordingly, the exclusions allow copying where this is compelled by design constraints.

The effect of both exclusions will vary depending on the circumstances. For example, for a pump for an aircraft, the design is mainly free standing but it has to be connected to the aircraft. The 1988 Act allows the connecting features to be copied so that others could compete with their own pump designs. But it would not allow the free-standing parts of the pump to be copied. As a result there would in general be protection for parts. Where, however, the designer is entirely dependent on the design of the equipment to which the article is to be fitted, then the 1988 Act would allow the entire article to be copied. See *Hansard*, H.L. Vol 491, cols. 1111, 1112.

(c) *Must-match exclusion*

20–74   The must-match exclusion is also necessary to avoid the situation where design right could completely shut competitors out of the market. However, the exclusion applies only to parts of a single object.

The effect is that the exclusion would not apply to individual items in a set of cutlery or a suite of furniture. In other words, it would not apply to families of articles but only within a single article. See *Hansard*, H.L. Vol. 494, col. 109.

The equivalent subsection (1(1)(b)(ii)) in the Registered Designs Act 1949 as amended was considered in *Ford Motor Company Limited and Iveco Fiat SpA's Design Applications* [1993] R.P.C. 399, where the Registered Designs Appeal Tribunal commented that the Registered Designs Act 1949 is undoubtedly ambiguous and obscure and thus it is proper to look at the Parliamentary debates for clarification. The Tribunal therefore considered comments made during the committee stage in the House of Lords where an example of a situation in which the Act would allow copying of an entire article was given as a car body panel. In this kind of case competitors have no choice but to copy the entire article. Where the circumstances compel copying, the need for competition in the after-market must prevail. (*Hansard*, H.L. Vol 491, cols. 1111–1112.) This was followed in *Ford*. The decision in *Ford* was subject to judicial review where the decision of the Registered Designs Appeal Tribunal was upheld: *R. v. The Registered Designs Appeal Tribunal ex parte Ford Motor Co. Ltd*, 2 March 1994, noted at I.P.D. 17049. Although this case concerns registrability of designs, the exclusion is in almost identical terms to section 213(3)(b)(ii) of the Copyright, Designs and Patents Act 1988. The court commented that an "article" has to have an independent life as an article of commerce, while the "another article" must refer to the vehicle as a whole. That is, the "article" is part of the "another article". In view of the importance of this case to the spare parts industry, leave to appeal direct to the House of Lords was given.

Designer's intention. The must-match exclusion requires that regard　　**20–74A** must be had to the intention of the designer as to the other article of which the article is to form an integral part. This was to avoid the exclusion taking away design protection in a wide range of cases where an independently designed item is subsequently used with other items in some larger article. The question of whether the must-match exclusion applies is to be answered at the moment when the design is created, not at some later time.

For example, suppose that a new shape of an all-purpose strut is designed. If that is all that is designed, then it is quite clear that, at the moment of creation, the shape or design of the strut is not dependent on anything else. The must-match exclusion would not apply. The strut may subsequently be used by someone else, for example in a protective grill where there are a number of matching struts. At this point the shape of any one of the struts matches that of the others and any replacement would also need to match the others. In debate, the Government's view was expressed to the effect that the must-match exclusion should not apply in these circumstances. See *Hansard*, H.L. Vol. 495, cols. 699, 700.

(d) *Surface decoration*

20–75   Decoration is a matter for copyright and registered design law. Any additional protection provided by design right would cause difficulty and confuse the nature of design right. Design right is intended to protect the overall form of an article not decoration applied to a surface. See *Hansard* H.L. Vol. 491, col. 1112.

(iii) Originality

20–76   "Original" has the same meaning as that used in Part I of the 1988 Act: that is independently created and not a copy: see *Hansard* H.C. Vol. 138, col. 69. See also *C & H Engineering v. F. Klucznik & Sons Ltd.* [1992] F.S.R. 421 confirming that for a design to be original it must be the work of the creator.

The word "commonplace" is not defined but appears to introduce a consideration akin to novelty. (*C & H Engineering v. F. Klucznik & Sons Ltd, ibid.*). For a comment on *C & H Engineering*, see Turner in [1993] 1 EIPR 24.

Some clarification of the meaning of "commonplace" as a limitation on the meaning of "original" can also be found in *Hansard*. It was the government's intention to avoid giving design right to mundane, routine designs of the kind which are common in the particular field in question: see *Hansard* H.L. Vol. 494, col. 112 and H.C., SCE cols. 575, 576.

(iv) Subsistence of design right

(a) *Recording of design in design document*

20–79   The creator of a design is not necessarily the person who records the design but usually will be: see *C & H Engineering v. F. Klucznik & Sons Ltd.* [1992] F.S.R. 421.

G. *Infringement of design right*

(i) Primary Infringement

20–124   **Exclusive right of design right owner.** Section 226(2) was added by amendment to the original Bill to clarify the meaning of "reproduction" as being limited to copying and not extending to independent creation of the same design: see *Hansard* H.L. Vol. 495, col. 703. For other Parliamentary discussion on this point, see *Hansard* H.L. Vol. 491, cols. 1132, 1133; and H.L. Vol. 494, cols. 125, 126.

The test for infringement requires:

(1) that the alleged infringing article be compared with the document or article embodying the design;

(2) that it then be decided whether copying took place; and, if so,

(3) that it then be decided whether or not the alleged infringing article is made exactly or substantially to the plaintiff's design.

This must be an objective test to be decided through the eyes of the person to whom the design is directed. See *C & H Engineering v. F. Klucznik & Sons Ltd.* [1992] F.S.R. 421 and a similar approach in *Billhöfer Maschinenfabrik GmbH v. T.H. Dixon & Co. Limited* [1990] F.S.R. 105, see *ante*, para. 8–55 *et seq.*

I. *Remedies for infringement of design right*

NOTE 79. The Trade Marks Act 1938 is prospectively repealed by the **20–147** Trade Marks Act 1994 (c. 26).

L. *Crown use*

(i) General

The term "arrangement" was included to cover any memorandum **20–180** of understanding with a foreign Government since the United Kingdom has very few formal "agreements" with other countries. See *Hansard* H.C. Vol. 138, col. 87.

M. *Jurisdiction*

(i) Comptroller

Rules of procedure before Comptroller. **20–204**

NOTE 51. The rules have been further amended by The Design Right (Proceedings before Comptroller) (Amendment) Rules 1992,[1] see *post*, para. B–167.

---

[1] (S.I. 1992 No. 615)

(ii) Court

20–207   **Infringement.** The Patents County Court has special jurisdiction to hear and determine any action relating to designs over which the High Court would have jurisdiction (See §20–207, n.57 in the Main Work). In *PSM International plc v. Specialised Fastener Products (Southern) Limited.* [1992] F.S.R. 113 at 116 it was commented that, although "designs" is not defined, there seems to be no difficulty in embracing within the term "designs" both registered designs and designs which are protected under Part III of the 1988 Act. The Patents County Court went on to comment that it would be an absurd result if it has special jurisdiction to deal with cases involving designs recorded in engineering drawings which are design documents made on or after the date of commencement of Part III of the 1988 Act and not if they were recorded before that date. Thus, in addition, the Patents County Court has jurisdiction to hear actions for copyright infringement concerning designs recorded in design documents before August 1, 1989.

For a comment on *PSM v. Specialised Fastener,* see Jones in [1992] 12 EIPR 449.

NOTE 57. The designated Patents County Court is currently the Central London County Court. See the Patents County Court (Designation and Jurisdiction) Order 1994,[2] *post,* para. B–233.

N. *Semiconductor topographies*

(i) General

20–208   See, generally, Carr, H. and Arnold, R., *Computer Software: Legal Protection in the U.K.* (Sweet & Maxwell, 1992), chapter 6.

NOTE 60. For the Directive, see *post,* para. H–1.

NOTE 65. Further amendments have been made by the Design Right (Semiconductor Topographies) Regulations 1991,[3] 1992[4] and 1993.[5] (See *infra,* paras. 20–215 and 20–216, and *post,* para. A–577L).

---

[2] (S.I. 1994 No. 1609)
[3] (S.I. 1991 No. 2237)
[4] (S.I. 1992 No. 400)
[5] (S.I. 1993 No. 2497)

(iii) Qualification for design right protection

Qualifying person. Delete: the references to Part III of the Schedule **20–215**
(see *post*, para. A–577L).

Whole paragraph. **Delete**, and **Substitute**: The countries in Part II **20–216**
of the Schedule to the Regulations as amended are Australia, Austria,
Finland, French overseas territories, Iceland, Japan, Liechtenstein,
Norway, Sweden, Switzerland and the United States of America (see
post, para. A–577L).

Chapter 21

RELATED FORMS OF PROTECTION—2

BREACH OF CONFIDENCE, PASSING OFF AND MALICIOUS FALSEHOOD

Contents   *Para.*

1. Breach of Confidence

A. *Rule stated*

NOTE 1.   See, now, Goff and Jones, *Law of Restitution* (4th ed., Sweet &   **21–1**
Maxwell, 1993), chapter 35. See also Coleman A., *The Legal Protection of
Trade Secrets* (Sweet & Maxwell, 1992); and Wright in [1993] EIPR 237.

C. *Elements of action for breach of confidence*

(i) Definition of information

NOTE 27.   See also *J.A. Mont (UK) Ltd. v. Mills* [1993] F.S.R. 577 at 590.   **21–4**

End of paragraph. **Add**: If the covenant in the contract of
employment of service is, on its true construction, wider than is
reasonable in the public interest and between the parties, it is void and
of no effect: *J.A. Mont (UK) Ltd. v. Mills* [1993] F.S.R. 577, at 587 and
590.

(ii) Requirements of confidentiality

End of paragraph. **Add**: If the information is in fact false, it cannot be   **21–5**
the subject of a confidential information claim: see *Mainmet Holdings
plc v. Austin* [1991] F.S.R. 538 following *Berkeley Administration Inc. v.
McClelland* [1990] F.S.R. 505.

(iii)Private or secret information

21–6 Line 7 on page 725. The obligation of confidence cannot survive publication of a patent specification by which a plaintiff voluntarily puts the information into the possession of the public. See *Prout v. British Gas plc* [1992] F.S.R. 478.

(v) Examples of confidential information

21–8 In *Times Newspapers Ltd. v. MGN Ltd.* [1993] E.M.L.R. 443 it was doubted whether information which is intended to be published but in which the publishers have a commercial interest to maintain the secrecy until publication can be the subject of a duty of confidence. But *c.f.*, *Shelley Films Ltd. v. Rex Features Ltd.* [1994] E.M.L.R. 134, where it was held that the physical appearance of a "closed" film set which formed part of the backdrop in scenes of a film intended to be released to the public could be the subject matter of confidential information.

Line 3 on page 728. A contractually enforceable obligation of confidence may be created in relation to suggestions of a potentially patentable nature disclosed by an employee to an employer under an employees suggestion scheme. See *Prout v. British Gas plc* [1992] F.S.R. 478.

(vi) Confidential relationships

21–6 **Confidence in contracts.** Line 6 on page 723. Where a contract of employment provided that the employee would not disclose "trade secrets" or "information of a confidential nature" about his employer's affairs, it was held that "trade secrets" meant information which, if disclosed to a competitor, would be liable to cause real or significant harm to the owner of the trade secret. The information must, however, be information used in a trade or business and the owner must have limited the dissemination of it or at least had not encouraged or permitted its widespread publication. The expression "trade secrets" in that context included not only secret formulae for manufactured products, but also the names of customers and of the goods which they would buy. See *Lansing Linde Ltd. v. Kerr* [1991] 1 W.L.R. 251.

21–17 **Contracts of service.** End of second paragraph. **Add**: Whether the confidential information qualifies as a trade secret is a matter of degree: *P.S.M. International Ltd. v. Whitehouse* [1992] F.S.R. 489, following *Faccenda Chicken Ltd. v. Fowler* [1987] Ch. 117. It is arguable that the designs of machines and quotations are of a sufficiently high degree of confidentiality to amount to a trade secret, within the meaning of that expression as defined in a contract of service, even though it may not be a trade secret in the strict sense: *P.S.M. International Ltd. v. Whitehouse, ibid.*

Line 2 on page 735. An employee is not entitled to steal documents or, after his employment ends, to use for his own purposes (for example, for soliciting orders) information which could sensibly be regarded as confidential information contained in the stolen documents regarding the plaintiff's customers, customer contacts, requirements or prices charged. Neither is an employee entitled to copy such information on to scrap paper and take it away with him and use for his own purposes. See *Universal Thermosensors Ltd. v. Hibben* [1992] 1 W.L.R. 840.

Second paragraph on page 736. **Add**: Where there is no restraint of trade clause, no injunction will be granted to restrain the use of customers' names for which the defendant relies on his memory. See *Roberts v. Northwest Fixing* [1993] F.S.R. 281, C.A.

Note 7. **Add**: *Austin Knight (U.K.) Ltd. v. Hinds* [1994] F.S.R. 52 at 59.

Other examples of confidential relationships. In *Shelley Films v. Rex* **21–18** *Features Ltd.* [1994] F.M.L.R. 134, following *Franklin v. Giddins* [1977] Q.R. 72 (Queensland), it was held arguable that a photographer who gained access to a "closed" film set without consent and may have seen notices prohibiting the taking of photographs became subject to an obligation of confidence. This was so notwithstanding that he had no pre-existing relationship with those alleging the duty of confidence.

Third paragraph, line 7. **Add**: A duty of confidence can exist between a private investigator and a client. No illegality is necessarily involved: see *House of Fraser Holdings plc. v. New* noted at [1993] I.P.D. 16016.

Note 19. **Add**: *The Lubrizoil Corp. v. Esso Petroleum Ltd (No.2)* [1993] F.S.R. 53 (an order was made to protect documents of a sensitive nature disclosed in pre-trial discovery).

(vii) Wrongful use of confidential information

After note 21 in the text. **Add**: The principles relating to confidential **21–19** information apply just as much where the defendant is misusing the information maliciously (*e.g.* to harm the plaintiff's connections) as where the defendant is misusing the information for his own gain. See *Mainmet Holdings plc v. Austin* [1991] F.S.R. 538.

21–20 **Justifiable use and public interest.** End of first main paragraph on page 741. **Add**: Information which has been obtained pursuant to statutory powers may be received under an obligation of confidence and a third party may be restrained from using it, even if he has come by the information innocently. But there will be no impropriety in the disclosure of the information to a person for whom the information was of mutual concern under the provisions of the statute. There is no breach of confidence or of statutory duty in such a disclosure, because it is to a person envisaged by the terms of the statute. See *Hoechst U.K. Ltd. v. Chemiculture Ltd.* [1993] F.S.R. 270.

NOTE 40. **Substitute**: 565 and 568 for 505 and 528, respectively. **Add**: *Roberts v. Northwest Fixings* [1993] F.S.R. 281.

(ix) Liability of third parties

21–22 Second line. **Substitute**: the words "an equitable duty" for the words "a duty". See *Andersen Consulting v. C.H.P. Consulting Ltd.* noted at [1991] I.P.D. 15024.

D. *Remedies*

(i) Injunction

21–23 End of the first sentence. **Add**: Where the likelihood of the future misuse of confidential information is established, the following principles apply:

(1) A plaintiff is entitled to an injunction to protect him from *further* misuse of the information, but the plaintiff is not entitled to be protected by injunction for misuse which has already taken place. That is a matter for damages. If, for example, the defendant has already misused information by making contact with a customer and has received an order from him, an injunction to restrain him from fulfilling the order or any future order will go too far. That would not be a case of *further* use of the confidential information.

(2) There may be circumstances in which an injunction is justified as a means of putting the parties back into the position that they

would have been in had there been no misuse of information. An injunction may be fair and just if it has the effect of restoring the parties to the competitive position which they each ought to occupy and which each would have occupied but for the defendant's misconduct. An order of that kind will prevent a defendant from benefiting from the springboard effect of his use of the confidential information. An injunction will not, however, be appropriate if its effect would be to put the plaintiff into a better position for the future than he would have been if there had been no misuse, such as where a defendant would eventually have been able to create the information for himself.

(3) An interlocutory or final injunction is in too wide a form if it is framed so as to restrain a defendant simply from soliciting or entering into or fulfilling a contract with a person whose name is on the plaintiff's confidential list of customers with whom the defendant had contact while he was in possession of the list.

(4) If it is impossible to undo what has already occurred, it may be appropriate to make an award of damages to the plaintiff for the use of the information, even though the plaintiff cannot prove that he has suffered any pecuniary loss as a result of the breach.

See *Universal Thermosensors Ltd. v. Hibben* [1992] 1 W.L.R. 840.

There is jurisdiction to grant an injunction which interferes with the contractual rights of innocent third parties by, for example, restraining an ex-employee from fulfilling a contract which he has made with the third party by the misuse of confidential information. The jurisdiction may be exercised pending trial if, for example:

(1) The contract was made by the defendant with the third party when he was still employed by the plaintiff and he has acted in breach of his duty of fidelity to the plaintiff.

(2) It is arguable that the third party had notice of the breach of duty on the part of the defendant.

See *P.S.M. International Ltd. v. Whitehouse* [1992] F.S.R. 489. The court rejected the argument that no injunction should be granted because all the damage had been done and the contract had already been placed. It was arguable that the third party might return to the plaintiff if the defendant could not fulfil the contract he had made with him. It was not necessary for the plaintiff to *prove* that he would suffer damages occurring after the date of the hearing.

After note 56 in the text. **Add**: Injunctions against misusing trade secrets must be drawn with precision, so that the defendant knows what he is prevented from doing. See *P.S.M. International Ltd. v.*

Whitehouse [1992] F.S.R. 489, applying *Lawrence David Ltd. v. Ashton* [1989] F.S.R. 87 and *Lock International plc v. Beswick* [1989] 1 W.L.R. 1268.

NOTE 54. **Add**: *C.f. Graham v. Deldafield* [1992] F.S.R. 313 (commercial information).

(ii) Damages

21–24   End of paragraph. **Add**: Even where it is established that the defendant has stolen documents containing confidential information and has used that information in soliciting orders, there is no irrebuttable presumption that business resulted from the orders derived from wrongful use of the information, so as to make the defendant liable. The court looks further than the fact that the document was stolen to see whether the information was used. The plaintiff is entitled to fair compensation for the wrong done to him by the defendant's misuse of confidential information. Whether any particular piece of business was obtained by a defendant as a result of misuse of the plaintiff's confidential information is a question of fact in each case. In answering that question, the court may look with scepticism at the defendant's evidence about the actual use he has made of the information. Any doubts about his evidence are likely to be resolved in favour of the plaintiff: *Roger Bullivant Ltd. v. Ellis* [1987] I.C.R. 464. A defendant cannot complain if he finds that it has become impossible to distinguish between potential customers whom he could have contacted lawfully and those whom he could not.

Where it has been possible to examine closely the circumstances in which the defendant dealt with the plaintiff's customers, it will not be appropriate to make an award of damages under the general head for loss of profit by reason of diminution in a plaintiff's trade or damage to its goodwill, in the absence of evidence justifying such a claim. *F. Robb v. Green* [1895] 2 Q.B. 315 and *Universal Thermosensors Ltd. v. Hibben* [1992] 1 W.L.R. 840.

(v) Procedure

21–27   End of paragraph. **Add**: The court may order inspection, for example, of a computerised data base alleged to have been made by a defendant in breach of copyright and confidence, prior to the service of a Statement of Claim in order to enable a plaintiff to plead a full and proper Statement of Claim: *Dun & Bradstreet Ltd. v. Typesetting Facilities Ltd.* [1992] F.S.R. 320.

2. Passing Off

C. *Actions for passing off*

Note 99. **Add**: *Games Workshop Ltd. v. Transworld Publishers Ltd.* [1993]   **21–32**
F.S.R. 705 ("Dark Future" as a title of a series of books). Note that the
Trade Marks Act 1938 is prospectively repealed by the Trade Marks
Act 1994 (c. 26).

(i) Elements of passing off

Note 2.   See, now, *Associated Newspapers plc. v. Insert Media Ltd.* [1991]   **21–33**
W.L.R. 571, C.A., and also *Tattinger v. Allbev Ltd.* [1993] F.S.R. 641.

End of first paragraph. **Add**: It has been pointed out that the
formulation of the principles in *Erven Warnink v. J. Townend & Sons
(Hull) Ltd.* [1979] A.C. 731, does not give the same degree of assistance
in analysis and decision-making as the "classical trinity" of requirements, namely:

(1) a reputation (or goodwill) acquired by the plaintiff for his goods,
    name or mark;

(2) a misrepresentation by the defendant leading to confusion (or
    deception), causing

(3) damage to the plaintiff.

See *Consorzio Del Prosciutto di Parma v. Marks & Spencer plc* [1991]
R.P.C. (alleged passing off of Parma ham) following the remarks of
Lord Oliver in *Reckitt & Coleman Products Inc. v. Borden Inc.* [1990] 1
W.L.R. 491 at 499, and confirming a "welcome return" to the classical
approach. In analysing the particular facts of a passing off action, it is
usually advantageous to take these three elements of passing off one
by one, even though they are often interactive. See *County Sound plc v.
Ocean Sound Ltd.* [1991] F.S.R. 367, in which it was also pointed out that
mere copying, however deliberate and however provocative, of a name
or style which another trader has used for his goods or services is not
enough to found a passing off action. See the discussion of descriptive
names at § 21–38 in the Main Work, from which it appears that if the
name is descriptive of goods or services and there is no evidence to
establish a secondary meaning, no action for passing off will lie.

Note 5. **Substitute**: n. 94 for n.17.

(ii) Goodwill

21–34   NOTE 12.   See also *Kaye v. Robertson* [1991] F.S.R. 62, in which a well known actor had no claim in passing off because he was not a trader in respect of his interest in the story about an accident in which he had been injured.

After note 13 in the text. **Add**: Whether goodwill is essentially local or is actually or potentially national in extent depends on the facts of the case: *Computa Tune v. Computatunes Ltd.* noted at [1991] I.P.D. 14180.

NOTE 14.   **Add**: There is no rule that a joint owner of goodwill which has become severed can never sue the other. Neither is entitled to appropriate to himself the name. If, however, one used the name so as to trade on the reputation of the other, an injunction might be granted. See *Cotton T.V. Rentals Ltd. v. Cottons of Lincoln Road Ltd.* noted at [1993] I.P.D. 16014.

NOTE 15.   **Add**: Whether a non-trading charity plaintiff can sue another non-trading charity in respect of use of a similar name has not been decided: *British Diabetic Association v. Diabetic Society Ltd.* noted at [1992] I.P.D. 15103. See also *British Legion v. British Legion Club (Street)* (1931) 48 R.P.C. 555.

NOTE 16.   See also *Mirage Studios v. Counter-Feat Clothing Co. Ltd.* [1991] F.S.R. 145 in which it was held that a sufficient reputation had been established over a period of four months by television and radio broadcasts to a large audience, by press coverage and sales of goods.

21–35   Goodwill of foreign business or publication

NOTE 20. For a full review of the Commonwealth and American authorities, see *Conagra v. McCain Foods (Aust) Pty. Ltd.* (1992) 23 I.P.R. 193 (Fed. Ct. of Australia).

Line 6 in the text. **Add**: A foreign manufacturer who does not trade in England but whose goods are sold here, may acquire a sufficient goodwill. Whether the goodwill is that of the manufacturer or of the importer is a question of fact. See *Nishika Corporation v. Goodchild* noted at [1990] I.P.D. 13090.

After note 21 in the text. **Add**: In the case of cross-frontier claims of passing off, it is not generally possible to confine the legal disputes between the parties to one set of proceedings brought in one country. In general, an English court has no jurisdiction to determine claims against a defendant who is not domiciled in the United Kingdom in respect of acts of passing off committed outside the United Kingdom. See *L.A. Gear Inc. v. Gerald Whelan & Sons Ltd.* [1991] F.S.R. 670. *Cf. An Bord Trachtala v. Waterford Foods plc* [1994] F.S.R. 316 (High Ct. of Ireland) (defendant domiciled in the jurisdiction of the Court).

(iii) Misrepresentation

End of main paragraph. **Add**: Sometimes a defendant offers to **21–36** publish a disclaimer to the effect that his goods or business has no connection with the plaintiff's. Once, however, a misrepresentation has been made by a defendant, a disclaimer will not have the effect of converting his false representation into a true one. On the contrary, a disclaimer may increase the confusion. It may simply reinforce the representation that what the defendant had been doing was authorised, but subject to a condition that such a disclaimer should be made: *Associated Newspapers plc v. Inset Media Ltd.* [1991] 1 W.L.R. 571.

Where the shape, finish and general appearance of an article was found to be distinctive of the plaintiff's product, the fact that the defendant's rival product bore a different name and carried prominent disclaimers was not enough to prevent deception. It was the shape, finish and general appearance which was distinctive. The name and notices did not enable the potential purchaser to tell which was the genuine article: *Weber-Stephen Products Co. v. Alrite Engineering (Pty) Ltd.* [1992] R.P.C. 549 (Sup. Ct. of S.A.).

NOTE 40. In *Ciba Geigy plc v. Parke Davis & Co. Ltd* noted at [1993] I.P.D. 16045, it was held arguable that any misrepresentation that may deceive a purchaser into the belief that he is getting something which he is not, is actionable; for example, a representation that the defendant's drug was equivalent to the plaintiff's was arguably a misrepresentation.

(v) Descriptive names

End of first paragraph on page 756. **Add**: Where the defendant has **21–38** adopted the very name by which the plaintiff is known, the principles that the use of a descriptive name cannot be restrained is inapplicable: see *The British Diabetic Association v. The Diabetic Society Ltd.* noted at [1992] I.P.D. 15103.

End of second paragraph on page 756. **Add**: In *McCain International Ltd v. Country Fair Foods Ltd.* [1981] R.P.C. 69 the use of the words "Oven Chips" was alleged to have constituted passing off. The plaintiff consistently used the name "McCain Oven Chips" and the defendant proposed to use its own brand name in relation to the words "Oven Chips". An interlocutory injunction was refused. The decision would have been the same, even if the defendant proposed to use the name

"Oven Chips" alone. See the analysis in *County Sound plc v. Ocean Sound Ltd.* [1991] F.S.R. 367. The words "Oven Chips" were predominantly descriptive. There was no evidence that they had become distinctive by acquiring a secondary meaning. In *County Sound plc v. Ocean Sound Ltd.* [1991] F.S.R. 367 the words "The Gold AM " were descriptive of the plaintiff's radio program consisting of the broadcast of popular hits from the 1950s, 60s and 70s. The expression meant "Golden Oldies on the AM radio frequency."

Goodwill in a descriptive name may be acquired by the exclusive use of that name over a substantial period of time. Where a descriptive name has often been used in conjunction with another, distinctive name, the acquisition of the goodwill in the descriptive name is hard to establish. This is because the use of the descriptive name in conjunction with the distinctive name does not amount to the exclusive use of the descriptive name. See *County Sound plc v. Ocean Sound Ltd.* [1991] F.S.R. 367.

The fact that there has been some confusion between two names does not mean that there will be any misrepresentation amounting to passing off. Such confusion as may arise may be due to the use of the descriptive name rather than to the existence of any passing off. See *Tamworth Herald Co. Ltd. v. Thomson Free Newspapers Ltd.* [1991] F.S.R. 337.

NOTE 58. **Add**: *Advance Magazine Publishing Inc. v. Redwood Publishing Ltd.* [1993] F.S.R. 449 ("Gourmet" vs. "BBC Gourmet Good Food" – injunction refused).

(vi) Get up

21–39   NOTE 64. **Add**: *Weber-Stephen Products Ltd. v. Alrite Engineering (Pty) Ltd.* [1992] R.P.C. 549 (Sup. Ct. of S.A.) (shape of barbecue grill).

After note 64 in the text. **Add**: The product itself or part of it may constitute or contribute to the get up which may include distinctive features of an article indicating that it is the product of a particular manufacturer.

End of second paragraph. **Add**: There is no rule of law that get up cannot form part of the article itself, as opposed to the wrapping of an article. It does, however, require an exceptionally strong case to justify the conclusion that the particular shape of an article has become so identified with a particular manufacturer or seller of such the article as to give him the right to claim that such shape means to the relevant sector of the public his goods and no one else's. See *Drayton Controls (Engineering) Ltd. v. Honeywell Control Systems Ltd.* [1992] F.S.R. 245 (thermostatic radiator valves). Further, a case of passing off based on get up may be weakened by evidence which shows that purchasers identify the goods by name rather than by shape or appearance: *c.f. Navan Carpets Ltd. v. Furlong Carpets (Wholesale) Ltd.* noted at [1990] 12 EIPR D–235 where the High Court of Ireland held that it was arguable that a floral design of a carpet had become distinctive of the plaintiff's carpets.

(vii) Deception of the public

After first sentence. **Add**: It is unnecessary to prove reliance on the misrepresentation, for example, by proving that the public would not buy the defendant's goods if they knew that they were buying counterfeit and not genuine articles. Once the misrepresentation is made, the court may infer, in the absence of other evidence, that the public have acted on a misrepresentation. See *Mirage Studios v. Counter-Feat Clothing Co. Ltd.* [1991] F.S.R. 145.   **21–40**

After second sentence. **Add**: No protection is available against confusion as such, only against confusion caused by misrepresentation. Where two traders carry on business in their own name, the representation made is that the goods which the trader markets are his own goods. That line is overstepped only when he represents that the goods are those of the other trader. See *Marengo v. Daily Sketch and Sunday Graphic Ltd.* [1992] F.S.R. 1, C.A., followed in *County Sound plc v. Ocean Sound Ltd.* [1991] F.S.R. 367. See also the report of the *Marengo* case in the House of Lords at 65 R.P.C. 242.

NOTE 71. See now *Associated Newspapers plc v. Insert Media Ltd.* [1991] 1 W.L.R. 571, C.A.

After note 76 in the text. **Add**: In this context, the court may well view with scepticism a claim that a plaintiff is likely to suffer damage as a result of confusion amongst potential advertisers: See *Tamworth Herald Co. Ltd. v. Thomson Free Newspapers Ltd.* [1991] F.S.R. 337.

End of second paragraph. **Add**: Evidence of deception may properly be obtained by means of a "trap order", and is admissible, even though the plaintiff, with the assistance of his legal advisers, has misrepresented himself as a bona fide customer in the course of executing the trap order. See *Marie Claire Album S.A. v. Hartstone Hosiery Ltd.* [1993] F.S.R. 692 at 696.

(viii) Evidence

NOTE 78: For a review of the admissibility of market survey evidence in passing off actions, see Pattinson in [1990] 3 EIPR 99.   **21–41**

After note 81 in the text. **Add**: In *United Biscuits (U.K.) Ltd. v. Burtons Biscuits Ltd.* [1992] F.S.R. 14 evidence of street surveys conducted by market research interviewers was held not to be reliable for the purposes of deciding whether or not to grant an interlocutory injunction. In the survey, the questions were not well designed and the answers were insufficiently well analysed to be of any value. See similar criticisms in *Imperial Group v. Phillip Morris Ltd.* [1984] R.P.C. 293 and *Laura Ashley v. Coloroll* [1987] R.P.C. 1.

Before penultimate sentence. **Add**: The question whether or not there is a real likelihood of deception is ultimately for the court and not the witnesses to decide. *Spalding Bros. v. Gamage Ltd.* (1915) 32 R.P.C. 286; *Parker-Knoll Ltd. v. Knoll International Ltd.* [1962] R.P.C. 265 at 285 and *The Financial Times Ltd. v. Evening Standard Co. Ltd.* [1991] F.S.R. 7 at 11 (use of pink coloured paper for the business section of the *Evening Standard* was held not to create a likelihood of confusion with the Financial Times, which is printed on pink paper).

Before final sentence. **Add**: Evidence is admissible from trade witnesses, as distinct from ordinary witnesses, as to their opinion as experts in the relevant market, on the likely reaction of others who are within the sphere of their work: *Sodastream Ltd. v. Thorn Cascade Ltd.* [1982] R.P.C. 459 at 468; *Guccio Guccia Spa v. Paolo Gucci* [1991] F.S.R. 89; *Tattinger S.A. v. Allbev Ltd.* [1993] F.S.R. 641 at 663 (interlocutory proceedings reported at [1992] F.S.R. 647).

End of paragraph. **Add**: The courts have also criticised the proliferation of affidavits and exhibits on interlocutory applications as "overkill". They add to the costs of the litigation and the time spent by the court in hearing such cases. See *Mothercare U.K. Ltd. v. Penguin Books Ltd.* [1988] R.P.C. 113 at 119; *Games Workshop Ltd. v. Transworld Publishers Ltd.* [1993] F.S.R. 705 at 715.

(ix) Damage

21–42   After note 86 in text. **Add**: Erosion or dilution of the distinctiveness or exclusiveness of a name or mark is a form of damage to the goodwill of a business. A tendency to impair distinctiveness may lead to an inference of damage to goodwill. See *Tattinger S.A. v. Allbev Ltd.* [1993] F.S.R. 641 at 670, 674 and 678. In that case Champagne producers complained of the use of the word "Champagne" in connection with a non-alcoholic elder flower cordial made by the defendant. It was held that the dilution of the plaintiffs' reputation by the defendant's use of the word "Champagne" could cause serious damage to the reputation or goodwill attached to the name. The plaintiffs were entitled to be protected against such damage by falsehoods which represented that the defendant's goods were of a class or shared the characteristics of a class to which the goodwill attached.

If goodwill or reputation is established, and a misrepresentation proved, it may not be difficult for the court to infer damage: see *Walt Disney Productions v. Triple 5 Corp.* (1992) 43 C.P.R. (3d) 321.

(x) Characters and character merchandising

After note 93 in the text. **Add**: The right to bring a passing off action **21–43** to protect a character merchandising operation, where the character is fictitious and the defendant's use does not amount to an infringement of copyright, was established in *Mirage Studios v. Counter-Feat Clothing Co. Ltd.* [1991] F.S.R. 145.

In that case, the defendant copied the concept of the plaintiff's humanoid turtle cartoon design. The following principles were stated:

(1) The evidence was that a substantial number of the purchasing public now expect and know that, where a famous cartoon or television character is reproduced on goods, reproduction is normally governed by a licence granted by the owner of the copyright or other rights in the character. There is a link between the plaintiff and the goods which are sold. Passing off protection is not limited to those who themselves market and sell the goods.

(2) It is not necessary that the reproduction is so similar as to amount to an infringement of copyright, provided that members of the public in fact mistake the defendant's goods for the plaintiff's.

(3) The marketing of such goods involves a representation, namely, that they are licensed goods.

(4) If the goods are in fact unlicensed, their marketing amounts to a misrepresentation. The misrepresentation is calculated to injure the business or goodwill of the owner of the reproduction or other rights in a character, provided his business includes that of licensing the use of such characters for profit. Unauthorised use of the character would result in a reduction of royalties for the owner. The unauthorised application of the character to inferior goods might also seriously and foreseeably damage the licensing rights.

(5) It is important that the plaintiff's business is dual in nature namely that it consists both of the creation and exploitation of the character or cartoon or film in question, and the licensing of the right to use such creations on goods sold by other people.

(6) It does not matter that the plaintiff is not himself a manufacturer of the goods of the type which the defendant is marketing.

It is sufficient if he is in the business of licensing such use, provided that the public assume the character would not normally appear without the licence of some person, such as the plaintiff.

(7) If there is a misrepresentation, there is no requirement to adduce evidence to show that the misrepresentation is the cause of the public buying the goods in question. The court may infer that the intention of the buyer will be to acquire the genuine article.

The present position is that the Australian cases of *Children's Television Workshop Inc. v. Woolworths (New South Wales) Ltd.* [1981] R.P.C. 187 ("The Muppets") and *Fido Dido Inc. v. Venture Stores (Retailers) Pty. Ltd.* (1988) 16 I.P.R. 365. ("Fido and Dido") are regarded as sound decisions on the law.

The previous English decisions on the subject were considered not to touch the case where the plaintiff has copyright in the relevant drawings and is in the business on a large scale in this country of licensing the use of the copyright in the drawings. For example, in *Wombles Ltd. v. Womble Skips Ltd.* [1977] R.P.C. 99, the plaintiff's claim had been dismissed because there was no common field of activity and only the name "Womble" had been taken. As to these reasons, the first is now a matter of evidence rather than a necessary requirement of a passing-off action. The second might still be a valid point. There was no copyright in a name, so that the plaintiffs could not have had a business in licensing the copyright in a name alone. In *Tavener Rutledge Ltd. v. Trexapalm Ltd.* [1975] F.S.R. 179 ("Kojak"), the claim failed on the ground that there was no common field of activity. In addition, the evidence did not establish that the system of character merchandising was known to the man in the street. It is now doubtful whether it is an essential ingredient of this kind of passing off to show that the public is aware that licensors are concerned to uphold the quality of goods on which the characters appear. In *Lyngstad v. Annabas Products Ltd.* [1975] F.S.R. 488, the court was again mainly concerned with use of a name ("Abba"). Further, there was no evidence in that case of substantial exploitation by the plaintiffs of licensing rights.

On the present state of authorities, it is unresolved whether a passing-off action based only on the use of a name of a character would succeed. It is thought that it may do, if the plaintiff establishes as a matter of evidence that the public makes or assumes a connection between the use of the name and someone having the right to license it and if the plaintiff establishes that he or other parties are able to command royalties for licensing the use of the name. See *Paramount Pictures Corp. v. Howley* [1991] C.P.R. (3d) 419; (1992) 5 O.R. (3d) 573 ("Crocodile Dundee"), following *Mirage Studios v. Counter-Feat Clothing Co. Ltd.* [1991] F.S.R. 145 where the plaintiff had no existing goodwill or business in merchandising the character in question, although it owned the exploitation rights and had previously engaged in the licensing of merchandise relating to other motion pictures. There was a misrepresentation that the defendant's product was licensed.

The whole area of character merchandising has generated much periodical literature. See "United Kingdom and character rights and merchandising rights today" in (1993) J.B.L. 444; "Character Merchandising" in 13 J.M.L. 229; Burley in [1991] EIPR 227; Chon and Maniatis in [1991] EIPR 253; Elmslie and Lewis in [1992] EIPR 270; Hull in [1991] Ent. L.R. 124.

(xi) Other instances of passing off

Beginning of first paragraph. **Add**: no one is entitled to be protected   **21–45** against confusion as such. Confusion may result from the collision of two independent rights and where that is the case neither party can complain. They must put up with the results of the confusion as one of the misfortunes which occur in life. The protection to which a man is entitled is protection against passing off, which is quite a different thing from mere confusion.

For example, an artist cannot complain if another artist chooses to adopt a similar style or some of its characteristics, except perhaps where some particular characteristic, trick or style has become associated with an artist and another has dishonestly and with intent to deceive so nearly copied it as to lead to confusion. See *Marengo v. Daily Sketch and Daily Graphic Ltd.* [1992] F.S.R. 1, C.A., and (1948) 65 R.P.C. 242, H.L.

NOTE 6. See [1991] Ent L.R. E–13 and 27.

NOTE 10. **Add**: *Conjeso Regulador, etc. v. Mathew Clark & Sons Ltd.* [1992] F.S.R. 525 (sherry).

End of second paragraph. Where Champagne producers complained of the use of the word "Champagne" in connection with a non-alcoholic elder flower cordial made by the defendant, it was held that the dilution of the plaintiffs' reputation by the defendant's use of the word "Champagne" could cause serious damage to the reputation or goodwill attached to the name. The plaintiffs were entitled to be protected against damage by falsehoods which represented that the defendant's goods were of a class or shared the characteristics of a class to which the goodwill attached. Damage to the goodwill was caused by diffusion or dilution: see *Tattinger S.A. v. Allbev Ltd.* [1993] F.S.R. 641.

(xii) "Nom de plume"

End of first sentence. **Add**: The fact that the name in issue is not the   **21–46** plaintiff's true name is no bar to relief: see *The British Diabetic*

Association v. The Diabetic Society Ltd. noted at [1992] I.P.D. 15103 following *Heels v. Stafford Heels* (1927) 44 R.P.C. 299.

NOTE 13. See also *Marengo v. Daily Sketch & Daily Graphic Ltd.* [1992] F.S.R. 1, C.A., and (1948) 65 R.P.C. 242, H.L. The principle that a man may honestly carry on business under his own name also applies to a case where he has carried on business under a nom de plume or any other name he adopts or acquires by reputation.

(xiii) Examples where injunctions granted

21–47   **Add**: "Management Today" and "Security Management Today". *Management Publications Ltd. v. Blenheim Exhibitions Group plc.* [1991] F.S.R. 550 where it was held that the publishers of "Management Today" had an arguable case on the evidence that the defendant's publication using the title "Security Management Today" would lead the public to think that both magazines were published by the same proprietor or that there was some other form of connection, giving rise to some general damage to the plaintiff's reputation.

"What's New in . . . ", "What's New in Training": *Morgan-Grampion plc v. Training Personnel Ltd.* [1992] F.S.R. 267 where an injunction was granted to a plaintiff who published a series of controlled circulation magazines with titles commencing "What's New in . . . " against the defendant's controlled circulation magazine originally entitled "Training Personnel" but then changed to "What's New in Training".

(xiv) Examples where injunctions refused

21–48   "Tamworth Herald", "Tamworth Herald and Post": *Tamworth Herald Company Ltd. v. Thomson Free Newspapers Ltd.* [1991]F.S.R. 337 where it was said that "Herald" was descriptive of a newspaper.

"Gourmet", "BBC Gourmet Good Food": *Advance Magazine Publishing Inc. v. Redwood Publishing Ltd.* [1993] F.S.R. 449.

(xv) Remedies

21–49   After note 53 in the text. **Add**: It is unlikely that in a passing off action damages would be awarded on a royalty basis: see *Dormeuil Freres S.A. v. Fera Glow* [1990] R.P.C. 449.

After note 55 in the text. **Add**: The principles laid down by the House of Lords in *American Cyanamid* apply to passing-off actions as much as to any other application for an interim injunction. Earlier cases, such as *Fellowes & Son v. Fisher* [1976] Q.B. 122 (a restraint of trade case) were decided when the principles of *American Cyanamid* were still being developed. See *The County Sound plc v. Ocean Sound Ltd.* [1991] F.S.R. 367.

Although the *American Cyanamid* principles apply to an application for an interim injunction in a passing-off action, where the action concerns get up, the judge at the interim stage is in a position to compare the rival goods and will often be able to decide that there is no serious question as to confusion which needs a trial to decide it. He can see that there is no real possibility that ordinary, sensible members of the public would be likely to be confused; or he may see that there is no real possibility that the defence will succeed because he can see at once that ordinary, sensible members of the public will be confused. Even if after making all the allowances for further evidence that may be adduced at trial, the judge at the interim stage can see that the trial judge would come to the same conclusion and he may either refuse or grant an injunction accordingly: see *County Sound plc v. Ocean Sound Ltd.* [1991] F.S.R. 367.

The fact that a defendant has changed the name under which he originally sold his product to a name to which the plaintiff objects and may therefore be in a position to change back to the original name pending trial and trade on his existing goodwill, may be an important factor in deciding to grant an injunction. See *Morgan-Grampion plc. v. Training Personnel Ltd.* [1992] F.S.R. 267.

If the effect of an interim injunction will be to force the defendant to change his name pending trial, then prima facie the status quo will not be preserved and an injunction may be refused as less injustice may be caused by withholding it than by granting it. See *Blazer plc v. Yardley & Co. Ltd.* [1992] F.S.R. 501, where the plaintiff had no plans to market immediately under its name in the same area as the objectionable use of the name by the defendant.

3. Malicious Falsehood

A. *Nature of action*

End of first paragraph. **Add**: The essentials of the tort of injurious   **21–50**
falsehood have recently been restated by the Court of Appeal as follows:

(1) Publication by the defendant of a false statement about the plaintiff. The test to be applied is whether a jury could reasonably conclude that the statement was true.

(2) Malicious publication of the statement. Malice will be inferred if it is proved that the words of the statement were calculated to produce damage and that the defendant knew when he published the statement that it was false or was reckless as to whether it was false or not.

(3) Special damage following as a direct and natural result of the publication. If the statement is published in writing and calculated to cause pecuniary damage to the plaintiff, that is sufficient under section 3(1) of the Defamation Act 1952.

See *Kaye v. Robertson* [1991] F.S.R. 62 at 67, followed in *Compaq Computer Corp. v. Dell Computer Corp. Ltd.* [1992] F.S.R. 93 (a case on comparative advertising).

In another recent case, the Court of Appeal emphasised that falsity is an essential ingredient of the tort. The plaintiff must establish the untruth of the statement of which he complains and that the statement was made maliciously. A person who makes a false statement in good faith is not liable. The Court of Appeal also distinguished the action for malicious falsehood from the action for defamation. The latter provides a remedy for words which injure a person's reputation. A false statement may, however, be both defamatory and a malicious falsehood, though damages cannot be recovered twice over for the same loss: *Joyce v. Sengupta* [1993] 1 W.L.R. 337; *C.H.C. Software Cure Ltd. v. Hopkins and Wood* [1993] F.S.R. 241.

B. *Whether necessary to prove damage*

21–51 Penultimate sentence in the text and NOTE 66. **Delete** both, and **substitute**: Damages may not necessarily be limited to financial loss. It has not been settled by authority whether damages for anxiety and distress are recoverable. It has been recognised that, if such damages are not recoverable, the result will be unsatisfactory and productive of injustice in some cases. See *Joyce v. Sengupta* [1993] 1 W.L.R. 337 at 347, 348.

C. *Examples*

21–52 End of second paragraph. **Add**: On an application for an interlocutory injunction to restrain repetition of a trade libel, the court may be faced with a dilemma that there is a serious issue to be tried, namely whether the statement makes injurious falsehoods which the defendant cannot justify, but an injunction would in practice prevent the defendant continuing to publish the statement which he intends to justify. The dilemma may be resolved by applying the *American Cyanamid* principles but taking into account, when considering the balance of justice, the question of interference with freedom of speech. See *Compaq Computer Corp. v. Dell Computer Corp. Ltd.* [1992] F.S.R. 93, following *Consorzio del Prosciutto di Parma v. Marks & Spencer plc* [1991] R.P.C. 351. If an injunction can be framed which will prevent the alleged injurious falsehood, but will not prevent the defendant from making statements which he believes can be justified, there will be no material prejudice to the right of freedom of speech. In the *Compaq* case it was possible to devise an injunction which would prevent the defendant from infringing one of the plaintiff's trade marks, but did not interfere with freedom of speech in advertisements.

The mere fact that the plaintiff's claim can be pleaded in defamation makes no difference unless the court concludes that the plaintiff's principal purpose is in fact to seek damages for defamation. If, however, there is some other serious interest to be protected, such as confidentiality or legal relations with third parties, an injunction will be granted. The court has to balance the right of free speech against the legal or equitable right asserted by the plaintiff: see *Microdata Information Services Ltd. v. Rivendale Ltd.* [1991] F.S.R. 681.

CHAPTER 22

RELATED FORMS OF PROTECTION—3

MORAL RIGHTS

Contents   *Para.*

1. Introduction

A. *Historical*

Droit moral. For an account of the background to the "droit moral" **22–1**
legislation, see Durie in [1991] 2 Ent. L.R. 40.

B. *Chapter IV of the 1988 Act*

For a table listing the Parliamentary debates on these and other
provisions of the 1988 Act, see *post*, Appendix I.

2. Right to be Identified as Author or Director

B. *The Circumstances in which the right exists*

(iii) Adaptations of Literary, Dramatic and Musical Works

22–13   Third sentence. Note the amendment to the definition of adaptation in relation to a computer program made by the Copyright (Computer Programs) Regulations 1992, discussed at *ante*, para. 8–126 *et seq.*

3. Right to Object to Derogatory Treatment of a Work

B. *Derogatory treatment*

22–37   After first sentence. **Add**: In *Morrison Leahy Music Ltd. v. Lightbond Ltd.* [1993] E.M.L.R. 144, the defendant took 10, 32 and 28 seconds from compositions of the plaintiffs' which lasted four minutes, four minutes 30 seconds and three minutes two seconds respectively. In two instances the defendant altered a word in the lyric. This was a "treatment" of the plaintiff's work. It was also arguably a distortion or mutilation of the work (see § 22–38 in the Main Work).

4. False Attribution of Authorship or Directorship

A. *Summary of the position under the 1956 Act*

22–51   Subparagraph (2). **Add**: To qualify as a "literary work", the work must afford sufficient information, instruction or literary enjoyment: *Noah v. Shuba* [1991] F.S.R. 14 at 33 applying *Exxon Corporation v. Exxon Insurance Consultants International Ltd.* [1982] Ch. 119. The following words were held not to constitute a literary work: "Follow clinic procedure for aftercare. If proper procedures are followed, no risk of viral infection can occur."

Subparagraph (7). **Add**: Where words have been added to a plaintiff's work and the whole passage attributed to the plaintiff, the author's rights are infringed. For the purposes of section 43, the "work" is the whole passage, not simply the added words of which the plaintiff was not the author: *Noah v. Shuba* [1991] F.S.R. 14 at 32.

D. *Other causes of action*

NOTE 45. **Add**: *Noah v. Shuba* [1991] F.S.R. 14 at 32.   **22–56**

Add: The assessment of damages for breach of duty should, however, take into account damages awarded for another cause of action (*e.g.* libel) arising out of the same facts: *Noah v. Shuba, ibid.*

5. Right to Privacy of Certain Photographs and Films

A. *General*

First sentence. The Lord Chancellor's Department has made propo-   **22–57**
sals for a new statutory tort of infringement of privacy. In *Kaye v. Robertson* [1991] F.S.R. 62 an actor was photographed in hospital without his consent. The Court of Appeal pointed out the desirability of providing some form of statutory protection for the privacy of individuals.

6. Duration of Moral Rights

E.C. Directive 93/98 for the harmonising of the term of protection of   **22–61**
copyright and certain related rights does not apply to moral rights (see Art. 9).

8. Remedies for Infringement of Moral Rights

See, for example, *Amar Nath Sehgal v. Union of India* (1992; unre-   **22–69**
ported), noted at [1992] 4 Ent. L.R. E-58 (*ex parte* injunction under s.57 of the Indian Copyright Act restraining the causing of further deterioration or damage to mural).

10. Transitional Provisions

B. *Existing works*

22–78 **Add**: In *Morrison Leahy Music Ltd. v. Lightbond Ltd.* [1993] E.M.L.R. 144, a composer entered into a publishing agreement whereby the copyright in certain future compositions was to be vested in the publisher. The court assumed that, for the purposes of Schedule 1, paragraph 23(3), the copyright first vested in the publisher, not in the composer.

CHAPTER 23

RELATED FORMS OF PROTECTION—4

PERFORMERS' RIGHTS AND RECORDING RIGHTS

Contents

1. Introduction

A. *Historical*

NOTE 1. See also Groves in [1990] 6 Ent. L.R. 202 and Sherrard in   **23–1**
[1992] 6 Ent. L.R. 57.

On November 19, 1992, E.C. Directive 92/100 was issued (see *post*,   **23–3A**
para. H–27 *et seq.*). The Directive relates to rental right, lending right
and certain rights relating to copyright in the field of intellectual
property. A consultation paper on the implementation of the Directive
has been published by the Patent Office. By Article 15(1) of the
Directive, Member States are required to bring into force laws,
regulations and administrative provisions necessary to comply with the
Directive not later than July 1, 1994. To date no proposals have been
put forward for the implementation of the Directive.

The object of the Directive is to harmonise protection in the field of
rental and lending rights and also other rights such as those which
belong to performing artists and record producers. The main points to
note in connection with performers' rights are as follows:

(1) The exclusive right to authorise or prohibit rental or lending
belongs to various persons, including performers, in respect of
the fixation of their performances (Art. 2(1)). This is not a right
which performers at present enjoy under the United Kingdom
law. Section 182 of the 1988 Act gives the performer the right to

259

control the making of a recording of his performance, but once an authorised recording has been made of his performance, then the Act gives the performer no right to prevent the rental of that copy (see ss.183 and 184 and §§ 23–37 to 23–41 in the Main Work). At present, therefore, under United Kingdom law the performer is left to stipulate what use may be made of recordings of his performance only as a matter of contract as between himself and the party to whom he gives his consent to the making of the recording. United Kingdom law will therefore need to be changed to accord with this requirement of the Directive.

(2) Those rights may be transferred, assigned or subject to the granting of contractual licences (Art. 2(4)). Under United Kingdom law, performers' rights are capable of being the subject of a grant of a contractual licence, and are transmissible on death of the performer, but are not capable of assignment (s.192 of the 1988 Act and see §§ 23–51 and 23–52 in the Main Work). Amendment will therefore be required to the Act to make such rights assignable.

(3) When a contract concerning film production is concluded, individually or collectively, by performers with a film producer, the performer covered by this contract is presumed, subject to contractual clauses to the contrary, to have transferred his rental right. That is, however, subject to the provisions in Article 4 which concern unwaivable rights to equitable remuneration for the rental. (Arts. 2(5), 4(1) and 4(2)). United Kingdom law will require to be changed to provide for this presumption, since, as stated above, such rights are not at present capable of assignment. Amendment will also be required to provide for the unwaivable right to equitable remuneration for rental in accordance with Article 4(2).

(4) Member States may provide that the signing of a contract concluded between a performer and a film producer concerning the production of a film has the effect of authorising rental, provided that the contract provides for equitable remuneration within the meaning of Article 4 (see Art. 2(7)). As with the point made under (3) above, United Kingdom legislation will require amendment if advantage is to be taken of this provision.

(5) The Directive also provides that Member States shall provide for performers to have the exclusive right to do various other things including the right to authorise or prohibit the fixation of their performances (Art. 6); the exclusive right for performers to authorise or prohibit the direct or indirect reproduction of fixations of their performances (Art. 7); the exclusive right for performers to authorise or prohibit communication to the public of their performances (Art. 8); and also for performers in respect of fixations of their performances, to have the exclusive

right to make available copies to the public by sale or otherwise (the distribution right) (Art. 9). The rights to be provided for under Articles 6, 7 and 8 already exist under United Kingdom law (see §§ 23–36 to 23–41 in the Main Work) and no amendment to the Act is required in these respects. However, the exclusive distribution right to be accorded under Article 9 is not at present a right accorded to performers under United Kingdom law (see the discussion under (1) above), and amendment will be required to give effect to this right.

3. Conditions for Subsistence

A. *General*

For a table listing the Parliamentary debates on these and other provisions of the 1988 Act, see *post*, Appendix I.   **23–21**

NOTE 32.   See S.I. 1994 No. 264 (*post*, para. D–41 *et seq.*) which **23–22** designates countries as enjoying reciprocal protection under Part II of the 1988 Act, revoking the earlier 1993 Order (S.I. 1993 No. 943).

4. Performers' Rights

A. *Qualifying performances of performers*

(vi) Ships, aircraft and hovercraft

Note that section 2 of the Merchant Shipping Act 1988 has been **23–25** repealed by the Merchant Shipping (Registration, etc) Act 1993. See *post*, para. A–165.

B. *Infringement of performers' rights*

(i) Recording

Add: In *Mad Hat Music Ltd. v. Pulse 8 Records Ltd.* [1993] E.M.L.R. 172 **23–37** it was considered, on the wording of section 183(1), that it was "not clear" whether the performer's consent was required not only for the making of the first recording but also for the making of subsequent recordings. It is difficult to see the ground for any doubt on this matter, since in both the cases of the first recording and any subsequent recordings the alleged offender "makes" a recording of the performance. No such point was taken in *Stansfield v. Sovereign Music Ltd.* [1994] E.M.L.R. 224, where the issue was whether a consent granted by a performer could be relied on by an assignee from the record company.

6. Duration of Rights

23–50 **Add**: On October 23, 1993, E.C. Directive 93/98 was issued for harmonising the term of protection of copyright and certain related rights (see *post*, para. H–62 *et seq.*). Article 3(1) of the Directive provides that the rights of performers shall expire 50 years after the date of the performance. If a fixation of the performance is lawfully published or lawfully communicated to the public within this period, the rights shall expire 50 years from the date of the first such publication or the first such communication to the public, whichever is the earlier. In each case the period of 50 years is to be calculated from January 1 of the year following the relevant event (Art. 8; see *post*, para. H–71). Member States are required to bring into force the laws, regulations and administrative provision necessary to comply with the Directive before July 1, 1995.

As regards the duration of performers' rights, therefore, the United Kingdom legislation is in accordance with the requirements of the Directive, and no changes will need to be made in this respect.

8. Consent

B. *Power of Copyright Tribunal*

(i) Jurisdiction

23–58 NOTE 1. For an example of an application under section 190(1)(a), see *Ex parte Sianel Pedwar Cymru* [1993] E.M.L.R. 251 (*Under Milk Wood*).

10. Remedies for Infringement of Rights

(iv) Disposal order

Note that the Trade Marks Act 1938 is prospectively repealed by the   **23–99**
Trade Marks Act 1994 (c. 26).

CHAPTER 24

RELATED FORMS OF PROTECTION—5

DEVICES DESIGNED TO CIRCUMVENT COPY-
PROTECTION AND FRAUDULENT RECEPTION OF
TRANSMISSIONS

Contents *Para.*

1. Devices Designed to Circumvent Copy-Protection

B. *The 1988 Act*

24–3 **Offences under section 296.** The description in the Main Work of section 296 providing for offences is inaccurate. The 1988 Act in several places specifically refers to the commission of certain prohibited acts as being offences, which may be punished by criminal proceedings in the criminal courts: see, for example, in Part I (Copyright), sections 107 to 112, in Part II (Rights in Performances), sections 198 to 202, and in Part IV (Patent Agents and Trade Mark Agents), sections 276 (6) and 283 (6). Elsewhere the Act provides a remedy against certain prohibited acts by giving a right to the appropriate person to take civil proceedings for injunctive relief and damages in respect of the commission of such act. The distinction between creating a criminal offence and a civil cause of action may be important in a number of different respects, not least as to whether the provision is to be interpreted as extending to acts committed outside the United Kingdom (see *per* Staughton L.J. in *BBC Enterprises Limited v. Hi-Tech Xtravision Limited* [1992] R.P.C. 167 at 186, lines 4–10).

In Part VII (Miscellaneous and General) itself, section 297(1) provides for the offence of fraudulently receiving programmes and section 297A provides for the offence of making, importing, selling or hiring unauthorised decoders. The other sections grouped together under this heading of "Devices designed to circumvent copy-protection", namely sections 296, 296A and 298, do not create offences, but are actionable by civil proceedings.

NOTE 17. **Add**: s.296 has been amended by the addition of a new subs. 2A (see *post*, para. A–283), which provides that the prohibited acts specified in s.296 (2)(a) in relation to any device or means designed to circumvent the form of copy-protection employed in relation to a copy of a computer program are to include possessing such a device or means in the course of a business. The amendment was made by the Copyright (Computer Programs) Regulations 1992[1] (see *post*, para. B-279) in order to implement Article 7 (1)(c) of Directive 91/250 on the legal protection of computer programs (see, generally, *ante*, paras. 1–54 and 2–2 and *post*, para. H–14 *et seq.*).

NOTE 21. See, as to the amendments made to s.18(2) by the Copyright (Computer Programs) Regulations 1992, *ante*, para. 8–92.

Relief where offence committed. As to the use of the term offence,   **24–4**
see the comments under *supra*, para. 24–3.

Section 296 not retrospective? As to the use of the term offence, see   **24–5**
the comments under *ante*, para. 24–3.

2. Fraudulent Reception of Transmissions

A. *Position before the 1988 Act*

History. As to the use of the term offence, see the comments under   **24–6**
ante, para. 24–3.

---

[1] (S.I. 1992 No. 3233).

B. *Position under the 1988 Act*

(iii) Apparatus for unauthorised reception of transmissions

24–13   **Offences under section 298.** As to the use of the term offence, see the comments under *ante*, para. 24–3.

    Add: The section is aimed at regulating the conduct in the United Kingdom of makers and sellers of decoding equipment (not at regulating the conduct of television users outside the U.K.) (*BBC Enterprises Limited v. Hi-Tech Xtravision Limited* [1992] R.P.C. 167 at 202, H.L., lines 15–20). It follows that the section can easily be by-passed by decoders being made and sold in other countries (*ibid.*, at 202, lines 38–30).

    The phrase "when they are not entitled to do so" in section 298 (2)(a) and (b) means "not authorised by the provider of the programmes or the sender of the other encrypted transmissions to do so" (*ibid.*, at 203, lines 5–10).

NOTE 46. The House of Lords affirmed the decision of the Court of Appeal in *BBC Enterprises Limited v. Hi-Tech Xtravision Limited* [1992] R.P.C. 167.

24–14   **Relief where offence is committed.** As to the use of the term offence, see the comments under *ante*, para. 24–4.

NOTE 47. **Add**: s. 298(1)(a) is dealing with a person who provides programmes included in a broadcasting or cable service for members of the public or part of it, and who makes charges for the reception of such programmes; s.298(1)(b) is dealing with a person who sends other kinds of transmissions in an encrypted form to one or more persons (but not to the public or part of it) and does not necessarily charge for it (*BBC Enterprises Limited v. Hi-Tech Xtravision Limited* [1992] R.P.C. 167 at 201, lines 24–30).

NOTE 51. **Add**: The problem raised by the phrase "the same rights and remedies . . . as a copyright owner has in respect of an infringement of copyright" was discussed by Scott J. in *BBC Enterprises Limited v. Hi-Tech Xtravision Limited* [1992] R.P.C. 167 at 201, line 24. The Court of Appeal appear not to have encountered the same difficulty with the phrase (see *per* Staughton L.J. at 188, lines 20–30 and *per* Beldam L.J. at 193, lines 44–52). The decision in the House of Lords was concerned only with two points of contention raised on the appeal, and did not address this point.

APPENDICES

Appendix A

UNITED KINGDOM STATUTES SEMICONDUCTOR REGULATIONS, PUBLIC LENDING RIGHT SCHEME

Copyright, Designs and Patents Act 1988

Literary, dramatic and musical works

The definition of "literary work" in section 3(1) has now been amended to read as follows:

  A–6

> "literary work" means any work, other than a dramatic or musical work, which is written, spoken or sung, and accordingly includes—
> (a) a table or compilation,
> (b) a computer program, and
> (c) preparatory design material for a computer program.

See the Copyright (Computer Programs) Regulations 1992 (S.I. 1992 No. 3233), *post*, para. B-279.

Sound recordings and films

Note that the final two lines of the definition of "sound recording" are part of the whole definition and not just of paragraph (b).

  A–8

Infringement by issue of copies to the public

Section 18(2) has been amended and a new subsection (3) added, to read as follows:

  A–21

> "(2) References in this Part to the issue to the public of copies of a work are except where the work is a computer program to the act of putting into circulation copies not previously put into circulation, in the United Kingdom or elsewhere, and not to—
> (a) any subsequent distribution, sale, hiring or loan of those copies, or
> (b) any subsequent importation of those copies into the United Kingdom;
> except that in relation to sound recordings and films the restricted act of issuing copies to the public includes any rental of copies to the public.
> (3) References in this Part to the issue to the public of copies of a work where the work is a computer program are to the act of putting into

269

circulation copies of that program not previously put into circulation in the United Kingdom or any other member State, by or with the consent of the copyright owner, and not to—
  (a) any subsequent distribution, sale, hiring or loan of those copies, or
  (b) any subsequent importation of those copies into the United Kingdom;
except that the restricted act of issuing copies to the public includes any rental of copies to the public."

See The Copyright (Computer Programs) Regulations 1992 (S.I. 1992 No. 3233), *post*, para. B–279.

Infringement by making adaptation or act done in relation to adaptation

A–24   Sections 21(3) and (4) have now been amended to read as follows:

"(3) In this Part "adaptation"—
  (a) in relation to a literary work, other than a computer program, or dramatic work, means—
    (i)   a translation of the work;
    (ii) a version of a dramatic work in which it is converted into a non-dramatic work or, as the case may be, of a non-dramatic work in which it is converted into a dramatic work;
    (iii) a version of the work in which the story or action is conveyed wholly or mainly by means of pictures in a form suitable for reproduction in a book, or in a newspaper, magazine or similar periodical;
  (ab) in relation to a computer program, means an arrangement or altered version of the program or a translation of it;
  (b) in relation to a musical work, means an arrangement or transcription of the work.
  (4) In relation to a computer program a "translation" includes a version of the program in which it is converted into or out of a computer language or code or into a different computer language or code."

See The Copyright (Computer Programs) Regulations, 1992 (S.I. 1992 No. 3233), *post*, para. B-279).

Meaning of "infringing copy"

A–30   Subsection 27(3) has been amended and a new subsection 27(3)(A) has been added as follows:

"(3) Subject to subsection (3A) an article is also an infringing copy if—
  (a) it has been or is proposed to be imported into the United Kingdom, and
  (b) its making in the United Kingdom would have constituted an infringement of the copyright in the work in question, or a breach of an exclusive licence agreement relating to that work.

(3A) A copy of a computer program which has previously been sold in any other member State by or with the consent of the copyright owner, is not an infringing copy for the purposes of subsection (3)."

See The Copyright (Computer Programs) Regulations, 1992 (S.I. 1992 No. 3233), *post*, para. B-279).

Research and private study

A new subsection 29(4) has been added as follows: **A–32**

"(4) It is not fair dealing—
(a) to convert a computer program expressed in a low level language into a version expressed in a higher level language, or
(b) incidentally in the course of so converting the program, to copy it,
(these being acts permitted if done in accordance with section 50B (decompilation))."

See The Copyright (Computer Programs) Regulations, 1992 (S.I. 1992 No. 3233), *post*, para. B-279).

Material communicated to the Crown in the course of public business

Delete: Note at end of paragraph. **Add**: A new subsection (6) was added by the **A–51**
National Health Service and Community Care Act 1990, section 60, Schedule 8, paragraph 3, as follows:

"(6) In this section "the Crown" includes a health service body, as defined in section 60(7) of the National Health Service and Community Care Act 1990, and a National Health Service trust established under Part I of that Act or the National Health Service (Scotland) Act 1978; and the reference in subsection (1) above to public business shall be construed accordingly."

New sections 50A, 50B and 50C have been added after section 50, as follows: **A–53A**

"Computer programs: lawful users

Back up copies

50A.—(1) It is not an infringement of copyright for a lawful user of a copy of a computer program to make any back up copy of it which it is necessary for him to have for the purposes of his lawful use.
(2) For the purposes of this section and sections 50B and 50C a person is a lawful user of a computer program if (whether under a licence to do any acts restricted by the copyright in the program or otherwise), he has a right to use the program.
(3) Where an act is permitted under this section, it is irrelevant whether or not there exists any term or condition in an agreement which purports

to prohibit or restrict the act (such terms being, by virtue of section 296A, void).

Decompilation

50B.—(1) It is not an infringement of copyright for a lawful user of a copy of a computer program expressed in a low level language—
    (a) to convert it into a version expressed in a higher level language, or
    (b) incidentally in the course of so converting the program, to copy it,
(that is, to "decompile" it), provided that the conditions in subsection (2) are met.
    (2) The conditions are that—
    (a) it is necessary to decompile the program to obtain the information necessary to create an independent program which can be operated with the program decompiled or with another program ("the permitted objective"); and
    (b) the information so obtained is not used for any purpose other than the permitted objective.
    (3) In particular, the conditions in subsection (2) are not met if the lawful user—
    (a) has readily available to him the information necessary to achieve the permitted objective;
    (b) does not confine the decompiling to such acts as are necessary to achieve the permitted objective;
    (c) supplies the information obtained by the decompiling to any person to whom it is not necessary to supply it in order to achieve the permitted objective; or
    (d) uses the information to create a program which is substantially similar in its expression to the program decompiled or to do any act restricted by copyright.
    (4) Where an act is permitted under this section, it is irrelevant whether or not there exists any term or condition in an agreement which purports to prohibit or restrict the act (such terms being, by virtue of section 296A, void).

Other acts permitted to lawful users

50C.—(1) It is not an infringement of copyright for a lawful user of a copy of a computer program to copy or adapt it, provided that the copying or adapting—
    (a) is necessary for his lawful use; and
    (b) is not prohibited under any term or condition of an agreement regulating the circumstances in which his use is lawful.
    (2) It may, in particular, be necessary for the lawful use of a computer program to copy it or adapt it for the purpose of correcting errors in it.
    (3) This section does not apply to any copying or adapting permitted under section 50A or 50B."

See The Copyright (Computer Programs) Regulations, 1992 (S.I. 1992 No. 3233), *post*, para. B-279).

Order as to disposal of infringing copy or other article

Section 114(6). This subsection is prospectively amended by the substitution of **A–117** the words "section 19 of the Trade Marks Act 1994" for the words "section 58C of the Trade Marks Act 1938". See section 106(1) and Schedule 4 of the Trade Marks Act 1994 (c. 26).

Jurisdiction of county court and sheriff court

The reference in section 115(1) to section 10(5) should be to section 101(5). **A–118**

The Copyright Tribunal

Section 145(3) has been amended as follows: **A–148**

4"(3) A person is not eligible for appointment as chairman or deputy chairman
  unless—
  (a) he has a 7 year general qualification, within the meaning of section
      71 of the Courts and Legal Services Act 1990;
  (b) he is an advocate or solicitor in Scotland of at least 7 year's standing;
  (c) he is a member of the Bar of Northern Ireland or solicitor of the
      Supreme Court of Northern Ireland of at least 7 year's standing; or
  (d) he has held judicial office."

See the Courts and Legal Services Act 1990, section 71(2) and Schedule 10, paragraph 73.

Membership of the Tribunal

A new subsection 146(3A) is prospectively added by the Judicial Pensions and **A–149** Retirement Act 1993, Schedule 6, paragraph 49, as follows:

"(3A) A person who is the chairman or a deputy chairman of the Tribunal shall vacate his office on the day on which he attains the age of 70 years; but this subsection is subject to section 26(4) to (6) of the Judicial Pensions and Retirement Act 1993 (power to authorise continuance in office up to the age of 75 years)."

British ships, aircraft and hovercraft

Note that section 2 of the Merchant Shipping Act 1988 has been repealed by **A–165** the Merchant Shipping (Registration, etc.) Act 1993. As to what is a British ship for the purposes of the Merchant Shipping Acts, see now section 8(2) and Schedule 3 of the 1993 Act.

Index of defined expressions

A–182   The following further definition has been inserted by amendment.

"lawful user (in sections 50A to 50C) section 50A(2)".

See The Copyright (Computer Programs) Regulations, 1992 (S.I. 1992 No. 3233), *post*, para. B-279).

Order as to disposal of illicit recording

A–207   Subsection 204(4). This subsection is prospectively amended by the substitution of the words "section 19 of the Trade Marks Act 1994" for the words "section 58C of the Trade Marks Act 1938". See section 106(1) and Schedule 4 of the Trade Marks Act 1994 (c.26).

British ships, aircraft and hovercraft

A–213   As to section 2 of the Merchant Shipping Act 1988, see *ante*, para. A–165.

Order as to disposal of infringing articles, &c.

A–234   Subsection 231(6). This subsection is prospectively amended by the substitution of the words "section 19 of the Trade Marks Act 1994" for the words "section 58C of the Trade Marks Act 1938". See section 106(1) and Schedule 4 of the Trade Marks Act 1994 (c.26).

Limitation of costs where pecuniary claim could have been brought in patents county court

A–280   Section 290 is prospectively repealed by the Courts and Legal Services Act 1990, section 125(7) and Schedule 20.

Devices designed to circumvent copy-protection

A–283   A new subsection 296(2A) has been inserted as follows:

"(2A) Where the copies being issued to the public as mentioned in subsection (1) are copies of a computer program, subsection (2) applies as if for the words "or advertises for sale or hire" there were substituted "advertises for sale or hire or possesses in the course of a business"."

See The Copyright (Computer Programs) Regulations, 1992 (S.I. 1992 No. 3233), *post*, para. B-279).

A new section 296A has been inserted by amendment after section 296, as   **A–283A**
follows:

"Computer programs

Avoidance of certain terms

296A.—(1) Where a person has the use of a computer program under an
agreement, any term or condition in the agreement shall be void in so far
as it purports to prohibit or restrict—
   (a) the making of any back up copy of the program which it is necessary
   for him to have for the purposes of the agreed use;
   (b) where the conditions in section 50B(2) are met, the decompiling of
   the program; or
   (c) the use of any device or means to observe, study or test the
   functioning of the program in order to understand the ideas and
   principles which underlie any element of the program.
   (2) In this section, decompile, in relation to a computer program, has
the same meaning as in section 50B."

See The Copyright (Computer Programs) Regulations, 1992 (S.I. 1992 No.
3233), *post*, para. B-279).

SCHEDULE 6

Right only for the benefit of the Hospital

Paragraph 7(3). For "the Charities Act 1960", **substitute**: "the Charities Act   **A–439**
1993". See the Charities Act 1993, Schedule 6, paragraph 30.

SCHEDULE 7

Merchant Shipping Act 1970 (c. 36)

Note that section 87 of the Merchant Shipping Act 1970 was repealed by the   **A–451**
Merchant Shipping (Registration, etc.) Act 1993, section 8(4), Schedule 5.

Tribunals and Inquiries Act 1971 (c. 62)

Paragraph 14 has been repealed by the Tribunals and Inquiries Act 1992,   **A–453**
section 18(2), Schedule 4.

Capital Gains Tax Act 1979 (c. 14)

Paragraph 26 has been repealed by the Taxation of Chargeable Gains Act   **A–462**
1992, section 290, Schedule 12.

Companies Act 1985 (c. 6)

A–467 Paragraph 31 of Schedule 7 is prospectively repealed by the Companies Act 1989, section 213, Schedule 24. Consequential amendments to Part XII of the Companies Act 1985 are made by the Companies Act 1989.

The Design Right (Semiconductor Topographies) Regulations 1989

A–577L   Schedule. **Delete**, and **substitute**:

SCHEDULE

REGULATION (4)2

ADDITIONAL CLASSES OF QUALIFYING PERSONS

PART 1

DESCRIPTIONS OF ADDITIONAL CLASSES

1. British Dependent Territory citizens.

2. Citizens and subjects of any country specified in Part II below.

3. Habitual residents of any country specified in Part II below, the Isle of Man, the Channel Islands or any colony.

4. Firms and bodies corporate formed under the law of, or of any part of, the United Kingdom, Gibraltar, another member State of the European Economic Community or any country specified in Part II below with a place of business within any country so specified at which substantial business activity is carried on.

PART II

SPECIFIED COUNTRIES: CITIZENS, SUBJECTS, HABITUAL RESIDENTS, BODIES CORPORATE AND OTHER BODIES HAVING LEGAL PERSONALITY

Australia

Austria

Finland

French overseas territories (French Polynesia; French Southern and Antarctic Territories; Mayotte; New Caledonia and dependencies; Saint-Pierre and Miquelon; Wallis and Futuna Islands)

Iceland

Japan

Liechtenstein

Norway

Sweden

Switzerland

United States of America

See the Design Right (Semiconductor Topographies) (Amendment) Regulations 1993 (S.I. 1993 No. 2497). Note that Australia had previously been added to Part II and the French overseas territories transferred from Part III to Part II. See the Design Right (Semiconductor Topographies) (Amendment) Regulations 1991 (S.I. 1991 No. 2237). Note further that Finland had previously been transferred from Part III to Part II of the Schedule by the Design Right (Semiconductor Topographies) (Amendment) Regulations 1992 (S.I.1992 No. 400).

The Public Lending Right Scheme 1982 (Commencement of Variations) Order 1990

Further amendments to the Scheme have been made by Statutory Instruments: 1991 No. 2618, 1992 No. 3049 and 1993 No. 3049. These amendments are noted up, *post*, paras. A–661 to A–665.   **A–657**

Authors

Article 4(1)(a)(ii). After the words "whichever is the less", **Add**: the words: **A–661**

", or who is entitled to a royalty payment from the publisher in respect of the book"

In Article 4(2), substitute for subparagraph (b) the following new subparagraphs:
"(b) is evidenced by his entitlement to a royalty payment from the publisher in respect of the book; or
(c) in the case of a book without a title page, is evidenced—

> (i) by his being named elsewhere in the book and in the view of the Registrar his contribution to the book was such that he would have merited a mention on the title page had there been one, or
>
> (ii) by his entitlement to a royalty payment from the publisher in respect of the book; or
>
> (d) is evidenced by a statement, signed by all the other authors of the book in respect of whom the fact that they are authors of the book is evidenced in accordance with paragraphs (a) to (c), that his contribution to the book was such that it is appropriate that he should be treated as an author of the book and the Registrar is satisfied that it is appropriate so to treat him."

In Article 6(2). **Delete**: subparagraph (b).

Determination of the sum due in respect of Public Lending Right

A–664   In Article 46(1)(a), the figure of 1.37p was substituted by the figure of 1.81p with effect from December 18, 1991, by the figure of 1.86p with effect from December 30, 1992 and by the figure of 2.00p with effect from December 30, 1993.

SCHEDULE 1

A–665   In Schedule 1, Part I. **Delete**: paragraph 2, and **substitute**:

> "2. The name of every author (within the meaning of Article 4) and the evidence on which each author relies for the purpose of being treated as an author in accordance with article 4(2)."

Appendix B

UNITED KINGDOM ORDERS

Delete introductory heading: "PRACTICE DIRECTION GENERAL NOTICE".

The Copyright Tribunal Rules 1989

Interpretation

Note the amendments to rule 2(1) made by the Copyright Tribunal (Amendment) Rules 1991 cited at § B-267 in the Main Work. **B–52**

Note the further rules 26A to 26D added by the Copyright Tribunal (Amendment) Rules 1991 cited at § B–267 in the Main Work. **B–76A**

Note the new rules 41A to 41D inserted by the Copyright Tribunal (Amendment) Rules 1991 cited at § B-267 in the Main Work. **B–91A**

SCHEDULE 1 **B–106**

Rule 49

Note that this Schedule was replaced by a new Schedule inserted by the Copyright Tribunal (Amendment) Rules 1991, referred to in the Main Work at § B-268.

The Design Right (Proceedings before Comptroller) Rules 1989   B–167

SCHEDULE 2   Rule 24

With effect from May 11, 1992, a new Schedule 2 has been substituted by the Design Right (Proceedings before Comptroller) (Amendment) Rules 1992 (S.I. 1992 No. 615) as follows:

FEES

1. On reference of dispute (Form 1) under rule 3(1).............................£65
2. On application (Form 2) under rule 7(1)...£40
3. On application (Form 3) under rule 10(1)...£65
4. On application (Form 4) under rule 14(1)...£65

B–208   ## The Copyright (Recording for Archives of Designated Class of Broadcasts and Cable Programmes) (Designated Bodies) (No. 2) Order 1989

This Order has been revoked. The present Order is as follows:

The Copyright (Recording for Archives of Designated Class of Broadcasts and Cable Programmes) (Designated Bodies) Order 1993

(S.I. 1993 No. 74)

Made	*18th January 1993*
Laid before Parliament	*21st January 1993*
Coming into force	*12th February 1993*

The Secretary of State, in exercise of powers conferred upon him by section 75 of the Copyright, Designs and Patents Act 1988 ("the Act"), and upon being satisfied that the bodies designated by this Order are not established or conducted for profit, hereby makes the following Order:

1. This Order may be cited as the Copyright (Recording for Archives of Designated Class of Broadcasts and Cable Programmes) (Designated Bodies) Order 1993 and shall come into force on 12th February 1993.

2. Each of the bodies specified in the Schedule to this Order is designated as a body for which a recording of a broadcast or cable programme of the class designated by article 3 below, or a copy thereof, may be made for the purpose of placing the same in any archive maintained by it.

3. All broadcasts other than encrypted transmissions and all cable programmes are designated as a class for the purposes of section 75 of the Act.

4. The Copyright (Recording for Archives of Designated Class of Broadcasts and Cable Programmes) (Designated Bodies) Order 1991 is hereby revoked.

SCHEDULE   Article 2

DESIGNATED BODIES

The British Film Institute
The British Library
The British Medical Association
The British Music Information Centre
The Imperial War Museum
The Music Performance Research Centre
The National Library of Wales
The Scottish Film Council

Patents County Court (Designation and Jurisdiction) Order 1990   B–233

This Order has been revoked and replaced by:

Patents County Court (Designation and Jurisdiction) Order 1994

Made   *17th June 1994*
Coming into force   *11th July 1994*

The Lord Chancellor, in exercise of the powers conferred on him by section 287 of the Copyright, Designs and Patents Act 1988, hereby makes the following Order:-

Citation and commencment

1. This Order may be cited as the Patents County Court (Designation and Jurisdiction) Order 1994 and shall come into force on 11th July 1994.

Designation as Patents County Court

2. The Central London County Court is hereby designated as a patents county court.

3. As a patents county court, the Central London County Court shall have jurisdiction, subject to article 4 below, to hear and determine any action or matter relating to patents or designs over which the High Court would have jurisdiction, together with any claims or matters ancillary to, or arising from, such proceedings.

4. The jurisdiction conferred by article 3 above shall not include jurisdiction to hear appeals from the comptroller.

Discontinuance and transitional provision

5.—(1) The Edmonton County Court shall cease to be a patents county court and accordingly the Patents County Court (Designation and Jurisdiction) Order 1990 is hereby revoked.

(2) The patents county court at the Central London County Court shall have jurisdiction in proceedings commenced in the patents county court at the Edmonton County Court before the coming into force of this Order.

The Copyright Tribunal (Amendment) Rules 1991

B–267 Rule 50A of the Copyright Tribunal Rules 1989 was revoked by the Copyright Tribunal (Amendment) Rules 1992 (S.I. 1992 No. 467), which explains that Rule 50A was inserted in error.

B–279 # The Copyright (Computer Programs) Regulations 1992

(S.I. 1992 No. 3233)

Made	*16th December 1992*
Coming into force	*1st January 1993*

Whereas a draft of the following Regulations has been approved by resolution of each House of Parliament:

Now, therefore, the Secretary of State, being a Minister designated for the purposes of section 2(2) of the European Communities Act 1972 in relation to measures relating to the protection by copyright of computer programs, in exercise of the powers conferred by section 2(2) and (4) of the said Act of 1972, hereby makes the following Regulations:—

Citation, commencement and extent

1.—(1) These Regulations may be cited as the Copyright (Computer Programs) Regulations 1992 and shall come into force on 1st January 1993.

(2) These Regulations extend to Northern Ireland.

2. The Copyright, Designs and Patents Act 1988 shall be amended as follows.

[The various amendments to the 1988 Act are noted at *ante*, para. A-6 *et seq.*]

Transitional provisions and savings

Computer programs created before 1st January 1993

12.—(1) Subject to paragraph (2), the amendments of the Copyright, Designs and Patents Act 1988 made by these Regulations apply in relation to computer programs created before 1st January 1993 as they apply to computer programs created on or after that date.

(2) Nothing in these Regulations affects any agreement or any term or condition of an agreement where the agreement, term or condition is entered into before 1st January 1993.

Appendix C

COPYRIGHT CONVENTIONS AND AGREEMENTS

AGREEMENT ON TRADE-RELATED ASPECTS OF INTELLECTUAL PROPERTY RIGHTS, INCLUDING TRADE IN COUNTERFEIT GOODS[a]

C–205

TABLE OF CONTENTS

---

[a] Concluded at Geneva on December 15, 1993, GATT document MTN/FA II–AIC.

Part V: Dispute Prevention and Settlement

Part VI: Transitional Arrangements

Part VII: Institutional Arrangements; Final Provisions

C–206   **Members**

Desiring to reduce distortions and impediments to international trade, and taking into account the need to promote effective and adequate protection of intellectual property rights, and to ensure that measures and procedures to enforce intellectual property rights do not themselves become barriers to legitimate trade:

Recognizing, to this end, the need for new rules and disciplines concerning:
(a) the applicability of the basic principles of the GATT 1994 and of relevant international intellectual property agreements or conventions;
(b) the provision of adequate standards and principles concerning the availability, scope and use of trade-related intellectual property rights;
(c) the provision of effective and appropriate means for the enforcement of trade-related intellectual property rights, taking into account differences in national legal systems;
(d) the provision of effective and expeditious procedures for the multilateral prevention and settlement of disputes between governments; and
(e) transitional arrangements aiming at the fullest participation in the results of the negotiations;

Recognizing the need for a multilateral framework of principles, rules and disciplines dealing with international trade in counterfeit goods;

Recognizing that intellectual property rights are private rights;

Recognizing the underlying public policy objectives of national systems for the protection of intellectual property, including developmental and technological objectives;

Recognizing also the special needs of the least-developed country Members in respect of maximum flexibility in the domestic implementation of laws and regulations in order to enable them to create a sound and viable technological base;

Emphasizing the importance of reducing tensions by reaching strengthened commitments to resolve disputes on trade-related intellectual property issues through multilateral procedures;

Desiring to establish a mutually supportive relationship between the MTO and the World Intellectual Property Organization (WIPO) as well as other relevant international organisations;

Hereby agree as follows:

PART I: GENERAL PROVISIONS AND BASIC PRINCIPLES

Article 1
Nature and Scope of Obligations   **C–207**

1.   Members shall give effect to the provisions of this Agreement. Members may, but shall not be obliged to, implement in their domestic law more extensive protection than is required by this Agreement, provided that such protection does not contravene the provisions of this Agreement. Members shall be free to determine the appropriate method of implementing the provisions of this Agreement within their own legal system and practice.

2.   For the purposes of this Agreement, the term "intellectual property" refers to all categories of intellectual property that are the subject of Sections 1 to 7 of Part II.

3.   Members shall accord the treatment provided for in this Agreement to the nationals of other Members.[1] In respect of the relevant intellectual property right, the nationals of other Members shall be understood as those natural or legal persons that would meet the criteria for eligibility for protection provided for in the Paris Convention (1967), the Berne Convention (1971), the Rome Convention and the Treaty on Intellectual Property in Respect of Integrated Circuits, were all Members of the MTO members of those conventions.[2] Any Member availing itself of the possibilities provided in paragraph 3 of Article 5 of paragraph 2 of Article 6 of the Rome Convention shall make a notification as foreseen in those provisions to the Council for Trade-Related Aspects of Intellectual Property Rights.

Article 2
Intellectual Property Conventions   **C–208**

1.   In respect of Parts II, III and IV of this Agreement, Members shall comply with Articles 1–12 and 19 of the Paris Convention (1967).

---

[1] When "nationals" are referred to in this Agreement, they shall be deemed, in the case of a separate customs territory Member of the MTO, to mean persons, natural or legal, who are domiciled or who have a real and effective industrial or commercial establishment in that customs territory.

[2] In this Agreement, "Paris Convention" refers to the Paris Convention for the Protection of Industrial Property: "Paris Convention (1967)" refers to the Stockholm Act of this Convention of 14 July 1967. "Berne Convention" refers to the Berne Convention for the Protection of Literary and Artistic Works: "Berne Convention (1971)" refers to the Paris Act of this Convention of 24 July 1971. "Rome Convention" refers to the International Convention for the Protection of Performers. Producers of Phonograms and Broadcasting Organisations, adopted at Rome on 26 October 1961. "Treaty on Intellectual Property in Respect of Integrated Circuits" (IPIC Treaty) refers to the Treaty on Intellectual Property in Respect of Integrated Circuits, adopted at Washington on 26 May 1989.

2. Nothing in Parts I to IV of this Agreement shall derogate from existing obligations that Members may have to each other under the Paris Convention, the Berne Convention, the Rome Convention and the Treaty on Intellectual Property in Respect of Integrated Circuits.

Article 3
National Treatment

C–209

1. Each Member shall accord to the nationals of other Members treatment no less favourable than that it accords to its own nationals with regard to the protection[3] of intellectual property, subject to the exceptions already provided in, respectively, the Paris Convention (1967), the Berne Convention (1971), the Rome Convention and the Treaty on Intellectual Property in Respect of Integrated Circuits. In respect of performers, producers of phonograms and broadcasting organizations, this obligation only applies in respect of the rights provided under this Agreement. Any Member availing itself of the possibilities provided in Article 6 of the Berne Convention and paragraph 1(b) of Article 16 of the Rome Convention shall make a notification as foreseen in those provisions to the Council for Trade-Related Aspects of Intellectual Property Rights.

2. Members may avail themselves of the exceptions permitted under paragraph 1 above in relation to judicial and administrative procedures, including the designation of an address for service or the appointment of an agent within the jurisdiction of a Member, only where such exceptions are necessary to secure compliance with laws and regulations which are not inconsistent with the provisions of this Agreement and where such practices are not applied in a manner which would constitute a disguised restriction on trade.

Article 4
Most-Favoured-Nation Treatment

C–210

With regard to the protection of intellectual property, any advantage, favour, privilege or immunity granted by a Member to the nationals of any other country shall be accorded immediately and unconditionally to the nationals of all other Members. Exempted from this obligation are any advantage, favour, privilege or immunity accorded by a Member:

 (a) deriving from international agreements on judicial assistance and law enforcement of a general nature and not particularly confined to the protection of intellectual property;

 (b) granted in accordance with the provisions of the Berne Convention (1971) or the Rome Convention authorizing that the treatment accorded

---

[3] For the purposes of Articles 3 and 4 of this Agreement, protection shall include matters affecting the availability, acquisition, scope, maintenance and enforcement of intellectual property rights as well as those matters affecting the use of intellectual property rights specifically addressed in this Agreement.

be a function not of national treatment but of the treatment accorded in another country;

(c) in respect of the rights of performers, producers of phonongrams and broadcasting organizations not provided under this Agreement;

(d) deriving from international agreements related to the protection of intellectual property which entered into force prior to the entry into force of the Agreement Establishing the MTO, provided that such agreements are notified to the Council for Trade-Related Aspects of Intellectual Property Rights and do not constitute an arbitrary or unjustifiable discrimination against nationals of other Members.

Article 5
Multilateral Agreements on Acquisition or Maintenance of Protection **C–211**

The obligations under Articles 3 and 4 above do not apply to procedures provided in multilateral agreements concluded under the auspices of the World Intellectual Property Organization relating to the acquisition or maintenance of intellectual property rights.

Article 6
Exhaustion **C–212**

For the purposes of dispute settlement under this Agreement, subject to the provisions of Articles 3 and 4 above nothing in this Agreement shall be used to address the issue of the exhaustion of intellectual property rights.

Article 7
Objectives **C–213**

The protection and enforcement of intellectual property rights should contribute to the promotion of technological innovation and to the transfer and dissemination of technology, to the mutual advantage of producers and users of technological knowledge and in a manner conducive to social and economic welfare, and to a balance of rights and obligations.

Article 8
Principles **C–214**

1. Members may, in formulating or amending their national laws and regulations, adopt measures necessary to protect public health and nutrition, and to promote the public interest in sectors of vital importance to their socio-economic and technological development, provided that such measures are consistent with the provisions of this Agreement.

2. Appropriate measures, provided that they are consistent with the provisions of this Agreement, may be needed to prevent the abuse of intellectual

property rights by right holders or the resort to practices which unreasonably restrain trade or adversely affect the international transfer of technology.

PART II: STANDARDS CONCERNING THE AVAILABILITY, SCOPE AND USE OF INTELLECTUAL PROPERTY RIGHTS

SECTION 1: COPYRIGHT AND RELATED RIGHTS

C–215

Article 9
Relation to Berne Convention

1.   Members shall comply with Articles 1–21 and the Appendix of the Berne Convention (1971). However, members shall not have rights or obligations under this Agreement in respect of the rights conferred under Article 6*bis* of that Convention or of the rights derived therefrom.

2.   Copyright protection shall extend to expressions and not to ideas, procedures, methods of operation or mathematical concepts as such.

C–216

Article 10
Computer Programs and Compilations of Data

1.   Computer programs, whether in source or object code, shall be protected as literary works under the Berne Convention (1971).

2.   Compilations of data or other material, whether in machine readable or other form, which by reason of the selection or arrangement of their contents constitute intellectual creations shall be protected as such. Such protection, which shall not extend to the data or material itself, shall be without prejudice to any copyright subsisting in the data or material itself.

C–217

Article 11
Rental Rights

In respect of at least computer programs and cinematographic works, a Member shall provide authors and their successors in title the right to authorize or to prohibit the commercial rental to the public of originals or copies of their copyright works. A Member shall be excepted from this obligation in respect of cinematographic works unless such rental has led to widespread copying of such works which is materially impairing the exclusive right of reproduction conferred in that Member on authors and their successors in title. In respect of computer programs, this obligation does not apply to rentals where the program itself is not the essential object of the rental.

Article 12
Term of Protection   C–218

Whenever the term of protection of a work, other than a photographic work or a work of applied art, is calculated on a basis other than the life of a natural person, such term shall be no less than fifty years from the end of the calendar year of authorized publication, or, failing such authorised publication within fifty years from the making of the work, fifty years from the end of the calendar year of making.

Article 13
Limitations and Exceptions   C–219

Members shall confine limitations or exceptions to exclusive rights to certain special cases which do not conflict with a normal exploitation of the work and do not unreasonably prejudice the legitimate interests of the right holder.

Article 14
Protection of Performers, Producers of Phonograms (Sound Recordings) and   C–220
Broadcasting Organizations

1.   In respect of a fixation of their performance on a phonogram, performers shall have the possibility of preventing the following acts when undertaken without their authorization: the fixation of their unfixed performance and the reproduction of such fixation. Performers shall also have the possibility of preventing the following acts when undertaken without their authorization: the broadcasting by wireless means and the communication to the public of their live performance.

2.   Producers of phonograms shall enjoy the right to authorize or prohibit the direct or indirect reproduction of their phonograms.

3.   Broadcasting organizations shall have the right to prohibit the following acts when undertaken without their authorization: the fixation, the reproduction of fixations, and the rebroadcasting by wireless means of broadcasts, as well as the communication to the public of television broadcasts of the same. Where Members do not grant such rights to broadcasting organizations, they shall provide owners of copyright in the subject matter of broadcasts with the possibility of preventing the above acts, subject to the provisions of the Berne Convention (1971).

4.   The provisions of Article 11 in respect of computer programs shall apply *mutatis mutandis* to producers of phonograms and any other right holders in phonograms as determined in domestic law. If, on the date of the Ministerial Meeting concluding the Uruguay Round of Multilateral Trade Negotiations, a Member has in force a system of equitable remuneration of right holders in respect of the rental of phonograms, it may maintain such system provided

that the commercial rental of phonograms is not giving rise to the material impairment of the exclusive rights of reproduction of right holders.

5.   The term of the protection available under this Agreement to performers and producers of phonograms shall last at least until the end of a period of fifty years computed from the end of the calendar year in which the fixation was made or the performance took place. The term of protection granted pursuant to paragraph 3 above shall last for at least twenty years from the end of the calendar year in which the broadcast took place.

6.   Any Member may, in relation to the rights conferred under paragraphs 1–3 above, provide for conditions, limitations, exceptions and reservations to the extent permitted by the Rome Convention. However, the provisions of Article 18 of the Berne Convention (1971) shall also apply, *mutatis mutandis*, to the rights of performers and producers of phonograms in phonograms.

SECTION 2: TRADEMARKS

C–221

Article 15
Protectable Subject Matter

1.   Any sign, or any combination of signs, capable of distinguishing the goods or services of one undertaking from those of other undertakings, shall be capable of constituting a trademark. Such signs, in particular words including personal names, letters, numerals, figurative elements and combinations of colours as well as any combination of such signs, shall be eligible for registration as trademarks. Where signs are not inherently capable of distinguishing the relevant goods or services, Members may make registrability depend on distinctiveness acquired through use. Members may require, as a condition of registration, that signs be visually perceptible.

2.   Paragraph 1 above shall not be understood to prevent a Member from denying registration of a trademark on other grounds, provided that they do not derogate from the provisions of the Paris Convention (1967).

3.   Members may make registrability depend on use. However, actual use of a trademark shall not be a condition for filing an application for registration. An application shall not be refused solely on the ground that intended use has not taken place before the expiry of a period of three years from the date of application.

4.   The nature of the goods or services to which a trademark is to be applied shall in no case form an obstacle to registration of the trademark.

5.   Members shall publish each trademark either before it is registered or promptly after it is registered and shall afford a reasonable opportunity for petitions to cancel the registration. In addition, Members may afford an opportunity for the registration of a trademark to be opposed.

Article 16
Rights Conferred **C–222**

1.   The owner of a registered trademark shall have the exclusive right to prevent all third parties not having his consent from using in the course of trade identical or similar signs for goods or services which are identical or similar to those in respect of which the trademark is registered where such use would result in a likelihood of confusion. In case of the use of an identical sign for identical goods or services, a likelihood of confusion shall be presumed. The rights described above shall not prejudice any existing prior rights, nor shall they affect the possibility of Members making rights available on the basis of use.

2.   Article 6*bis* of the Paris Convention (1967) shall apply, *mutatis mutandis*, to services. In determining whether a trademark is well-known, account shall be taken of the knowledge of the trademark in the relevant sector of the public, including knowledge in that Member obtained as a result of the promotion of the trademark.

3.   Article 6*bis* of the Paris Convention (1967) shall apply, *mutatis mutandis*, to goods or services which are not similar to those in respect of which a trademark is registered, provided that use of that trademark in relation to those goods or services would indicate a connection between those goods or services and the owner of the registered trademark and provided that the interests of the owner of the registered trademark are likely to be damaged by such use.

Article 17
Exceptions **C–223**

Members may provide limited exceptions to the rights conferred by a trademark, such as fair use of descriptive terms, provided that such exceptions take account of the legitimate interests of the owner of the trademark and of third parties.

Article 18
Term of Protection **C–224**

Initial registration, and each renewal of registration, of a trademark shall be for a term of no less than seven years. The registration of a trademark shall be renewable indefinitely.

Article 19
Requirement of Use **C–225**

1.   If use is required to maintain a registration, the registration may be cancelled only after an uninterrupted period of at least three years of non-use,

unless valid reasons based on the existence of obstacles to such use are shown by the trademark owner. Circumstances arising independently of the will of the owner of the trademark which constitute an obstacle to the use of the trademark, such as import restrictions on or other government requirements for goods or services protected by the trademark, shall be recognized as valid reasons for non-use.

2.   When subject to the control of its owner, use of a trademark by another person shall be recognized as use of the trademark for the purpose of maintaining the registration.

Article 20
Other Requirements

C–226

The use of a trademark in the course of trade shall not be unjustifiably encumbered by special requirements, such as use with another trademark, use in a special form or use in a manner detrimental to its capability to distinguish the goods or services of one undertaking from those of other undertakings. This will not preclude a requirement prescribing the use of the trademark identifying the undertaking producing the goods or services along with, but without linking it to, the trademark distinguishing the specific goods or services in question of that undertaking.

Article 21
Licensing and Assignment

C–227

Members may determine conditions on the licensing and assignment of trademarks, it being understood that the compulsory licensing of trademarks shall not be permitted and that the owner of a registered trademark shall have the right to assign his trademark with or without the transfer of the business to which the trademark belongs.

SECTION 3: GEOGRAPHICAL INDICATIONS

Article 22
Protection of Geographical Indications

C–228

1.   Geographical indications are, for the purposes of this Agreement, indications which identify a good as originating in the territory of a Member, or a region or locality in that territory, where a given quality, reputation or other characteristic of the good is essentially attributable to its geographical origin.

2.   In respect of geographical indications, Members shall provide the legal means for interested parties to prevent:

(a) the use of any means in the designation or presentation of a good that indicates or suggests that the good in question originates in a geographical area other than the true place of origin in a manner which misleads the public as to the geographical origin of the good;

(b) any use which constitutes an act of unfair competition within the meaning of Article 10*bis* of the Paris Convention (1967).

3.   A Member shall, *ex officio* if its legislation so permits or at the request of an interested party, refuse or invalidate the registration of a trademark which contains or consists of a geographical indication with respect to goods not originating in the territory indicated, if use of the indication in the trademark for such goods in that member is of such a nature as to mislead the public as to the true place of origin.

4.   The provisions of the preceding paragraphs of this Article shall apply to a geographical indication which, although literally true as to the territory, region or locality in which the goods originate, falsely represents to the public that the goods originate in another territory.

Article 23
Additional Protection for Geographical Indications for Wines and Spirits   **C–229**

1.   Each Member shall provide the legal means for interested parties to prevent use of a geographical indication identifying wines for wines not originating in the place indicated by the geographical indication in question or identifying spirits for spirits not originating in the place indicated by the geographical indication in question, even where the true origin of the goods is indicated or the geographical indication is used in translation or accompanied by expressions such as "kind", "type", "style", "imitation" or the like.[4]

2.   The registration of a trademark for wines which contains or consists of a geographical indication identifying wines or for spirits which contains or consists of a geographical indication identifying spirits shall be refused or invalidated, *ex officio* if domestic legislation so permits or at the request of an interested party, with respect to such wines or spirits not having this origin.

3.   In the case of homonymous geographical indications for wines, protection shall be accorded to each indication, subject to the provisions of paragraph 4 of Article 22 above. Each Member shall determine the practical conditions under which the homonymous indications in question will be differentiated from each other, taking into account the need to ensure equitable treatment of the producers concerned and that consumers are not misled.

4.   In order to facilitate the protection of geographical indications for wines, negotiations shall be undertaken in the Council for Trade-Related Aspects of Intellectual Property Rights concerning the establishment of a multilateral

---

[4] Notwithstanding the first sentence of Article 42, Members may, with respect to these obligations, instead provide for enforcement by administrative action.

system of notification and registration of geographical indications for wines eligible for protection in those Members participating in the system.

Article 24
International Negotiations; Exceptions

1.   Members agree to enter into negotiations aimed at increasing the protection of individual geographical indications under Article 23. The provisions of paragraphs 4–8 below shall not be used by a Member to refuse to conduct negotiations or to conclude bilateral or multilateral agreements. In the context of such negotiations, Members shall be willing to consider the continued applicability of those provisions to individual geographical indications whose use was the subject of such negotiations.

2.   The Council for Trade-Related Aspects of Intellectual Property Rights shall keep under review the application of the provisions of this Section; the first such review shall take place within two years of the entry into force of the Agreement Establishing the MTO. Any matter affecting the compliance with the obligations under these provisions may be drawn to the attention of the Council, which, at the request of a Member, shall consult with any Member or Members in respect of such matter in respect of which it has not been possible to find a satisfactory solution through bilateral or plurilateral consultations between the Members concerned. The Council shall take such action as may be agreed to facilitate the operation and further the objectives of this Section.

3.   In implementing this Section, a Member shall not diminish the protection of geographical indications that existed in that Member immediately prior to the date of entry into force of the Agreement Establishing the MTO.

4.   Nothing in this Section shall require a Member to prevent continued and similar use of a particular geographical indication of another Member identifying wines or spirits in connection with goods or services by any of its nationals or domiciliaries who have used that geographical indication in a continuous manner with regard to the same or related goods or services in the territory of that Member either (a) for at least ten years preceding the date of the Ministerial Meeting concluding the Uruguay Round of Multilateral Trade Negotiations or (b) in good faith preceding that date.

5.   Where a trademark has been applied for or registerèd in good faith, or where rights to a trademark have been acquired through use in good faith either:
   (a) before the date of application of these provisions in that Member as defined in Part VI below; or
   (b) before the geographical indication is protected in its country of origin; measures adopted to implement this Section shall not prejudice eligibility for or the validity of the registration of a trademark, or the right to use a trademark, on the basis that such a trademark is identical with, or similar to, a geographical indication.

6.   Nothing in this Section shall require a Member to apply its provisions in respect of a geographical indication of any other Member with respect to

goods or services for which the relevant indication is identical with the term customary in common language as the common name for such goods or services in the territory of that Member. Nothing in this Section shall require a Member to apply its provisions in respect of a geographical indication of any other member with respect to products of the vine for which the relevant indication is identical with the customary name of a grape variety existing in the territory of that Member as of the date of entry into force of the Agreement Establishing the MTO.

7.   A Member may provide that any request made under this Section in connection with the use or registration of a trademark must be presented within five years after the adverse use of the protected indication has become generally known in that Member or after the date of registration of the trademark in that Member provided that the trademark has been published by that date, if such date is earlier than the date on which the adverse use became generally known in that Member, provided that the geographical indication is not used or registered in bad faith.

8.   The provisions of this Section shall in no way prejudice the right of any person to use, in the course of trade, his name or the name of his predecessor in business, except where such name is used in such a manner as to mislead the public.

9.   There shall be no obligation under this Agreement to protect geographical indications which are not or cease to be protected in their country of origin, or which have fallen into disuse in that country.

SECTION 4: INDUSTRIAL DESIGNS

Article 25
Requirements for Protection

1.   Members shall provide for the protection of independently created industrial designs that are new or original. Members may provide that designs are not new or original if they do not significantly differ from known designs or combinations of known design features. Members may provide that such protection shall not extend to designs dictated essentially by technical or functional considerations.

2.   Each Member shall ensure that requirements for securing protection for textile designs, in particular in regard to any cost, examination or publication, do not unreasonably impair the opportunity to seek and obtain such protection. Members shall be free to meet this obligation through industrial design law or through copyright law.

Article 26
Protection

1.   The owner of a protected industrial design shall have the right to prevent third parties not having his consent from making, selling or importing articles bearing or embodying a design which is a copy, or substantially a copy, of the protected design, when such acts are undertaken for commercial purposes.

2.   Members may provide limited exceptions to the protection of industrial designs, provided that such exceptions do not unreasonably conflict with the normal exploitation of protected industrial designs and do not unreasonably prejudice the legitimate interests of the owner of the protected design, taking account of the legitimate interests of third parties.

3.   The duration of protection available shall amount to at least ten years.

SECTION 5: PATENTS

C–233

Article 27
Patentable Subject Matter

1.   Subject to the provisions of paragraphs 2 and 3 below, patents shall be available for any inventions, whether products or processes, in all fields of technology, provided that they are new, involve an inventive step and are capable of industrial application.[5] Subject to paragraph 4 of Article 65, paragraph 8 of Article 70 and paragraph 3 of this Article, patents shall be available and patent rights enjoyable without discrimination as to the place of invention, the field of technology and whether products are imported or locally produced.

2.   Members may exclude from patentability inventions, the prevention within their territory of the commercial exploitation of which is necessary to protect *ordre public* or morality, including to protect human, animal or plant life or health or to avoid serious prejudice to the environment, provided that such exclusion is not made merely because the exploitation is prohibited by domestic law.

3.   Members may also exclude from patentability:
  (a) diagnostic, therapeutic and surgical methods for the treatment of humans or animals;
  (b) plants and animals other than microorganisms, and essentially biological processes for the production of plants or animals other than non-biological and microbiological processes. However, Members shall provide for the protection of plant varieties either by patents or by an

---

[5]   For the purposes of this Article, the terms "inventive step" and "capable of industrial application" may be deemed by a Member to be synonymous with the terms "non-obvious" and "useful" respectively.

effective *sui generis* system or by any combination thereof. The provisions of this sub-paragraph shall be reviewed four years after the entry into force of the Agreement Establishing the MTO.

Article 28
Rights Conferred

1. A patent shall confer on its owner the following exclusive rights:
    (a) where the subject matter of a patent is a product, to prevent third parties not having his consent from the acts of: making, using, offering for sale, selling, or importing[6] for these purposes that product;
    (b) where the subject matter of a patent is a process, to prevent third parties not having his consent from the act of using the process, and from the acts of: using, offering for sale, selling, or importing for these purposes at least the product obtained directly by that process.

2. Patent owners shall also have the right to assign, or transfer by succession, the patent and to conclude licensing contracts.

Article 29
Conditions on Patent Applicants

1. Members shall require that an applicant for a patent shall disclose the invention in a manner sufficiently clear and complete for the invention to be carried out by a person skilled in the art and may require the applicant to indicate the best mode for carrying out the invention known to the inventor at the filing date or, where priority is claimed, at the priority date of the application.

2. Members may require an applicant for a patent to provide information concerning his corresponding foreign applications and grants.

Article 30
Exceptions to Rights Conferred

Members may provide limited exceptions to the exclusive rights conferred by a patent, provided that such exceptions do not unreasonably conflict with a normal exploitation of the patent and do not unreasonably prejudice the legitimate interests of the patent owner, taking account of the legitimate interests of third parties.

---

[6] This right, like all other rights conferred under this Agreement in respect of the use, sale, importation or other distribution of goods, is subject to the provisions of Article 6 above.

299

Article 31
Other Use Without Authorization of the Right Holder

Where the law of a Member allows for other use[7] of the subject matter of a patent without the authorization of the right holder, including use by the government or third parties authorized by the government, the following provisions shall be respected:

(a) authorization of such use shall be considered on its individual merits;

(b) such use may only be permitted if, prior to such use, the proposed user has made efforts to obtain authorization from the right holder on reasonable commercial terms and conditions and that such efforts have not been successful within a reasonable period of time. This requirement may be waived by a Member in the case of a national emergency or other circumstances of extreme urgency or in cases of public non-commercial use. In situations of national emergency or other circumstances of extreme urgency, the right holder shall, nevertheless, be notified as soon as reasonably practicable. In the case of public non-commercial use, where the government or contractor, without making a patent search, knows or has demonstrable grounds to know that a valid patent is or will be used by or for the government, the right holder shall be informed promptly;

(c) the scope and duration of such use shall be limited to the purpose for which it was authorized, and in the case of semi-conductor technology shall only be for public non-commercial use or to remedy a practice determined after judicial or administrative process to be anti-competitive.

(d) such use shall be non-exclusive;

(e) such use shall be non-assignable, except with that part of the enterprise or goodwill which enjoys such use;

(f) any such use shall be authorized predominantly for the supply of the domestic market of the Member authorizing such use;

(g) authorization for such use shall be liable, subject to adequate protection of the legitimate interests of the persons so authorized, to be terminated if and when the circumstances which led to it cease to exist and are unlikely to recur. The competent authority shall have the authority to review, upon motivated request, the continued existence of these circumstances;

(h) the right holder shall be paid adequate remuneration in the circumstances of each case, taking into account the economic value of the authorization;

(i) the legal validity of any decision relating to the authorization of such use shall be subject to judicial review or other independent review by a distinct higher authority in that Member;

(j) any decision relating to the remuneration provided in respect of such use shall be subject to judicial review or other independent review by a distinct higher authority in that Member;

(k) Members are not obliged to apply the conditions set forth in sub-paragraphs (b) and (f) above where such use is permitted to remedy a practice determined after judicial or administrative process to be

---

[7] "Other use" refers to use other than that allowed under Article 30.

anti-competitive. The need to correct anti-competitive practices may be taken into account in determining the amount of remuneration in such cases. Competent authorities shall have the authority to refuse termination of authorization if and when the conditions which led to such authorization are likely to recur;

(l) where such use is authorized to permit the exploitation of a patent ("the second patent") which cannot be exploited without infringing another patent ("the first patent"), the following additional conditions shall apply:

    (i)   the invention claimed in the second patent shall involve an important technical advance of considerable economic significance in relation to the invention claimed in the first patent;

    (ii) the owner of the first patent shall be entitled to a cross-licence on reasonable terms to use the invention claimed in the second patent; and

    (iii) the use authorized in respect of the first patent shall be non-assignable except with the assignment of the second patent.

Article 32
Revocation/Forfeiture   **C–238**

An opportunity for judicial review of any decision to revoke or forfeit a patent shall be available.

Article 33
Term of Protection   **C–239**

The term of protection available shall not end before the expiration of a period of twenty years counted from the filing date.[8]

Article 34
Process Patents: Burden of Proof   **C–240**

1.   For the purposes of civil proceedings in respect of the infringement of the rights of the owner referred to in paragraph 1(b) of Article 28 above, if the subject matter of a patent is a process for obtaining a product, the judicial authorities shall have the authority to order the defendant to prove that the process to obtain an identical product is different from the patented process. Therefore, Members shall provide, in at least one of the following circumstances, that any identical product when produced without the consent of the patent owner shall, in the absence of proof to the contrary, be deemed to have been obtained by the patented process:

   (a) if the product obtained by the patented process is new;

---

[8] It is understood that those Members which do not have a system of original grant may provide that the term of protection shall be computed from the filing date in the system of original grant.

(b) if there is a substantial likelihood that the identical product was made by the process and the owner of the patent has been unable through reasonable efforts to determine the process actually used.

2.   Any Member shall be free to provide that the burden of proof indicated in paragraph 1 shall be on the alleged infringer only if the condition referred to in sub-paragraph (a) is fulfilled or only if the condition referred to in sub-paragraph (b) is fulfilled.

3.   In the adduction of proof to the contrary, the legitimate interests of the defendant in protecting his manufacturing and business secrets shall be taken into account.

SECTION 6: LAYOUT-DESIGNS (TOPOGRAPHIES) OF INTEGRATED CIRCUITS

C–241

Article 35
Relation to IPIC Treaty

Members agree to provide protection to the layout-designs (topographies) of integrated circuits (hereinafter referred to as "layout-designs") in accordance with Articles 2–7 (other than paragraph 3 of Article 6), Article 12 and paragraph 3 of Article 16 of the Treaty on Intellectual Property in Respect of Integrated Circuits and, in addition, to comply with the following provisions.

C–242

Article 36
Scope of the Protection

Subject to the provisions of paragraph 1 of Article 37 below, Members shall consider unlawful the following acts if performed without the authorization of the right holder:[9] importing, selling, or otherwise distributing for commercial purposes a protected layout-design, an integrated circuit in which a protected layout-design is incorporated, or an article incorporating such an integrated circuit only insofar as it continues to contain an unlawfully reproduced layout-design.

C–243

Article 37
Acts not Requiring the Authorization of the Right Holder

1.   Notwithstanding Article 36 above, no Member shall consider unlawful the performance of any of the acts referred to in that Article in respect of an

---

[9] The term "right holder" in this Section shall be understood as having the same meaning as the term "holder of the right" in the IPIC Treaty.

integrated circuit incorporating an unlawfully reproduced layout-design or any article incorporating such an integrated circuit where the person performing or ordering such acts did not know and had no reasonable ground to know, when acquiring the integrated circuit or article incorporating such an integrated circuit, that it incorporated an unlawfully reproduced layout-design. Members shall provide that, after the time that such person has received sufficient notice that the layout-design was unlawfully reproduced, he may perform any of the acts with respect to the stock on hand or ordered before such time, but shall be liable to pay to the right holder a sum equivalent to a reasonable royalty such as would be payable under a freely negotiated licence in respect of such a layout-design.

2.   The conditions set out in sub-paragraphs (a)-(k) of Article 31 above shall apply *mutatis mutandis* in the event of any non-voluntary licensing of a layout-design or of its use by or for the government without the authorization of the right holder.

Article 38
Term of Protection

C–244

1.   In Members requiring registration as a condition of protection, the term of protection of layout-designs shall not end before the expiration of a period of ten years counted from the date of filing an application for registration or from the first commercial exploitation wherever in the world it occurs.

2.   In Members not requiring registration as a condition for protection, layout-designs shall be protected for a term of no less than ten years from the date of the first commercial exploitation wherever in the world it occurs.

3.   Notwithstanding paragraphs 1 and 2 above, a Member may provide that protection shall lapse fifteen years after the creation of the layout-design.

SECTION 7: PROTECTION OF UNDISCLOSED INFORMATION

Article 39

C–245

1. In the course of ensuring effective protection against unfair competition as provided in Article 10*bis* of the Paris Convention (1967), Members shall protect undisclosed information in accordance with paragraph 2 below and data submitted to governments or governmental agencies in accordance with paragraph 3 below.

2.   Natural and legal persons shall have the possibility of preventing information lawfully within their control from being disclosed to, acquired by,

or used by others without their consent in a manner contrary to honest commercial practices[10] so long as such information:
  — is secret in the sense that it is not, as a body or in the precise configuration and assembly of its components, generally known among or readily accessible to persons within the circles that normally deal with the kind of information in question;
  — has commercial value because it is secret; and
  — has been subject to reasonable steps under the circumstances, by the person lawfully in control of the information, to keep it secret.

3.   Members, when requiring, as a condition of approving the marketing of pharmaceutical or of agricultural chemical products which utilize new chemical entities, the submission of undisclosed test or other data, the origination of which involves a considerable effort, shall protect such data against unfair commercial use. In addition, Members shall protect such data against disclosure, except where necessary to protect the public, or unless steps are taken to ensure that the data are protected against unfair commercial use.

SECTION 8: CONTROL OF ANTI-COMPETITIVE PRACTICES IN CONTRACTUAL LICENCES

C–246   *Article 40*

1.   Members agree that some licensing practices or conditions pertaining to intellectual property rights which restrain competition may have adverse effects on trade and may impede the transfer and dissemination of technology.

2.   Nothing in this Agreement shall prevent Members from specifying in their national legislation licensing practices or conditions that may in particular cases constitute an abuse of intellectual property rights having an adverse effect on competition in the relevant market. As provided above, a Member may adopt, consistently with the other provisions of this Agreement, appropriate measures to prevent or control such practices, which may include for example exclusive grantback conditions, conditions preventing challenges to validity and coercive package licensing, in the light of the relevant laws and regulations of that Member.

3.   Each Member shall enter, upon request, into consultations with any other Member which has cause to believe that an intellectual property right owner that is a national or domiciliary of the Member to which the request for consultations has been addressed is undertaking practices in violation of the requesting Member's laws and regulations on the subject matter of this

---

[10] For the purpose of this provision, "a manner contrary to honest commercial practices" shall mean at least practices such as breach of contract, breach of confidence and inducement to breach, and includes the acquisition of undisclosed information by third parties who knew, or were grossly negligent in failing to know, that such practices were involved in the acquisition.

Section, and which wishes to secure compliance with such legislation, without prejudice to any action under the law and to the full freedom of an ultimate decision of either Member. The Member addressed shall accord full and sympathetic consideration to, and shall afford adequate opportunity for, consultations with the requesting Member, and shall co-operate through supply of publicly available non-confidential information of relevance to the matter in question and of other information available to the Member, subject to domestic law and to the conclusion of mutually satisfactory agreements concerning the safeguarding of its confidentiality by the requesting Member.

4.   A Member whose nationals or domiciliaries are subject to proceedings in another Member concerning alleged violation of that other Member's laws and regulations on the subject matter of this Section shall, upon request, be granted an opportunity for consultations by the other Member under the same conditions as those foreseen in paragraph 3 above.

PART III: ENFORCEMENT OF INTELLECTUAL PROPERTY RIGHTS

SECTION 1: GENERAL OBLIGATIONS

Article 41   **C–247**

1.   Members shall ensure that enforcement procedures as specified in this Part are available under their national laws so as to permit effective action against any act of infringement of intellectual property rights covered by this Agreement, including expeditious remedies to prevent infringements and remedies which constitute a deterrent to further infringements. These procedures shall be applied in such a manner as to avoid the creation of barriers to legitimate trade and to provide for safeguards against their abuse.

2.   Procedures concerning the enforcement of intellectual property rights shall be fair and equitable. They shall not be unnecessarily complicated or costly, or entail unreasonable time-limits or unwarranted delays.

3.   Decisions on the merits of a case shall preferably be in writing and reasoned. They shall be made available at least to the parties to the proceeding without undue delay. Decisions on the merits of a case shall be based only on evidence in respect of which parties were offered the opportunity to be heard.

4.   Parties to a proceeding shall have an opportunity for review by a judicial authority of final administrative decisions and, subject to jurisdictional provisions in national laws concerning the importance of a case, of at least the legal aspects of initial judicial decisions on the merits of a case. However, there shall be no obligation to provide an opportunity for review of acquittals in criminal cases.

5.   It is understood that this Part does not create any obligation to put in place a judicial system for the enforcement of intellectual property rights distinct

from that for the enforcement of laws in general, nor does it affect the capacity of Members to enforce their laws in general. Nothing in this Part creates any obligation with respect to the distribution of resources as between enforcement of intellectual property rights and the enforcement of laws in general.

SECTION 2: CIVIL AND ADMINISTRATIVE PROCEDURES AND REMEDIES

Article 42
C–248   *Fair and Equitable Procedures*

Members shall make available to right holders[11] civil judicial procedures concerning the enforcement of any intellectual property right covered by this Agreement. Defendants shall have the right to written notice which is timely and contains sufficient detail, including the basis of the claims. Parties shall be allowed to be represented by independent legal counsel, and procedures shall not impose overly burdensome requirements concerning mandatory personal appearances. All parties to such procedures shall be duly entitled to substantiate their claims and to present all relevant evidence. The procedure shall provide a means to identify and protect confidential information, unless this would be contrary to existing constitutional requirements.

Article 43
C–249   *Evidence of Proof*

1.   The judicial authorities shall have the authority, where a party has presented reasonably available evidence sufficient to support its claims and has specified evidence relevant to substantiation of its claims which lies in the control of the opposing party, to order that this evidence be produced by the opposing party, subject in appropriate cases to conditions which ensure the protection of confidential information.

2.   In cases in which a party to a proceeding voluntarily and without good reason refuses access to, or otherwise does not provide necessary information within a reasonable period, or significantly impedes a procedure relating to an enforcement action, a Member may accord judicial authorities the authority to make preliminary and final determinations, affirmative or negative, on the basis of the information presented to them, including the complaint or the allegation presented by the party adversely affected by the denial of access to information, subject to providing the parties an opportunity to be heard on the allegations or evidence.

---

[11] For the purpose of this Part, the term "right holder" includes federations and associations having legal standing to assert such rights.

Article 44
Injunctions   C–250

1.   The judicial authorities shall have the authority to order a party to desist from an infringement, *inter alia* to prevent the entry into the channels of commerce in their jurisdiction of imported goods that involve the infringement of an intellectual property right, immediately after customs clearance of such goods. Members are not obliged to accord such authority in respect of protected subject-matter acquired or ordered by a person prior to knowing or having reasonable grounds to know that dealing in such subject-matter would entail the infringement of an intellectual property right.

2.   Notwithstanding the other provisions of this Part and provided that the provisions of Part II specifically addressing use by governments, or by third parties authorized by a government, without the authorization of the right holder are complied with, Members may limit the remedies available against such use to payment of remuneration in accordance with sub-paragraph (h) of Article 31 above. In other cases, the remedies under this Part shall apply or, where these remedies are inconsistent with national law, declaratory judgments and adequate compensation shall be available.

Article 45
Damages   C–251

1.   The judicial authorities shall have the authority to order the infringer to pay the right holder damages adequate to compensate for the injury the right holder has suffered because of an infringement of his intellectual property right by an infringer who knew or had reasonable grounds to know that he was engaged in infringing activity.

2.   The judicial authorities shall also have the authority to order the infringer to pay the right holder expenses, which may include appropriate attorney's fees. In appropriate cases, Members may authorize the judicial authorities to order recovery of profits and/or payment of pre-established damages even where the infringer did not know or had no reasonable grounds to know that he was engaged in infringing activity.

Article 46
Other Remedies   C–252

In order to create an effective deterrent to infringement, the judicial authorities shall have the authority to order that goods that they have found to be infringing be, without compensation of any sort, disposed of outside the channels of commerce in such a manner as to avoid any harm caused to the right holder, or, unless this would be contrary to existing constitutional requirements, destroyed. The judicial authorities shall also have the authority to order that materials and implements the predominant use of which has been in the creation of the infringing goods be, without compensation of any sort, disposed of outside the channels of commerce in such a manner as to minimize the risks of further infringements. In considering such requests, the need for proportionality between the seriousness of the infringement and the remedies ordered as well as the interests of third parties shall be taken into account. In regard to counterfeit trademark goods, the simple removal of the trademark unlawfully affixed shall not be sufficient, other than in exceptional cases, to permit release of the goods into the channels of commerce.

Article 47
Right of Information

C–253

Members may provide that the judicial authorities shall have the authority, unless this would be out of proportion to the seriousness of the infringement, to order the infringer to inform the right holder of the identity of third persons involved in the production and distribution of the infringing goods or services and of their channels of distribution.

Article 48
Indemnification of the Defendant

C–254

1.   The judicial authorities shall have the authority to order a party at whose request measures were taken and who has abused enforcement procedures to provide to a party wrongfully enjoined or restrained adequate compensation for the injury suffered because of such abuse. The judicial authorities shall also have the authority to order the applicant to pay the defendant expenses, which may include appropriate attorney's fees.

2.   In respect of the administration of any law pertaining to the protection or enforcement of intellectual property rights, Members shall only exempt both public authorities and officials from liability to appropriate remedial measures where actions are taken or intended in good faith in the course of the administration of such laws.

Article 49
Administrative Procedures

C–255

To the extent that any civil remedy can be ordered as a result of administrative procedures on the merits of a case, such procedures shall conform to principles equivalent in substance to those set forth in this Section.

SECTION 3: PROVISIONAL MEASURES

Article 50 **C–256**

1. The judicial authorities shall have the authority to order prompt and effective provisional measures:
    (a) to prevent an infringement of any intellectual property right from occurring, and in particular to prevent the entry into the channels of commerce in their jurisdiction of goods, including imported goods immediately after customs clearance;
    (b) to preserve relevant evidence in regard to the alleged infringement.

2. The judicial authorities shall have the authority to adopt provisional measures *inaudita altera parte* where appropriate, in particular where any delay is likely to cause irreparable harm to the right holder, or where there is a demonstrable risk of evidence being destroyed.

3. The judicial authorities shall have the authority to require the applicant to provide any reasonably available evidence in order to satisfy themselves with a sufficient degree of certainty that the applicant is the right holder and that his right is being infringed or that such infringement is imminent, and to order the applicant to provide a security or equivalent assurance sufficient to protect the defendant and to prevent abuse.

4. Where provisional measures have been adopted *inaudita altera parte*, the parties affected shall be given notice, without delay after the execution of the measures at the latest. A review, including a right to be heard, shall take place upon request of the defendant with a view to deciding, within a reasonable period after the notification of the measures, whether these measures shall be modified, revoked or confirmed.

5. The applicant may be required to supply other information necessary for the identification of the goods concerned by the authority that will execute the provisional measures.

6. Without prejudice to paragraph 4 above, provisional measures taken on the basis of paragraphs 1 and 2 above shall, upon request by the defendant, be revoked or otherwise cease to have effect, if proceedings leading to a decision on the merits of the case are not initiated within a reasonable period, to be determined by the judicial authority ordering the measures where national law so permits or, in the absence of such a determination, not to exceed twenty working days or thirty-one calendar days, whichever is the longer.

7. Where the provisional measures are revoked or where they lapse due to any act or omission by the applicant, or where it is subsequently found that there has been no infringement or threat of infringement of an intellectual property right, the judicial authorities shall have the authority to order the applicant, upon request of the defendant, to provide the defendant appropriate compensation for any injury caused by these measures.

8.   To the extent that any provisional measure can be ordered as a result of administrative procedures, such procedures shall conform to principles equivalent in substance to those set forth in this Section.

SECTION 4: SPECIAL REQUIREMENTS RELATED TO BORDER MEASURES[12]

C–257

Article 51
Suspension of Release by Customs Authorities

Members shall, in conformity with the provisions set out below, adopt procedures[13] to enable a right holder, who has valid grounds for suspecting that the importation of counterfeit trademark or pirated copyright goods[14] may take place, to lodge an application in writing with competent authorities, administrative or judicial, for the suspension by the customs authorities of the release into free circulation of such goods. Members may enable such an application to be made in respect of goods which involve other infringements of intellectual property rights, provided that the requirements of this Section are met. Members may also provide for corresponding procedures concerning the suspension by the customs authorities of the release of infringing goods destined for exportation from their territories.

C–258

Article 52
Application

Any right holder initiating the procedures under Article 51 above shall be required to provide adequate evidence to satisfy the competent authorities that, under the laws of the country of importation, there is *prima facie* an

---

[12] Where a Member has dismantled substantially all controls over movement of goods across its border with another member with which it forms part of a customs union, it shall not be required to apply the provisions of this Section at that border.

[13] It is understood that there shall be no obligation to apply such procedures to imports of goods put on the market in another country by or with the consent of the right holder, or to goods in transit.

[14] For the purposes of this Agreement:
  — counterfeit trademark goods shall mean any goods, including packaging, bearing without authorization a trademark which is identical to the trademark validly registered in respect of such goods, or which cannot be distinguished in its essential aspects from such a trademark, and which thereby infringes the rights of the owner of the trademark in question under the law of the country of importation;
  — pirated copyright goods shall mean any goods which are copies made without the consent of the right holder or person duly authorized by him in the country of production and which are made directly or indirectly from an article where the making of that copy would have constituted an infringement of a copyright or a related right under the law of the country of importation.

infringement of his intellectual property right and to supply a sufficiently detailed description of the goods to make them readily recognizable by the customs authorities. The competent authorities shall inform the applicant within a reasonable period whether they have accepted the application and, where determined by the competent authorities, the period for which the customs authorities will take action.

Article 53
Security or Equivalent Assurance

C–259

1.   The competent authorities shall have the authority to require an applicant to provide a security or equivalent assurance sufficient to protect the defendant and the competent authorities and to prevent abuse. Such security or equivalent assurance shall not unreasonably deter recourse to these procedures.

2.   Where pursuant to an application under this Section the release of goods involving industrial designs, patents, layout-designs or undisclosed information into free circulation has been suspended by customs authorities on the basis of a decision other than by a judicial or other independent authority, and the period provided for in Article 55 has expired without the granting of provisional relief by the duly empowered authority, and provided that all other conditions for importation have been complied with, the owner, importer, or consignee of such goods shall be entitled to their release on the posting of a security in an amount sufficient to protect the right holder for any infringement. Payment of such security shall not prejudice any other remedy available to the right holder, it being understood that the security shall be released if the right holder fails to pursue his right of action within a reasonable period of time.

Article 54
Notice of Suspension

C–260

The importer and the applicant shall be promptly notified of the suspension of the release of goods according to Article 51 above.

Article 55
Duration of Suspension

C–261

If, within a period not exceeding ten working days after the applicant has been served notice of the suspension, the customs authorities have not been informed that proceedings leading to a decision on the merits of the case have been initiated by a party other than the defendant, or that the duly empowered authority has taken provisional measures prolonging the suspension of the release of the goods, the goods shall be released, provided that all other conditions for importation or exportation have been complied with; in appropriate cases, this time-limit may be extended by another ten working days. If proceedings leading to a decision on the merits of the case have been initiated, a review, including a right to be heard, shall take place upon request of the defendant with a view to deciding, within a reasonable period, whether these measures shall be modified, revoked or confirmed. Notwithstanding the above, where the suspension of the release of goods is carried out or continued in accordance with a provisional judicial measure, the provisions of Article 50, paragraph 6 above shall apply.

C–262

Article 56

Indemnification of the Importer and of the Owner of the Goods

Relevant authorities shall have the authority to order the applicant to pay the importer, the consignee and the owner of the goods appropriate compensation for any injury caused to them through the wrongful detention of goods or through the detention of goods released pursuant to Article 55 above.

C–263

Article 57

Right of Inspection and Information

Without prejudice to the protection of confidential information, Members shall provide the competent authorities the authority to give the right holder sufficient opportunity to have any product detained by the customs authorities inspected in order to substantiate his claims. The competent authorities shall also have authority to give the importer an equivalent opportunity to have any such product inspected. Where a positive determination has been made on the merits of a case, Members may provide the competent authorities the authority to inform the right holder of the names and addresses of the consignor, the importer and the consignee and of the quantity of the goods in question.

C–264

Article 58

Ex Officio Action

Where Members require competent authorities to act upon their own initiative and to suspend the release of goods in respect of which they have acquired *prima facie* evidence that an intellectual property right is being infringed:

(a) the competent authorities may at any time seek from the right holder any information that may assist them to exercise these powers:

(b) the importer and the right holder shall be promptly notified of the suspension. Where the importer has lodged an appeal against the suspension with the competent authorities, the suspension shall be subject to the conditions, *mutatis mutandis*, set out at Article 55 above;

(b) Members shall only exempt both public authorities and officials from liability to appropriate remedial measures where actions are taken or intended in good faith.

Article 59
Remedies

Without prejudice to other rights of action open to the right holder and subject to the right of the defendant to seek review by a judicial authority, competent authorities shall have the authority to order the destruction or disposal of infringing goods in accordance with the principles set out in Article 46 above. In regard to counterfeit trademark goods, the authorities shall not allow the re-exportation of the infringing goods in an unaltered state or subject them to a different customs procedure, other than in exceptional circumstances.

Article 60
De Minimis Imports

Members may exclude from the application of the above provisions small quantities of goods of a non-commercial nature contained in travellers' personal luggage or sent in small consignments.

SECTION 5: CRIMINAL PROCEDURES

Article 61

Members shall provide for criminal procedures and penalties to be applied at least in cases of wilful trademark counterfeiting or copyright piracy on a commercial scale. Remedies available shall include imprisonment and/or monetary fines sufficient to provide a deterrent, consistently with the level of penalties applied for crimes of a corresponding gravity. In appropriate cases, remedies available shall also include the seizure, forfeiture and destruction of the infringing goods and of any materials and implements the predominant use of which has been in the commission of the offence. Members may provide for criminal procedures and penalties to be applied in other cases of infringement of intellectual property rights, in particular where they are committed wilfully and on a commercial scale.

PART IV: ACQUISITION AND MAINTENANCE OF INTELLECTUAL PROPERTY RIGHTS AND RELATED INTER-PARTES PROCEDURES

Article 62

1.   Members may require, as a condition of the acquisition or maintenance of the intellectual property rights provided for under Sections 2–6 of Part II of this Agreement, compliance with reasonable procedures and formalities. Such

313

procedures and formalities shall be consistent with the provisions of this Agreement.

2.   Where the acquisition of an intellectual property right is subject to the right being granted or registered, Members shall ensure that the procedures for grant or registration, subject to compliance with the substantive conditions for acquisition of the right, permit the granting or registration of the right within a reasonable period of time so as to avoid unwarranted curtailment of the period of protection.

3.   Article 4 of the Paris Convention (1967) shall apply *mutatis mutandis* to service marks.

4.   Procedures concerning the acquisition or maintenance of intellectual property rights and, where the national law provides for such procedures, administrative revocation and *inter partes* procedures such as opposition, revocation and cancellation, shall be governed by the general principles set out in paragraphs 2 and 3 of Article 41.

5.   Final administrative decisions in any of the procedures referred to under paragraph 4 above shall be subject to review by a judicial or quasi-judicial authority. However, there shall be no obligation to provide an opportunity for such review of decisions in cases of unsuccessful opposition or administrative revocation, provided that the grounds for such procedures can be the subject of invalidation procedures.

PART V: DISPUTE PREVENTION AND SETTLEMENT

Article 63
C–269
Transparency

1.   Laws and regulations, and final judicial decisions and administrative rulings of general application, made effective by any Member pertaining to the subject matter of this Agreement (the availability, scope, acquisition, enforcement and prevention of the abuse of intellectual property rights) shall be published, or where such publication is not practicable made publicly available, in a national language, in such a manner as to enable governments and right holders to become acquainted with them. Agreements concerning the subject matter of this Agreement which are in force between the government or a governmental agency of any Member and the government or a governmental agency of any other Member shall also be published.

2.   Members shall notify the laws and regulations referred to in paragraph 1 above to the Council for Trade-Related Aspects of Intellectual Property Rights in order to assist that Council in its review of the operation of this Agreement. The Council shall attempt to minimize the burden on Members in carrying out this obligation and may decide to waive the obligation to notify such laws and regulations directly to the Council if consultations with the World Intellectual Property Organization on the establishment of a common register containing

these laws and regulations are successful. The Council shall also consider in this connection any action required regarding notifications pursuant to the obligations under this Agreement stemming from the provisions of Article 6*ter* of the Paris Convention (1967).

3. Each Member shall be prepared to supply, in response to a written request from another Member, information of the sort referred to in paragraph 1 above. A Member, having reason to believe that a specific judicial decision or administrative ruling or bilateral agreement in the area of intellectual property rights affects its rights under this Agreement, may also request in writing to be given access to or be informed in sufficient detail of such specific judicial decisions or administrative rulings or bilateral agreements.

4. Nothing in paragraphs 1 to 3 above shall require Members to disclose confidential information which would impede law enforcement or otherwise be contrary to the public interest or would prejudice the legitimate commercial interests of particular enterprises, public or private.

Article 64
Dispute Settlement

C–270

1. The provisions of Articles XXII and XXIII of the General Agreement on Tariffs and Trade 1994 as elaborated and applied by the Understanding on Rules and Procedures Governing the Settlement of Disputes shall apply to consultations and the settlement of disputes under this Agreement except as otherwise specifically provided herein.

2. Sub-paragraphs XXIII: 1(b) and XXIII:1(c) of the General Agreement on Tariffs and Trade 1994 shall not apply to the settlement of disputes under this Agreement for a period of five years from the entry into force of the Agreement establishing the Multilateral Trade Organization.

3. During the time period referred to in paragraph 2, the TRIPS Council shall examine the scope and modalities for Article XXIII:1(b) and Article XXIII:1(c)-type complaints made pursuant to this Agreement, and submit its recommendations to the Ministerial Conference for approval. Any decision of the Ministerial Conference to approve such recommendations or to extend the period in paragraph 2 shall be made only by consensus, and approved recommendations shall be effective for all Members without further formal acceptance process.

PART VI: TRANSITIONAL ARRANGEMENTS

Article 65
Transitional Arrangements

C–271

1. Subject to the provisions of paragraphs 2, 3 and 4 below, no Member shall be obliged to apply the provisions of this Agreement before the expiry of a

general period of one year following the date of entry into force of the Agreement Establishing the MTO.

2.   Any developing country Member is entitled to delay for a further period of four years the date of application, as defined in paragraph 1 above, of the provisions of this Agreement other than Articles 3, 4 and 5 of Part I.

3.   Any other Member which is in the process of transformation from a centrally-planned into a market, free-enterprise economy and which is undertaking structural reform of its intellectual property system and facing special problems in the preparation and implementation of intellectual property laws, may also benefit from a period of delay as foreseen in paragraph 2 above.

4.   To the extent that a developing country Member is obliged by this Agreement to extend product patent protection to areas of technology not so protectable in its territory on the general date of application of this Agreement for that member, as defined in paragraph 2 above, it may delay the application of the provisions on product patents of Section 5 of Part II of this Agreement to such areas of technology for an additional period of five years.

5.   Any Member availing itself of a transitional period under paragraphs 1, 2, 3 or 4 above shall ensure that any changes in its domestic laws, regulations and practice made during that period do not result in a lesser degree of consistency with the provisions of this Agreement.

C–272

Article 66
Least-Developed Country Members

1.   In view of their special needs and requirements, their economic, financial and administrative constraints, and their need for flexibility to create a viable technological base, least-developed country Members shall not be required to apply the provisions of this Agreement, other than Articles 3, 4 and 5, for a period of 10 years from the date of application as defined under paragraph 1 of Article 65 above. The Council shall, upon duly motivated request by a least-developed country Member, accord extensions of this period.

2.   Developed country Members shall provide incentives to enterprises and institutions in their territories for the purpose of promoting and encouraging technology transfer to least-developed country Members in order to enable them to create a sound and viable technological base.

C–273

Article 67
Technical Cooperation

In order to facilitate the implementation of this Agreement, developed country Members shall provide, on request and on mutually agreed terms and conditions, technical and financial cooperation in favour of developing and least-developed country Members. Such cooperation shall include assistance in the preparation of domestic legislation on the protection and enforcement of intellectual property rights as well as on the prevention of their abuse, and shall include support regarding the establishment or reinforcement of domestic offices and agencies relevant to these matters, including the training of personnel.

PART VII: INSTITUTIONAL ARRANGEMENTS; FINAL PROVISIONS

Article 68
Council for Trade-Related Aspects of Intellectual Property Rights   **C–274**

The Council for Trade-Related Aspects of Intellectual Property Rights shall monitor the operation of this Agreement and, in particular, Members' compliance with their obligations hereunder, and shall afford Members the opportunity of consulting on matters relating to the trade-related aspects of intellectual property rights. It shall carry out such other responsibilities as assigned to it by the Members, and it shall, in particular, provide any assistance requested by them in the context of dispute settlement procedures. In carrying out its functions, the Council may consult with and seek information from any source it deems appropriate. In consultation with the World Intellectual Property Organization, the Council shall seek to establish, within one year of its first meeting, appropriate arrangements for cooperation with bodies of that Organization.

Article 69
International Co-operation   **C–275**

Members agree to cooperate with each other with a view to eliminating international trade in goods infringing intellectual property rights. For this purpose, they shall establish and notify contact points in their national administrations and be ready to exchange information on trade in infringing goods. They shall, in particular, promote the exchange of information and cooperation between customs authorities with regard to trade in counterfeit trademark goods and pirated copyright goods.

Article 70
Protection of Existing Subject-Matter   **C–276**

1. This Agreement does not give rise to obligations in respect of acts which occurred before the date of application of the Agreement for the Member in question.

2.   Except as otherwise provided for in this Agreement, this Agreement gives rise to obligations in respect of all subject matter existing at the date of application of this Agreement for the Member in question, and which is protected in that Member on the said date, or which meets or comes subsequently to meet the criteria for protection under the terms of this Agreement. In respect of this paragraph and paragraphs 3 and 4 below, copyright obligations with respect to existing works shall be solely determined under Article 18 of the Berne Convention (1971), and obligations with respect to the rights of producers of phonograms and performers in existing phonograms shall be determined solely under Article 18 of the Berne Convention (1971) as made applicable under paragraph 6 of Article 14 of this Agreement.

3.   There shall be no obligation to restore protection to subject matter which on the date of application of this Agreement for the member in question has fallen into the public domain.

4.   In respect of any acts in respect of specific objects embodying protected subject matter which become infringing under the terms of legislation in conformity with this Agreement, and which were commenced, or in respect of which a significant investment was made, before the date of acceptance of the Agreement Establishing the MTO by that Member, any member may provide for a limitation of the remedies available to the right holder as to the continued performance of such acts after the date of application of the Agreement for that member. In such cases the Member shall, however, at least provide for the payment of equitable remuneration.

5.   A Member is not obliged to apply the provisions of Article 11 and of paragraph 4 of Article 14 with respect to originals or copies purchased prior to the date of application of this Agreement for that Member.

6.   Members shall not be required to apply Article 31, or the requirement in paragraph 1 of Article 27 that patent rights shall be enjoyable without discrimination as to the field of technology, to use without the authorization of the right holder where authorization for such use was granted by the government before the date this Agreement became known.

7.   In the case of intellectual property rights for which protection is conditional upon registration, applications for protection which are pending on the date of application of this Agreement for the Member in question shall be permitted to be amended to claim any enhanced protection provided under the provisions of this Agreement. Such amendments shall not include new matter.

8.   Where a Member does not make available as of the date of entry into force of the Agreement Establishing the MTO patent protection for pharmaceutical and agricultural chemical products commensurate with its obligations under Article 27, that Member shall:
   (i) notwithstanding the provisions of Part VI above, provide as from the date of entry into force of the Agreement Establishing the MTO a means by which applications for patents for such inventions can be filed;

(ii) apply to these applications, as of the date of application of this Agreement, the criteria for patentability as laid down in this Agreement as if those criteria were being applied on the date of filing in that Member or, where priority is available and claimed, the priority date of the application;

(iii) provide patent protection in accordance with this Agreement as from the grant of the patent and for the remainder of the patent term, counted from the filing date in accordance with Article 33 of this Agreement, for those of these applications that meet the criteria for protection referred to in sub- paragraph (ii) above.

9. Where a product is the subject of a patent application in a Member in accordance with paragraph 8(i) above, exclusive marketing rights shall be granted, notwithstanding the provisions of Part VI above, for a period of five years after obtaining market approval in that Member or until a product patent is granted or rejected in that Member, whichever period is shorter, provided that, subsequent to the entry into force of the Agreement Establishing the MTO, a patent application has been filed and a patent granted for that product in another Member and marketing approval obtained in such other Member.

Article 71
Review and Amendment   **C–277**

1. The Council for Trade-Related Aspects of Intellectual Property Rights shall review the implementation of this Agreement after the expiration of the transitional period referred to in paragraph 2 of Article 65 above. The Council shall, having regard to the experience gained in its implementation, review it two years after that date, and at identical intervals thereafter. The Council may also undertake reviews in the light of any relevant new developments which might warrant modification or amendment of this Agreement.

2. Amendments merely serving the purpose of adjusting to higher levels of protection of intellectual property rights achieved, and in force, in other multilateral agreements and accepted under those agreements by all Members of the MTO may be referred to the Ministerial Conference for action in accordance with Article X, paragraph 6, of the Agreement Establishing the MTO on the basis of a consensus proposal from the Council for Trade-Related Aspects of Intellectual Property Rights.

Article 72
Reservations   **C–278**

Reservations may not be entered in respect of any of the provisions of this Agreement without the consent of the other Members.

C–279

Article 73
Security Exceptions

Nothing in this Agreement shall be construed:
(a) to require any Member to furnish any information the disclosure of which it considers contrary to its essential security interests; or
(b) to prevent any Member from taking any action which it considers necessary for the protection of its essential security interests:
 (i) relating to fissionable materials or the materials from which they are derived;
 (ii) relating to the traffic in arms, ammunition and implements of war and to such traffic in other goods and materials as is carried on directly or indirectly for the purpose of supplying a military establishment;
 (iii) taken in time of war or other emergency in international relations; or
(c) to prevent any Member from taking any action in pursuance of its obligations under the United Nations Charter for the maintenance of international peace and security.

Appendix D

UNITED KINGDOM ORDERS IN COUNCIL

The Copyright (Application to Other Countries) (No. 2) Order 1989

D–22

This Order has now been revoked and replaced by:

The Copyright (Application to Other Countries) Order 1993

D–23

(S.I. 1993 No. 942)

Made	*31st March 1993*
Laid before Parliament	*13th April 1993*
Coming into force	*4th May 1993*

At the Court at Buckingham Palace, the 31st day of March 1993
Present,
The Queen's Most Excellent Majesty in Council

Whereas Her Majesty is satisfied that provision has been or will be made—

  (a) in respect of literary, dramatic, musical and artistic works, films and typographical arrangements of published editions, under the law of Uganda,
  (b) in respect of sound recordings, under the laws of Bangladesh, Ghana, Malawi and Thailand,
  (c) in respect of broadcasts, under the law of Malawi,

giving adequate protection to the owners of copyright under Part I of the Copyright, Designs and Patents Act 1988:

Now, therefore, Her Majesty, by and with the advice of Her Privy Council, and by virtue of the authority conferred upon Her by section 159 of the said Act, is pleased to order, and it is hereby ordered as follows:—

  1.—(1) This Order may be cited as the Copyright (Application to Other Countries) Order 1993 and shall come into force on 4th May 1993.

D–24

(2) In this Order—

"the Act" means the Copyright, Designs and Patents Act 1988, and

"first published" shall be construed in accordance with section 155(3) of the Act.

D–25   **2.**—(1) In relation to literary, dramatic, musical and artistic works, films and the typographical arrangements of published editions, sections 153, 154 and 155 of the Act (qualification for copyright protection) apply in relation to—

(a) persons who are citizens or subjects of a country specified in Schedule 1 to this Order or are domiciled or resident there as they apply to persons who are British citizens or are domiciled or resident in the United Kingdom;

(b) bodies incorporated under the law of such a country as they apply in relation to bodies incorporated under the law of a part of the United Kingdom; and

(c) works first published in such a country as they apply in relation to works first published in the United Kingdom;

but subject to paragraph (2) and article 5 below.

(2) Copyright does not subsist—

(a) in a literary, dramatic, musical or artistic work by virtue of section 154 of the Act as applied by paragraph (1) above (qualification by reference to author) if it was first published—
  (i) before 1st June 1957 (commencement of Copyright Act 1956), or
  (ii) before 1st August 1989 (commencement of Part I of the Act) and at the material time (as defined in section 154(4)(b) of the Act) the author was not a relevant person; or

(b) in any work by virtue of paragraph (1) above if—
  (i) a date is, or dates are, specified in Schedule 1 to this Order in respect of the only country or countries relevant to the work for the purposes of paragraph (1) above, and
  (ii) the work was first published before that date or (as the case may be) the earliest of those dates;

and for the purposes of sub-paragraph (a)(ii) of this paragraph, a "relevant person" is a Commonwealth citizen, a British protected person, a citizen or subject of any country specified in Schedule 1 to this Order, or a person resident or domiciled in the United Kingdom, another country to which the relevant provisions of Part I of the Act extend or (subject to article 5 below) a country specified in Schedule 1 to this Order.

(3) Where copyright subsists in a work by virtue of paragraph (1) above, the whole of Part I of the Act (including Schedule 1 to the Act) applies in relation to the work, save that in relation to an artistic work consisting of the design of a typeface—

(a) section 54(2) (articles for producing material in particular typeface) does not apply,

(b) section 55 (making such articles not an infringement) applies as if the words in subsection (2) from the beginning to "marketed" were omitted, and

(c) paragraph 14(5) of Schedule 1 (transitional provision) does not apply, and subject also to articles 5 and 7 below.

3. In relation to sound recordings, article 2 above shall apply as it applies in **D–26** relation to films, subject to the following modifications—
- (a) section 19, 20, 26 and 107(3) of the Act (infringement by playing in public, broadcasting or inclusion in a cable programme service and related provisions) apply only if—
  - (i) at least one of the countries relevant to the work for the purposes of article 2(1) above is specified in Schedule 2 to this Order, or
  - (ii) the sound recording in question is a film sound-track accompanying a film.

4.—(1) In relation to broadcasts, sections 153, 154 and 156 of the Act **D–27** (qualification for copyright protection) apply in relation to—
- (a) persons who are citizens or subjects of a country specified in Schedule 3 to this Order or are domiciled or resident there as they apply to persons who are British citizens or are domiciled or resident in the United Kingdom;
- (b) bodies incorporated under the law of such a country as they apply in relation to bodies incorporated under the law of a part of the United Kingdom; and
- (c) broadcasts made from such a country as they apply to broadcasts made from the United Kingdom;
but subject to paragraphs (2) and (3) and article 5 below.

(2) If the only country or countries relevant to a broadcast for the purposes of paragraph (1) above are identified in Schedule 3 to this Order by the words "television only", copyright subsists in the broadcast only if it is a television broadcast.

(3) Copyright does not subsist in a broadcast by virtue of paragraph (1) above if it was made before the relevant date.

(4) Where copyright subsists in a broadcast by virtue of paragraph (1) above, the whole or Part I of the Act (including Schedule 1 to the Act) applies in relation to the broadcast, save that for the purposes of section 14(2) (duration of copyright in repeats)—
- (a) a broadcast shall be disregarded if it was made before the relevant date, and
- (b) a cable programme shall be disregarded if it was included in a cable programme service before the later of the relevant date and 1st January 1985;
and subject also to article 7 below.

(5) For the purposes of paragraphs (3) and (4) above, the "relevant date" is the date or (as the case may be) the earliest of the dates specified in Schedule 3 to this Order in respect of the country or countries relevant to the broadcast for the purposes of paragraph (1) above, being (where different dates are specified for television and non-television broadcasts) the date appropriate to the type of broadcast in question.

(6) In respect of [Indonesia and] Singapore, this article applies in relation to cable programmes as it applies in relation to broadcasts, subject to article 5 below.

D–28   **5.** Schedule 4 to this Order shall have effect so as to modify the application of this Order in respect of certain countries.

6. Nothing in this Order shall be taken to derogate from the effect of paragraph 35 of Schedule 1 to the Act (continuation of existing qualification for copyright protection).

7.—(1) This article applies in any case in which—
(a) a work was made before 1st August 1989 (commencement of Part I of the Act) and copyright under the Copyright Act 1956 did not subsist in it when it was made, or
(b) a work is made on or after 1st August 1989 and copyright under the Act does not subsist in it when it is made,
but copyright subsequently subsists in it by virtue of article 2(1), 3 or 4(1) above.

(2) Where in any such case a person incurs or has incurred any expenditure or liability in connection with, for the purpose of or with a view to the doing of an act which at the time is not or was not an act restricted by any copyright in the work, the doing, or continued doing, of that act after copyright subsequently subsists in the work by virtue of article 2(1), 3 or 4(1) above shall not be an act restricted by the copyright unless the owner of the copyright or his exclusive licensee (if any) pays such compensation as, failing agreement, may be determined by arbitration.

8. The Orders listed in Schedule 5 to this Order are hereby revoked.

SCHEDULE 1   Article 2(1) and (2)

D–29   COUNTRIES ENJOYING PROTECTION IN RESPECT OF ALL WORKS EXCEPT BROADCASTS AND CABLE PROGRAMMES

(The countries specified in this Schedule either are parties to the Berne Copyright Convention and/or the Universal Copyright Convention or otherwise give adequate protection under their law.)

[Albania]
Algeria (28th August 1973)
Andorra (27th September 1957)
Argentina
Australia (including Norfolk Island)
Austria
Bahamas
Bangladesh
Barbados
Belgium

Belize
Benin
Bolivia
[Bosnia-Herzegovina]
Brazil
Bulgaria
Burkina Faso
Cameroon
Canada
Central African Republic
Chad
Chile
China
Colombia
Congo
Costa Rica
Côte d'Ivoire
Croatia
Cuba (27th September 1957)
Cyprus, Republic of
[Czech Republic]
Denmark (including Greenland and the Faeroe Islands)
Dominican Republic (8th May 1983)
Ecuador
Egypt
El Salvador
Fiji
Finland
France (including all Overseas Departments and Territories)
Gabon
Gambia
Germany
Ghana
Greece
Guatemala (28th October 1964)
Guinea, Republic of
Guinea-Bissau
Haiti (27th September 1957)
Holy See
Honduras
Hungary
Iceland
India
[Indonesia]
Ireland, Republic of
Israel
Italy
[Jamaica]
Japan
Kampuchea (27th September 1957)
[Kazakhstan (25th December 1991)]
Kenya
Korea, Republic of (1st October 1987)

Laos (27th September 1957)
Lebanon
Lesotho
Liberia
Libya
Liechtenstein
Luxembourg
[Macedonia]
Madagascar
Malawi
Malaysia
Mali
Malta
Mauritania
Mauritius
Mexico
Monaco
Morocco
[Namibia]
Netherlands (including Aruba and the Netherlands Antilles)
New Zealand
Nicaragua (16th August 1961)
Niger
Nigeria
Norway
Pakistan
Panama (17th October 1962)
Paraguay
Peru
Philippines
Poland
Portugal
Romania
[Russian Federation (25th December 1991)]
Rwanda
[Saint Lucia]
St. Vincent and the Grenadines
Senegal
Singapore
[Slovak Republic]
Slovenia
South Africa
Soviet Union (27th May 1973)
Spain
Sri Lanka
Suriname
Sweden
Switzerland
Taiwan, territory of (10th July 1985)
[Tajikistan (25 December 1991)]
Thailand
Togo
Trinidad and Tobago

Tunisia
Turkey
Uganda (20th July 1964)
United States of America (including Puerto Rico and all territories and
    possessions)
Uruguay
Venezuela
Yugoslavia
Zaire
Zambia
Zimbabwe

SCHEDULE 2   Article 3(a)(1)

COUNTRIES ENJOYING FULL PROTECTION FOR SOUND · **D–30**
RECORDINGS

(The countries specified in this Schedule either are parties to the Rome
Convention for the Protection of Performers, Producers of Phonograms and
Broadcasting Organisations or otherwise give adequate protection under their
law.)

Argentina
Australia (including Norfolk Island)
Austria
Bangladesh
Barbados
[Bolivia]
Brazil
Burkina Faso
Chile
Colombia
Congo
Costa Rica
[Czech Republic]
Denmark (including Greenland and the Faeroe Islands)
Dominican Republic
Ecuador
El Salvador
Fiji
Finland
France (including all Overseas Departments and Territories)
Germany
Ghana
Greece
Guatemala
Honduras
India
Indonesia
Ireland, Republic of

Italy
Japan
Lesotho
Luxembourg
Malawi
Malaysia
Mexico
Monaco
[Netherlands]
New Zealand
Niger
[Nigeria]
Norway
Pakistan
Panama
Paraguay
Peru
Philippines
[Slovak Republic]
Spain
Sweden
[Switzerland]
Taiwan, territory of
Thailand
Uruguay

SCHEDULE 3   Article 4(1), (2) and (5)

D–31   COUNTRIES ENJOYING PROTECTION IN RESPECT OF
BROADCASTS

(The countries specified in this Schedule either are parties to the Rome
Convention for the Protection of Performers, Producers of Phonograms and
Broadcasting Organisations and/or the European Agreement on the Protection of Television Broadcasts or otherwise give adequate protection under
their law.)

Argentina (2nd March 1992)
Australia (30th September 1992)
Austria (9th June 1973)
Barbados (18th September 1983)
Belgium (8th March 1968—television only)
[Bolivia (24th November 1993)]
Brazil (29th September 1965)
Burkina Faso (14th January 1988)
Chile (5th September 1974)
Colombia (17th September 1976)
Congo (18th May 1964)
Costa Rica (9th September 1971)
Cyprus, Republic of (5th May 1970—television only)
[Czech Republic (1st January 1993)]

Denmark (including Greenland and the Faeroe Islands) (1st February 1962—television; 1st July 1965—non-television)
Dominican Republic (27th January 1987)
Ecuador (18th May 1964)
El Salvador (29th June 1979)
Fiji (11th April 1972)
Finland (21st October 1983)
France (including all Overseas Departments and Territories) (1st July 1961—television; 3rd July 1987—non-television)
Germany (21st October 1966)
Greece (6th January 1993)
Guatemala (14th January 1977)
Honduras (16th February 1990)
[Indonesia (1st June 1957)]
Ireland, Republic of (19th September 1979)
Italy (8th April 1975)
Japan (26th October 1989)
Lesotho (26th January 1990)
Luxembourg (25th February 1976)
Malawi (22nd June 1989)
Malaysia (1st June 1957)
Mexico (18th May 1964)
Monaco (6th December 1985)
[Netherlands (7th October 1993)]
Niger (18th May 1964)
[Nigeria (29th October 1993)]
Norway (10th August 1968—television; 10th July 1978—non-television)
Panama (2nd September 1983)
Paraguay (26th February 1970)
Peru (7th August 1985)
Philippines (25th September 1984)
Singapore (1st June 1957)
[Slovak Republic (1st January 1993)]
Spain (19th November 1971—television; 14th November 1991—non-television)
Sweden (1st July 1961—television; 18th May 1964—non-television)
[Switzerland (24th September 1993)]
Uruguay (4th July 1977)

SCHEDULE 4   Article 5

MODIFICATIONS

[**1.** In respect of Indonesia—
  (a) sub-paragraph (c) of article 2(1) shall not apply except as applied by article 3(a) in relation to sound recordings, and
  (b) in the application of article 4(3) above in relation to cable programmes by virtue of article 4(6), the relevant date is 1st January 1985.]
2. In respect of Singapore—
  (a) articles 2(1)(a) and (2) and 4(1)(a) above shall apply as if the references to persons domiciled in Singapore were omitted, and

(b) in the application of article 4(3) above in relation to cable programmes by virtue of article 4(6), the relevant date is 1st January 1985.

3. In respect of the territory of Taiwan—
   (a) article 2(1)(a) and (2) above shall apply as if the reference to persons domiciled or resident in the territory of Taiwan were limited to such persons who are also citizens or subjects of China, and
   (b) in the application of Part I of the Act by virtue of article 2(3) above, subsection (1) of section 21 (infringement by making adaptation) applies as if subsection (3)(a)(i) of that section (translation of literary of dramatic work) were omitted.

SCHEDULE 5 Article 8

D–33 ORDERS IN COUNCIL REVOKED

Number	Title
S.I. 1989/1293	The Copyright (Application to Other Countries) (No. 2) Order 1989
S.I. 1989/2415	The Copyright (Application to Other Countries) (No. 2) (Amendment) Order 1989
S.I. 1990/2153	The Copyright (Application to Other Countries) (No. 2) (Amendment) Order 1990

AMENDMENT: This order is printed as amended by the Copyright (Application to Other Countries) (Amendment) Order 1994 (S.I. 1994 No. 263), the words in square brackets being added. Presumably the words ". . . (translation of literary of dramatic work) . . " in para. 3(b) of Schedule 4 is an error for " . . . (translation of literary or dramatic work) . . .".

The Performances (Reciprocal Protection) (Convention Countries) (No. 2)   D–40

This Order has been revoked and replaced by:

The Performances (Reciprocal Protection) (Convention Countries) Order 1994   D–41

(S.I. 1994 No. 2621)

Made	*8th February 1994*
Laid before Parliament	*18th February 1994*
Coming into force	*11th March 1994*

At the Court at Buckingham Palace, the 8th day of February 1994
Present,
The Queen's Most Excellent Majesty in Council

Her Majesty, by virtue of the authority conferred upon Her by section 208(1)(a) of the Copyright, Designs and Patents Act 1988 is pleased, by and with the advice of Her Privy Council, to order, and it is hereby ordered, as follows:

1. This Order may be cited as the Performances (Reciprocal Protection) (Convention Countries) Order 1994 and shall come into force on 11th March 1994.

2. The following countries are hereby designated as enjoying reciprocal   **D–42** protection under Part II of the Copyright, Designs and Patents Act 1988 (rights in performances)—

Argentina
Australia
Austria
Barbados
Bolivia
Brazil
Burkina Faso
Chile
Columbia
Congo
Costa Rica
Czech Republic
Denmark (including Greenland and the Faeroe Islands)
Dominican Republic

Ecuador
El Salvador
Fiji
Finland
France (including all Overseas Departments and Territories)
Germany
Greece
Guatemala
Honduras
Ireland, Republic of
Italy
Japan
Lesotho
Luxembourg
Mexico
Monaco
Netherlands
Niger
Nigeria
Norway
Panama
Paraguay
Peru
Philippines
Spain
Slovak Republic
Sweden
Switzerland
Uruguay

3. The Performances (Reciprocal Protection) (Convention Countries) Order 1993 is hereby revoked.

The Copyright (Isle of Man) (Revocation) Order 1992   D–50

(S.I. 1992 No. 1306)

Made	*4th June 1992*
Coming into force	*1st July 1992*

At the Court at Buckingham Palace, the 4th day of June 1992
Present,
The Queen's Most Excellent Majesty in Council

Whereas it appears to Her Majesty that provision with respect to copyright has been made in the law of the Isle of Man otherwise than by extending the provisions of Part I of the Copyright, Designs and Patents Act 1988;

Now, therefore, Her Majesty, in pursuance of paragraph 36(3) of Schedule 1 to that Act, is pleased, by and with the advice of Her Privy Council, to order, and it is hereby ordered, as follows:

1. This Order may be cited as the Copyright (Isle of Man) (Revocation) Order 1992 and shall come into force on 1st July 1992.

2. The Copyright (Isle of Man) Order 1986 is hereby revoked.

The Copyright (Application to the Isle of Man) Order   D–51 1992

(S.I. 1992 No. 1313)

Made	*4th June 1992*
Laid before Parliament	*9th June 1992*
Coming into force	*1st July 1992*

At the Court at Buckingham Palace, the 4th day of June 1992
Present,
The Queen's Most Excellent Majesty in Council

Whereas Her Majesty is satisfied that, in respect of the classes of works to which this Order relates, provision has been or will be made under the laws of the Isle of Man giving adequate protection to the owners of copyright under Part I of the Copyright, Designs and Patents Act 1988;

Now, therefore, Her Majesty, in pursuance of section 159 of the said Act, is pleased, by and with the advice of Her Privy Council, to order, and it is hereby ordered, as follows:

1. This Order may be cited as the Copyright (Application to the Isle of Man) Order 1992 and shall come into force on 1st July 1992.

2. Sections 153 to 156 of the Act (qualification for copyright protection) apply in relation to:

(a) persons who are domiciled or resident in the Isle of Man as they apply to persons who are domiciled or resident in the United Kingdom;

(b) bodies incorporated under the law of the Isle of Man as they apply in relation to bodies incorporated under the law of a part of the United Kingdom;

(c) works first published in the Isle of Man as they apply in relation to works first published in the United Kingdom; and

(d) broadcasts made from, or cable programmes sent from, the Isle of Man as they apply in relation to broadcasts made from, or cable programmes sent from, the United Kingdom.

Appendix E

UNITED STATES OF AMERICA CODE

101. Definitions   E–4

Section 101 is amended as follows:

Added definition:

An "architectural work" is the design of a building as embodied in any tangible medium of expression, including a building, architectural plans, or drawings. The work includes the overall form as well as the arrangement and composition of spaces and elements in the design, but does not include individual standard features.
(PL 101–650, 104 Stat. 5133, December 1, 1990)

Amended definition of "Berne Convention work":

A work is a "Berne Convention work" if:

(1) in the case of an unpublished work, one or more of the authors is a national of a nation adhering to the Berne Convention, or in the case of a published work, one or more of the authors is a national of a nation adhering to the Berne Convention on the date of first publication;
(2) the work was first published in a nation adhering to the Berne Convention, or was simultaneously first published in a nation adhering to the Berne Convention and in a foreign nation that does not adhere to the Berne Convention;
(3) in the case of an audiovisual work:
    (A) if one or more of the authors is a legal entity, that author has its headquarters in a nation adhering to the Berne Convention; or
    (B) if one or more of the authors is an individual, that author is domiciled, or has his or her habitual residence in, a nation adhering to the Berne Convention;
(4) in the case of a pictorial, graphic, or sculptural work that is incorporated in a building or other structure, the building or structure is located in a nation adhering to the Berne Convention; or
(5) in the case of an architectural work embodied in a building, such building is erected in a country adhering to the Berne Convention. For purposes of paragraph (1), an author who is domiciled in or has his or her habitual residence in, a nation adhering to the Berne Convention is considered to be a national of that nation. For purposes of paragraph (2), a work is considered to

have been simultaneously published in two or more nations if its dates of publication are within 30 days of one another.
(PL 101–650, 104 Stat. 5133, December 1, 1990)

Added definition:

A "work of visual art" is:

(1) a painting, drawing, print, or sculpture, existing in a single copy, in a limited edition of 200 copies or fewer that are signed and consecutively numbered by the author, or, in the case of a sculpture, in multiple cast, carved, or fabricated sculptures of 200 or fewer that are consecutively numbered by the author and bear the signature or other identifying mark of the author; or (2) a still photographic image produced for exhibition purposes only, existing in a single copy that is signed by the author, or in a limited edition of 200 copies or fewer that are signed and consecutively numbered by the author.

A "work of visual art" does not include:
   (A)(i)   any poster, map, globe, chart, technical drawing, diagram, model, applied art, motion picture or other audiovisual work, book, magazine, newspaper, periodical, data base, electronic information service, electronic publication, or similar publication;
      (ii)   any merchandising item or advertising, promotional, descriptive, covering, or packaging material or container;
      (iii)   any portion or part of any item described in clause (i) or (ii);
   (B) any work made for hire; or
   (C) any work not subject to copyright protection under this title.
(PL 101–650, 104 Stat. 5128, December 1, 1990)

Added Definition:

"Registration", for purposes of sections 205(c)(2), 405, 406, 410(d), 411, 412, and 506(e), means a registration of a claim in the original or renewed and extended term of copyright.
(PL 102–307, 106 Stat. 266, June 26, 1992)

E–5   102. Subject matter of copyright: in general

Section 102(a) has been amended as follows:

End of paragraph (6). **Delete**: "and".

End of paragraph (7). **Add**: "and".

After paragraph (7). **Add**: "(8) architectural works."

E–8   105. Subject matter of copyright: United States Government works

Before section 105. **Add**:

104A. Copyright in certain motion pictures

(*a*) RESTORATION OF COPYRIGHT.

Subject to subsections (b) and (c):

  (1) any motion picture that is first fixed or published in the territory of a NAFTA country as defined in section 2(4) of the North American Free Trade Agreement Implementation Act to which Annex 1705.7 of the North American Free Trade Agreement applies, and

  (2) any work included in such motion picture that is first fixed in or published with such motion picture, that entered the public domain in the United States because it was first published on or after January 1, 1978, and before March 1, 1989, without the notice required by section 401, 402, or 403 of this title, the absence of which has not been excused by the operation of section 405 of this title, as such sections were in effect during that period, shall have copyright protection under this title for the remainder of the term of copyright protection to which it would have been entitled in the United States had it been published with such notice.

(*b*) EFFECTIVE DATE OF PROTECTION

The protection provided under subsection (a) shall become effective, with respect to any motion picture or work included in such motion picture meeting the criteria of that subsection, one year after the date on which the North American Free Trade Agreement enters into force with respect to, and the United States applies the Agreement to, the country in whose territory the motion picture was first fixed or published if, before the end of that one-year period, the copyright owner in the motion picture or work files with the Copyright Office a statement of intent to have copyright protection restored under subsection (a). The Copyright Office shall publish in the Federal Register promptly after that effective date a list of motion pictures, and works included in such motion pictures, for which protection is provided under subsection (a).

(*c*) USE OF PREVIOUSLY OWNED COPIES.

A national or domiciliary of the United States who, before the date of the enactment of the North American Free Trade Agreement Implementation Act, made or acquired copies of a motion picture, or other work included in such motion picture, that is subject to protection under subsection (a), may sell or distribute such copies or continue to perform publicly such motion picture and other work without liability for such sale, distribution, or performance, for a period of one year after the date on which the list of motion pictures, and works included in such motion pictures, that are subject to protection under subsection (a) is published in the Federal Registration under subsection (b). (PL 103–182, 107 Stat. 2115, December 8, 1993)

106. Exclusive rights in copyrighted works   **E–9**

Section 106 has been amended by deleting "118" and substituting "120". (PL 101–318, 104 Stat. 288, July 3, 1990; PL 101–650, 04 Stat. 5134, December 1, 1990)

Before section 107. **Add**:

106A. Rights of certain authors to attribution and integrity

(*a*) RIGHTS OF ATTRIBUTION AND INTEGRITY.

Subject to section 107 and independent of the exclusive rights provided in section 106, the author of a work of visual art:

(1) shall have the right:
   (A) to claim authorship of that work, and
   (B) to prevent the use of his or her name as the author of any work of visual art which he or she did not create;
(2) shall have the right to prevent the use of his or her name as the author of the work of visual art in the event of a distortion, mutilation, or other modification of the work which would be prejudicial to his or her honor or reputation; and
(3) subject to the limitations set forth in section 113(d), shall have the right:
   (A) to prevent any intentional distortion, mutilation, or other modification of that work which would be prejudicial to his or her honor or reputation, and any intentional distortion, mutilation, or modification of that work is a violation of that right, and
   (B) to prevent any destruction of a work of recognized stature, and any intentional or grossly negligent destruction of that work is a violation of that right.

(*b*) SCOPE AND EXERCISE OF RIGHTS.

Only the author of a work of visual art has the rights conferred by subsection (a) in that work, whether or not the author is the copyright owner. The authors of a joint work of visual art are co-owners of the rights conferred by subsection (a) in that work.

(*c*) EXCEPTIONS.

(1) The modification of a work of visual art which is a result of the passage of time or the inherent nature of the materials is not a distortion, mutilation, or other modification described in subsection (a)(3)(A).
(2) The modification of a work of visual art which is the result of conservation, or of the public presentation, including lighting and placement, of the work is not a destruction, distortion, mutilation, or other modification described in subsection (a)(3) unless the modification is caused by gross negligence.
(3) The rights described in paragraphs (1) and (2) of subsection (a) shall not apply to any reproduction, depiction, portrayal, or other use of a work in, upon, or in any connection with any item described in subparagraph (A) or (B) of the definition of "work of visual art" in section 101, and any such reproduction, depiction, portrayal, or other use of a work is not a destruction, distortion, mutilation, or other modification described in paragraph (3) of subsection (a).

(*d*) DURATION OF RIGHTS.

(1) With respect to works of visual art created on or after the effective date set forth in section 610(a) of the Visual Artists Rights Act of 1990, the

338

rights conferred by subsection (a) shall endure for a term consisting of the life of the author.

(2) With respect to works of visual art created before the effective date set forth in section 610(a) of the Visual Artists Rights Act of 1990, but title to which has not, as of such effective date, been transferred from the author, the rights conferred by subsection (a) shall be coextensive with, and shall expire at the same time as, the rights conferred by section 106.

(3) In the case of a joint work prepared by two or more authors, the rights conferred by subsection (a) shall endure for a term consisting of the life of the last surviving author.

(4) All terms of the rights conferred by subsection (a) run to the end of the calendar year in which they would otherwise expire.

(*e*) TRANSFER AND WAIVER.

(1) The rights conferred by subsection (a) may not be transferred, but those rights may be waived if the author expressly agrees to such waiver in a written instrument signed by the author. Such instrument shall specifically identify the work, and uses of that work, to which the waiver applies, and the waiver shall apply only to the work and uses so identified. In the case of a joint work prepared by two or more authors, a waiver of rights under this paragraph made by one such author waives such rights for all such authors.

(2) Ownership of the rights conferred by subsection (a) with respect to a work of visual art is distinct from ownership of any copy of that work, or of a copyright or any exclusive right under a copyright in that work. Transfer of ownership of any copy of a work of visual art, or of a copyright or any exclusive right under a copyright, shall not constitute a waiver of the rights conferred by subsection (a). Except as may otherwise be agreed by the author in a written instrument signed by the author, a waiver of the rights conferred by subsection (a) with respect to a work of visual art shall not constitute a transfer of ownership of any copy of that work, or of ownership of a copyright or of any exclusive right under a copyright in that work.

(Added PL 101–650, 104 Stat. 5128, December 1, 1990)

107. Limitations on exclusive rights: Fair use　　　　　　　　　　**E–10**

End of Section 107. **Add**:

The fact that a work is unpublished shall not itself bar a finding of fair use if such finding is made upon consideration of all the above factors.
(PL 101–650, 104 Stat. 5132, December 1, 1990; PL 102–492, 106 Stat. 3145, October 24, 1992)

108. Limitations on exclusive rights: Reproduction by libraries and archives　E–11

Section 108(i) has been repealed.
(PL 102–307, 106 Stat. 272, June 26, 1992)

E–12   109. Limitations on exclusive rights: Effect of transfer of particular copy or phonorecord

Section 109 has been amended to read as follows:

(*a*) Notwithstanding the provisions of section 106(3), the owner of a particular copy or phonorecord lawfully made under this title, or any person authorized by such owner, is entitled, without the authority of the copyright owner, to sell or otherwise dispose of the possession of that copy or phonorecord.

(*b*)(1)(A) Notwithstanding the provisions of subsection (a), unless authorized by the owners of copyright in the sound recording or the owner of copyright in a computer program (including any tape, disk, or other medium embodying such program), and in the case of a sound recording in the musical works embodied therein, neither the owner of a particular phonorecord nor any person in possession of a particular copy of a computer program (including any tape, disk, or other medium embodying such program), may, for the purposes of direct or indirect commercial advantage, dispose of, or authorize the disposal of, the possession of that phonorecord or computer program (including any tape, disk, or other medium embodying such program) by rental, lease, or lending, or by any other act or practice in the nature of rental, lease, or lending. Nothing in the preceding sentence shall apply to the rental, lease, or lending of a phonorecord for nonprofit purposes by a nonprofit library or nonprofit educational institution. The transfer of possession of a lawfully made copy of a computer program by a nonprofit educational institution to another nonprofit educational institution or to faculty, staff, and students does not constitute rental, lease, or lending for direct or indirect commercial purposes under this subsection.

    (B) This subsection does not apply to:
        (i) a computer program which is embodied in a machine or product and which cannot be copied during the ordinary operation or use of the machine or product; or
        (ii) a computer program embodied in or used in conjunction with a limited purpose computer that is designed for playing video games and may be designed for other purposes.
    (C) Nothing in this subsection affects any provision of chapter 9 of this title.
    (2)(A) Nothing in this subsection shall apply to the lending of a computer program for nonprofit purposes by a nonprofit library, if each copy of a computer program which is lent by such library has affixed to the packaging containing the program a warning of copyright in accordance with requirements that the Register of Copyrights shall prescribe by regulation.
    (B) Not later than three years after the date of the enactment of the Computer Software Rental Amendments Act of 1990, and at such times thereafter as the Register of Copyright considers appropriate, the Register of Copyrights, after consultation with representatives of copyright owners and librarians, shall submit to the Congress a report stating whether this paragraph has achieved its intended purpose of maintaining the integrity of the copyright system while providing nonprofit libraries the capability to fulfill their function. Such report shall advise the Congress as to any information or recommendations

that the Register of Copyrights considers necessary to carry out the purposes of this subsection.

(3) Nothing in this subsection shall affect any provision of the antitrust laws. For purposes of the preceding sentence, "antitrust laws" has the meaning given that term in the first section of the Clayton Act and includes section 5 of the Federal Trade Commission Act to the extent that section relates to unfair methods of competition.

(4) Any person who distributes a phonorecord or a copy of a computer program (including any tape, disk, or other medium embodying such program) in violation of paragraph (1) is an infringer of copyright under section 501 of this title and is subject to the remedies set forth in sections 502, 503, 504, 505, and 509. Such violation shall not be a criminal offense under section 506 or cause such person to be subject to the criminal penalties set forth in section 2319 of title 18.

(c) Notwithstanding the provisions of section 106(5), the owner of a particular copy lawfully made under this title, or any person authorized by such owner, is entitled, without the authority of the copyright owner, to display that copy publicly, either directly or by the projection of no more than one image at a time, to viewers present at the place where the copy is located.

(d) The privileges prescribed by subsections (a) and (c) do not, unless authorized by the copyright owner, extend to any person who has acquired possession of the copy or phonorecord from the copyright owner, by rental, lease, loan, or otherwise, without acquiring ownership of it.

(e) Notwithstanding the provisions of sections 106(4) and 106(5), in the case of an electronic audiovisual game intended for use in coin-operated equipment, the owner of a particular copy of such a game lawfully made under this title, is entitled, without the authority of the copyright owner of the game, to publicly perform or display that game in coin-operated equipment, except that this subsection shall not apply to any work of authorship embodied in the audiovisual game if the copyright owner of the electronic audiovisual game is not also the copyright owner of the work of authorship.

(PL 101–650, 104 Stat. 5134, December 1, 1990)

111. Limitations on exclusive rights: Secondary transmissions   E–14

Section 111 has been amended as follows:

Subsection (c)(2)(B). **Delete** the words "recorded the notice specified by subsection (d) and".

Subsections (d)(1) and (d)(1)(A). In each case **delete** the words "after consultation with the Copyright Royalty Tribunal (if and when the Tribunal has been constituted)".

Subsection (d)(2). Last four lines. **Delete** and **substitute**: "Librarian of Congress in the event no controversy over distribution exists, or by a copyright arbitration royalty panel in the event a controversy over such distribution exists."

Subsection (d)(4)(A). For the words "Copyright Royalty Tribunal" and "Tribunal" **substitute** in each case the words "Librarian of Congress".

Subsection (d)(4)(B). **Delete** existing clause and substitute:

(B) After the first day of August of each year, the Librarian of Congress shall, upon the recommendation of the Register of Copyrights, determine whether there exists a controversy concerning the distribution of royalty fees. If the Librarian determines that no such controversy exists, the Librarian shall, after deducting reasonable administrative costs under this section, distribute such fees to the copyright owners entitled to such fees, or to their designated agents. If the Librarian finds the existence of a controversy, the Librarian shall, pursuant to chapter 8 of this title, convene a copyright arbitration royalty panel to determine the distribution of royalty fees.

Subsection (*d*)(4)(C). For the words "Copyright Royalty Tribunal" **substitute** the words "Librarian of Congress".

Subsection (*f*). Definition of "secondary transmission", **delete** the second sentence. Definition of "local service area of a primary transmitter", **delete** last two sentences.
(PL 101–318, 104 Stat. 287, July 3, 1990; PL 103–198, 107 Stat. 2311, December 17, 1993)

E–16   113. Scope of exclusive rights in pictorial, graphic, and sculptural works

A new subsection (*d*) has been inserted, as follows:

(*d*)(1) In a case in which:
  (A) a work of visual art has been incorporated in or made part of a building in such a way that removing the work from the building will cause the destruction, distortion, mutilation, or other modification of the work as described in section 106A(*a*)(3), and
  (B) the author consented to the installation of the work in the building either before the effective date set forth in section 610(a) of the Visual Artists Rights Act of 1990, or in a written instrument executed on or after such effective date that is signed by the owner of the building and the author and that specifies that installation of the work may subject the work to destruction, distortion, mutilation, or other modification, by reason of its removal, then the rights conferred by paragraphs (2) and (3) of section 106A(*a*) shall not apply.
  (2) If the owner of a building wishes to remove a work of visual art which is a part of such building and which can be removed from the building without the destruction, distortion, mutilation, or other modification of the work as described in section 106A(*a*)(3), the author's rights under paragraphs (2) and (3) of section 106A(*a*) shall apply unless:
  (A) the owner has made a diligent, good faith attempt without success to notify the author of the owner's intended action affecting the work of visual art, or
  (B) the owner did provide such notice in writing and the person so notified failed, within 90 days after receiving such notice, either to remove the work or to pay for its removal. For purposes of subparagraph (A), an owner shall be presumed to have made a diligent, good faith attempt to send notice if the owner sent such notice by registered mail to the author at the most recent address of the author that was recorded with the Register of Copyrights pursuant to paragraph (3). If the work is removed at the expense of the author, title to that copy of the work shall be deemed to be in the author.

(3) The Register of Copyrights shall establish a system of records whereby any author of a work of visual art that has been incorporated in or made part of a building, may record his or her identity and address with the Copyright Office. The Register shall also establish procedures under which any such author may update the information so recorded, and procedures under which owners of buildings may record with the Copyright Office evidence of their efforts to comply with this subsection.

(PL 101–650, 104 Stat. 5130, December 1, 1990)

116. Scope of exclusive rights in nondramatic musical works: **E–19**

Section 116 has been repealed.
(PL 103–198, 107 Stat. 2309, December 17, 1993)

116A. Negotiated licenses for public performances by means of coin-   **E–20**
operated phonorecord players

Section 116A has been redesignated as section 116. It has also been amended by striking subsection (*b*) and redesignating subsections (*c*) and (*d*) as subsections (*b*) and (*c*), respectively.

The words "Copyright Royalty Tribunal" have been replaced by "Librarian of Congress".
(PL 103–198, 107 Stat. 2309, December 17, 1993)

118. Scope of exclusive rights. Use of certain works in connection with   **E–22**
noncommercial broadcasting

Subsections 118(*b*) and (c) have been amended as follows:

(*b*) Notwithstanding any provision of the antitrust laws, any owners of copyright in published nondramatic musical works and published pictorial, graphic, and sculptural works and any public broadcasting entities, respectively, may negotiate and agree upon the terms and rates of royalty payments and the proportionate division of fees paid among various copyright owners, and may designate common agents to negotiate, agree to, pay, or receive payments.

(1) Any owner of copyright in a work specified in this subsection or any public broadcasting entity may submit to the Librarian of Congress proposed licenses covering such activities with respect to such works. The Librarian of Congress shall proceed on the basis of the proposals submitted to it as well as any other relevant information. The Librarian of Congress shall permit any interested party to submit information relevant to such proceedings.

(2) License agreements, voluntarily negotiated at any time between one or more copyright owners and one or more public broadcasting entities shall be given effect in lieu of any determination by the Librarian of Congress: Provided, that copies of such agreements are filed in the Copyright Office within thirty days of execution in accordance with regulations that the Register of Copyrights shall prescribe.

(3) In the absence of license agreements negotiated under paragraph (2), the Librarian of Congress shall, pursuant to chapter 8, convene a copyright arbitration royalty panel to determine and publish in the Federal Register a schedule of rates and terms which, subject to paragraph (2), shall be binding on all owners of copyright in works specified by this subsection and public broadcasting entities, regardless of whether such copyright owners have submitted proposals to the Librarian of Congress. In establishing such rates and terms the copyright arbitration royalty panel may consider the rates for comparable circumstances under voluntary license agreements negotiated as provided in paragraph (2). The Librarian of Congress shall also establish requirements by which copyright owners may receive reasonable notice of the use of their works under this section, and under which records of such use shall be kept by public broadcasting entities.

(*c*) The initial procedure specified in subsection (*b*) shall be repeated and concluded between June 30 and December 31, 1997, and at five-year intervals thereafter, in accordance with regulations that the Librarian of Congress shall prescribe.

Subsection (*d*) has been amended by the deletion of the words "transitional provisions of subsection (*b*)(4), and to the" from the opening words.

119. Limitations on exclusive rights: Secondary transmissions of superstations and network stations for private home viewing

The word "secondary" should be added to the second line of subsection (*a*)(1), between the words "subsection," and "transmission".

Subsections (*b*)(1) and (*b*)(1)(A) have been amended by the **deletion** in each case of the words "after consultation with the Copyright Royalty Tribunal".

Subsections (*b*)(2) and (*b*)(4)(A) have been amended by the **substitution** in each case of the words "Librarian of Congress" for the words "Copyright Royalty Tribunal" and "Tribunal".

Subsection (*b*)(4)(B) has been amended to read as follows:

(B) Determination of controversy; distribution—After the first day of August of each year, the Librarian of Congress shall determine whether there exists a controversy concerning the distribution of royalty fees. If the Librarian of Congress determines that no such controversy exists, the Librarian of Congress shall, after deducting reasonable administrative costs under this paragraph, distribute such fees to the copyright owners entitled to receive them, or to their designated agents. If the Librarian of Congress finds the existence of a controversy, the Librarian of Congress shall, pursuant to chapter 8 of this title, convene a copyright arbitration royalty panel to determine the distribution of royalty fees.

Subsections (*b*)(4)(C), (*c*)(2)(A), (*c*)(2)(B), (*c*)(3)(A) have been amended by the **substitution** in each case of the words "Librarian of Congress" for the words "Copyright Royalty Tribunal".

119(*c*): the subsection heading is amended by deleting "DETERMINATION" and substituting "ADJUSTMENT".

Subsection (*c*)(3)(A) has been further amended by the **substitution** of the words "Such arbitration proceeding shall be conducted under chapter 8." for the final sentence.

Subsections (*c*)(3)(B) and (C) have been deleted, (*c*)(3)(D) redesignated as (*c*)(3)(B) and amended by the **substitution** of the words "copyright arbitration royalty panel appointed under chapter 8" for the words "Arbitration Panel".

Subsections (*c*)(3)(E) and (F) have been **deleted**, (*c*)(3)(G) and (H) redesignated as (*c*)(3)(C) and (D) respectively and amended to read as follows:
  (C) Period during which decision of arbitration panel or order of Librarian effective.—The obligation to pay the royalty fee established under a determination which—
      (i) is made by a copyright arbitration royalty panel in an arbitration proceeding under this paragraph and is adopted by the Librarian of Congress under section 802(f), or
      (ii) is established by the Librarian of Congress under section 802(f), shall become effective as provided in section 802(g).
  (D) Persons subject to royalty fee.—The royalty fee referred to in subparagraph (C) shall be binding on all satellite carriers, distributors, and copyright owners, who are not party to a voluntary agreement filed with the Copyright Office under paragraph (2).

Subsection (*c*)(4) has been **deleted**.

Before chapter headings. **Add**: the following new section.   **E–24**

120. Scope of exclusive rights in architectural works

(*a*) PICTORIAL REPRESENTATIONS PERMITTED.

The copyright in an architectural work that has been constructed does not include the right to prevent the making, distributing, or public display of pictures, paintings, photographs, or other pictorial representations of the work, if the building in which the work is embodied is located in or ordinarily visible from a public place.

(*b*) ALTERATIONS TO AND DESTRUCTION OF BUILDINGS.

Notwithstanding the provisions of section 106(2), the owners of a building embodying an architectural work may, without the consent of the author or copyright owner of the architectural work, make or authorize the making of alterations to such building, and destroy or authorize the destruction of such building. (Added PL 101–650, 104 Stat. 5133, December 1, 1990.)

CHAPTER 3

DURATION OF COPYRIGHT

301. Preemption with respect to other laws   **E–31**

A new subsection 301(f) has been inserted, as follows:

(*f*)(1) On or after the effective date set forth in section 610(a) of the Visual Artists Rights Act of 1990, all legal or equitable rights that are equivalent to any of the rights conferred by section 106A with respect to works of visual art to which the rights conferred by section 106A apply are governed exclusively by section 106A and section 113(d) and the provisions of this title relating to such sections. Thereafter, no person is entitled to any such right or equivalent right in any work of visual art under the common law or statutes of any State.

  (2) Nothing in paragraph (1) annuls or limits any rights or remedies under the common law or statutes of any State with respect to—

   (A) any cause of action from undertakings commenced before the effective date set forth in section 610(a) of the Visual Artists Rights Act of 1990;

   (B) activities violating legal or equitable rights that are not equivalent to any of the rights conferred by section 106A with respect to works of visual art; or

   (C) activities violating legal or equitable rights which extend beyond the life of the author.

(PL 101–650, 104 Stat. 5131, December 1, 1990)

E–34   304. Duration of copyright: subsisting copyrights

Section 304(*a*) has been amended to provide as follows:

(*a*) Copyrights in Their First Term on January 1, 1978.

   (1)(A) Any copyright, the first term of which is subsisting on January 1, 1978, shall endure for 28 years from the date it was originally secured.

     (B) In the case of—

       (i) any posthumous work or of any periodical, cyclopedic, or other composite work upon which the copyright was origin- ally secured by the proprietor thereof, or

       (ii) any work copyrighted by a corporate body (otherwise than as assignee or licensee of the individual author) or by an employer for whom such work is made for hire, the proprietor of such copyright shall be entitled to a renewal and extension of the copyright in such work for the further term of 47 years.

     (C) In the case of any other copyrighted work, including a contribution by an individual author to a periodical or to a cyclopedic or other composite work—

       (i) the author of such work, if the author is still living,

       (ii) the widow, widower, or children of the author, if the author is not living,

       (iii) the author's executors, if such author, widow, widower, or children are not living, or

       (iv) the author's next of kin, in the absence of a will of the author, shall be entitled to a renewal and extension of the copyright in such work for a further term of 47 years.

   (2)(A) At the expiration of the original term of copyright in a work specified in paragraph (1)(B) of this subsection, the copyright shall endure for a renewed and extended further term of 47 years, which—

    (i) if an application to register a claim to such further term has been made to the Copyright Office within one year before the expiration of the original term of copyright, and the claim is registered, shall vest, upon the beginning of such further term, in the proprietor of the copyright who is entitled to claim the renewal of copyright at the time the application is made; or

    (ii) if no such application is made or the claim pursuant to such application is not registered, shall vest, upon the beginning of such further term, in the person or entity that was the proprietor of the copyright as of the last day of the original term of copyright.

(B) At the expiration of the original term of copyright in a work specified in paragraph (1)(C) of this subsection, the copyright shall endure for a renewed and extended further term of 47 years, which—

    (i) if an application to register a claim to such further term has been made to the Copyright Office within one year before the expiration of the original term of copyright, and the claim is registered, shall vest, upon the beginning of such further term, in any person who is entitled under paragraph (1)(C) to the renewal and extension of the copyright at the time the application is made; or

    (ii) if no such application is made or the claim pursuant to such application is not registered, shall vest, upon the beginning of such further term, in any person entitled under paragraph (1)(C), as of the last day of the original term of copyright, to the renewal and extension of the copyright.

(3)(A) An application to register a claim to the renewed and extended term of copyright in a work may be made to the Copyright Office—

    (i) within one year before the expiration of the original term of copyright by any person entitled under paragraph (1)(B) or (C) to such further term of 47 years; and

    (ii) at any time during the renewed and extended term by any person in whom such further term vested, under paragraph (2)(A) or (B), or by any successor or assign of such person, if the application is made in the name of such person.

(B) Such an application is not a condition of the renewal and extension of the copyright in a work for a further term of 47 years.

(4)(A) If an application to register a claim to the renewed and extended term of copyright in a work is not made within one year before the expiration of the original term of copyright in a work, or if the claim pursuant to such application is not registered, then a derivative work prepared under authority of a grant of a transfer or license of the copyright that is made before the expiration of the original term of copyright may continue to be used under the terms of the grant during the renewed an extended term of copyright without infringing the copyright, except that such use does not extend to the preparation during such renewed and extended term of other derivative works based upon the copyrighted work covered by such grant.

(B) If an application to register a claim to the renewed and extended term of copyright in a work is made within one year before its expiration, and the claim is registered, the certificate of such registration shall constitute prima facie evidence as to the validity of the copyright during its renewed and extended term and of the facts stated in the certificate. The evidentiary weight to be accorded the certificates of a registration of a renewed and extended term of copyright made after the end of that one-year period shall be within the discretion of the court.

(PL 102–307, 106 Stat. 264, June 26, 1992)

Section 304(c) has been amended in the matter preceding paragraph (1) by striking "second proviso of subsection (*a*)" and inserting "subsection (*a*)(1)(C)".
(PL 102–307, 106 Stat. 266, June 26, 1992)

CHAPTER 4

COPYRIGHT NOTICE, DEPOSIT, AND REGISTRATION

E–44   408. Copyright registration in general

Section 408(*a*) has been amended by **deleting** "At" and all that follows up to "unpublished work," and **substituting**:

"At any time during the subsistence of the first term of copyright in any published or unpublished work in which the copyright was secured before January 1, 1978, and during the subsistence of any copyright secured on or after that date,"

(PL 102–307, 106 Stat 266, June 26, 1992)

E–45   409. Application for copyright registration

Section 409 has been amended by **adding** at the end the following:

"If an application is submitted for the renewed and extended term provided for in section 304(*a*)(3)(A) and an original term registration has not been made, the Register may request information with respect to the existence, ownership, or duration of the copyright for the original term."

(PL 102–307, 106 Stat. 266, June 26, 1992)

E–47   411. Registration and infringement actions

Section 411(*a*) has been amended in the first sentence by inserting after "United States" the following:

"and an action brought for a violation of the rights of the author under section 106A(*a*)".

(PL 101–650 104 Stat. 5131, December 1, 1990)

412. Registration as prerequisite to certain remedies for infringement   **E–48**

Section 412 has been amended by **inserting** after "other than" the following:

> "an action brought for a violation of the rights of the author under section 106A(*a*) or"

(PL 101–650, 104 Stat. 5131, December 1, 1990)

CHAPTER 5

COPYRIGHT INFRINGEMENT AND REMEDIES

501. Infringement of copyright   **E–50**

Section 501(*a*) has been amended to provide as follows:

(*a*) Anyone who violates any of the exclusive rights of the copyright owner as provided by sections 106 through 118, or of the author as provided in section 106A(*a*), or who imports copies or phonorecords into the United States in violation of section 602, is an infringer of the copyright or right of the author, as the case may be. For purposes of this chapter (other than section 506), any reference to copyright shall be deemed to include the rights conferred by section 106A(*a*). As used in this subsection, the term "anyone" includes any State, any instrumentality of a State, and any officer or employee of a State, any instrumentality of a State, and any officer or employee of a State or instrumentality of a State acting in his or her official capacity. Any State, and any such instrumentality, officer, or employee, shall be subject to the provisions of this title in the same manner and to the same extent as any nongovernmental entity.
(PL 101–553, 104 Stat. 2749, November 15, 1990; PL 101–650, 104 Stat. 5131, December 1, 1990)

Note further that subsection (*e*) ceases to be effective from December 31, 1994.
(PL 100–667, 102 Stat. 3960, November 16, 1988)

506. Criminal offences   **E–55**

A new subsection 506(*f*) has been inserted, as follows:

(*f*) RIGHTS OF ATTRIBUTION AND INTEGRITY.

Nothing in this section applies to infringement of the rights conferred by section 106A(*a*).
(PL 101–650, 104 Stat. 5131, December 1, 1990)

E–59   **510. Remedies for alteration of programming by cable systems**

A new section 511 has been inserted as follows:

511. Liability of States, instrumentalities of States, and State officials for infringement of copyright

(*a*) In General.

Any State, any instrumentality of a State, and any officer or employee of a State or instrumentality of a State acting in his or her official capacity, shall not be immune, under the Eleventh Amendment of the Constitution of the United States or under any other doctrine of sovereign immunity, from suit in Federal Court by any person, including any governmental or nongovernmental entity, for a violation of any of the exclusive rights of a copyright owner provided by sections 106 through 119, for importing copies of phonorecords in violation of section 602, or for any other violation under this title.

(*b*) Remedies.

In a suit described in subsection (*a*) for a violation described in that subsection, remedies (including remedies both at law and in equity) are available for the violation to the same extent as such remedies are available for such a violation in a suit against any public or private entity other than a State, instrumentality of a State, or officer or employee of a State acting in his or her official capacity. Such remedies include impounding and disposition of infringing articles under section 503, actual damages and profits and statutory damages under section 504, costs and attorney's fees under section 505, and the remedies provided in section 510.
(PL 101–553, 104 Stat. 2749, November 15, 1990)

Chapter 7

Copyright Office

E–65   **701. The Copyright Office: General responsibilities and organisation**

A new subsection 701(*e*) has been inserted, as follows:
(*e*) The Register of Copyrights shall be compensated at the rate of pay in effect for Level IV of the Executive Schedules under section 5315 of Title 5. The Librarian of Congress shall establish not more than four positions for Associate Registers of Copyrights, in accordance with the recommendations of the Register of Copyrights. Each Associate Register of Copyrights shall be paid at a rate not to exceed the maximum annual rate of basic pay payable for GS-18 of the General Schedule under section 5332 of title 5.
(PL 101–319, 104 Stat. 290, July 3, 1990)

E–68   **704. Retention and disposition of articles deposited in Copyright Office**

Section 704(*e*) has been amended by **deleting** "708(*a*)(11)" and **substituting** "708(*a*)(10)".
(PL 101–318, 104 Stat. 288, July 3, 1990)

708. Copyright Office fees   **E–72**

Section 708(*a*) has been amended to read as follows:

(*a*) The following fees shall be paid to the Register of Copyrights:
(1) on filing each application under section 408 for registration of a copyright claim or for a supplementary registration, including the issuance of a certificate of registration if registration is made, $20;
(2) on filing each application for registration of a claim for renewal of a subsisting copyright under section 304(a), including the issuance of a certificate of registration if registration is made, $20;
(3) for the issuance of a receipt for a deposit under section 407, $4;
(4) for the recordation, as provided by section 205, of a transfer of copyright ownership or other document covering not more than one title, $20; for additional titles, $10 for each group of not more than 10 titles;
(5) for the filing, under section 115(*b*), of a notice of intention to obtain a compulsory license, $12;
(6) for the recordation, under section 302(*c*), of a statement revealing the identity of an author of an anonymous or pseudonymous work, or for the recordation, under section 302(*d*), of a statement relating to the death of an author, $20 for a document covering not more than one title; for each additional title, $2;
(7) for the issuance, under section 706, of an additional certificate of registration, $8;
(8) for the issuance of any other certification, $20 for each hour or fraction of an hour consumed with respect thereto;
(9) for the making and reporting of a search as provided by section 705, and for any related services, $20 for each hour or fraction of an hour consumed with respect thereto; and
(10) for any other special services requiring a substantial amount of time or expense, such fees as the Register of Copyrights may fix on the basis of the cost of providing the service.
The Register of Copyrights is authorized to fix the fees for preparing copies of Copyright Office records, whether or not such copies are certified, on the basis of the cost of such preparation.
(PL 101–318, 104 Stat. 287, July 3, 1990; 102–307, 106 Stat. 266, June 26, 1992)

CHAPTER 8

COPYRIGHT ROYALTY TRIBUNAL

801. Copyright Royalty Tribunal: Establishment and purpose   **E–76**

The opening words of section 801 have been amended to read as follows:

(*a*) ESTABLISHMENT.

The Librarian of Congress, upon the recommendation of the Register of Copyrights, is authorized to appoint and convene copyright arbitration royalty panels.

(*b*) PURPOSES.

Subject to the provisions of this chapter, the purposes of the copyright arbitration royalty panels shall be—

Subsection (*b*)(2)(A) has been amended by the **substitution** of the words "copyright arbitration royalty panels" for the word "Commission".

Subsection (*b*)(2)(B) has been amended by the **substitution** of the words "copyright arbitration royalty panels" for the words "Copyright Royalty Tribunal".

Subsections (*b*)(3) and (*c*) have been amended and a new subsection (*d*) **added** as follows:
(3) to distribute royalty fees deposited with the Register of Copyrights under sections 111, 116, 119(*b*), and 1003, and to determine, in cases where controversy exists, the distribution of such fees.

(*c*) RULINGS.

The Librarian of Congress, upon the recommendation of the Register of Copyrights, may, before a copyright arbitration royalty panel is convened, make any necessary procedural or evidentiary rulings that would apply to the proceedings conducted by such panel.

(*d*) ADMINISTRATIVE SUPPORT OF COPYRIGHT ARBITRATION ROYALTY PANELS.

The Library of Congress, upon the recommendation of the Register of Copyrights, shall provide the copyright arbitration royalty panels with the necessary administrative services related to proceedings under this chapter. (PL 101–318, 104 Stat. 288, July 3, 1990; PL 102–563, 106 Stat. 4247, October 28, 1992; PL 103–198, 107 Stat. 2304, December 17, 1993)

E–77   802. Membership of the Tribunal

Section 802 has been amended to provide as follows:

802. Membership and proceedings of copyright arbitration royalty panels.

(*a*) COMPOSITION OF COPYRIGHT ARBITRATION ROYALTY PANELS.

A copyright arbitration royalty panel shall consist of 3 arbitrators selected by the Librarian of Congress pursuant to subsection (*b*).

(*b*) SELECTION OF ARBITRATION PANEL.

Not later than ten days after publication of a notice in the Federal Register initiating an arbitration proceeding under section 803, and in accordance with procedures specified by the Register of Copyrights, the Librarian of Congress shall, upon the recommendation of the Register of Copyrights, select two arbitrators from lists provided by professional arbitration associations. Qualifications of the arbitrators shall include experience in conducting arbitration proceedings and facilitating the resolution and settlement of disputes, and any qualifications which the Librarian of Congress, upon the recommendation of the Register of Copyrights, shall adopt by regulation. The two arbitrators so selected shall, within ten days after their selection, choose a third arbitrator from the same lists, who shall serve as the chairperson of the arbitrators. If such two arbitrators fail to agree upon the selection of a third arbitrator, the Librarian of Congress shall promptly select the third arbitrator. The Librarian of Congress, upon the recommendation of the Register of Copyrights, shall adopt regulations regarding standards of conduct which shall govern arbitrators and the proceedings under this chapter.

(*c*) ARBITRATION PROCEEDINGS.

Copyright arbitration royalty panels shall conduct arbitration proceedings, subject to subchapter II of chapter five of title five, for the purpose of making their determinations in carrying out the purposes set forth in section 801. The arbitration panels shall act on the basis of a fully documented written record, prior decisions of the Copyright Royalty Tribunal, prior copyright arbitration panel determinations, and rulings by the Librarian of Congress under section 801(*c*). Any copyright owner who claims to be entitled to royalties under section 111, 116, or 119, or any interested copyright party who claims to be entitled to royalties under section 1006, may submit relevant information and proposals to the arbitration panels in proceedings applicable to such copyright owner or interested copyright party, and any other person participating in arbitration proceedings may submit such relevant information and proposals to the arbitration panel conducting the proceedings. In ratemaking proceedings, the parties to the proceedings shall bear the entire cost thereof in such manner and proportion as the arbitration panels shall direct. In distribution proceedings, the parties shall bear the cost in direct proportion to their share of the distribution.

(*d*) PROCEDURES.

Effective on the date of the enactment of the Copyright Royalty Tribunal Reform Act of 1993, the Librarian of Congress shall adopt the rules and regulations set forth in chapter three of title 37 of the Code of Federal Regulations to govern proceedings under this chapter. Such rules and regulations shall remain in effect unless and until the Librarian, upon the recommendation of the Register of Copyrights, adopts supplemental or superseding regulations under subchapter II of chapter five of title five.

(*e*) REPORT TO THE LIBRARIAN OF CONGRESS.

Not later than 180 days after publication of the notice in the Federal Register initiating an arbitration proceeding, the copyright arbitration royalty panel conducting the proceeding shall report to the Librarian of Congress its determination concerning the royalty fee or distribution of royalty fees, as the case may be. Such report shall be accompanied by the written record, and shall set forth the facts that the arbitration panel found relevant to its determination.

(*f*) ACTION BY LIBRARIAN OF CONGRESS.

Within 60 days after receiving the report of a copyright arbitration royalty panel under subsection (*e*), the Librarian of Congress, upon the recommendation of the Register of Copyrights, shall adopt or reject the determination of the arbitration panel. The Librarian shall adopt the determination of the arbitration panel unless the Librarian finds that the determination is arbitrary or contrary to the applicable provisions of this title. If the Librarian rejects the determination of the arbitration panel, the Librarian shall, before the end of that 60-day period, and after full examination of the record created in the arbitration proceeding, issue an order setting the royalty fee or distribution of fees, as the case may be. The Librarian shall cause to be published in the Federal Register the determination of the arbitration panel, and the decision of the Librarian (including an order issued under the preceding sentence). The Librarian shall also publicize such determination and decision in such other manner as the Librarian considers appropriate. The Librarian shall also make the report of the arbitration panel and the accompanying record available for public inspection and copying.

(*g*) JUDICIAL REVIEW.

Any decision of the Librarian of Congress under subsection (*f*) with respect to a determination of an arbitration panel may be appealed, by any aggrieved party who would be bound by the determination, to the United States Court of Appeals for the District of Columbia Circuit, within 30 days after the publication of the decision in the Federal Register. If no appeal is brought within such 30-day period, the decision of the Librarian is final, and the royalty fee or determination with respect to the distribution of fees, as the case may be, shall take effect as set forth in the decision. The pendency of an appeal under this paragraph shall not relieve persons obligated to make royalty payments under sections 111, 115, 116, 118, 119, or 1003 who would be affected by the determination on appeal to deposit the statement of account and royalty fees specified in those sections. The court shall have jurisdiction to modify or vacate a decision of the Librarian only if it finds, on the basis of the record before the Librarian, that the Librarian acted in an arbitrary manner. If the court modifies the decision of the Librarian, the court shall have jurisdiction to enter its own determination with respect to the amount or distribution of royalty fees and costs, to order the repayment of any excess fees, and to order the payment of any underpaid fees, and the interest pertaining respectively thereto, in accordance with its final judgment. The court may further vacate the decision of the arbitration panel and remand the case to the Librarian for arbitration proceedings in accordance with subsection (*c*).

(*h*) ADMINISTRATIVE MATTERS.

(1) Deduction of costs from royalty fees.—The Librarian of Congress and the Register of Copyrights may, to the extent not otherwise provided

under this title, deduct from royalty fees deposited or collected under this title the reasonable costs incurred by the Library of Congress and the Copyright Office under this chapter. Such deduction may be made before the fees are distributed to any copyright claimants. If no royalty pool exists from which their costs can be deducted, the Librarian of Congress and the Copyright Office may assess their reasonable costs directly to the parties to the most recent relevant arbitration proceeding.

(2) Positions required for administration of compulsory licensing.—Section 307 of the Legislative Branch Appropriations Act, 1994, shall not apply to employee positions in the Library of Congress that are required to be filled in order to carry out section 111, 115, 116, 118, or 119 or chapter 10.

(PL 101–319, 104 Stat. 290, July 3, 1990; PL 103–198, 107 Stat. 2305, December 17, 1993)

803. Procedures of the Tribunal E-78

Section 803 has been amended to provide as follows:

(a)(1) With respect to proceedings under section 801(*b*)(1) concerning the adjustment of royalty rates as provided in sections 115 and 116, and with respect to proceedings under subparagraphs (A) and (D) of section 801(*b*)(2), during the calendar years specified in the schedule set forth in paragraphs (2), (3), and (4), any owner or user of a copyrighted work whose royalty rates are specified by this title, established by the Copyright Royalty Tribunal before the date of the enactment of the Copyright Royalty Tribunal Reform Act of 1993, or established by a copyright arbitration royalty panel after such date of enactment, may file a petition with the Librarian of Congress declaring that the petitioner requests an adjustment of the rate. The Librarian of Congress shall, upon the recommendation of the Register of Copyrights, make a determination as to whether the petitioner has such a significant interest in the royalty rate in which an adjustment is requested. If the Librarian determines that the petitioner has such a significant interest, the Librarian shall cause notice of this determination, with the reasons therefor, to be published in the Federal Register, together with the notice of commencement of proceedings under this chapter.

(2) In proceedings under section 801(*b*)(2)(A) and (D), a petition described in paragraph (1) may be filed during 1995 and in each subsequent fifth calendar year.

(3) In proceedings under section 801(*b*)(1) concerning the adjustment of royalty rates as provided in section 115, a petition described in paragraph (1) may be filed in 1997 and in each subsequent tenth calendar year.

(4)(A) In proceedings under section 801(*b*)(1) concerning the adjustment of royalty rates as provided in section 116, a petition described in paragraph (1) may be filed at any time within one year after negotiated licenses authorized by section 116 are terminated or expire and are not replaced by subsequent agreements.

(B) If a negotiated license authorized by section 116 is terminated or expires and is not replaced by another such license agreement which provides permission to use a quantity of musical works not substantially smaller than the quantity of such works performed on coin-operated phonorecord players during the one-year period ending March 1, 1989, the Librarian of Congress shall, upon petition filed under paragraph (1) within one year after such termination or expiration, convene a copyright arbitration royalty panel. The arbitration panel shall promptly establish an interim royalty rate or rates for the public performance by means of a coin-operated phonorecord player of non-dramatic musical works embodied in phonorecords which had been subject to the terminated or expired negotiated license agreement. Such rate or rates shall be the same as the last such rate or rates and shall remain in force until the conclusion of proceedings by the arbitration panel, in accordance with section 802, to adjust the royalty rates applicable to such works, or until superseded by a new negotiated license agreement, as provided in section 116(*b*).

(*b*) With respect to proceedings under subparagraph (B) or (C) of section 801(*b*)(2), following an event described in either of those subsections, any owner or user of a copyrighted work whose royalty rates are specified by section 111, or by a rate established by the Copyright Royalty Tribunal or the Librarian of Congress, may, within 12 months, file a petition with the Librarian declaring that the petitioner requests an adjustment of the rate. In this event the Librarian shall proceed as in subsection (*a*) of this section. Any change in royalty rates made by the Copyright Royalty Tribunal or the Librarian of Congress pursuant to this subsection may be reconsidered in 1980, 1985, and each fifth calendar year thereafter, in accordance with the provisions in section 801(*b*)(2)(B) or (C), as the case may be.

(*c*) With respect to proceedings under section 801(*b*(1), concerning the determination of reasonable terms and rates of royalty payments as provided in section 118, the Librarian of Congress shall proceed when and as provided by that section.

(*d*) With respect to proceedings under section 801(*b*)(3) or (4), concerning the distribution of royalty fees in certain circumstances under section 111, 116, 119, or 1007 the Librarian of Congress shall, upon a determination that a controversy exists concerning such distribution, cause to be published in the Federal Register notice of commencement of proceedings under this chapter. (PL 101–318, Sec., 104 Stat. 288, July 3, 1990; PL 102–563, 106 Stat. 4248, October 28, 1992, 106 Stat. 4248; renumbered Section 803 and amended PL 103–198, 107 Stat. 2307, December 17, 1993)

E–79   804. Institution and conclusion of proceedings

Section 804(*a*)(2)(c)(i) has been amended by **deleting** "115" and **substituting** "116".
(PL 101–318, 104 Stat. 288, July 3, 1990)

E–80/ E–85

Sections 805 to 810 have been repealed.
(PL 103–198, 107 Stat. 2308, December, 18, 1993)

After section 914. **Add**:   **E–100**

1001. Definitions   **E–100/1**

As used in this chapter, the following terms have the following meanings:

(1) A "digital audio copied recording" is a reproduction in a digital recording format of a digital musical recording, whether that reproduction is made directly from another digital musical recording or indirectly from a transmission.

(2) A "digital audio interface device" is any machine or device that is designed specifically to communicate digital audio information and related interface data to a digital audio recording device through a nonprofessional interface.

(3) A "digital audio recording device" is any machine or device of a type commonly distributed to individuals for use by individuals, whether or not included with or as part of some other machine or device, the digital

recording function of which is designed or marketed for the primary purpose of, and that is capable of, making a digital audio copied recording for private use, except for—

(A) professional model products, and

(B) dictation machines, answering machines, and other audio recording equipment that is designed and marketed primarily for the creation of sound recordings resulting from the fixation of nonmusical sounds.

(4) (A) A "digital audio recording medium" is any material object in a form commonly distributed for use by individuals, that is primarily marketed or most commonly used by consumers for the purpose of making digital audio copied recordings by use of a digital audio recording device.

(B) Such term does not include any material object—

(i) that embodies a sound recording at the time it is first distributed by the importer or manufacturer; or

(ii) that is primarily marketed and most commonly used by consumers either for the purpose of making copies of motion pictures or other audiovisual works or for the purpose of making copies of nonmusical literary works, including computer programs or data bases.

(5) (A) A "digital musical recording" is a material object—

(i) in which are fixed, in a digital recording format, only sounds, and material, statements, or instructions incidental to those fixed sounds, if any, and

(ii) from which the sounds and material can be perceived, reproduced, or otherwise communicated, either directly or with the aid of a machine or device.

(B) A "digital musical recording" does not include a material object—

(i) in which the fixed sounds consist entirely of spoken word recordings, or

(ii) in which one or more computer programs are fixed, except that a digital musical recording may contain statements or instructions constituting the fixed sounds and incidental material, and statements or instructions to be used directly or indirectly in order to bring about the perception, reproduction, or communication of the fixed sounds and incidental material.

(C) For purposes of this paragraph—

(i) a "spoken word recording" is a sound recording in which are fixed only a series of spoken words, except that the spoken words may be accompanied by incidental musical or other sounds, and

(ii) the term "incidental" means related to and relatively minor by comparison.

(6) "Distribute" means to sell, lease, or assign a product to consumers in the United States, or to sell, lease, or assign a product in the United States for ultimate transfer to consumers in the United States.

(7) An "interested copyright party" is—

(A) the owner of the exclusive right under section 106(1) of this title to reproduce a sound recording of a musical work that has been embodied in a digital musical recording or analog musical recording lawfully made under this title that has been distributed;

(B) the legal or beneficial owner of, or the person that controls, the right to reproduce in a digital musical recording or analog musical recording a musical work that has been embodied in a digital musical recording or analog musical recording lawfully made under this title that has been distributed;

(C) a featured recording artist who performs on a sound recording that has been distributed; or

(D) any association or other organization—

   (i) representing persons specified in subparagraph (A), (B), or (C), or

   (ii) engaged in licensing rights in musical works to music users on behalf of writers and publishers.

(8) To "manufacture" means to produce or assemble a product in the United States. A "manufacturer" is a person who manufactures.

(9) A "music publisher" is a person that is authorized to license the reproduction of a particular musical work in a sound recording.

(10) A "professional model product" is an audio recording device that is designed, manufactured, marketed, and intended for use by recording professionals in the ordinary course of a lawful business, in accordance with such requirements as the Secretary of Commerce shall establish by regulation.

(11) The term "serial copying" means the duplication in a digital format of a copyrighted musical work or sound recording from a digital reproduction of a digital musical recording. The term "digital reproduction of a digital musical recording" does not include a digital musical recording as distributed, by authority of the copyright owner, for ultimate sale to consumers.

(12) The "transfer price" of a digital audio recording device or a digital audio recording medium—

(A) is, subject to subparagraph (B)—

   (i) in the case of an imported product, the actual entered value at United States Customs (exclusive of any freight, insurance, and applicable duty), and

   (ii) in the case of a domestic product, the manufacturer's transfer price (FOB the manufacturer, and exclusive of any direct sales taxes or excise taxes incurred in connection with the sale); and

(B) shall, in a case in which the transferor and transferee are related entities or within a single entity, not be less than a reasonable arms-length price under the principles of the regulations adopted pursuant to section 482 of the Internal Revenue Code of 1986, or any successor provision to such section.

(13) A "writer" is the composer or lyricist of a particular musical work.

(Added PL 102–563, 106 Stat. 4237, October 28, 1992.)

SUBCHAPTER B—COPYING CONTROLS

1002. Incorporation of copying controls   **E–100/2**

(*a*) PROHIBITION ON IMPORTATION, MANUFACTURE, AND DISTRIBUTION.

No person shall import, manufacture, or distribute any digital audio recording device or digital audio interface device that does not conform to—

(1) the Serial Copy Management System;
(2) a system that has the same functional characteristics as the Serial Copy Management System and requires that copyright and generation status information be accurately sent, received, and acted upon between devices using the system's method of serial copying regulation and devices using the Serial Copy Management System; or
(3) any other system certified by the Secretary of Commerce as prohibiting unauthorized serial copying.

(*b*) DEVELOPMENT OF VERIFICATION PROCEDURE.

The Secretary of Commerce shall establish a procedure to verify, upon the petition of an interested party, that a system meets the standards set forth in subsection (*a*)(2).

(*c*) PROHIBITION ON CIRCUMVENTION OF THE SYSTEM.

No person shall import, manufacture, or distribute any device, or offer or perform any service, the primary purpose or effect of which is to avoid, bypass, remove, deactivate, or otherwise circumvent any program or circuit which implements, in whole or in part, a system described in subsection (*a*).

(*d*) ENCODING OF INFORMATION ON DIGITAL MUSICAL RECORDINGS.

(1) Prohibition on encoding inaccurate information.—No person shall encode a digital musical recording of a sound recording with inaccurate information relating to the category code, copyright status, or generation status of the source material for the recording.
(2) Encoding of copyright status not required.—Nothing in this chapter requires any person engaged in the importation or manufacture of digital musical recordings to encode any such digital musical recording with respect to its copyright status.

(*e*) INFORMATION ACCOMPANYING TRANSMISSIONS IN DIGITAL FORMAT.

Any person who transmits or otherwise communicates to the public any sound recording in digital format is not required under this chapter to transmit or otherwise communicate the information relating to the copyright status of the sound recording. Any such person who does transmit or otherwise communicate such copyright status information shall transmit or communicate such information accurately.
(Added PL 102–563, 106 Stat. 4240, October 28, 1992)

SUBCHAPTER C—ROYALTY PAYMENTS

E–100/3   1003. Obligation to make royalty payments

(*a*) PROHIBITION ON IMPORTATION AND MANUFACTURE.

No person shall import into and distribute, or manufacture and distribute, any digital audio recording device or digital audio recording medium unless such person records the notice specified by this section and subsequently deposits the statements of account and applicable royalty payments for such device or medium specified in section 1004.

(*b*) Filing of Notice.

The importer or manufacturer of any digital audio recording device or digital audio recording medium, within a product category or utilizing a technology with respect to which such manufacturer or importer has not previously filed a notice under this subsection, shall file with the Register of Copyrights a notice with respect to such device or medium, in such form and content as the Register shall prescribe by regulation.

(*c*) Filing of Quarterly and Annual Statements of Account.

(1) Generally.—Any importer or manufacturer that distributes any digital audio recording device or digital audio recording medium that it manufactured or imported shall file with the Register of Copyrights, in such form and content as the Register shall prescribe by regulation, such quarterly and annual statements of account with respect to such distribution as the Register shall prescribe by regulation.
(2) Certification, verification, and confidentiality.—Each such statement shall be certified as accurate by an authorized officer or principal of the importer or manufacturer. The Register shall issue regulations to provide for the verification and audit of such statements and to protect the confidentiality of the information contained in such statements. Such regulations shall provide for the disclosure, in confidence, of such statements to interested copyright parties.
(3) Royalty payments.—Each such statement shall be accompanied by the royalty payments specified in section 1004.
(Added PL 102–563, 106 Stat. 4240, Oct. 28, 1992.)

1004. Royalty payments   **E–100/4**

(*a*) Digital Audio Recording Devices.

(1) Amount of payment.—The royalty payment due under section 1003 for each digital audio recording device imported into and distributed in the United States, or manufactured and distributed in the United States, shall be two per cent. of the transfer price. Only the first person to manufacture and distribute or import and distribute such device shall be required to pay the royalty with respect to such device.
(2) Calculation for devices distributed with other devices.—With respect to a digital audio recording device first distributed in combination with one or more devices, either as a physically integrated unit or as separate components, the royalty payment shall be calculated as follows:
(A) If the digital audio recording device and such other devices are part of a physically integrated unit, the royalty payment shall be based on the transfer price of the unit, but shall be reduced by any royalty payment made on any digital audio recording device included within the unit that was not first distributed in combination with the unit.

    (B) If the digital audio recording device is not part of a physically integrated unit and substantially similar devices have been distributed separately at any time during the preceding four calendar quarters, the royalty payment shall be based on the average transfer price of such devices during those 4 quarters.

    (C) If the digital audio recording device is not part of a physically integrated unit and substantially similar devices have not been distributed separately at any time during the preceding four calendar quarters, the royalty payment shall be based on a constructed price reflecting the proportional value of such device to the combination as a whole.

  (3) Limits on royalties.—Notwithstanding paragraph (1) or (2), the amount of the royalty payment for each digital audio recording device shall not be less than $1 nor more than the royalty maximum. The royalty maximum shall be $8 per device, except that in the case of a physically integrated unit containing more than one digital audio recording device, the royalty maximum for such unit shall be $12. During the sixth year after the effective date of this chapter, and not more than once each year thereafter, any interested copyright party may petition the Librarian of Congress to increase the royalty maximum and, if more than 20 per cent. of the royalty payments are at the relevant royalty maximum, the Librarian of Congress shall prospectively increase such royalty maximum with the goal of having no more than 10 per cent. of such payments at the new royalty maximum; however the amount of any such increase as a percentage of the royalty maximum shall in no event exceed the percentage increase in the Consumer Price Index during the period under review.

(*b*) DIGITAL AUDIO RECORDING MEDIA.

The royalty payment due under section 1003 for each digital audio recording medium imported into and distributed in the United States, or manufactured and distributed in the United States, shall be three per cent. of the transfer price. Only the first person to manufacture and distribute or import and distribute such medium shall be required to pay the royalty with respect to such medium.
(PL 102–563, 106 Stat. 4241, October 28, 1992; PL 103–198, 107 Stat. 2312, December 17, 1993)

E100/5   1005. Deposit of royalty payments and deduction of expenses

The Register of Copyrights shall receive all royalty payments deposited under this chapter and, after deducting the reasonable costs incurred by the Copyright Office under this chapter, shall deposit the balance in the Treasury of the United States as offsetting receipts, in such manner as the Secretary of the Treasury directs. All funds held by the Secretary of the Treasury shall be invested in interest-bearing United States securities for later distribution with interest under section 1007. The Register may, in the Register's discretion, four years after the close of any calendar year, close out the royalty payments account for that calendar year, and may treat any funds remaining in such account and any subsequent deposits that would otherwise be attributable to that calendar year as attributable to the succeeding calendar year.

(PL 102–563, 106 Stat. 4242, October 28, 1992; PL 103–198,. 107 Stat. 2312, December 17, 1993)

1006. Entitlement to royalty payments

(*a*) INTERESTED COPYRIGHT PARTIES.

The royalty payments deposited pursuant to section 1005 shall, in accordance with the procedures specified in section 1007, be distributed to any interested copyright party—
  (1) whose musical work or sound recording has been—
      (A) embodied in a digital musical recording or an analog musical recording lawfully made under this title that has been distributed, and
      (B) distributed in the form of digital musical recordings or analog musical recordings or disseminated to the public in transmissions, during the period to which such payments pertain; and
  (2) who has filed a claim under section 1007.

(*b*) ALLOCATION OF ROYALTY PAYMENTS TO GROUPS.

The royalty payments shall be divided into two funds as follows:
  (1) The Sound Recordings Fund.—662/3 per cent. of the royalty payments shall be allocated to the Sound Recordings Fund. $2\frac{5}{8}$ per cent. of the royalty payments allocated to the Sound Recordings Fund shall be placed in an escrow account managed by an independent administrator jointly appointed by the interested copyright parties described in section 1001(7)(A) and the American Federation of Musicians (or any successor entity) to be distributed to nonfeatured musicians (whether or not members of the American Federation of Musicians or any successor entity) who have performed on sound recordings distributed in the United States. $1\frac{3}{8}$ per cent. of the royalty payments allocated to the Sound Recordings Fund shall be placed in an escrow account managed by an independent administrator jointly appointed by the interested copyright parties described in section 1001(7)(A) and the American Federation of Television and Radio Artists (or any successor entity) to be distributed to nonfeatured vocalists (whether or not members of the American Federation Television and Radio Artists or any successor entity) who have performed on sound recordings distributed in the United States. 40 per cent. of the remaining royalty payments in the Sound Recordings Fund shall be distributed to the interested copyright parties described in section 1001(7)(C), and 60 per cent. of such remaining royalty payments shall be distributed to the interested copyright parties described in section 1001(7)(A).
  (2) The Musical Works Fund.—
      (A) $33\frac{1}{3}$ per cent. of the royalty payments shall be allocated to the Musical Works Fund for distribution to interested copyright parties described in section 1001(7)(B).
      (B)   (i) Music publishers shall be entitled to 50 per cent. of the royalty payments allocated to the Musical Works Fund.
           (ii) Writers shall be entitled to the other 50 per cent. of the royalty payments allocated to the Musical Works Fund.

(*c*) ALLOCATION OF ROYALTY PAYMENTS WITHIN GROUPS.

If all interested copyright parties within a group specified in subsection (*b*) do not agree on a voluntary proposal for the distribution of the royalty payments within each group, the Librarian of Congress shall convene a copyright arbitration royalty panel which shall, pursuant to the procedures specified under section 1007(*c*), allocate royalty payments under this section based on the extent to which, during the relevant period—

    (1) for the Sound Recordings Fund, each sound recording was distributed in the form of digital musical recordings or analog musical recordings; and

    (2) for the Musical Works Fund, each musical work was distributed in the form of digital musical recordings or analog musical recordings or disseminated to the public in transmissions.

(PL 102–563, 106 Stat. 4242, October 28, 1992; PL 103–198, 107 Stat. 2312, December 17, 1993)

E–100/7   1007. Procedures for distributing royalty payments

(*a*) FILING OF CLAIMS AND NEGOTIATIONS.

    (1) Filing of claims.—During the first two months of each calendar year after the calendar year in which this chapter takes effect, every interested copyright party seeking to receive royalty payments to which such party is entitled under section 1006 shall file with the Librarian of Congress a claim for payments collected during the preceding year in such form and manner as the Librarian of Congress shall prescribe by regulation.

    (2) Negotiations.—Notwithstanding any provision of the antitrust laws, for purposes of this section interested copyright parties within each group specified in section 1006(*b*) may agree among themselves to the proportionate division of royalty payments, may lump their claims together and file them jointly or as a single claim, or may designate a common agent, including any organization described in section 1001(7)(D), to negotiate or receive payment on their behalf; except that no agreement under this subsection may modify the allocation of royalties specified in section 1006(*b*).

(*b*) DISTRIBUTION OF PAYMENTS IN THE ABSENCE OF A DISPUTE.

Within 30 days after the period established for the filing of claims under subsection (*a*), in each year after the year in which this section takes effect, the Librarian of Congress shall determine whether there exists a controversy concerning the distribution of royalty payments under section 1006(*c*). If the Librarian of Congress determines that no such controversy exists, the Librarian of Congress shall, within 30 days after such determination, authorize the distribution of the royalty payments as set forth in the agreements regarding the distribution of royalty payments entered into pursuant to subsection (*a*), after deducting its reasonable administrative costs under this section.

(*c*) RESOLUTION OF DISPUTES.

If the Librarian of Congress finds the existence of a controversy, the Librarian shall, pursuant to chapter 8 of this title, convene a copyright arbitration royalty panel to determine the distribution of royalty payments. During the pendency of such a proceeding, the Librarian of Congress shall withhold from distribution an amount sufficient to satisfy all claims with respect to which a controversy exists, but shall, to the extent feasible, authorize the distribution of any amounts that are not in controversy. The Librarian of Congress shall, before authorizing the distribution of such royalty payments, deduct the reasonable administrative costs incurred by the Librarian under this section. (PL 102–563, 106 Stat. 4244, October 28, 1992; PL 103–198, 107 Stat. 2312, December 17, 1993)

SUBCHAPTER D—PROHIBITION ON CERTAIN INFRINGEMENT ACTIONS, REMEDIES, AND ARBITRATION

1008. Prohibition on certain infringement actions   **E–100/8**

No action may be brought under this title alleging infringement of copyright based on the manufacture, importation, or distribution of a digital audio recording device, a digital audio recording medium, an analog recording device, or an analog recording medium, or based on the noncommercial use by a consumer of such a device or medium for making digital musical recordings or analog musical recordings.
(Added PL 102–563, 106 Stat. 4244, October 28, 1992.)

1009. Civil remedies   **E–100/9**

(*a*) CIVIL ACTIONS.

Any interested copyright party injured by a violation of section 1002 or 1003 may bring a civil action in an appropriate United States district court against any person for such violation.

(*b*) OTHER CIVIL ACTIONS.

Any person injured by a violation of this chapter may bring a civil action in an appropriate United States district court for actual damages incurred as a result of such violation.

(*c*) POWERS OF THE COURT.

In an action brought under subsection (*a*), the court—
   (1) may grant temporary and permanent injunctions on such terms as it deems reasonable to prevent or restrain such violation;
   (2) in the case of a violation of section 1002, or in the case of an injury resulting from a failure to make royalty payments required by section 1003, shall award damages under subsection (*d*);

    (3) in its discretion may allow the recovery of costs by or against any party other than the United States or an officer thereof; and

    (4) in its discretion may award a reasonable attorney's fee to the prevailing party.

(*d*) AWARD OF DAMAGES.

    (1) Damages for section 1002 or 1003 violations.—

        (A) Actual damages.—

            (i) In an action brought under subsection (*a*), if the court finds that a violation of section 1002 or 1003 has occurred, the court shall award to the complaining party its actual damages if the complaining party elects such damages at any time before final judgment is entered.

            (ii) In the case of section 1003, actual damages shall constitute the royalty payments that should have been paid under section 1004 and deposited under section 1005. In such a case, the court, in its discretion, may award an additional amount of not to exceed 50 percent of the actual damages.

        (B) Statutory damages for section 1002 violations.—

            (i) Device.—A complaining party may recover an award of statutory damages for each violation of section 1002 (*a*) or (*c*) in the sum of not more than $2,500 per device involved in such violation or per device on which a service prohibited by section 1002(*c*) has been performed, as the court considers just.

            (ii) Digital musical recording.—A complaining party may recover an award of statutory damages for each violation of section 1002(d) in the sum of not more than $25 per digital musical recording involved in such violation, as the court considers just.

            (iii) Transmission.—A complaining party may recover an award of damages for each transmission or communication that violates section 1002(*e*) in the sum of not more than $10,000 as the court considers just.

    (2) Repeated violations.—In any case in which the court finds that a person has violated section 1002 or 1003 within three years after a final judgment against that person for another such violation was entered, the court may increase the award of damages to not more than double the amounts that would otherwise be awarded under paragraph (1), as the court considers just.

    (3) Innocent violations of section 1002.—The court in its discretion may reduce the total award of damages against a person violating section 1002 to a sum of not less than $250 in any case in which the court finds that the violator was not aware and had no reason to believe that its acts constituted a violation of section 1002.

(*e*) PAYMENT OF DAMAGES.

Any award of damages under subsection (*d*) shall be deposited with the Register pursuant to section 1005 for distribution to interested copyright parties as though such funds were royalty payments made pursuant to section 1003.

(*f*) Impounding of Articles.

At any time while an action under subsection (*a*) is pending, the court may order the impounding, on such terms as it deems reasonable, of any digital audio recording device, digital musical recording, or device specified in section 1002(*c*) that is in the custody or control of the alleged violator and that the court has reasonable cause to believe does not comply with, or was involved in a violation of, section 1002.

(*g*) Remedial Modification and Destruction of Articles.

In an action brought under subsection (*a*), the court may, as part of a final judgment or decree finding a violation of section 1002, order the remedial modification or the destruction of any digital audio recording device, digital musical recording, or device specified in section 1002(*c*) that—
    (1) does not comply with, or was involved in a violation of, section 1002, and
    (2) is in the custody or control of the violator or has been impounded under subsection (*f*).
(Added PL 102–563, 106 Stat. 4245, October 28, 1992)

1010. Arbitration of certain disputes

(*a*) Scope of Arbitration.

Before the date of first distribution in the United States of a digital audio recording device or a digital audio interface device, any party manufacturing, importing, or distributing such device, and any interested copyright party may mutually agree to binding arbitration for the purpose of determining whether such device is subject to section 1002, or the basis on which royalty payments for such device are to be made under section 1003.

(*a*) Initiation of Arbitration Proceedings.

Parties agreeing to such arbitration shall file a petition with the Librarian of Congress requesting the commencement of an arbitration proceeding. The petition may include the names and qualifications of potential arbitrators. Within two weeks after receiving such a petition, the Librarian of Congress shall cause notice to be published in the Federal Register of the initiation of an arbitration proceeding. Such notice shall include the names and qualifications of three arbitrators chosen by the Librarian of Congress from a list of available arbitrators obtained from the American Arbitration Association or such similar organization as the Librarian of Congress shall select, and from potential arbitrators listed in the parties' petition. The arbitrators selected under this subsection shall constitute an Arbitration Panel.

(*c*) Stay of Judicial Proceedings.

Any civil action brought under section 1009 against a party to arbitration under this section shall, on application of one of the parties to the arbitration, be stayed until completion of the arbitration proceeding.

(*d*) ARBITRATION PROCEEDING.

The Arbitration Panel shall conduct an arbitration proceeding with respect to the matter concerned, in accordance with such procedures as it may adopt. The Panel shall act on the basis of a fully documented written record. Any party to the arbitration may submit relevant information and proposals to the Panel. The parties to the proceeding shall bear the entire cost thereof in such manner and proportion as the Panel shall direct.

(*e*) REPORT TO LIBRARIAN OF CONGRESS.

Not later than 60 days after publication of the notice under subsection (*b*) of the initiation of an arbitration proceeding, the Arbitration Panel shall report to the Librarian of Congress its determination concerning whether the device concerned is subject to section 1002, or the basis on which royalty payments for the device are to be made under section 1003. Such report shall be accompanied by the written record, and shall set forth the facts that the Panel found relevant to its determination.

(*f*) ACTION BY THE LIBRARIAN OF CONGRESS.

Within 60 days after receiving the report of the Arbitration Panel under subsection (*e*), the Librarian of Congress shall adopt or reject the determination of the Panel. The Librarian of Congress shall adopt the determination of the Panel unless the Librarian of Congress finds that the determination is clearly erroneous. If the Librarian of Congress rejects the determination of the Panel, the Librarian of Congress shall, before the end of that 60-day period, and after full examination of the record created in the arbitration proceeding, issue an order setting forth the Librarian's decision and the reasons therefor. The Librarian of Congress shall cause to be published in the Federal Register the determination of the Panel and the decision of the Librarian of Congress under this subsection with respect to the determination (including any order issued under the preceding sentence).

(*g*) JUDICIAL REVIEW.

Any decision of the Librarian of Congress under subsection (*f*) with respect to a determination of the Arbitration Panel may be appealed, by a party to the arbitration, to the United States Court of Appeals for the District of Columbia Circuit, within 30 days after the publication of the decision in the Federal Register. The pendency of a appeal under this subsection shall not stay the decision of the Librarian of Congress. The Court shall have jurisdiction to modify or vacate a decision of the Librarian of Congress only if it finds, on the basis of the record before the Librarian of Congress, that the Arbitration Panel or the Librarian of Congress acted in an arbitrary manner. If the Court modifies the decision of the Librarian of Congress, the Court shall have jurisdiction to enter its own decision in accordance with its final judgment. The Court may further vacate the decision of the Librarian of Congress and remand the case for arbitration proceedings as provided in this section.
(PL. 102–563, 106 Stat. 4246, October 28, 1992; PL 103–198, 107 Stat. 2312, December 17, 1993)

**"2318. Transportation, sale or receipt of phonograph records bearing   E–111
forged or counterfeit labels**

Section 2318 of title 18 of the United States Code has been amended to
provide as follows:
Trafficking in counterfeit labels for phonorecords and copies of motion
pictures or other audiovisual works

(*a*) Whoever, in any of the circumstances described in subsection (*c*) of
this section, knowingly traffics in a counterfeit label affixed or designed to
be affixed to a phonorecord, or a copy of a motion picture or other
audiovisual work, shall be fined not more than $250,000 or imprisoned for
not more than five years, or both.

(*b*) As used in this section—

(1) the term "counterfeit label" means an identifying label or container
that appears to be genuine, but is not;

(2) the term "traffic" means to transport, transfer or otherwise dispose of, to
another, as consideration for anything of value or to make or obtain
control of with intent to so transport, transfer or dispose of; and

(3) the terms "copy", "phonorecord", "motion picture", and "audiovisual
work" have, respectively, the meanings given those terms in section 101
(relating to definitions) of title 17.

(*c*) The circumstances referred to in subsection (*a*) of this section are—

(1) the offense is committed within the special maritime and territorial
jurisdiction of the United States; or within the special aircraft jurisdiction of the United States (as defined in section 101 of the Federal
Aviation Act of 1958);

(2) the mail or a facility of interstate or foreign commerce is used or
intended to be used in the commission of the offense; or

(3) the counterfeit label is affixed to or encloses, or is designed to be affixed
to or enclose, a copyrighted motion picture or other audiovisual work,
or a phonorecord of a copyrighted sound recording.

(*d*) When any person is convicted of any violation of subsection (*a*), the court
in its judgment of conviction shall in addition to the penalty therein
prescribed, order the forfeiture and destruction or other disposition of all
counterfeit labels and all articles to which counterfeit labels have been affixed
or which were intended to have had such labels affixed.

(*e*) Except to the extent they are inconsistent with the provisions of this title,
all provisions of section 509, title 17, United States Code, are applicable to
violations of subsection (*a*).
(PL 101–647, 104 Stat. 4928, November 29, 1990)

Appendix F

TREATY OF ROME

(As amended by the Single European Act of February 1986 and the Maastricht Treaty of February 1992)

Delete: ARTICLE 2, and **substitute**:   **F–1**

ARTICLE 2

The Community shall have as its task, by establishing a common market and an economic and monetary union and by implementing the common policies or activities referred to in Articles 3 and 3a, to promote throughout the Community a harmonious and balanced development of economic activities, sustainable and non-inflationary growth respecting the environment, a high degree of convergence of economic performance, a high level of employment and of social protection, the raising of the standard of living and quality of life, and economic and social cohesion and solidarity among Member States.

Delete: ARTICLE 3, and **substitute**:   **F–2**

ARTICLE 3

For the purposes set out in Article 2, the activities of the Community shall include, as provided in this Treaty and in accordance with the timetable set out therein:
- (a) the elimination, as between Member States, of customs duties and quantitative restrictions on the import and export of goods, and of all other measures having equivalent effect;
- (b) a common commercial policy;
- (c) an internal market characterised by the abolition, as between Member States, of obstacles to the free movement of goods, persons, services and capital;
- (d) measures concerning the entry and movement of persons in the internal market as provided for in Article 100c;
- (e) a common policy in the sphere of agriculture and fisheries;
- (f) a common policy in the sphere of transport;
- (g) a system ensuring that competition in the internal market is not distorted;
- (h) the approximation of the laws of Member States to the extent required for the functioning of the common market;
- (i) a policy in the social sphere comprising a European Social Fund;
- (j) the strengthening of economic and social cohesion;
- (k) a policy in the sphere of the environment;
- (l) the strengthening of the competitiveness of Community industry;

(*m*) the promotion of research and technological development;

(*n*) encouragement for the establishment and development of trans-European networks;

(*o*) a contribution to the attainment of a high level of health protection;

(*p*) a contribution to education and training of quality and to the flowering of the cultures of the Member States;

(*q*) a policy in the sphere of development cooperation;

(*r*) the association of the overseas countries and territories in order to increase trade and promote jointly economic and social development;

(*s*) a contribution to the strengthening of consumer protection;

(*t*) measures in the spheres of energy, civil protection and tourism.

F–2A   Insert:

ARTICLE 3a

1. For the purposes set out in Article 2, the activities of the Member States and the Community shall include, as provided in this Treaty and in accordance with the timetable set out therein, the adoption of an economic policy which is based on the close coordination of Member States' economic policies, on the internal market and on the definition of common objectives, and conducted in accordance with the principle of an open market economy with free competition.

2. Concurrently with the foregoing, and as provided in this Treaty and in accordance with the timetable and the procedures set out therein, these activities shall include the irrevocable fixing of exchange rates leading to the introduction of a single currency, the ECU, and the definition and conduct of a single monetary policy and exchange rate policy the primary objective of both of which shall be to maintain price stability and, without prejudice to this objective, to support the general economic policies in the Community, in accordance with the principle of an open market economy with free competition.

3. These activities of the Member States and the Community shall entail compliance with the following guiding principles: stable prices, sound public finances and monetary conditions and a sustainable balance of payments.

F–3A   Insert:

ARTICLE 6

Within the scope of application of this Treaty, and without prejudice to any special provisions contained therein, any discrimination on grounds of nationality shall be prohibited.

The Council, acting in accordance with the procedure referred to in Article 189c, may adopt rules designed to prohibit such discrimination.

F–4   The text of this Article (renumbered 7a due to the deletion of the former Article 6) remains the same, but the references to Articles 8b and 8c have been amended to refer to Articles 7b and 7c.

Insert:

ARTICLE 100

The Council shall, acting unanimously on a proposal from the Commission and after consulting the European Parliament and the Economic and Social Committee, issue directives for the approximation of such laws, regulations or administrative provisions of the Member States as directly affect the establishment or functioning of the common market.

Insert:

ARTICLE 100a

1. By way of derogation from Article 100 and save where otherwise provided in this Treaty, the following provisions shall apply for the achievement of the objectives set out in Article 7a. The Council shall, acting in accordance with the procedure referred to in Article 189b and after consulting the Economic and Social Committee, adopt the measures for the approximation of the provisions laid down by law, regulation or adminstrative action in Member States which have as their object the establishment and functioning of the internal market.

2. Paragraph 1 shall not apply to fiscal provisions, to those relating to the free movement of persons nor to those relating to the rights and interests of employed persons.

3. The Commission, in its proposals envisaged in paragraph 1 concerning health, safety, environmental protection and consumer protection, will take as a base a high level of protection.

4. If, after the adoption of a harmonisation measure by the Council acting by a qualified majority, a Member State deems it necessary to apply national provisions on grounds of major needs referred to in Article 36, or relating to protection of the environment or the working environment, it shall notify the Commission of these provisions.

The Commission shall confirm the provisions involved after having verified that they are not a means of arbitrary discrimination or a disguised restriction on trade between Member States.

By way of derogation from the procedure laid down in Articles 169 and 170, the Commission or any Member State may bring the matter directly before the Court of Justice if it considers that another Member State is making improper use of the powers provided for in this Article.

5. The harmonisation measures referred to above shall, in appropriate cases, include a safeguard clause authorising the Member States to take for one or more of the non-economic reasons referred to in Article 36, provisional measures subject to a Community control procedure.

F–10A   **Insert**:

ARTICLE 189

In order to carry out their task and in accordance with the provisions of this Treaty, the European Parliament acting jointly with the Council, the Council and the Commission shall make regulations and issue directives, take decisions, make recommendations or deliver opinions.

A regulation shall have general application. It shall be binding in its entirety and directly applicable in all Member States.

A directive shall be binding, as to the result to be achieved, upon each Member State to which it is addressed, but shall leave to the national authorities the choice of form and methods.

A decision shall be binding in its entirety upon those to whom it is addressed.

Recommendations and opinions shall have no binding force.

Appendix G

PRECEDENTS AND COURT FORMS

(F) NOTICE OF MOTION	**G–12**

It is now sufficient if the Notice of Motion states that the Court will be moved before "the Chancery Motions Judge" rather than a named judge. See Practice Direction (Chancery Division: Forms) [1992] 1 W.L.R. 791.

(H) ANTON PILLER ORDER	**G–14**

Delete form H, and **substitute**:

[Heading—see Court Form (G)]

ORDER TO ALLOW ENTRY AND SEARCH OF PREMISES

IMPORTANT:-

NOTICE TO THE DEFENDANT

(1) This Order orders you to allow the persons mentioned below to enter the premises described in the Order and to search for, examine and remove or copy the articles specified in the Order. This part of the Order is subject to restrictions. The Order also requires you to hand over any of the articles which are under your control and to provide information to the Plaintiff's solicitors, and prohibits you from doing certain acts. You should read the terms of the Order very carefully. You are advised to consult a solicitor as soon as possible.

(2) Before you the Defendant or the person appearing to be in control of the premises allow anybody onto the premises to carry out this Order you are entitled to have the solicitor who serves you with this Order explain to you what it means in every day language.

(3) You are entitled to insist that there is nobody or nobody except Mr [   ] present who could gain commercially from anything he might read or see on your premises.

(4) You are entitled to refuse to permit entry before 9.30 am or after 5.30 pm or at all on Saturday or Sunday.

(5) You are entitled to seek legal advice, and to ask the Court to vary or discharge this Order, provided you do so at once, and provided that meanwhile you permit the Supervising Solicitor (who is a solicitor acting independently of the Plaintiff) and the Plaintiff's solicitor to enter, but not start to search: see paragraph 3.

(6) If you   the Defendant disobey this Order you will be guilty of contempt of Court and may be (sent to prison or) fined or your assets seized.[1]

THE ORDER

An application was made today [date] by counsel [or solicitors] for . . . the Plaintiff to Mr Justice [   ]. Mr Justice [   ] heard the application and read the affidavits listed in Schedule 6 at the end of this Order. As a result of the application **IT IS ORDERED** by Mr Justice [   ] that:

Entry and search of premises and vehicles on the premises.

1.(1) The Defendant must allow Mr/Mrs/Miss   :('the Supervising Solicitor'), together with Mr   a solicitor of the Supreme Court, and a partner in the firm of the Plaintiff's solicitors   and up to   other persons being   [their capacity] accompanying them, to enter the premises mentioned in Schedule 1 to this Order and any vehicles on the premises so that they can search for, inspect, photograph or photocopy, and deliver into the safekeeping of the Plaintiff's solicitors all the documents and articles which are listed in Schedule 2 to this Order ('the listed items') or which Mr   believes to be listed items. The Defendant must allow those persons to remain on the premises until the search is complete, and if necessary to re-enter the premises on the same or the following day in order to complete the search.

(2) This Order must be complied with either by the Defendant himself or by a responsible employee of the Defendant or by the person appearing to be in control of the premises.

(3) This Order requires the Defendant or his employee or the person appearing to be in control of the premises to permit entry to the premises immediately the Order is served upon him, except as stated in paragraph 3 below.

Restrictions on the service and carrying out of paragraph 1 of this Order

2.   Paragraph 1 of this Order is subject to the following restrictions:—

(1) This Order may only be served between 9.30 am and 5.30 pm on a weekday.

(2) This Order may not be carried out at the same time as any police search warrant.

---

[1] Delete the words "sent to prison" in the case of a corporate Defendant. This notice is not a substitute for the indorsement of a penal notice.

(3) This Order must be served by the Supervising Solicitor, and paragraph 1 of the Order must be carried out in his presence and under his supervision. [At least one of the persons accompanying him as provided by paragraph 1 of this Order shall be a woman.][2]

(4) This Order does not require the person served with the Order to allow anyone [or anyone except Mr   who could gain commercially from anything he might read or see on the premises if the person served with the Order objects.

(5) No item may be removed from the premises until a list of the items to be removed has been prepared, and a copy of the list has been supplied to the person served with the Order, and he has been given a reasonable opportunity to check the list.

(6) The premises must not be searched, and items must not be removed from them, except in the presence of the Defendant or a person appearing to be a responsible employee of the Defendant.

(7) If the Supervising Solicitor is satisfied that full compliance with subparagraph (5) or (6) above is impracticable, he may permit the search to proceed and items to be removed without compliance with the impracticable requirements.

Obtaining legal advice and applying to the Court

3. Before permitting entry to the premises by any person other than the Supervising Officer and the Plaintiff's solicitors, the Defendant or other person appearing to be in control of the premises may seek legal advice, and apply to the Court to vary or discharge this Order, provided he does so at once. While this is being done, he may refuse entry to the premises by any other person, and may refuse to permit the search to begin, for a short time (not to exceed two hours, unless the Supervising Solicitor agrees to a longer period).

Delivery of listed items and computer print-outs

4. (1) The Defendant must immediately hand over to the Plaintiff's solicitors any of the listed items which are in his possession or under his control.

(2) If any of the listed items exists only in computer readable form, the Defendant must immediately give the Plaintiff's solicitors effective access to the computers, with all necessary passwords, to enable them to be searched, and cause the listed items to be printed out. A print out of the items must be given to the Plaintiff's solicitors or displayed on the computer screen so that they can be read and copied. All reasonable steps shall be taken by the Plaintiff to ensure that no damage is done to any computer or data. The Plaintiff and his representatives may not themselves search the Defendant's computers unless they have sufficient expertise to do so without damaging the Defendant's system.

Disclosure of information by the Defendant

5.(1) The Defendant must immediately inform the Plaintiff's solicitors:–

---

[2] The words in brackets in (3) are to be included in a case where the premises are likely to be occupied by an unaccompanied woman and the Supervising Solicitor is a man.

    (a) where all the listed items are; and
    (b) so far as he is aware
        (i)   the name and address of everyone who has supplied him, or offered to supply him, with listed items;
        (ii) the name and address of everyone to whom he has supplied, or offered to supply, listed items; and
        (iii) full details of the dates and quantities of every such supply and offer.

  (2) Within   days after being served with this Order the Defendant must prepare and swear an affidavit confirming the above information.

Prohibited acts

6.(1) Except for the purpose of obtaining legal advice, the Defendant must not directly or indirectly inform anyone of these proceedings or of the contents of this Order, or warn anyone that proceedings have been or may be brought against him by the Plaintiff until [   ].[3]

  (2) [Insert any negative injunctions].

EFFECT OF THIS ORDER

1) A Defendant who is an individual who is ordered not to do something must not do it himself or in any other way. He must not do it through others acting on his behalf or on his instructions or with his encouragement.

2) A Defendant which is a corporation and which is ordered not to do something must not do it itself or by its directors officers employees or agents or in any other way.

UNDERTAKINGS

The Plaintiff, the Plaintiff's solicitors and the Supervising Solicitor gave to the Court the undertakings contained in Schedules 3, 4 and 5 respectively to this Order.

DURATION OF THIS ORDER

Paragraph 6(2) of this Order will remain in force up to and including [: :19] (which is 'the Return Date'), unless before then it is varied or discharged by a further Order of the Court.[4] The application in which this Order is made shall come back to the Court for further hearing on the Return Date.

VARIATION OR DISCHARGE OF THIS ORDER

The Defendant (or anyone notified of this Order) may apply to the Court at any time to vary or discharge this Order (or so much of it as affects that person), but anyone wishing to do so must first inform the Plaintiff's solicitors.

NAME AND ADDRESS OF PLAINTIFF'S SOLICITORS

The Plaintiff's solicitors are:–
[Name, address and telephone numbers both in and out of office hours.]

---

[3] The date to be inserted here should be the Return Date or, if sooner, 7 days from the date of the Order.
[4] The date should be the earliest practicable return date.

[INTERPRETATION OF THIS ORDER

1) In this Order "he" "him" or "his" include "she" or "her" and "it" or "its".

2) Where there are two or more Defendants then (unless the context indicates differently)

   (a) References to "the Defendants" means both or all of them.
   (b) An Order requiring "the Defendants" to do or not to do anything requires each Defendant to do or not to do it.
   (c) A requirement relating to service of this Order, or of any legal proceedings, on "the Defendants" means on each of them.
   (d) Any other requirement that something shall be done to or in the presence of "the Defendants" means to or in the presence of one of them.]

SCHEDULE 1

The Premises

SCHEDULE 2

The listed items

SCHEDULE 3

Undertakings given by the Plaintiff

1) If the Court later finds that this Order or carrying it out has caused loss to the Defendant, and decides that the Defendant should be compensated for that loss, the Plaintiff will comply with any Order the Court may make.

2) As soon as practicable to issue a writ of summons [in the form of the draft writ produced to the Court] [claiming appropriate relief].

3) To [swear and file an affidavit] [cause an affidavit to be sworn and filed] [substantially in the terms of the draft produced to the Court] [confirming the substance of what was said to the Court by the Plaintiff's counsel/solicitors].

4) To serve on the Defendant at the same time as this Order is served upon him (i) the writ (ii) a notice of motion/summons for   19   and (iii) copies of the affidavits and copiable exhibits containing the evidence relied on by the Plaintiff. [Copies of the confidential exhibits   need not be served, but they must be made available for inspection by or on behalf of the Defendant in the presence of the Plaintiff's solicitors while the Order is carried out. Afterwards they must be provided to a solicitor representing the Defendant who gives a written undertaking not to permit the Defendant to see them or copies of them except in his presence and not to permit the Defendant to make or take away any note or record of the exhibits.]

5) To serve on the Defendant a copy of the Supervising Solicitor's report on the carrying out of this Order as soon as it is received and to produce a copy of the report to the Court.

6) Not, without the leave of the Court, to use any information or documents obtained as a result of carrying out this Order except for the purposes of these proceedings or to inform anyone else of these proceedings until after the Return Date.

[7)[5]]

SCHEDULE 4

Undertakings given by the Plaintiff's solicitors

1) To answer at once to the best of their ability any question whether a particular item is a listed item.

2) To return the originals of all documents obtained as a result of this Order (except original documents which belong to the Plaintiff) as soon as possible and in any event within two working days of their removal.

3) While ownership of any item obtained as a result of this Order is in dispute, to deliver the article into the keeping of solicitors acting for the Defendant within two working days from receiving a written undertaking by them to retain the article in safe keeping and to produce it to the Court when required.

4) To retain in their own safe keeping all other items obtained as a result of this Order until the Court directs otherwise.

SCHEDULE 5

Undertakings given by the Supervising Solicitor

1) To offer to explain to the person served with the Order its meaning and effect fairly and in everyday language, and to inform him of his right to seek legal advice and apply to vary or discharge the Order as mentioned in paragraph 3 of the Order.

2) To make and provide to the Plaintiff's solicitors a written report on the carrying out of the Order.

SCHEDULE 6

Affidavits

The Judge read the following affidavits before making this Order:

1)

2)

---

[5] In appropriate cases an undertaking to insure the items removed from the premises shall be included.

All communications to the Court about this Order should be sent to [**Room ,**] **Royal Courts of Justice, Strand, London WC2A 2LL quoting the case number**. The office is open between 10 am and 4.30 pm Monday to Friday. The telephone numbers are [ ].

See *Practice Direction, The Times*, August 2, 1994.

G–15   (I) Mareva Order

Delete form I, and **substitute**:

[Heading — see Court Form (G)]

INJUNCTION PROHIBITING DISPOSAL OF ASSETS IN ENGLAND AND WALES[6]

IMPORTANT:—
NOTICE TO THE DEFENDANT

(1) This Order prohibits you from dealing with your assets up to the amount stated. The Order is subject to the exceptions at the end of the Order. You should read it all carefully. You are advised to consult a solicitor as soon as possible. You have a right to ask the Court to vary or discharge this Order.

(2) If you disobey this Order you will be guilty of contempt of Court and may be [sent to prison or] fined or your assets may be seized.[7]

THE ORDER

An Application was made today [date] by counsel [or solicitors] for . . . the Plaintiff to Mr Justice [   ]. Mr Justice [   ] heard the application and read the affidavits listed in Schedule 2 to this Order. As a result of the application **IT IS ORDERED** by Mr Justice [   ] that:

1. Disposal of assets

1) The Defendant must not remove from England and Wales or in any way dispose of or deal with or diminish the value of any of his assets which are in England and Wales whether in his own name or not and whether solely or jointly owned up to the value of £   . This prohibition includes the following assets in particular:-
   (a) the property known as   for the net sale money after payment of any mortgages if it has been sold;
   (b) the property and assets of the Defendant's business known as   (or carried on at   ) or the sale money if any of them have been sold; and
   (c) any money in the accounts numbered   at

---

[6] See *infra* for a worldwide Mareva Order.
[7] Delete the words "sent to prison" in the case of a corporate Defendant. This notice is not a substitute for the indorsement of a penal notice.

2) If the total unincumbered value of the Defendant's assets in England and Wales exceeds £   , the Defendant may remove any of those assets from England and Wales or may dispose of or deal with them so long as the total unincumbered value of his assets still in England and Wales remains above £   .

2. Disclosure of information

1) The Defendant must inform the Plaintiff in writing at once of all his assets in England and Wales whether in his own name or not and whether solely or jointly owned, giving the value, location and details of all such assets. The information must be confirmed in an Affidavit which must be served on the Plaintiffs' solicitors within   days after this Order has been served on the Defendant.

EXCEPTIONS TO THIS ORDER

1) This Order does not prohibit the Defendant from spending £   a week towards his ordinary living expenses [and £   a week towards his ordinary and proper business expenses] and also £   a week [*or* a reasonable sum] on legal advice and representation. But before spending any money the Defendant must tell the Plaintiff's solicitors where the money is to come from.

2) This Order does not prohibit the Defendant from dealing with or disposing of any of his assets in the ordinary and proper course of business].

3) The Defendant may agree with the Plaintiff's solicitors that the above spending limits should be increased or that this Order should be varied in any other respect but any such agreement must be in writing.

EFFECT OF THIS ORDER

1) A Defendant who is an individual who is ordered not to do something must not do it himself or in any other way. He must not do it through others acting on his behalf or on his instructions or with his encouragement.

2) A Defendant which is a corporation and which is ordered not to do something must not do it itself or by its directors officers employees or agents or in any other way.

THIRD PARTIES

1) *Effect of this Order.* It is a contempt of Court for any person notified of this Order knowingly to assist in or permit a breach of the Order. Any person doing so may be sent to prison, fined, or have his assets seized.

2) *Set off by Banks.* This injunction does not prevent any bank from exercising any right of set off it may have in respect of any facility which it gave to the Defendant before it was notified of the Order.

3) *Withdrawals by the Defendant.* No bank need enquire as to the application or proposed application of any money withdrawn by the Defendant if the withdrawal appears to be permitted by this Order.

[SERVICE OUT OF THE JURISDICTION AND SUBSTITUTED SERVICE

1) The Plaintiff may serve the Writ of Summons on the Defendant at by

2) If the Defendant wishes to defend the Action he must acknowledge service within   days of being served with the Writ of Summons.]

UNDERTAKINGS

The Plaintiff gives to the Court the undertakings set out in Schedule 1 to this Order.

DURATION OF THIS ORDER

This Order will remain in force up to and including : : 19 ("the Return Date") unless before then it is varied or discharged by a further Order of the Court.[8] The application in which this Order is made shall come back to the Court for further hearing on the Return Date.

VARIATION OR DISCHARGE OF THIS ORDER

The Defendant (or anyone notified of this Order) may apply to the Court at any time to vary or discharge this Order (or so much of it as affects that person), but anyone wishing to do so must first inform the Plaintiff's solicitors.

NAME AND ADDRESS OF PLAINTIFF'S SOLICITORS

The Plaintiff's solicitors are:–

   Name, address and telephone numbers both in and out of office hours].

[INTERPRETATION OF THIS ORDER

1) In this Order "he" "him" or "his" include "she" or "her" and "it" or "its".

2) Where there are two or more Defendants then (unless otherwise stated)
    (a) References to "the Defendants" means both or all of them.
    (b) An Order requiring "the Defendants" to do or not to do anything requires each Defendant to do or not to do it.
    (c) A requirement relating to service of this Order or of any legal proceedings on "the Defendants" means on each of them.]

SCHEDULE 1

Undertakings given to the Court by the Plaintiff

1) If the Court later finds that this Order has caused loss to the Defendant, and decides that the Defendant should be compensated for that loss, the Plaintiff will comply with any Order the Court may make.

2) As soon as practicable the Plaintiff will [issue and] serve on the Defendant [a] [the] Writ of Summons [in the form of the draft writ produced to the Court] [claiming appropriate relief] together with this Order.

---

[8] The date should be the earliest practicable return date.

3) The Plaintiff will cause an affidavit to be sworn and filed [substantially in the terms of the draft affidavit produced to the Court] [confirming the substance of what was said to the Court by the Plaintiff's counsel/solicitors].

4) As soon as practicable the Plaintiff will serve on the Defendant a [notice of motion] [summons] for the Return Date together with a copy of the affidavits and exhibits containing the evidence relied on by the Plaintiff.

5) Anyone notified of this Order will be given a copy of it by the Plaintiff's solicitors.

6) The Plaintiff will pay the reasonable costs of anyone other than the Defendant which have been incurred as a result of this Order including the costs of ascertaining whether that person holds any of the Defendant's assets and that if the Court later finds that this Order has caused such person loss, and decides that such person should be compensated for that loss, the Plaintiff will comply with any Order the Court may make.

SCHEDULE 2

Affidavits

The Judge read the following affidavits before making this Order:

1)

2)

*All communications to the Court about this Order should be sent to [**Room ,] Royal Courts of Justice, Strand, London WC2A 2LL quoting the case number**. The office is open between 10 am and 4.30 pm Monday to Friday. The telephone numbers are [ ].*

See *Practice Direction*, *The Times*, August 2, 1994.

(I) Mareva Order (Worldwide)

[Heading—See Court Form (G)]

INJUNCTION PROHIBITING DISPOSAL OF ASSETS WORLDWIDE

IMPORTANT:–

NOTICE TO THE DEFENDANT

(1) This Order prohibits you from dealing with your assets up to the amount stated. The Order is subject to the exceptions at the end of the Order. You should read it all carefully. You are advised to consult a solicitor as soon as possible. You have a right to ask the Court to vary or discharge this Order.

(2) If you disobey this Order you will be guilty of contempt of Court and may be [sent to prison or] fined or your assets may be seized.[9]

THE ORDER

An application was made today [date] by counsel [or solicitors] for . . . the Plaintiff to Mr Justice [   ]. Mr Justice [   ] heard the application and read the affidavits listed in Schedule 2 at the end of this Order.

As a result of the application **IT IS ORDERED** by Mr Justice [   ] that:

1. Disposal of assets

1) The Defendant must not (i) remove from England and Wales any of his assets which are in England and Wales whether in his own name or not and whether solely or jointly owned up to the value of £   or (ii) in any way dispose of or deal with or diminish the value of any of his assets whether they are in or outside England or Wales whether in his own name or not and whether solely or jointly owned up to the same value. This prohibition includes the following assets in particular:-
   (a) the property known as   or the net sale money after payment of any mortgages if it has been sold;
   (b) the property and assets of the Defendant's business known as   (or carried on at   ) or the sale money if any of them have been sold; and
   (c) any money in the accounts numbered   at

---

[9] Delete the words "sent to prison" in the case of a corporate Defendant. This notice is not a substitute for the indorsement of a penal notice.

2. If the total unincumbered value of the Defendant's assets in England and Wales exceeds £   the Defendant may remove any of those assets from England and Wales or may dispose of or deal with them so long as the total unincumbered value of his assets still in England and Wales remains above £   . If the total unincumbered value of the Defendant's assets in England and Wales does not exceed £   , the Defendant must not remove any of those assets from England and Wales and must not dispose of or deal with any of them, but if he has other assets outside England and Wales the Defendant may dispose of or deal with those assets so long as the total unincumbered value of all his assets whether in or outside England and Wales remains above £

2.   Disclosure of information

1) The Defendant must inform the Plaintiff in writing at once of all his assets whether in or outside England and Wales and whether in his own name or not and whether solely or jointly owned, giving the value, location and details of all such assets.

2) The information must be confirmed in an affidavit which must be served on the Plaintiff's solicitors within   days after this Order has been served on the Defendant.

EXCEPTIONS TO THIS ORDER

1) This Order does not prohibit the Defendant from spending £   a week towards his ordinary living expenses [and £   a week towards his ordinary and proper business expenses] and also £   a week [*or* a reasonable sum] on legal advice and representation. But before spending any money the Defendant must tell the Plaintiff's solicitors where the money is to come from.

2) This Order does not prohibit the Defendant from dealing with or disposing of any of his assets in the ordinary and proper course of business.

3) The Defendant may agree with the Plaintiff's Solicitors that the above spending limits should be increased or that this Order should be varied in any other respect but any such agreement must be in writing.

EFFECT OF THIS ORDER

1) A Defendant who is an individual who is ordered not to do something must not do it himself or in any other way. He must not do it through others acting on his behalf or on his instructions or with his encouragement.

2) A Defendant which is a corporation and which is ordered not to do something must not do it itself or by its directors officers employees or agents or in any other way.

THIRD PARTIES

1) Effect of this Order. It is a contempt of Court for any person notified of this Order knowingly to assist in or permit a breach of the Order. Any person doing so may be sent to prison, fined, or have his assets seized.

2) Effect of this Order outside England and Wales. The terms of this Order do not affect or concern anyone outside the jurisdiction of this Court until it is declared enforceable or is enforced by a Court in the relevant country and

then they are to affect him only to the extent they have been declared enforceable or have been enforced **UNLESS** such person is:

>   (a)   a person to whom this Order is addressed or an officer or an agent appointed by power of attorney of such a person; or
>   (b)   a person who is subject to the jurisdiction of this Court and (i) has been given written notice of this Order at his residence or place of business within the jurisdiction of this Court and (ii) is able to prevent acts or omissions outside the jurisdiction of this Court which constitute or assist in a breach of the terms of this Order.

3)   <u>Set off by Banks</u>. This injunction does not prevent any bank from exercising any right of set off it may have in respect of any facility which it gave to the Defendant before it was notified of the Order.

4)   <u>Withdrawals by the Defendant</u>. No bank need enquire as to the application or proposed application of any money withdrawn by the Defendant if the withdrawal appears to be permitted by this Order.

[SERVICE OUT OF THE JURISDICTION AND SUBSTITUTED SERVICE

1)   The Plaintiff may serve the Writ of Summons on the Defendant at
by

2)   If the Defendant wishes to defend the Action he must acknowledge service
within   days of being served with the Writ of Summons.]

UNDERTAKINGS

The Plaintiff gives to the Court the undertakings set out in Schedule 1 to this Order.

DURATION OF THIS ORDER

This Order will remain in force up to and including   : 19 ("the Return Date"), unless before then it is varied or discharged by a further Order of the Court.[10] The application in which this Order is made shall come back to the Court for further hearing on the Return Date.

VARIATION OR DISCHARGE OF THIS ORDER

The Defendant (or anyone notified of this Order) may apply to the Court at any time to vary or discharge this Order (or so much of it as affects that person), but anyone wishing to do so must first inform the Plaintiff's solicitors.

NAME AND ADDRESS OF PLAINTIFF'S SOLICITORS

The Plaintiff's solicitors are:–

>   [Name, address and telephone numbers both in and out of office hours].

[INTERPRETATION OF THIS ORDER

1)   In this Order "he" "him" or "his" include "she" or "her" and "it" or "its".

---

[10]   The date should be the earliest practicable return date.

2) (Where there are two or more Defendants then (unless the context indicates differently)
    (a) References to "the Defendants" means both or all of them;
    (b) An Order requiring "the Defendants" to do or not to do anything requires each Defendant to do or not to do it;
    (c) A requirement relating to service of this Order, or of any legal proceedings, on "the Defendants" means on each of them.]

SCHEDULE 1

Undertakings given to the Court by the Plaintiff

1) If the Court later finds that this Order has caused loss to the Defendant, and decides that the Defendant should be compensated for that loss, the Plaintiff will comply with any Order the Court may make.

2) As soon as practicable the Plaintiff will [issue and] serve on the Defendant [a] [the] Writ of Summons [in the form of the draft writ produced to the Court] [claiming appropriate relief] together with this Order.

3) The Plaintiff will cause an affidavit to be sworn and filed [substantially in the terms of the draft affidavit produced to the Court] [confirming the substance of what was said to the Court by the Plaintiff's counsel/solicitors].

4) As soon as practicable the Plaintiff will serve on the Defendant a [notice of motion] [summons] for the Return Date together with a copy of the affidavits and exhibits containing the evidence relied on by the Plaintiff.

5) Anyone notified of this Order will be given a copy of it by the Plaintiff's solicitors.

6) The Plaintiff will pay the reasonable costs of anyone other than the Defendant which have been incurred as a result of this Order including the costs of ascertaining whether that person holds any of the Defendant's assets and that if the Court later finds that this Order has caused such a person loss, and decides that the person should be compensated for that loss, the Plaintiff will comply with any Order the Court may make.

7) The Plaintiff will not without the leave of the Court begin proceedings against the Defendant in any other jurisdiction or use information obtained as a result of an Order of the Court in this jurisdiction for the purpose of civil or criminal proceedings in any other jurisdiction.

8) The Plaintiff will not without the leave of the Court seek to enforce this Order in any country outside England and Wales [or seek an Order of a similar nature including Orders conferring a charge or other security against the Defendant or the Defendant's assets].]

SCHEDULE 2

Affidavits

The Judge read the following affidavits before making this Order:

1)

2)

See *Practice Direction, The Times,* August 2, 1994.

Appendix H

E.C. DIRECTIVES

COUNCIL DIRECTIVE 87/54/EEC

of December 16, 1986
on the legal protection of topographies of semiconductor products

([1987] O.J. L24/36)

THE COUNCIL OF THE EUROPEAN COMMUNITIES, **H–1**

Having regard to the Treaty establishing the European Economic Community and in particular Article 100 thereof,

Having regard to the proposal from the Commission,

Having regard to the opinion of the European Parliament,

Having regard to the opinion of the Economic and Social Committee,

(1) Whereas semiconductor products are playing an increasingly important role in a broad range of industries and semiconductor technology can accordingly be considered as being of fundamental importance for the Community's industrial development;

(2) Whereas the functions of semiconductor products depend in large part on the topographies of such products and whereas the development of such topographies requires the investment of considerable resources, human, technical and financial, while topographies of such products can be copied at a fraction of the cost needed to develop them independently;

(3) Whereas topographies of semiconductor products are at present not clearly protected in all Member States by existing legislation and such protection, where it exists, has different attributes;

(4) Whereas certain existing differences in the legal protection of semiconductor products offered by the laws of the Member States have direct and negative effects on the functioning of the common market as regards semiconductor products and such differences could well become greater as Member States introduce new legislation on this subject;

(5) Whereas existing differences having such effects need to be removed and new ones having a negative effect on the common market prevented from arising;

391

(6) Whereas, in relation to extension of protection to persons outside the Community, Member States should be free to act on their own behalf in so far as Community decisions have not been taken within a limited period of time;

(7) Whereas the Community's legal framework on the protection of topographies of semiconductor products can, in the first instance, be limited to certain basic principles by provisions specifying whom and what should be protected, the exclusive rights on which protected persons should be able to rely to authorize or prohibit certain acts, exceptions to these rights and for how long the protection should last;

(8) Whereas other matters can for the time being be decided in accordance with national law, in particular, whether registration or deposit is required as a condition for protection and, subject to an exclusion of licences granted for the sole reason that a certain period of time has elapsed, whether and on what conditions non-voluntary licences may be granted in respect of protected topographies;

(9) Whereas protection of topographies of semiconductor products in accordance with this Directive should be without prejudice to the application of some other forms of protection;

(10) Whereas further measures concerning the legal protection of topographies of semiconductor products in the Community can be considered at a later stage, if necessary, while the application of common basic principles by all Member States in accordance with the provisions of this Directive is an urgent necessity,

HAS ADOPTED THIS DIRECTIVE:

CHAPTER 1

Definitions

Article 1

1. For the purposes of this Directive:

(a) a "semiconductor product" shall mean the final or an intermediate form of any product:
  (i) consisting of a body of material which includes a layer of semiconducting material; and
  (ii) having one or more other layers composed of conducting, insulating or semiconducting material, the layers being arranged in accordance with a predetermined three-dimensional pattern; and
  (iii) intended to perform, exclusively or together with other functions, an electronic function;
(b) the "topography" of a semiconductor product shall mean a series of related images, however fixed or encoded;
  (i) representing the three-dimensional pattern of the layers of which a semiconductor product is composed; and

(ii) in which series, each image has the pattern or part of the pattern of a surface of the semiconductor product at any stage of its manufacture;
(c) "commercial exploitation" means the sale, rental, leasing or any other method of commercial distribution, or an offer for these purposes. However, for the purposes of Articles 3(4), 4(1), 7(1), (3) and (4) "commercial exploitation" shall not include exploitation under conditions of confidentiality to the extent that no further distribution to third parties occurs, except where exploitation of a topography takes place under conditions of confidentiality required by a measure taken in conformity with Article 223(1)(b) of the Treaty.

2. The Council acting by qualified majority on a proposal from the Commission, may amend paragraph 1 (a)(i) and (ii) in order to adapt these provisions in the light of technical progress.

CHAPTER 2

Protection of topographies of semiconductor products

Article 2   **H–3**

1. Member States shall protect the topographies of semiconductor products by adopting legislative provisions conferring exclusive rights in accordance with the provisions of the Directive.

2. The topography of a semiconductor product shall be protected in so far as it satisfies the conditions that it is the result of its creator's own intellectual effort and is not commonplace in the semiconductor industry. Where the topography of a semiconductor product consists of elements that are commonplace in the semiconductor industry, it shall be protected only to the extent that the combination of such elements, taken as a whole, fulfils the abovementioned conditions.

Article 3   **H–4**

1. Subject to paragraphs 2 to 5, the right to protection shall apply in favour of persons who are the creators of the topographies of semiconductor products.

2. Member States may provide that,
(a) where a topography is created in the course of the creator's employment, the right to protection shall apply in favour of the creator's employer unless the terms of employment provide to the contrary;
(b) where a topography is created under a contract other than a contract of employment, the right to protection shall apply in favour of a party to the contract by whom the topography has been commissioned, unless the contract provides to the contrary.

3a As regards the persons referred to in paragraph 1, the right to protection shall apply in favour of natural persons who are nationals of a Member

State or who have their habitual residence on the territory of a Member State.

(b) Where Member States make provision in accordance with paragraph 2, the right to protection shall apply in favour of:

    (i) natural persons who are nationals of a Member State or who have their habitual residence on the territory of a Member State;

    (ii) companies or other legal persons which have a real and effective industrial or commercial establishment on the territory of a Member State.

4. Where no right to protection exists in accordance with other provisions of this Article, the right to protection shall also apply in favour of the persons referred to in paragraphs 3(b)(i) and (ii) who:

(a) first commercially exploit within a Member State a topography which has not yet been exploited commercially anywhere in the world; and

(b) have been exclusively authorised to exploit commercially the topography throughout the Community by the person entitled to dispose of it.

5. The right to protection shall also apply in favour of the successors in title of the persons mentioned in paragraphs 1 to 4.

6. Subject to paragraph 7, Member States may negotiate and conclude agreements or understandings with third States and multilateral Conventions concerning the legal protection of topographies of semiconductor products whilst respecting Community law and in particular the rules laid down in this Directive.

7. Member States may enter into negotiations with[1] third States with a view to extending the right to protection to persons who do not benefit from the right to protection according to the provisions of this Directive. Member States who enter into such negotiations shall inform the Commission thereof.

When a Member State wishes to extend protection to persons who otherwise do not benefit from the right to protection according to the provisions of this Directive or to conclude an agreement or understanding on the extension of protection with a non-Member State it shall notify the Commission. The Commission shall inform the other Member States thereof.

The Member State shall hold the extension of protection or the conclusion of the agreement or understanding in abeyance for one month from the date on which it notifies the Commission. However, if within that period the Commission notifies the Member State concerned of its intention to submit a proposal to the Council for all Member States to extend protection in respect of the persons or non-Member State concerned, the Member State shall hold the extension of protection or the conclusion of the agreement or understanding in abeyance for a period of two months from the date of the notification by the Member State.

Where, before the end of this two-month period, the Commission submits such a proposal to the Council, the Member State shall hold the extension of protection or the conclusion of the agreement or understanding in abeyance for a further period of four months from the date on which the proposal was submitted.

---

[1] O.J. text has "which".

In the absence of a Commission notification or proposal or a Council decision within the time limits prescribed above, the Member State may extend protection or conclude the agreement or understanding.

A proposal by the Commission to extend protection, whether or not it is made following a notification by a Member State in accordance with the preceding paragraphs shall be adopted by the Council acting by qualified majority.

A Decision of the Council on the basis of a Commission proposal shall not prevent a Member State from extending protection to persons, in addition to those to benefit from protection in all Member States, who were included in the envisaged extension, agreement or understanding as notified, unless the Council acting by qualified majority has decided otherwise.

8. Commission proposals and Council decisions pursuant to paragraph 7 shall be published for information in the *Official Journal of the European Communities*.

Article 4 **H–5**

1. Member States may provide that the exclusive rights conferred in conformity with Article 2 shall not come into existence or shall no longer apply to the topography of a semiconductor product unless an application for registration in due form has been filed with a public authority within two years of its first commercial exploitation. Member States may require in addition to such registration that material identifying or exemplifying the topography or any combination thereof has been deposited with a public authority, as well as a statement as to the date of first commercial exploitation of the topography where it precedes the date of the application for registration.

2. Member States shall ensure that material deposited in conformity with paragraph 1 is not made available to the public where it is a trade secret. This provision shall be without prejudice to the disclosure of such material pursuant to an order of a court or other competent authority to persons involved in litigation concerning the validity or infringement of the exclusive rights referred to in Article 2.

3. Member States may require that transfers of rights in protected topographies be registered.

4. Member States may subject registration and deposit in accordance with paragraphs 1 and 3 to the payment of fees not exceeding their administrative costs.

5. Conditions prescribing the fulfilment of additional formalities for obtaining or maintaining protection shall not be admitted.

6. Member States which require registration shall provide for legal remedies in favour of a person having the right to protection in accordance with the provisions of this Directive who can prove that another person has applied for or obtained the registration of a topography without his authorisation.

Article 5 **H–6**

1. The exclusive rights referred to in Article 2 shall include the rights to authorise or prohibit any of the following acts:

395

(a) reproduction of a topography in so far as it is protected under Article 2(2);

(b) commercial exploitation or the importation for that purpose of a topography or of a semiconductor product manufactured by using the topography.

2. Notwithstanding paragraph 1, a Member State pay permit the reproduction of a topography privately for non commercial aims.

3. The exclusive rights referred to in paragraph 1(a) shall not apply to reproduction for the purpose of analysing, evaluating or teaching the concepts, processes, systems or techniques embodied in the topography or the topography itself.

4. The exclusive rights referred to in paragraph 1 shall not extend to any such act in relation to a topography meeting the requirements of Article 2(2) and created on the basis of an analysis and evaluation of another topography, carried out in conformity with paragraph 3.

5. The exclusive rights to authorise or prohibit the acts specified in paragraph 1(b) shall not apply to any such act committed after the topography or the semiconductor product has been put on the market in a Member State by the person entitled to authorise its marketing or with his consent.

6. A person who, when he acquires a semiconductor product, does not know, or has no reasonable grounds to believe, that the product is protected by an exclusive right conferred by a Member State in conformity with this Directive shall not be prevented from commercially exploiting that product.

However, for acts committed after that person knows, or has reasonable grounds to believe, that the semiconductor product is so protected, Member States shall ensure that on the demand of the rightholder a tribunal may require, in accordance with the provisions of the national law applicable, the payment of adequate remuneration.

7. The provisions of paragraph 6 shall apply to the successors in title of the person referred to in the first sentence of that paragraph.

H–7   *Article 6*

Member States shall not subject the exclusive rights referred to in Article 2 to licences granted, for the sole reason that a certain period of time has elapsed, automatically, and by operation of law.

H–8   *Article 7*

1. Member States shall provide that the exclusive rights referred to in Article 2 shall come into existence:

(a) where registration is the condition for the coming into existence of the exclusive rights in accordance with Article 4, on the earlier of the following dates:

(i) the date when the topography is first commercially exploited anywhere in the world;

(ii) the date when an application or registration has been filed in due form; or

(b) when the topography is first commercially exploited anywhere in the world; or

(c) when the topography is first fixed or encoded.

2. Where the exclusive rights come into existence in accordance with paragraph 1(a) or (b), the Member States shall provide, for the period prior to those rights coming into existence, legal remedies in favour of a person having the right to protection in accordance with the provisions of this Directive who can prove that another person has fraudulently reproduced or commercially exploited or imported for that purpose a topography. This paragraph shall be without prejudice to legal remedies made available to enforce the exclusive rights conferred in conformity with Article 2.

3. The exclusive rights shall come to an end 10 years from the end of the calendar year in which the topography is first commercially exploited anywhere in the world or, where registration is a condition for the coming into existence or continuing application of the exclusive rights, 10 years from the earlier of the following dates:

(a) the end of the calendar year in which the topography is first commercially exploited anywhere in the world;

(b) the end of the calendar year in which the application for registration has been filed in due form.

4. Where a topography has not been commercially exploited anywhere in the world within a period of 15 years from its first fixation or encoding, any exclusive rights in existence pursuant to paragraph 1 shall come to an end and no new exclusive rights shall come into existence unless an application for registration in due form has been filed within that period in those Member States where registration is a condition for the coming into existence or continuing application of the exclusive rights.

Article 8   **H–9**

The protection granted to the topographies of semiconductor products in accordance with Article 2 shall not extend to any concept, process, system, technique or encoded information embodied in the topography other than the topography itself.

Article 9   **H–10**

Where the legislation of Member States provides that semiconductor products manufactured using protected topographies may carry an indication, the indication to be used shall be a capital T as follows: T, "T", [T], "T" or [T].

CHAPTER 3

Continued application of other legal provisions

H–11 *Article 10*

1. The provisions of this Directive shall be without prejudice to legal provisions concerning patent and utility model rights.

2. The provisions of this Directive shall be without prejudice:
(a) to rights conferred by the Member States in fulfilment of their obligations under international agreements, including provisions extending such rights to nationals of, or residents in, the territory of the Member State concerned;
(b) to the law of copyright in Member States, restricting the reproduction of drawing or other artistic representations of topographies by copying them in two dimensions.

3. Protection granted by national law to topographies of semiconductor products fixed or encoded before the entry into force of the national provisions enacting the Directive, but no later than the date set out in Article 11 (1), shall not be affected by the provisions of this Directive.

CHAPTER 4

Final provisions

H–12 *Article 11*

1. Member States shall bring into force the laws, regulations or administrative provisions necessary to comply with this Directive by November 7 1987.

2. Member States shall ensure that they communicate to the Commission the texts of the main provisions of national law which they adopt in the field covered by this Directive.

H–13 *Article 12*

This Directive is addressed to the Member States.

Done at Brussels, 16 December 1986.

COUNCIL DIRECTIVE 91/250/EEC

of May 14, 1991
on the legal protection of computer programs

([1991] O.J. L122/42)

THE COUNCIL OF THE EUROPEAN COMMUNITIES, **H–14**

Having regard to the Treaty establishing the European Economic Community and in particular Article 100a thereof,

Having regard to the proposal from the Commission,

In cooperation with the European Parliament,

Having regard to the opinion of the Economic and Social Committee[3],

(1) Whereas computer programs are at present not clearly protected in all Member States by existing legislation and such protection, where it exists, has different attributes;

(2) Whereas the development of computer programs requires the investment of considerable human, technical and financial resources while computer programs can be copied at a fraction of the cost needed to develop them independently;

(3) Whereas computer programs are playing an increasingly important role in a broad range of industries and computer program technology can accordingly be considered as being of fundamental importance for the Community's industrial development;

(4) Whereas certain differences in the legal protection of computer programs offered by the laws of the Member States have direct and negative effects on the functioning of the common market as regards computer programs and such differences could well become greater as Member States introduce new legislation on this subject;

(5) Whereas existing differences having such effects need to be removed and new ones prevented from arising, while differences not adversely affecting the functioning of the common market to a substantial degree need not be removed or prevented from arising;

(6) Whereas the Community's legal framework on the protection of computer programs can accordingly in the first instance be limited to establishing that Member States should accord protection to computer programs under copyright law as literary works and, further, to establishing who and what should be protected, the exclusive rights on which protected persons should be able to rely in order to authorize or prohibit certain acts and for how long the protection should apply;

(7) Whereas, for the purpose of this Directive, the term "computer program" shall include programs in any form, including those which are incorporated

399

into hardware; whereas this term also includes preparatory design work leading to the development of a computer program provided that the nature of the preparatory work is such that a computer program can result from it at a later stage;

(8) Whereas, in respect of the criteria to be applied in determining whether or not a computer program is an original work, no tests as to the qualitative or aesthetic merits of the program should be applied;

(9) Whereas the Community is fully committed to the promotion of international standardizations;

(10) Whereas the function of a computer program is to communicate and work together with other components of a computer system and with users and, for this purpose, a logical and, where appropriate, physical interconnection and interaction is required to permit all elements of software and hardware to work with other software and hardware and with users in all the ways in which they are intended to function;

(11) Whereas the parts of the program which provide for such interconnection and interaction between elements of software and hardware are generally known as "interfaces";

(12) Whereas this functional interconnection and interaction is generally known as "interoperability"; whereas such interoperability can be defined as the ability to exchange information and mutually to use the information which has been exchanged;

(13) Whereas, for the avoidance of doubt, it has to be made clear that only the expression of a computer program is protected and that ideas and principles which underlie any element of a program, including those which underlie its interfaces, are not protected by copyright under this Directive;

(14) Whereas, in accordance with this principle of copyright, to the extent that logic, algorithms and programming languages comprise ideas and principles, those ideas and principles are not protected under this Directive;

(15) Whereas, in accordance with the legislation and jurisprudence of the Member States and the international copyright conventions, the expression of those ideas and principles is to be protected by copyright;

(16) Whereas, for the purposes of this Directive, the term "rental" means the making available for use, for a limited period of time and for profit-making purposes, of a computer program or a copy thereof; whereas this term does not include public lending, which, accordingly, remains outside the scope of this Directive;

(17) Whereas the exclusive rights of the author to prevent the unauthorized reproduction of his work have to be subject to a limited exception in the case of a computer program to allow the reproduction technically necessary for the use of that program by the lawful acquirer;

(18) Whereas this means that the acts of loading and running necessary for the use of a copy of a program which has been lawfully acquired, and the act of correction of its errors, may not be prohibited by contract; whereas, in the absence of specific contractual provisions, including when a copy of the program has been sold, any other act necessary for the use of the copy of a program may be performed in accordance with its intended purpose by a lawful acquirer of that copy;

(19) Whereas a person having a right to use a computer program should not be prevented from performing acts necessary to observe, study or test the functioning of the program, provided that these acts do not infringe the copyright in the program;

(20) Whereas the unauthorised reproduction, translation, adaptation or transformation of the form of the code in which a copy of a computer program has been made available constitutes an infringement of the exclusive rights of the author;

(21) Whereas, nevertheless, circumstances may exist when such a reproduction of the code and translation of its form within the meaning of Article 4(a) and (b) are indispensable to obtain the necessary information to achieve the interoperability of an independently created program with other programs;

(22) Whereas it has therefore to be considered that in these limited circumstances only, performance of the acts of reproduction and translation by or on behalf of a person having a right to use a copy of the program is legitimate and compatible with fair practice and must therefore be deemed not to require the authorization of the rightholder;

(23) Whereas an objective of this exception is to make it possible to connect all components of a computer system, including those of different manufacturers, so that they can work together;

(24) Whereas such an exception to the author's exclusive rights may not be used in a way which prejudices the legitimate interests of the rightholder or which conflicts with a normal exploitation of the program;

(25) Whereas, in order to remain in accordance with the provisions of the Berne Convention for the Protection of Literary and Artistic Works, the term of protection should be the life of the author and fifty years from the first of January of the year following the year of his death or, in the case of an anonymous or pseudonymous work, 50 years from the first of January of the year following the year in which the work is first published;

(26) Whereas protection of computer programs under copyright laws should be without prejudice to the application, in appropriate cases, of other forms of protection; whereas, however, any contractual provisions contrary to Article 6 or to the exceptions provided for in Article 5 (2) and (3) should be null and void;

(27) Whereas the provisions of this Directive are without prejudice to the application of the competition rules under Articles 85 and 86 of the Treaty if a dominant supplier refuses to make information available which is necessary for interoperability as defined in this Directive;

(28) Whereas the provisions of this Directive should be without prejudice to specific requirements of Community law already enacted in respect of the publication of interfaces in the telecommunications sector or Council Decisions relating to standardization in the field of information technology and telecommunication;

(29) Whereas this Directive does not affect derogations provided for under national legislation in accordance with the Berne Convention on points not covered by this Directive,

HAS ADOPTED THIS DIRECTIVE:

Article 1

Object of protection

1. In accordance with the provisions of this Directive, Member States shall protect computer programs, by copyright, as literary works within the meaning of the Berne Convention for the Protection of Literary and Artistic Works. For the purposes of this Directive, the term "computer programs" shall include their preparatory design material.

2. Protection in accordance with this Directive shall apply to the expression in any form of a computer program. Ideas and principles which underlie any element of a computer program, including those which underlie its interfaces, are not protected by copyright under this Directive.

3. A computer program shall be protected if it is original in the sense that it is the author's own intellectual creation. No other criteria shall be applied to determine its eligibility for protection.

H–17   *Article 2*

Authorship of computer programs

1. The author of a computer program shall be the natural person or group of natural persons who has created the program or, where the legislation of the Member State permits, the legal person designated as the rightholder by that legislation. Where collective works are recognized by the legislation of a Member State, the person considered by the legislation of the Member State to have created the work shall be deemed to be its author.

2. In respect of a computer program created by a group of natural persons jointly, the exclusive rights shall be owned jointly.

3. Where a computer program is created by an employee in the execution of his duties or following the instructions given by his employer, the employer exclusively shall be entitled to exercise all economic rights in the program so created, unless otherwise provided by contract.

H–18   *Article 3*

Beneficiaries of protection

Protection shall be granted to all natural or legal persons eligible under national copyright legislation as applied to literary works.

H–19   *Article 4*

Restricted Acts

Subject to the provisions of Articles 5 and 6, the exclusive rights of the rightholder within the meaning of Article 2, shall include the right to do or to authorize:

(a) the permanent or temporary reproduction of a computer program by any means and in any form, in part or in whole. Insofar as loading, displaying, running, transmission or storage of the computer program necessitate such reproduction, such acts shall be subject to authorization by the rightholder;

(b) the translation, adaptation, arrangement and any other alteration of a computer program and the reproduction of the results thereof, without prejudice to the rights of the person who alters the program;

(c) any form of distribution to the public, including the rental, of the original computer program or of copies thereof. The first sale in the Community of a copy of a program by the rightholder or with his consent shall exhaust the distribution right within the Community of that copy, with the exception of the right to control further rental of the program or a copy thereof.

Article 5   **H–20**

Exceptions to the restricted acts

1. In the absence of specific contractual provisions, the acts referred to in Article 4 (a) and (b) shall not require authorization by the rightholder where they are necessary for the use of the computer program by the lawful acquirer in accordance with its intended purpose, including for error correction.

2. The making of a back-up copy by a person having a right to use the computer program may not be prevented by contract insofar as it is necessary for that use.

3. The person having a right to use a copy of a computer program shall be entitled, without the authorization of the rightholder, to observe, study or test the functioning of the program in order to determine the ideas and principles which underlie any element of the program if he does so while performing any of the acts of loading, displaying, running, transmitting or storing the program which he is entitled to do.

Article 6   **H–21**

Decompilation

1. The authorization of the rightholder shall not be required where reproduction of the code and translation of its form within the meaning of Article 4 (a) and (b) are indispensable to obtain the information necessary to achieve the interoperability of an independently created computer program with other programs, provided that the following conditions are met:

(a) these acts are performed by the licensee or by another person having a right to use a copy of a program, or on their behalf by a person authorized to do so;

(b) the information necessary to achieve interoperability has not previously been readily available to the persons referred to in subparagraph (a); and

(c) these acts are confined to the parts of the original program which are necessary to achieve interoperability.

2. The provisions of paragraph 1 shall not permit the information obtained through its application:
  (a) to be used for goals other than to achieve the interoperability of the independently created computer program;
  (b) to be given to others, except when necessary for the interoperability of the independently created computer program; or
  (c) to be used for the development, production or marketing of a computer program substantially similar in its expression, or for any other act which infringes copyright.

3. In accordance with the provisions of the Berne Convention for the protection of Literary and Artistic Works, the provisions of this Article may not be interpreted in such a way as to allow its application to be used in a manner which unreasonably prejudices the rightholder's legitimate interests or conflicts with a normal exploitation of the computer program.

H–22   *Article 7*

Special measures of protection

1. Without prejudice to the provisions of Articles 4, 5 and 6, Member States shall provide, in accordance with their national legislation, appropriate remedies against a person committing any of the acts listed in subparagraphs (a), (b) and (c) below;
  (a) any act of putting into circulation a copy of a computer program knowing, or having reason to believe, that it is an infringing copy;
  (b) the possession, for commercial purposes, of a copy of a computer program knowing, or having reason to believe, that it is an infringing copy;
  (c) any act of putting into circulation, or the possession for commercial purposes, of any means the sole intended purpose of which is to facilitate the unauthorized removal or circumvention of any technical device which may have been applied to protect a computer program.

2. Any infringing copy of a computer program shall be liable to seizure in accordance with the legislation of the Member State concerned.

3. Member States may provide for the seizure of any means referred to in paragraph 1 (c).

H–23   *Article 8*

Term of protection

1. Protection shall be granted for the life of the author and for fifty years after his death or after the death of the last surviving author; where the computer program is an anonymous or pseudonymous work, or where a legal person is designated as the author by national legislation in accordance with Article 2 (1), the term of protection shall be fifty years from the time that the computer program is first lawfully made available to the public. The term of protection shall be deemed to begin on the first of January of the year following the abovementioned events.

2. Member States which already have a term of protection longer than that provided for in paragraph 1 are allowed to maintain their present term until such time as the term of protection for copyright works is harmonized by Community law in a more general way.

[**Article 8 has been repealed by Article 11(1) of Directive 93/98: see** *post*, **para. H–74.**]

Article 9   **H–24**

Continued application of other legal provisions

1. The provisions of this Directive shall be without prejudice to any other legal provisions such as those concerning patent rights, trade-marks, unfair competition, trade secrets, protection of semi-conductor products or the law of contract. Any contractual provisions contrary to Article 6 or to the exceptions provided for in Article 5 (2) and (3) shall be null and void.

2. The provisions of this Directive shall apply also to programs created before 1 January 1993 without prejudice to any acts concluded and rights acquired before that date.

Article 10   **H–25**

Final provisions

1. Member States shall bring into force the laws, regulations and administrative provisions necessary to comply with this Directive before 1 January 1993.

When Member States adopt these measures, the latter shall contain a reference to this Directive or shall be accompanied by such reference on the occasion of their official publication. The methods of making such a reference shall be laid down by the Member States.

2. Member States shall communicate to the Commission the provisions of national law which they adopt in the field governed by this Directive.

Article 11

This Directive is addressed to the Member States.   **H–26**

Done at Brussels, May 14, 1991.

COUNCIL DIRECTIVE 92/100/EEC

of November 19, 1992
on rental right and lending right and on certain rights related to copyright in
the field of intellectual property

([1992] O.J. L346/61)

H–27 THE COUNCIL OF THE EUROPEAN COMMUNITIES,

Having regard to the Treaty establishing the European Economic Community, and in particular Articles 57 (2), 66 and 100a thereof,

Having regard to the proposal from the Commission

In cooperation with the European Parliament

Having regard to the opinion of the Economic and Social Committee

(1) Whereas differences exist in the legal protection provided by the laws and practices of the Member States for copyright works and subject matter of related rights protection as regards rental and lending; whereas such differences are sources of barriers to trade and distortions of competition which impede the achievement and proper functioning of the internal market;

(2) Whereas such differences in legal protection could well become greater as Member States adopt new and different legislation or as national case-law interpreting such legislation develops differently;

(3) Whereas such differences should therefore be eliminated in accordance with the objective of introducing an area without internal frontiers as set out in Article 8a of the Treaty so as to institute, pursuant to Article 3 (f) of the Treaty, a system ensuring that competition in the common market is not distorted;

(4) Whereas rental and lending of copyright works and the subject matter of related rights protection is playing an increasingly important role in particular for authors, performers and producers of phonograms and films; whereas piracy is becoming an increasing threat;

(5) Whereas the adequate protection of copyright works and subject matter of related rights protection by rental and lending rights as well as the protection of the subject matter of related rights protection by the fixation right, reproduction right, distribution right, right to broadcast and communication to the public can accordingly be considered as being of fundamental importance for the Community's economic and cultural development;

(6) Whereas copyright and related rights protection must adapt to new economic developments such as new forms of exploitation;

(7) Whereas the creative and artistic work of authors and performers necessitates an adequate income as a basis for further creative and artistic work, and the investments required particularly for the production of

phonograms and films are especially high and risky; whereas the possibility for securing that income and recouping that investment can only effectively be guaranteed through adequate legal protection of the rightholders concerned;

(8) Whereas these creative, artistic and entrepreneurial activities are, to a large extent, activities of self-employed persons; whereas the pursuit of such activities must be made easier by providing a harmonized legal protection within the Community;

(9) Whereas, to the extent that these activities principally constitute services, their provision must equally be facilitated by the establishment in the Community of a harmonized legal framework;

(10) Whereas the legislation of the Member States should be approximated in such a way so as not to conflict with the international conventions on which many Member States' copyright and related rights laws are based;

(11) Whereas the Community's legal framework on the rental right and lending right and on certain rights related to copyright can be limited to establishing that Member States provide rights with respect to rental and lending for certain groups of rightholders and further to establishing the rights of fixation, reproduction, distribution, broadcasting and communication to the public for certain groups of rightholders in the field of related rights protection;

(12) Whereas it is necessary to define the concepts of rental and lending for the purposes of this Directive;

(13) Whereas it is desirable, with a view to clarity, to exclude from rental and lending within the meaning of this Directive certain forms of making available, as for instance making available phonograms or films (cinematographic or audiovisual works or moving images, whether or not accompanied by sound) for the purpose of public performance or broadcasting, making available for the purpose of exhibition, or making available for on-the-spot reference use; whereas lending within the meaning of this Directive does not include making available between establishments which are accessible to the public;

(14) Whereas, where lending by an establishment accessible to the public gives rise to a payment the amount of which does not go beyond what is necessary to cover the operating costs of the establishment, there is no direct or indirect economic or commercial advantage within the meaning of this Directive;

(15) Whereas it is necessary to introduce arrangements ensuring that an unwaivable equitable remuneration is obtained by authors and performers who must retain the possibility to entrust the administration of this right to collecting societies representing them;

(16) Whereas the equitable remuneration may be paid on the basis of one or several payments at[2] any time on or after the conclusion of the contract;

(17) Whereas the equitable remuneration must take account of the importance of the contribution of the authors and performers concerned to the phonogram or film;

---

[2] O.J. text has "an".

(18) Whereas it is also necessary to protect the rights at least of authors as regards public lending by providing for specific arrangements; whereas, however, any measures based on Article 5 of this Directive have to comply with Community law, in particular with Article 7 of the Treaty;

(19) Whereas the provisions of Chapter II do not prevent Member States from extending the presumption set out in Article 2 (5) to the exclusive rights included in that chapter; whereas furthermore the provisions of Chapter II do not prevent Member States from providing for a rebuttable presumption of the authorization of exploitation in respect of the exclusive rights of performers provided for in those articles, in so far as such presumption is compatible with the International Convention for the Protection of Performers, Producers of Phonograms and Broadcasting Organizations (hereinafter referred to as the Rome Convention);

(20) Whereas Member States may provide for more far-reaching protection for owners of rights related to copyright than that required by Article 8 of this Directive;

(21) Whereas the harmonized rental and lending rights and the harmonized protection in the field of rights related to copyright should not be exercised in a way which constitutes a disguised restriction on trade between Member States or in a way which is contrary to the rule of media exploitation chronology, as recognized in the Judgment handed down in *Société Cinéthèque v. FNCF*[3],

HAS ADOPTED THIS DIRECTIVE

CHAPTER I

RENTAL AND LENDING RIGHT

H–28   *Article 1*

Object of harmonization

1. In accordance with the provisions of this Chapter, Member States shall provide, subject to Article 5, a right to authorize or prohibit the rental and lending of originals and copies of copyright works, and other subject matter as set out in Article 2 (1).

2. For the purposes of this Directive, "rental" means making available for use, for a limited period of time and for direct or indirect economic or commercial advantage.

3. For the purposes of this Directive, "lending" means making available for use, for a limited period of time and not for direct or indirect economic or

---

[3] Cases 60/84 and 61/84 [1985] E.C.R. 2605.

commercial advantage, when it is made through establishments which are accessible to the public.

4. The rights referred to in paragraph 1 shall not be exhausted by any sale or other act of distribution of originals and copies of copyright works and other subject matter as set out in Article 2 (1).

Article 2   **H-29**

Rightholders and subject matter of rental and lending right

1. The exclusive right to authorize or prohibit rental and lending shall belong:
— to the author in respect of the original and copies of his work,
— to the performer in respect of fixations of his performance,
— to the phonogram producer in respect of his phonograms, and
— to the producer of the first fixation of a film in respect of the original and copies of his film. For the purposes of this Directive, the term "film" shall designate a cinematographic or audiovisual work or moving images, whether or not accompanied by sound.

2. For the purposes of this Directive the principal director of a cinematographic or audiovisual work shall be considered as its author or one of its authors. Member States may provide for others to be considered as its co-authors.

3. This Directive does not cover rental and lending rights in relation to buildings and to works of applied art.

4. The rights referred to in paragraph 1 may be transferred, assigned or subject to the granting of contractual licences.

5. Without prejudice to paragraph 7, when a contract concerning film production is concluded, individually or collectively, by performers with a film producer, the performer covered by this contract shall be presumed, subject to contractual clauses to the contrary, to have transferred his rental right, subject to Article 4.

6. Member States may provide for a similar presumption as set out in paragraph 5 with respect to authors.

7. Member States may provide that the signing of a contract concluded between a performer and a film producer concerning the production of a film has the effect of authorizing rental, provided that such contract provides for an equitable remuneration within the meaning of Article 4. Member States may also provide that this paragraph shall apply *mutatis mutandis* to the rights included in Chapter II.

Article 3   **H-30**

Rental of computer programs

This Directive shall be without prejudice to Article 4 (c) of Council Directive 91/250/EEC of May 14, 1991 on the legal protection of computer programs.

409

H–31   *Article 4*

Unwaivable right to equitable remuneration

1. Where an author or performer has transferred or assigned his rental right concerning a phonogram or an original or copy of a film to a phonogram or film producer, that author or performer shall retain the right to obtain an equitable remuneration for the rental.

2. The right to obtain an equitable remuneration for rental cannot be waived by authors or performers.

3. The administration of this right to obtain an equitable remuneration may be entrusted to collecting societies representing authors or performers.

4. Member States may regulate whether and to what extent administration by collecting societies of the right to obtain an equitable remuneration may be imposed, as well as the question from whom this remuneration may be claimed or collected.

H–32   *Article 5*

Derogation from the exclusive public lending right

1. Member States may derogate from the exclusive right provided for in Article 1 in respect of public lending, provided that at least authors obtain a remuneration for such lending. Member States shall be free to determine this remuneration taking account of their cultural promotion objectives.

2. When Member States do not apply the exclusive lending right provided for in Article 1 as regards phonograms, films and computer programs, they shall introduce, at least for authors, a remuneration.

3. Member States may exempt certain categories of establishments from the payment of the remuneration referred to in paragraphs 1 and 2.

4. The Commission in cooperation with the Member States, shall draw up before July 1, 1997 a report on public lending in the Community. It shall forward this report to the European Parliament and to the Council.

CHAPTER II

RIGHTS RELATED TO COPYRIGHT

H–33   *Article 6*

Fixation right

1. Member States shall provide for performers the exclusive right to authorize or prohibit the fixation of their performances.

2. Member States shall provide for broadcasting organizations the exclusive right to authorize or prohibit the fixation of their broadcasts, whether these broadcasts are transmitted by wire or over the air, including by cable or satellite.

3. A cable distributor shall not have the right provided for in paragraph 2 where it merely retransmits by cable the broadcasts of broadcasting organizations.

Article 7 **H–34**

Reproduction right

1. Member States shall provide the exclusive right to authorize or prohibit the direct or indirect reproduction:
— for performers, of fixations of their performances,
— for phonogram producers, of their phonograms,
— for producers of the first fixations of films, in respect of the original and copies of their films, and
— for broadcasting organizations, of fixations of their broadcasts, as set out in Article 6 (2).

2. The reproduction right referred to in paragraph 1 may be transferred, assigned or subject to granting of contractual licences.

Article 8 **H–35**

Broadcasting and communication to the public

1. Member States shall provide for performers the exclusive right to authorize or prohibit the broadcasting by wireless means and the communication to the public of their performances, except where the performance is itself already a broadcast performance or is made from a fixation.

2. Member States shall provide a right in order to ensure that a single equitable remuneration is paid by the user, if a phonogram published for commercial purposes, or a reproduction of such phonogram, is used for broadcasting by wireless means or for any communication to the public, and to ensure that this remuneration is shared between the relevant performers and phonogram producers. Member States may, in the absence of agreement between the performers and phonogram producers, lay down the conditions as to the sharing of this remuneration between them.

3. Member States shall provide for broadcasting organizations the exclusive right to authorize or prohibit the rebroadcasting of their broadcasts by wireless means, as well as the communication to the public of their broadcasts if such communication is made in places accessible to the public against payment of an entrance fee.

Article 9

Distribution right

1. Member States shall provide
— for performers, in respect of fixations of their performances,
— for phonogram producers, in respect of their phonograms,
— for producers of the first fixations of films, in respect of the original and copies of their films,
— for broadcasting organizations, in respect of fixations of their broadcast as set out in Article 6 (2),
the exclusive right to make available these objects, including copies thereof, to the public by sale or otherwise hereafter referred to as the "distribution right".

2. The distribution right shall not be exhausted within the Community in respect of an object as referred to in paragraph 1, except where the first sale in the Community of that object is made by the rightholder or with his consent.

3. The distribution right shall be without prejudice to the specific provisions of Chapter I, in particular Article 1 (4).

4. The distribution right may be transferred, assigned or subject to the granting of contractual licences.

H–37   *Article 10*

Limitations to rights

1. Member States may provide for limitations to the rights referred to in Chapter II in respect of:
  (a) private use;
  (b) use of short excerpts in connection with the reporting of current events;
  (c) ephemeral fixation by a broadcasting organization by means of its own facilities and for its own broadcasts;
  (d) use solely for the purposes of teaching or scientific research.

2. Irrespective of paragraph 1, any Member State may provide for the same kinds of limitations with regard to the protection of performers, producers of phonograms, broadcasting organizations and of producers of the first fixations of films, as it provides for in connection with the protection of copyright in literary and artistic works. However, compulsory licences may be provided for only to the extent to which they are compatible with the Rome Convention.

3. Paragraph 1 (a) shall be without prejudice to any existing or future legislation on remuneration for reproduction for private use.

CHAPTER III

DURATION

Article 11   **H–38**

Duration of authors' rights

Without prejudice to further harmonization, the authors' rights referred to in this Directive shall not expire before the end of the term provided by the Berne Convention for the Protection of Literary and Artistic Works.

Article 12   **H–39**

Duration of related rights

Without prejudice to further harmonization, the rights referred to in this Directive of performers, phonogram producers and broadcasting organizations shall not expire before the end of the respective terms provided by the Rome Convention. The rights referred to in this Directive for producers of the first fixations of films shall not expire before the end of a period of 20 years computed from the end of the year in which the fixation was made.

[Articles 11 and 12 have been repealed by Article 11(2) of Directive 93/98: see *post*, para. H-74.]

CHAPTER IV

COMMON PROVISIONS

Article 13   **H–40**

Application in time

1. This Directive shall apply in respect of all copyright works, performances, phonograms, broadcasts and first fixations of films referred to in this Directive which are, on 1 July 1994, still protected by the legislation of the Member States in the field of copyright and related rights or meet the criteria for protection under the provisions of this Directive on that date.

2. This Directive shall apply without prejudice to any acts of exploitation performed before 1 July 1994.

3. Member States may provide that the rightholders are deemed to have given their authorization to the rental or lending of an object referred to in Article 2 (1) which is proven to have been made available to third parties for this purpose or to have been acquired before 1 July 1994. However, in particular where such an object is a digital recording, Member States may provide that rightholders shall have a right to obtain an adequate remuneration for the rental or lending of that object.

413

4. Member States need not apply to provisions of Article 2 (2) to cinematographic or audiovisual works created before 1 July 1994.

5. Member States may determine the date as from which the Article 2 (2) shall apply, provided that that date is not later than 1 July 1997.

6. This Directive shall, without prejudice to paragraph 3 and subject to paragraphs 8 and 9, not affect any contracts concluded before the date of its adoption.

7. Member States may provide, subject to the provisions of paragraphs 8 and 9, that when rightholders who acquire new rights under the national provisions adopted in implementation of this Directive have, before July 1, 1994, given their consent for exploitation, they shall be presumed to have transferred the new exclusive rights.

8. Member States may determine the date as from which the unwaivable right to an equitable remuneration referred to in Article 4 exists, provided that that date is no later than 1 July 1997.

9. For contracts concluded before July 1, 1994, the unwaivable right to an equitable remuneration provided for in Article 4 shall apply only where authors or performers or those representing them have submitted a request to that effect before 1 January 1997. In the absence of agreement between rightholders concerning the level of remuneration, Member States may fix the level of equitable remuneration.

H–41   *Article 14*

Relation between copyright and related rights

Protection of copyright-related rights under this Directive shall leave intact and shall in no way affect the protection of copyright.

H–42   *Article 15*

Final provisions

1. Member States shall bring into force the laws, regulations and administrative provisions necessary to comply with this Directive not later than 1 July 1994. They shall forthwith inform the Commission thereof.

When Member States adopt these measures, they shall contain a reference to this Directive or shall be accompanied by such reference at the time of their official publication. The methods of making such a reference shall be laid down by the Member States.

2. Member States shall communicate to the Commission the main provisions of domestic law which they adopt in the field covered by this Directive.

H–43   *Article 16*

This Directive is addressed to the Member States.

Done at Brussels, 19 November 1992.

COUNCIL DIRECTIVE 93/83/EEC

of September 27, 1993
on the coordination of certain rules concerning copyright and rights related to
copyright applicable to satellite broadcasting and cable retransmission

([1993] O.J. L248)

THE COUNCIL OF THE EUROPEAN COMMUNITIES,   **H–44**

Having regard to the Treaty establishing the European Economic Community, and in particular Articles 57 (2) and 66 thereof,

Having regard to the proposal from the Commission,

In cooperation with the European Parliament,

Having regard to the opinion of the Economic and Social Committee,

(1) Whereas the objectives of the Community as laid down in the Treaty include establishing an ever closer union among the peoples of Europe, fostering closer relations between the States belonging to the Community and ensuring the economic and social progress of the Community countries by common action to eliminate the barriers which divide Europe;

(2) Whereas, to that end, the Treaty provides for the establishment of a common market and an area without internal frontiers; whereas measures to achieve this include the abolition of obstacles to the free movement of services and the institution of a system ensuring that competition in the common market is not distorted; whereas, to that end, the Council may adopt directives for the coordination of the provisions laid down by law, regulation or administrative action in Member States concerning the taking up and pursuit of activities as self-employed persons;

(3) Whereas broadcasts transmitted across frontiers within the Community, in particular by satellite and cable, are one of the most important ways of pursuing these Community objectives, which are at the same time political, economic, social, cultural and legal;

(4) Whereas the Council has already adopted Directive 89/552/EEC of 3 October 1989 on the coordination of certain provisions laid down by law, regulation or administrative action in Member States concerning the pursuit of television broadcasting activities, which makes provision for the promotion of the distribution and production of European television programmes and for advertising and sponsorship, the protection of minors and the right of reply;

(5) Whereas, however, the achievement of these objectives in respect of cross-border satellite broadcasting and the cable retransmission of programmes from other Member States is currently still obstructed by a series of differences between national rules of copyright and some degree of legal uncertainty; whereas this means that holders of rights are exposed to the threat of seeing

their works exploited without payment of remuneration or that the individual holders of exclusive rights in various Member States block the exploitation of their rights; whereas the legal uncertainty in particular constitutes a direct obstacle in the free circulation of programmes within the Community;

(6) Whereas a distinction is currently drawn for copyright purposes between communication to the public by direct satellite and communication to the public by communications satellite; whereas, since individual reception is possible and affordable nowadays with both types of satellite, there is no longer any justification for this differing legal treatment;

(7) Whereas the free broadcasting of programmes is further impeded by the current legal uncertainty over whether broadcasting by a satellite whose signals can be received directly affects the rights in the country of transmission only or in all countries of reception together; whereas, since communications satellites and direct satelites are treated alike for copyright purposes, this legal uncertainty now affects almost all programmes broadcast in the Community by satellite;

(8) Whereas, furthermore, legal certainty, which is a prerequisite for the free movement of broadcasts within the Community, is missing where programmes transmitted across frontiers are fed into and retransmitted through cable networks;

(9) Whereas the development of the acquisition of rights on a contractual basis by authorization is already making a vigorous contribution to the creation of the desired European audiovisual area; whereas the continuation of such contractual agreements should be ensured and their smooth application in practice should be promoted wherever possible;

(10) Whereas at present cable operators in particular cannot be sure that they have actually acquired all the programme rights covered by such an agreement;

(11) Whereas, lastly, parties in different Member States are not all similarly bound by obligations which prevent them from refusing without valid reason to negotiate on the acquisition of the rights necessary for cable distribution or allowing such negotiations to fail;

H–45 (12) Whereas the legal framework for the creation of a single audiovisual area laid down in Directive 89/552/EEC must, therefore, be supplemented with reference to copyright;

(13) Whereas, therefore, an end should be put to the differences of treatment of the transmission of programmes by communications satellite which exist in the Member States, so that the vital distinction throughout the Community becomes whether works and other protected subject matter are communicated to the public; whereas this will also ensure equal treatment of the supplies of cross-border broadcasts, regardless of whether they use a direct broadcasting or a communications satellite;

(14) Whereas the legal uncertainty regarding the rights to be acquired which impedes cross-border satellite broadcasting should be overcome by defining the notion of communication to the public by satellite at a Community level; whereas this definition should at the same time specify where the act of communication takes place; whereas such a definition is necessary to avoid the cumulative application of several national laws to one single act of broadcasting; whereas communication to the public by satellite occurs only when, and in

the Member State where, the programme-carrying signals are introduced under the control and responsibility of the broadcasting organization into an uninterrupted chain of communication leading to the satellite and down towards the earth; whereas normal technical procedures relating to the programme-carrying signals should not be considered as interruptions to the chain of broadcasting;

(15) Whereas the acquisition on a contractual basis of exclusive broadcasting rights should comply with any legislation on copyright and rights related to copyright in the Member State in which communication to the public by satellite occurs;

(16) Whereas the principle of contractual freedom on which this Directive is based will make it possible to continue limiting the exploitation of these rights, especially as far as certain technical means of transmission or certain language versions are concerned;

(17) Whereas, in arriving at the amount of the payment to be made for the rights acquired, the parties should take account of all aspects of the broadcast, such as the actual audience, the potential audience and the language version;

(18) Whereas the application of the country-of-origin principle contained in this Directive could pose a problem with regard to existing contracts; whereas this Directive should provide for a period of five years for existing contracts to be adapted, where necessary, in the light of the Directive; whereas the said country-of-origin principle should not, therefore, apply to existing contracts which expire before 1 January 2000; whereas if by that date parties still have an interest in the contract, the same parties should be entitled to renegotiate the conditions of the contract;

(19) Whereas existing international co-production agreements must be interpreted in the light of the economic purpose and scope envisaged by the parties upon signature; whereas in the past international co-production agreements have often not expressly and specifically addressed communication to the public by satellite within the meaning of this Directive a particular form of exploitation; whereas the underlying philosophy of many existing international co-production agreements is that the rights in the co-production are exercised separately and independently by each co-producer, by dividing the exploitation rights between them along territorial lines; whereas, as a general rule, in the situation where a communication to the public by satellite authorized by one co-producer would prejudice the value of the exploitation rights of another co-producer, the interpretation of such an existing agreement would normally suggest that the latter co-producer would have to give his consent to the authorization, by the former co-producer, of the communication to the public by satellite; whereas the language exclusivity of the latter co-producer will be prejudiced where the language version or versions of the communication to the public, including where the version is dubbed or subtitled, coincide(s) with the language or the languages widely understood in the territory allotted by the agreement to the latter co- producer; whereas the notion of exclusivity should be understood in a wider sense where the communication to the public by satellite concerns a work which consists merely of images and contains no dialogue or subtitles; whereas a clear rule is necessary in cases where the international co-production agreement does not expressly regulate the division of rights in the specific case of communication to the public by satellite within the meaning of this Directive;

(20) Whereas communications to the public by satellite from non-member countries will under certain conditions be deemed to occur within a Member State of the Community;

(21) Whereas it is necessary to ensure that protection for authors, performers, producers of phonograms and broadcasting organizations is accorded in all Member States and that this protection is not subject to a statutory licence system; whereas only in this way is it possible to ensure that any difference in the level of protection within the common market will not create distortions of competition;

(22) Whereas the advent of new technologies is likely to have an impact on both the quality and the quantity of the exploitation of works and other subject matter;

(23) Whereas in the light of these developments the level of protection granted pursuant to this Directive to all rightholders in the areas covered by this Directive should remain under consideration;

H–46   (24) Whereas the harmonization of legislation envisaged in this Directive entails the harmonization of the provisions ensuring a high level of protection of authors, performers, phonogram producers and broadcasting organizations; whereas this harmonization should not allow a broadcasting organization to take advantage of differences in levels of protection by relocating activities, to the detriment of audiovisual productions;

(25) Whereas the protection provided for rights related to copyright should be aligned on that contained in Council Directive 92/100/EEC of 19 November 1992 on rental right and lending right and on certain rights related to copyright in the field of intellectual property for the purposes of communication to the public by satellite; whereas, in particular, this will ensure that performers and phonogram producers are guaranteed an appropriate remuneration for the communication to the public by satellite of their performances or phonograms;

(26) Whereas the provisions of Article 4 do not prevent Member States from extending the presumption set out in Article 2 (5) of Directive 92/100/EEC to the exclusive rights referred to in Article 4; whereas, furthermore, the provisions of Article 4 do not prevent Member States from providing for a rebuttable presumption of the authorization of exploitation in respect of the exclusive rights of performers referred to in that Article, in so far as such presumption is compatible with the International Convention for the Protection of Performers, Producers of Phonograms and Broadcasting Organizations;

(27) Whereas the cable retransmission of programmes from other Member States is an act subject to copyright and, as the case may be, rights related to copyright; whereas the cable operator must, therefore, obtain the authorization from every holder of rights in each part of the programme retransmitted; whereas, pursuant to this Directive, the authorizations should be granted contractually unless a temporary exception is provided for in the case of existing legal licence schemes;

(28) Whereas, in order to ensure that the smooth operation of contractual arrangements is not called into question by the intervention of outsiders holding rights in individual parts of the programme, provision should be made, through the obligation to have recourse to a collecting society, for the

exclusive collective exercise of the authorization right to the extent that this is required by the special features of cable retransmission; whereas the authorization right as such remains intact and only the exercise of this right is regulated to some extent, so that the right to authorize a cable retransmission can still be assigned; whereas this Directive does not affect the exercise of moral rights;

(29) Whereas the exemption provided for in Article 10 should not limit the choice of holders of rights to transfer their rights to a collecting society and thereby have a direct share in the remuneration paid by the cable distributor for cable retransmission;

(30) Whereas contractual arrangements regarding the authorization of cable retransmission should be promoted by additional measures; whereas a party seeking the conclusion of a general contract should, for its part, be obliged to submit collective proposals for an agreement; whereas furthermore, any party shall be entitled, at any moment, to call upon the assistance of impartial mediators whose task is to assist negotiations and who may submit proposals; whereas any such proposals and any opposition thereto should be served on the parties concerned in accordance with the applicable rules concerning the service of legal documents, in particular as set out in existing international conventions; whereas, finally, it is necessary to ensure that the negotiations are not blocked without valid justification or that individual holders are not prevented without valid justification from taking part in the negotiations; whereas none of these measures for the promotion of the acquisition of rights calls into question the contractual nature of the acquisition of cable retransmission rights;

(31) Whereas for a transitional period Member States should be allowed to retain existing bodies with jurisdiction in their territory over cases where the right to retransmit a programme by cable to the public has been unreasonably refused or offered on unreasonable terms by a broadcasting organization; whereas it is understood that the right of parties concerned to be heard by the body should be guaranteed and that the existence of the body should not prevent the parties concerned from having normal access to the courts;

(32) Whereas, however, Community rules are not needed to deal with all of those matters, the effects of which perhaps with some commercially insignificant exceptions, are felt only inside the borders of a single Member State;

(33) Whereas minimum rules should be laid down in order to establish and guarantee free and uninterrupted cross-border broadcasting by satellite and simultaneous, unaltered cable retransmission of programmes broadcast from other Member States, on an essentially contractual basis;

(34) Whereas this Directive should not prejudice further harmonization in the field of copyright and rights related to copyright and the collective administration of such rights; whereas the possibility for Member States to regulate the activities of collecting societies should not prejudice the freedom of contractual negotiation of the rights provided for in this Directive, on the understanding that such negotiation takes place within the framework of general or specific national rules with regard to competition law or the prevention of abuse of monopolies;

(35) Whereas it should, therefore, be for the Member States to supplement the general provisions needed to achieve the objectives of this Directive by taking legislative and administrative measures in their domestic law, provided that

these do not run counter to the objectives of this Directive and are compatible with Community law;

(36) Whereas this Directive does not affect the applicability of the competition rules in Articles 85 and 86 of the Treaty,

HAS ADOPTED THIS DIRECTIVE:

CHAPTER I

DEFINITIONS

H–47 *Article 1*

Definitions

1. For the purpose of this Directive, "satellite" means any satellite operating on frequency bands which, under telecommunications law, are reserved for the broadcast of signals for reception by the public or which are reserved for closed, point-to-point communication. In the latter case, however, the circumstances in which individual reception of the signals takes place must be comparable to those which apply in the first case.

2. (a) For the purpose of this Directive, "communication to the public by satellite" means the act of introducing, under the control and responsibility of the broadcasting organization, the programme-carrying signals intended for reception by the public into an uninterrupted chain of communication leading to the satelite and down towards the earth.

(b) The act of communication to the public by satellite occurs solely in the Member State where, under the control and responsibility of the broadcasting organization, the programme-carrying signals are introduced into an uninterrupted chain of communication leading to the satellite and down towards the earth.

(c) If the programme-carrying signals are encrypted, then there is communication to the public by satellite on condition that the means for decrypting the broadcast are provided to the public by the broadcasting organization or with its consent.

(d) Where an act of communication to the public by satellite occurs in a non-Community State which does not provide the level of protection provided for under Chapter II,

  (i) if the programme-carrying signals are transmitted to the satellite from an uplink station[4] situated in a Member State, that act of communication to the public by satellite shall be deemed to have occurred in that Member State and the rights provided for under Chapter II shall be exercisable against the person operating the uplink station; or

  (ii) if there is no use of an uplink station situated in a Member State but a broadcasting organization established in a Member State has commissioned the act of communication to the public by satellite,

---

[4] O.J. text has "situation".

that act shall be deemed to have occurred in the Member State in which the broadcasting organization has its principal establishment in the Community and the rights provided for under Chapter II shall be exercisable against the broadcasting organization.

3. For the purposes of this Directive, "cable retransmission" means the simultaneous, unaltered and unabridged retransmission by a cable or microwave system for reception by the public of an initial transmission from another Member State, by wire or over the air, including that by satellite, of television or radio programmes intended for reception by the public.

4. For the purposes of this Directive "collecting society" means any organization which manages or administers copyright or rights related to copyright as its sole purpose or as one of its main purposes.

5. For the purposes of this Directive, the principal director of a cinematographic or audiovisual work shall be considered as its author or one of its authors. Member States may provide for others to be considered as its co-authors.

CHAPTER II

BROADCASTING OF PROGRAMMES BY SATELLITE

Article 2 **H–48**

Broadcasting right

Member States shall provide an exclusive right for the author to authorize the communication to the public by satellite of copyright works, subject to the provisions set out in this chapter.

Article 3 **H–49**

Acquisition of broadcasting rights

1. Member States shall ensure that the authorization referred to in Article 2 may be acquired only be agreement.

2. A Member State may provide that a collective agreement between a collecting society and a broadcasting organization concerning a given category of works may be extended to rightholders of the same category who are not represented by the collecting society, provided that:
— the communication to the public by satellite simulcasts a terrestrial broadcast by the same broadcaster, and
— the unrepresented rightholder shall, at any time, have the possibility of excluding the extension of the collective agreement to his works and of exercising his rights either individually or collectively.

3. Paragraph 2 shall not apply to cinematographic works, including works created by a process analogous to cinematography.

4. Where the law of a Member State provides for the extension of a collective agreement in accordance with the provisions of paragraph 2, that Member State[5] shall inform the Commission which broadcasting organizations are entitled to avail themselves of that law. The Commission shall publish this information in the *Official Journal of the European Communities* (C series).

H–50   *Article 4*

Rights of performers, phonogram producers and broadcasting organizations

1. For the purposes of communication to the public by satellite, the rights of performers, phonogram producers and broadcasting organizations shall be protected in accordance with the provisions of Articles 6, 7, 8 and 10 of Directive 92/100/EEC.

2. For the purposes of paragraph 1, "broadcasting by wireless means" in Directive 92/100/EEC shall be understood as including communication to the public by satellite.

3. With regard to the exercise of the rights referred to in paragraph 1, Articles 2 (7) and 12 of Directive 92/100/EEC shall apply.

H–51   *Article 5*

Relation between copyright and related rights

Protection of copyright-related rights under this Directive shall leave intact and shall in no way affect the protection of copyright.

H–52   *Article 6*

Minimum protection

1. Member States may provide for more far-reaching protection for holders of rights related to copyright than that required by Article 8 of Directive 92/100/EEC.

2. In applying paragraph 1 Member States shall observe the definitions contained in Article 1 (1) and (2).

---

[5] O.J. text has "States".

Article 7   **H–53**

Transitional provisions

1. With regard to the application in time of the rights referred to in Article 4 (1) of this Directive, Article 13 (1), (2), (6) and (7) of Directive 92/100/EEC shall apply. Article 13 (4) and (5) of Directive 92/100/EEC shall apply *mutatis mutandis.*

2. Agreements concerning the exploitation of works and other protected subject matter which are in force on the date mentioned in Article 14 (1) shall be subject to the provisions of Articles 1 (2), 2 and 3 as from 1 January 2000 if they expire after that date.

3. When an international co-production agreement concluded before the date mentioned in Article 14 (1) between a co-producer from a Member State and one or more co-producers from other Member States or third countries expressly provides for a system of division of exploitation rights between the co-producers by geographical areas for all means of communication to the public, without distinguishing the arrangements applicable to communication to the public by satellite from the provisions applicable to the other means of communication, and where communication to the public by satellite of the co-production would prejudice the exclusivity, in particular the language exclusivity, of one of the co-producers or his assignees in a given territory, the authorization by one of the co-producers or his assignees for a communication to the public by satellite shall require the prior consent of the holder of that exclusivity, whether co-producer or assignee.

CHAPTER III

CABLE RETRANSMISSION

Article 8   **H–54**

Cable retransmission right

1. Member States shall ensure that when programmes from other Member States are retransmitted by cable in their territory the applicable copyright and related rights are observed and that such retransmission takes place on the basis of individual or collective contractual agreements between copyright owners, holders of related rights and cable operators.

2. Notwithstanding paragraph 1, Member States may retain until 31 December 1997 such statutory licence systems which are in operation or expressly provided for by national law on 31 July 1991.

Article 9   **H–55**

Exercise of the cable retransmission right

1. Member States shall ensure that the right of copyright owners and holders of related rights to grant or refuse authorization to a cable operator for a cable retransmission may be exercised only through a collecting society.

2. Where a rightholder has not transferred the management of his rights to a collecting society, the collecting society which manages rights of the same category shall be deemed to be mandated to manage his rights. Where more than one collecting society manages rights of that category, the rightholder shall be free to choose which of those collecting societies is deemed to be mandated to manage his rights. A rightholder referred to in this paragraph shall have the same rights and obligations resulting from the agreement between the cable operator and the collecting society which is deemed to be mandated to manage his rights as the rightholders who have mandated that collecting society and he shall be able to claim those rights within a period, to be fixed by the Member State concerned, which shall not be shorter than three years from the date of the cable retransmission which includes his work or other protected subject matter.

3. A Member State may provide that, when a rightholder authorizes the initial transmission within its territory of a work or other protected subject matter, he shall be deemed to have agreed not to exercise his cable retransmission rights on an individual basis but to exercise them in accordance with the provisions of this Directive.

H–56   *Article 10*

Exercise of the cable retransmission right by broadcasting organizations

Member States shall ensure that Article 9 does not apply to the rights exercised by a broadcasting organization in respect of its own transmission, irrespective of whether the rights concerned are its own or have been transferred to it by other copyright owners and/or holders of related rights.

H–57   *Article 11*

Mediators

1. Where no agreement is concluded regarding authorization of the cable retransmission of a broadcast, Member States shall ensure that either party may call upon the assistance of one or more mediators.

2. The task of the mediators shall be to provide assistance with negotiation. They may also submit proposals to the parties.

3. It shall be assumed that all the parties accept a proposal as referred to in paragraph 2 if none of them expresses its opposition within a period of three months. Notice of the proposal and of any opposition thereto shall be served on the parties concerned in accordance with the applicable rules concerning the service of legal documents.

4. The mediators shall be so selected that their independence and impartiality are beyond reasonable doubt.

Article 12

Prevention of the abuse of negotiating positions

1. Member States shall ensure by means of civil or administrative law, as appropriate, that the parties enter and conduct negotiations regarding authorization for cable retransmission in good faith and do not prevent or hinder negotiation without valid justification.

2. A Member State which, on the date mentioned in Article 14 (1), has a body with jurisdiction in its territory over cases where the right to retransmit a programme by cable to the public in that Member State has been unreasonably refused or offered on unreasonable terms by a broadcasting organization may retain that body.

3. Paragraph 2 shall apply for a transitional period of eight years from the date mentioned in Article 14 (1).

CHAPTER IV

GENERAL PROVISIONS

Article 13

Collective administration of rights

This Directive shall be without prejudice to the regulation of the activities of collecting societies by the Member States.

Article 14

Final provisions

1. Member States shall bring into force the laws, regulations and administrative provisions necessary to comply with this Directive before 1 January 1995. They shall immediately inform the Commission thereof.

When Member States adopt these measures, the latter shall contain a reference to this Directive or shall be accompanied by such reference at the time of their official publication. The methods of making such a reference shall be laid down by the Member States.

2. Member States shall communicate to the Commission the provisions of national law which they adopt in the field covered by this Directive.

3. Not later than 1 January 2000, the Commission shall submit to the European Parliament, the Council and the Economic and Social Committee a report on the application of this Directive and, if necessary, make further proposals to adapt it to developments in the audio and audiovisual sector.

Article 15

This Directive is addressed to the Member States.

Done at Brussels, 27 September 1993.

COUNCIL DIRECTIVE 93/98/EEC

of October 29, 1993
harmonizing the term of protection of copyright and certain related rights

H–62 THE COUNCIL OF THE EUROPEAN COMMUNITIES,

Having regard to the Treaty establishing the European Economic Community, and in particular Articles 57 (2), 66 and 100a thereof,

Having regard to the proposal from the Commission,

In cooperation with the European Parliament,

Having regard to the opinion of the Economic and Social Committee,

(1) Whereas the Berne Convention for the protection of literary and artistic works and the International Convention for the protection of performers, producers of phonograms and broadcasting organizations (Rome Convention) lay down only minimum terms of protection of the rights they refer to, leaving the Contracting States free to grant longer terms; whereas certain Member States have exercised this entitlement; whereas in addition certain Member States have not become party to the Rome Convention;

(2) Whereas there are consequently differences between the national laws governing the terms of protection of copyright and related rights, which are liable to impede the free movement of goods and freedom to provide services, and to distort competition in the common market; whereas therefore with a view to the smooth operation of the internal market, the laws of the Member States should be harmonized so as to make terms of protection identical throughout the Community;

(3) Whereas harmonization must cover not only the terms of protection as such, but also certain implementing arrangements such as the date from which each term of protection is calculated;

(4) Whereas the provisions of this Directive do not affect the application by the Member States of the provisions of Article 14a (2) (b), (c) and (d) and (3) of the Berne Convention;

(5) Whereas the minimum term of protection laid down by the Berne Convention, namely the life of the author and 50 years after his death, was intended to provide protection for the author and the first two generations of his descendants; whereas the average lifespan in the Community has grown longer, to the point where this term is no longer sufficient to cover two generations;

(6) Whereas certain Member States have granted a term longer than 50 years after the death of the author in order to offset the effects of world wars on the exploitation of authors' works;

(7) Whereas for the protection of related rights certain Member States have introduced a term of 50 years after lawful publication or lawful communication to the public;

(8) Whereas under the Community position adopted for the Uruguay Round negotiations under the General Agreement on Tariffs and Trade (GATT) the term of protection for producers of phonograms should be 50 years after first publication;

(9) Whereas due regard for established rights is one of the general principles of law protected by the Community legal order; whereas, therefore, a harmonization of the terms of protection of copyright and related rights cannot have the effect of reducing the protection currently enjoyed by rightholders in the Community; whereas in order to keep the effects of transitional measures to a minimum and to allow the internal market to operate in practice, the harmonization of the term of protection should take place on a long term basis;

(10) Whereas in its communication of 17 January 1991 "Follow-up to the Green Paper—Working programme of the Commission in the field of copyright and neighbouring rights" the Commission stresses the need to harmonize copyright and neighbouring rights at a high level of protection since these rights are fundamental to intellectual creation and stresses that their protection ensures the maintenance and development of creativity in the interest of authors, cultural industries, consumers and society as a whole;

(11) Whereas in order to establish a high level of protection which at the same time meets the requirements of the internal market and the need to establish a legal environment conducive to the harmonious development of literary and artistic creation in the Community, the term of protection for copyright should be harmonized at 70 years after the death of the author or 70 years after the work is lawfully made available to the public, and for related rights at 50 years after the event which sets the term running;

(12) Whereas collections are protected according to Article 2 (5) of the Berne Convention when, by reason of the selection and arrangement of their content, they constitute intellectual creations; whereas those works are protected as such, without prejudice to the copyright in each of the works forming part of such collections, whereas in consequence specific terms of protection may apply to works included in collections;

(13) Whereas in all cases where one or more physical persons are identified as authors the term of protection should be calculated after their death; whereas the question of authorship in the whole or a part of a work is a question of fact which the national courts may have to decide;

(14) Whereas terms of protection should be calculated from the first day of January of the year following the relevant event, as they are in the Berne and Rome Conventions; **H–63**

(15) Whereas Article 1 of Council Directive 91/250/EEC of May 14, 1991 on the legal protection of computer programs provides that Member States are to protect computer programs, by copyright, as literary works within the meaning of the Berne Convention; whereas this Directive harmonizes the term of protection of literary works in the Community; whereas Article 8 of Directive 91/250/EEC, which merely makes provisional arrangements governing the term of protection of computer programs, should accordingly be repealed;

(16) Whereas Articles 11 and 12 of Council Directive 92/100/EEC of November 19, 1992 on rental right and lending right and on certain rights

related to copyright in the field of intellectual property make provision for minimum terms of protection only, subject to any further harmonization; whereas this Directive provides such further harmonization; whereas these Articles should accordingly be repealed;

(17) Whereas the protection of photographs in the Member States is the subject of varying regimes; whereas in order to achieve a sufficient harmonization of the term of protection of photographic works, in particular of those which, due to their artistic or professional character, are of importance within the internal market, it is necessary to define the level of originality required in this Directive; whereas a photographic work within the meaning of the Berne Convention is to be considered original if it is the author's own intellectual creation reflecting his personality, no other criteria such as merit or purpose being taken into account; whereas the protection of other photographs should be left to national law;

(18) Whereas, in order to avoid differences in the term of protection as regards related rights it is necessary to provide the same starting point for the calculation of the term throughout the Community; whereas the performance, fixation, transmission, lawful publication, and lawful communication to the public, that is to say the means of making a subject of a related right perceptible in all appropriate ways to persons in general, should be taken into account for the calculation of the term of protection regardless of the country where this performance, fixation, transmission, lawful publication, or lawful comunication to the public takes place;

(19) Whereas the rights of broadcasting organizations in their broadcasts, whether these broadcasts are transmitted by wire or over the air, including by cable or satellite, should not be perpetual; whereas it is therefore necessary to have the term of protection running from the first transmission of a particular broadcast only; whereas this provision is understood to avoid a new term running in cases where a broadcast is identical to a previous one;

(20) Whereas the Member States should remain free to maintain or introduce other rights related to copyright in particular in relation to the protection of critical and scientific publications; whereas, in order to ensure transparency at Community level, it is however necessary for Member States which introduce new related rights to notify the Commission;

(21) Whereas it is useful to make clear that the harmonization brought about by this Directive does not apply to moral rights;

(22) Whereas, for works whose country of origin within the meaning of the Berne Convention is a third country and whose author is not a Community national, comparison of terms of protection should be applied, provided that the term accorded in the Community does not exceed the term laid down in this Directive;

(23) Whereas where a rightholder who is not a Community national qualifies for protection under an international agreement the term of protection of related rights should be the same as that laid down in this Directive, except that it should not exceed that fixed in the country of which the rightholder is a national;

(24) Whereas comparison of terms should not result in Member States being brought into conflict with their international obligations;

(25) Whereas, for the smooth functioning of the internal market this Directive should be applied as from 1 July 1995;

(26) Whereas Member States should remain free to adopt provisions on the interpretation, adaptation and further execution of contracts on the exploitation of protected works and other subject matter which were concluded before the extension of the term of protection resulting from this Directive;

(27) Whereas respect of acquired rights and legitimate expectations is part of the Community legal order; whereas Member States may provide in particular that in certain circumstances the copyright and related rights which are revived pursuant to this Directive may not give rise to payments by persons who undertook in good faith the exploitation of the works at the time when such works lay within the public domain,

HAS ADOPTED THIS DIRECTIVE:

Article 1 **H–64**

Duration of authors' rights

1. The rights of an author of a literary or artistic work within the meaning of Article 2 of the Berne Convention shall run for the life of the author and for 70 years after his death, irrespective of the date when the work is lawfully made available to the public.

2. In the case of a work of joint authorship the term referred to in paragraph 1 shall be calculated from the death of the last surviving author.

3. In the case of anonymous or pseudonymous works, the term of protection shall run for seventy years after the work is lawfully made available to the public. However, when the pseudonym adopted by the author leaves no doubt as to his identity, or if the author discloses his identity during the period referred to in the first sentence, the term of protection applicable shall be that laid down in paragraph 1.

4. Where a Member State provides for particular provisions on copyright in respect of collective works or for a legal person to be designated as the rightholder, the term of protection shall be calculated according to the provisions of paragraph 3, except if the natural persons who have created the work as such are identified as such in the versions of the work which are made available to the public. This paragraph is without prejudice to the rights of identified authors whose identifiable contributions are included in such works, to which contributions paragraph 1 or 2 shall apply.

5. Where a work is published in volumes, parts, instalments, issues or episodes and the term of protection runs from the time when the work was lawfully made available to the public, the term of protection shall run for each such item separately.

6. In the case of works for which the term of protection is not calculated from the death of the author or authors and which have not been lawfully made available to the public within seventy years from their creation, the protection shall terminate.

H–65   *Article 2*

Cinematographic or audiovisual works

1. The principal director of a cinematographic or audiovisual work shall be considered as its author or one of its authors. Member States shall be free to designate other co-authors.

2. The term of protection of cinematographic or audiovisual works shall expire 70 years after the death of the last of the following persons to survive, whether or not these persons are designated as co-authors: the principal director, the author of the screenplay, the author of the dialogue and the composer of music specifically created for use in the cinematographic or audiovisual work.

H–66   *Article 3*

Duration of related rights

1. The rights of performers shall expire 50 years after the date of the performance. However, if a fixation of the performance is lawfully published or lawfully communicated to the public within this period, the rights shall expire 50 years from the date of the first such publication or the first such communication to the public, whichever is the earlier.

2. The rights of producers of phonograms shall expire 50 years after the fixation is made. However, if the phonogram is lawfully published or lawfully communicated to the public during this period, the rights shall expire 50 years from the date of the first such publication or the first such communication to the public, whichever is the earlier.

3. The rights of producers of the first fixation of a film shall expire 50 years after the fixation is made. However, if the film is lawfully published or lawfully communicated to the public during this period, the rights shall expire 50 years from the date of the first such publication or the first such communication to the public, whichever is the earlier. The term "film" shall designate a cinematographic or audiovisual work or moving images, whether or not accompanied by sound.

4. The rights of broadcasting organizations shall expire 50 years after the first transmission of a broadcast, whether this broadcast is transmitted by wire or over the air, including by cable or satellite.

H–67   *Article 4*

Protection of previously unpublished works

Any person who, after the expiry of copyright protection, for the first time lawfully publishes or lawfully communicates to the public a previously unpublished work, shall benefit from a protection equivalent to the economic rights of the author. The term of protection of such rights shall be 25 years from the time when the work was first lawfully published or lawfully communicated to the public.

Article 5

H–68

Critical and scientific publication

Member States may protect critical and scientific publications of works which have come into the public domain. The maximum term of protection of such rights shall be 30 years from the time when the publication was first lawfully published.

Article 6

H–69

Protection of photographs

Photographs which are original in the sense that they are the author's own intellectual creation shall be protected in accordance with Article 1. No other criteria shall be applied to determine their eligibility for protection. Member States may provide for the protection of other photographs.

Article 7

H–70

Protection *vis-à-vis* third countries

1. Where the country of origin of a work, within the meaning of the Berne Convention, is a third country, and the author of the work is not a Community national, the term of protection granted by the Member States shall expire on the date of expiry of the protection granted in the country of origin of the work, but may not exceed the term laid down in Article 1.

2. The terms of protection laid down in Article 3 shall also apply in the case of rightholders who are not Community nationals, provided Member States grant them protection. However, without prejudice to the international obligations of the Member States, the term of protection granted by Member States shall expire no later than the date of expiry of the protection granted in the country of which the rightholder is a national and may not exceed the term laid down in Article 3.

3. Member States which, at the date of adoption of this Directive, in particular pursuant to their international obligations, granted a longer term of protection than that which would result from the provisions, referred to in paragraphs 1 and 2 may maintain this protection until the conclusion of international agreements on the term of protection by copyright or related rights.

431

H–71   *Article 8*

Calculation of terms

The terms laid down in this Directive are calculated from the first day of January of the year following the event which gives rise to them.

H–72   *Article 9*

Moral rights

This Directive shall be without prejudice to the provisions of the Member States regulating moral rights.

H–73   *Article 10*

Application in time

1. Where a term of protection, which is longer than the corresponding term provided for by this Directive, is already running in a Member State on the date referred to in Article 13 (1), this Directive shall not have the effect of shortening that term of protection in that Member State.

2. The terms of protection provided for in this Directive shall apply to all works and subject matter which are protected in at least one Member State, on the date referred to in Article 13 (1), pursuant to national provisions on copyright or related rights or which meet the criteria for protection under Directive 92/100/EEC.

3. This Directive shall be without prejudice to any acts of exploitation performed before the date referred to in Article 13 (1). Member States shall adopt the necessary provisions to protect in particular acquired rights of third parties.

4. Member States need not apply the provisions of Article 2 (1) to cinematographic or audiovisual works created before July 1, 1994.

5. Member States may determine the date as from which Article 2 (1) shall apply, provided that date is no later than July 1, 1997.

H–74   *Article 11*

Technical adaptation

1. Article 8 of Directive 91/250/EEC is hereby repealed.

2. Articles 11 and 12 of Directive 92/100/EEC are hereby repealed.

Article 12 **H–75**

Notification procedure

Member States shall immediately notify the Commission of any governmental plan to grant new related rights, including the basic reasons for their introduction and the term of protection envisaged.

Article 13 **H–76**

General provisions

1. Member States shall bring into force the laws, regulations and administrative provisions necessary to comply with Articles 1 to 11 of this Directive before 1 July 1995.

When Member States adopt these provisions, they shall contain a reference to this Directive or shall be accompanied by such reference at the time of their official publication. The methods of making such a reference shall be laid down by the Member States.

Member States shall communicate to the Commission the texts of the provisions of national law which they adopt in the field governed by this Directive.

2. Member States shall apply Article 12 from the date of notification of this Directive.

Article 14 **H–77**

This Directive is addressed to the Member States.

Done at Brussels, 29 October 1993.

Appendix I

PARLIAMENTARY DEBATES ON THE COPYRIGHT, DESIGNS AND PATENTS ACT

1988 AND SUBSEQUENT AMENDMENTS

The following is a table of the main debates on particular sections of the Bill and subsequent amendments. References to "H.C., SCE" and "H.C., SCF" are to the debates in the House of Commons of Standing Committee E in 1988 and Standing Committee F in 1990 respectively.

Section 1(1)	H.L. Vol. 490, cols. 822, 823; H.L. Vol 493, cols. 1054, 1055 (on removal of distinction between Parts I and II in 1956 Act).
Section 1(1)(a)	H.L. Vol 490, cols. 813–822; H.L. Vol. 493, cols. 1072–1074 (photograph).
Section 1(1)(b),(c)	H.L. vol. 493, cols. 1055–1058;
Section 1(1)(c)	H.L. Vol. 490, col. 823.
Section 1(3)	H.C., SCE col. 21.
Section 2	H.L. Vol. 490, cols. 827, 828; H.L. Vol. 494, cols. 607, 610.
Section 3(1)	"Literary work": H.L. Vol 490, cols. 828–832; H.C., SCE cols. 21–25, 36–39.
	"Table or compilation": H.L. Vol. 490, cols. 832, 834; H.C., SCE cols. 21–25.
	"Musical work": H.L. Vol. 490, cols. 828, 831; H.C., SCE cols. 36–39.
	"Dramatic work": H.L. Vol. 490, cols. 830, 836, 837; H.C., SCE cols. 33–38.

Section 3(2)	H.L. Vol. 490, col. 828, 834–836; H.L. Vol. 493, cols. 1058, 1059; H.C., SCE cols. 33–39; H.L. Vol. 501, cols. 197–200.
Section 3(3)	H.L. Vol. 490, col. 835; Vol. 493, cols. 1058–1059; H.C., SCE cols. 34–39; Vol. 495, cols. 610–611.
Section 4(1)(a)	H.L. Vol. 490, cols. 838–841 ("Irrespective of artistic quality")
	H.L. Vol. 490, cols. 843–847; Vol. 493, cols. 1067–1069 ("Typeface").
	H.L. Vol. 490, col. 849; Vol. 493, cols. 1066, 1067 ("Collage").
Section 4(1)(b)	H.L. Vol. 490, cols. 841–843.
Section 4(1)(c)	H.L. Vol. 490, cols. 846–848.
Section 4(2)	H.L. Vol. 493, cols. 1069–1071 ("Building").
	H.L. Vol. 490, cols. 852–854; Vol. 493, cols. 1071, 1072 ("Graphic work").
	H.L. Vol. 490, cols. 849–852; Vol. 493, cols. 1063–1066, 1072–1074; Vol 495, cols, 611–615 ("Photograph").
Section 5(1)	H.L. Vol. 490, col. 854, 856, 858–859; H.C., SCE Cols. 40–43 ("Sound recording").
	H.L. Vol. 490, cols. 856–859; Vol. 493, col. 1072; H.C., SCE cols. 40–43 ("Film").
Section 5(2)	H.L. Vol. 493, cols. 1072–1074.
Section 6(1)	H.L. Vol. 490, cols. 859–863; Vol. 493, cols. 1074, 1075; H.C., SCE cols. 44–48; H.L. Vol. 501, cols. 201–203.
Section 6(2)	H.L. Vol. 501, cols. 201–203.
Section 6(3)	H.L. Vol. 490, cols. 863–866; Vol. 493, cols. 1075–1076; Vol. 495, col. 615; H.C., SCE cols. 44–49; H.L. Vol. 501, cols. 201–203.
Section 6(6)	H.C., SCE cols. 49–51.

Section 7	H.C. Vol. 138, cols. 112–115; H.L. Vol. 501, cols. 203–206.
Section 7(1),(2)	H.L. Vol. 490, cols. 866–870; Vol. 495, cols, 615–617; H.C., SCE cols. 51–53.
Section 8(1)	H.L. Vol. 490, cols. 870–874.
Section 9(1)	H.L. Vol. 490, cols. 879–886 (photograph).
Section 9(2)(a)	H.L. Vol. 490, cols. 886–891; H.L. Vol. 493, cols. 1076–1081; H.C., SCE cols. 57–65.
Section 9(2)(d)	H.L. Vol. 490, cols. 891–893.
Sections 9(4),(5)	H.L. Vol. 490, cols. 893, 894; H.L. Vol. 493, cols. 1081–1084.
Section 10	H.C., SCE cols. 65–70.
Section 10(1)	H.L. Vol. 490, cols. 903, 904; H.L. Vol. 493, cols. 1084, 1085.
Section 11	(Commissioned works) H.L. Vol. 490, cols. 916–917; H.L. Vol.493, cols. 1095–1098.
Section 11(2)	H.L. Vol. 490, cols. 895–902, 904–911, 911–915 (photographs); H.C., SCE cols. 70–90; H.C. Vol. 138, cols. 115–127; H.L. Vol. 493, cols. 1085–1095.
Section 12(1)	H.L. Vol. 490, cols. 1149–1154, 1160; H.C., SCE Cols. 107–115.
	(Photographs): H.L. Vol. 490, cols. 1154–1158.
Section 12(2)	H.L. Vol. 490, cols. 1153, 1154, 1158–1160; H.L. Vol. 493, cols. 1081–1084, 1098, 1099; H.C., SCE cols. 115–120.
Section 12(3)	H.C., SCE cols. 120–121; H.L. Vol. 501, cols. 206–208.
Section 13(1)	H.L. Vol. 490, cols. 1160–1162; H.L. Vol. 493, cols. 1099–1103.
Section 14(1),(2)	H.L. Vol. 490, cols. 1162, 1163.
Section 15	H.L. Vol. 490, col. 1163–1165.

Appendix I: Hansard References

Section 16	H.L. Vol. 490, cols. 1165–1167 (knowledge).
Section 16(2)	H.L. Vol. 490, cols. 824–827 (authorise).
Section 16(3)	H.L. Vol. 493, cols. 1105, 1106.
Section 16(3)(a)	H.L. Vol. 490, cols. 1167–1174.
Section 16(3)(b)	H.L. Vol. 490, cols. 1184, 1185.
Section 17(1)	H.L. Vol.490, col. 1191 (parody).
Section 17(2)	H.L. Vol. 490, cols. 1177–1184, 1190; H.L. Vol. 493, cols. 1103–1105; H.C., SCE cols. 121–128; 130–136; H.L. Vol. 501, cols. 208–214 (storing by electronic means and transient copying).
Section 17(2)	H.L. Vol. 490, cols. 1186–1189 (photograph).
Section 17(4)	H.L. Vol. 490, cols. 1189, 1190, H.L. Vol. 493, cols. 1106–1109.
Section 17(5)	H.L. Vol. 490, cols. 1191, 1192.
Section 17(6)	[see *supra*, section 17(2)].
Section 18	H.L. Vol. 501, cols. 214–224; H.C. Vol 140, cols. 270, 271.
Section 18(2)	H.L. Vol. 490, cols. 1192–1205; H.L. Vol. 493, cols. 1109–1120; H.L. Vol. 495, cols. 619–623, 650; H.C., SCE cols. 139–149, 259–345 (rental); H.C. Vol. 138, cols. 128, 146–173; H.L. Vol. 501, cols. 217–224.
Section 19(1)	H.C., SCE cols. 150–162 ("in public").
Section 19(2)	H.L. Vol. 490, cols. 1205, 1206.
Section 21	H.C., SCE cols. 162–164 (sampling).
Section 21(3)(a)(iii)	H.L. Vol. 490, cols. 1206, 1208.
Section 22	H.L. Vol. 490, cols. 1208, 1209 ("export").
Sections 22, 23, 24	H.L. Vol. 490, cols. 1212–1214; H.L. Vol. 493, cols. 1129–1132 ("reason to believe", etc.).
Section 23(a)	H.L. Vol. 490, cols. 1214–1216; H.L. Vol. 493, cols. 1132–1133.

Section 24(1)	H.L. Vol. 490, cols. 1216, 1217. ("Specifically designed or adapted":) H.L. Vol. 490, cols. 1216, 1217; H.L. Vol. 493, cols. 1133–1135.
Section 24(1)(c)	H.L. Vol. 493, cols. 1135–1137.
Section 24(2)	H.L. Vol. 490, cols. 1209–1211; H.C., SCE cols. 165, 166; H.C. Vol. 138, col. 129.
Section 25	H.L. Vol. 490, cols. 1218–1221.
Section 25(1)	H.L. Vol. 490, col. 1218; H.L. Vol. 493, cols. 1140–1144; H.L. Vol. 495, col. 625 (grounds for belief).
Section 26	H.L. Vol. 490, cols. 1221, 1222.
Section 26(2)(b)	H.L. Vol. 493, cols. 1144, 1145.
Section 27(3)(b)	H.L. Vol. 490, cols. 1222, 1223; H.C., SCE cols. 169–174.
Section 27(5)	H.L. Vol. 490, cols. 1223–1227; H.L. Vol. 493, cols. 1145, 1146; H.C., SCE cols. 169–174.
Section 27(6)	H.L. Vol. 495, cols. 626, 627; H.C., SCE cols. 174–177; H.L. Vol. 501, cols. 225–227.
Section 28	H.L. Vol. 491, cols. 72–75; H.L. Vol. 501, cols. 227–232.
Section 28(1)	H.L. Vol. 493, cols. 1146–1152; H.L. Vol. 495, cols. 673, 674; H.C., SCE cols. 177–180; H.L. Vol. 501, cols. 227–232.
Section 29	H.L. Vol. 491, cols. 85–111; H.L. Vol. 493, cols. 1153–1162; H.L. Vol. 495, cols. 627, 628; H.C., SCE cols. 180–204; H.C. Vol. 138, cols. 129–136.
Section 29(3)	H.C., SCE cols. 197–199; H.C. Vol. 138, cols. 137–139; H.L. Vol. 501, cols. 232–236.
Section 30(2)	H.L. Vol. 491, cols. 111–115;.C., SCE cols. 205–217; H.C. Vol. 138, cols. 139–140; H.L. Vol. 501, cols. 236, 237.
Section 30(3)	H.L. Vol. 491, cols. 115, 116.
Section 31(1)	H.L. Vol. 491, cols. 120–124.

Section 31(3)	H.C., SCE cols. 217–220; H.L. Vol. 501, cols. 237, 238.
Section 32(2)	H.L. Vol. 491, cols. 124–127; H.L. Vol. 493, cols. 1164–1166.
Section 32(4)	H.C., SCE cols. 220, 221; H.L. Vol. 501, cols. 238, 239.
Section 32(5)	H.C Vol. 138, cols. 140, 141.
Section 33	H.L. Vol. 491, cols. 128–136; H.C., SCE cols. 221, 222; H.L. Vol. 501, cols. 239, 240.
Section 33(2)	H.L. Vol. 491, cols. 135–136.
Section 33(4)	H.L. Vol. 493, col. 1166.
Section 34(1),(2)	H.L. Vol. 493, cols. 1166–1168.
Section 34(2)	H.C., SCE cols. 222, 223.
Section 34	H.L. Vol. 491, cols. 148–151.
Section 35	H.C., SCE cols. 224, 225.
Section 36(2)	H.L. Vol. 491, cols. 151–159; H.L. Vol. 493, cols. 1169–1172.
Section 36(4)	H.L. Vol. 491, cols. 159–166.
Section 37(2)	H.L. Vol. 493, cols. 1171–1173.
Section 38	H.L. Vol. 491, col. 167–177; H.L. Vol. 495, cols. 635–637.
Section 39	H.L. Vol. 491, cols. 177–180; H.L. Vol. 495, cols. 637–640; H.C., SCE cols. 226–229.
Section 40	H.L. Vol. 491, cols. 180, 181; H.C., SCE cols. 229–231.
Section 42	H.C., SCE cols. 231, 232; H.L. Vol. 501, cols. 240, 241.
Section 43	H.C., SCE cols. 232, 233.
Section 45	H.L. Vol. 491, cols. 181–183.

Section 45(2)   H.L. Vol. 493, cols. 1173–1176.

Section 46(4)   H.L. Vol. 493, cols. 1176, 1177; H.L. Vol. 495, cols. 640, 641.

Section 47   H.C., SCE col. 234; H.L. Vol. 501, cols. 241, 242.

Section 48(2)   H.L. Vol. 493, cols. 1177, 1178; H.L. Vol. 495, cols. 641–643.

Section 50   H.L. Vol. 495, col. 643; H.C. Vol. 138, col. 142; H.L. Vol. 501, cols. 242–245.

Section 51   H.L. Vol. 490, cols. 1174–1176, 1184, 1185; H.L. Vol. 491, cols. 183–188; H.L. Vol. 493, cols. 1178–1180; H.L. Vol. 495, cols. 618, 619, 643–646; H.C., SCE cols. 237–249.

Section 52   H.L. Vol. 491, cols. 188, 189.

Section 52(6)   H.C., SCE cols. 249, 250; H.L. Vol. 501, cols. 245, 246.

Section 53   H.C., SCE col. 251.

Section 54   H.L. Vol. 493, cols. 1180, 1181; H.L. Vol. 495, col. 646.

Section 55   H.L. Vol. 493, cols. 1181, 1182.

Section 56   H.L. Vol. 495, cols. 647–648; H.C., SCE cols. 251–256; H.L. Vol. 501, cols. 208–214; 249.

Section 57   H.L. Vol. 493, col. 1182; H.C., SCE cols. 256, 257; H.L. Vol. 501, cols. 206–208.

Section 58   H.L. Vol. 491, cols. 116–120; H.L. Vol. 493, cols. 1060–1063; H.L. Vol. 495, cols. 648, 649; H.C., SCE cols. 25–33; H.C., SCE cols. 484, 485; H.L. Vol. 501, cols. 197–200.

Section 59   H.L. Vol. 491, cols. 189, 190; H.C., SCE cols. 257–259; H.C. Vol. 138, cols. 142–143; H.L. Vol. 501, cols. 197–200.

Section 60	H.L. Vol. 491, cols. 105–111; H.L. Vol. 495, cols. 628–630; H.C. Vol. 138, cols. 143–145; H.L. Vol. 501, cols. 251–252. (See also s.29).
Section 61	H.C. Vol. 138, cols. 104–112; H.L. Vol. 501, cols. 252–254.
Section 62	H.L. Vol. 491, col. 190; H.L. Vol. 493, cols. 1182–1184; H.C. Vol. 138, cols. 145, 146.
Section 63	H.L. Vol. 493, cols. 1184–1186; H.L. Vol. 495, cols. 626, 627; H.C. Vol. 138, col. 141.
Section 64	H.L. Vol. 491, cols. 190–192; H.L. Vol. 493, cols. 1186, 1187.
Section 66	H.L. Vol. 495, cols. 650, 651; H.C., SCE cols. 259–345; H.C. Vol. 138, cols. 146–173; H.L. Vol. 501, cols. 214–224.
Section 66(6)	H.L. Vol. 495, cols. 650.
Section 67	H.L. Vol. 493, cols. 1188, 1189; H.C., SCE cols. 345, 346.
Section 68	H.L. Vol. 495, cols. 654, 655; H.C., SCE cols. 346–348; H.L. Vol. 501, cols. 242–245.
Section 69	H.L. Vol. 495, cols. 655, 656.
Section 70	H.C., SCE cols. 348, 349, 470–482; H.C. Vol. 138, cols. 72–78; H.L. Vol. 501, cols. 255–270.
Section 72	H.L. Vol. 491, cols. 340–343; H.L. Vol. 493, cols. 1190–1192; H.C., SCE cols. 349–353.
Section 72(2)(b)	H.L. Vol. 493, col. 1192.
Section 73	H.L. Vol. 491, cols. 343–345; H.C., SCE cols. 353, 354.
Section 74	H.L. Vol. 491, cols. 345, 346; H.C., SCE cols. 354, 355; H.L. Vol. 501, cols. 271, 272; H.C. Vol. 140, cols. 271–272.
Section 75	H.C., SCE cols. 355, 356.

Section 76	H.L. Vol. 491, cols. 127, 128.
Section 77	H.L. Vol. 491, cols. 346–361; H.C., SCE cols. 357–367.
Section 77(4)(c),(5)	H.L. Vol. 493, cols. 1298–1300.
Section 77(8)	H.L. Vol. 493, col. 1300; H.L. Vol. 501, cols. 272, 273.
Section 78	H.L. Vol. 491, cols. 361–366; H.L. Vol. 493, cols. 1300–1303; H.C., SCE cols. 367, 368; H.C. Vol. 138, cols. 174, 175.
Section 79	H.L. Vol. 491, cols. 366, 367, 375–388; H.L. Vol. 493, cols. 1326–1329; H.L. Vol. 495, cols. 657–661; H.C., SCE cols. 368–386; H.C. Vol. 138, cols. 175–182.
Section 79(2)	H.L. Vol. 493, col. 1305.
Section 79(3)	H.L. Vol. 491, cols. 375–384; H.L. Vol. 493, cols. 1305–1314.
Section 79(4)	H.L. Vol. 491, cols. 385, 386; H.L. Vol. 501, col. 273.
Section 79(4),(5)	H.L. Vol. 495, cols. 657–660.
Section 79(4)(e)	H.L. Vol. 501, col. 273.
Section 79(4)(h)	H.L. Vol. 501, cols. 206–208.
Section 80	H.L. Vol. 491, cols. 387–391; H.C., SCE cols. 386–389; H.C. Vol. 138, cols. 182–184.
Section 80(2)(b)	H.L. Vol. 493, cols. 1329–1331; H.L. Vol. 495, cols. 661, 662.
Section 80(7)	H.L. Vol. 491, cols. 389–391.
Section 81	H.L. Vol. 491, cols. 391–394; H.C., SCE col. 389.
Section 81(6)	H.L. Vol. 493, cols. 1329–1331; H.L. Vol. 495, col. 664; H.L. Vol. 501, cols. 242–245.
Section 82	H.L. Vol. 493, cols. 1332, 1333; H.L. Vol. 495, cols. 662, 663.
Section 85	H.L. Vol. 495, cols. 607–610.

Section 87	H.L. Vol. 491, cols. 394–398; H.L. Vol. 493, cols. 1334–1342; H.C., SCE cols. 390, 391.
Section 88	H.L. Vol. 495, cols. 666, 667.
Section 90(2)	H.L. Vol. 491, cols. 398–401; H.L. Vol. 493, cols. 1342, 1343; H.L. Vol. 495, cols. 667, 668; H.C., SCE col. 392; H.L. Vol. 501, col. 275.
Section 95	H.L. Vol. 491, cols. 401–404; H.L. Vol. 493, cols. 1343–1345; H.L. Vol. 495, col. 666.
Section 95(4)	H.L. Vol. 501, cols. 276, 277.
Section 96	H.L. Vol. 491, cols. 404–406; H.C., SCE cols. 395, 396.
Section 97	H.L. Vol. 491, cols. 407, 408.
Section 97(1)	H.L. Vol. 491, cols. 406–407; H.L. Vol. 493, cols. 1345–1347.
Section 97(2)	H.C., SCE cols. 396–399.
Section 98	H.L. Vol. 501, cols. 277–283.
Section 98(1)	H.C., SCE cols. 486–488.
Section 99	H.L. Vol. 491, cols. 408–410; H.L. Vol. 493, cols. 1347–1350; H.C., SCE cols. 399–403; H.L. Vol. 501, cols. 246–249.
Section 100	H.L. Vol. 491, cols. 410–414; H.L. Vol. 493, cols. 1359–1363; H.L. Vol. 495, col. 669; H.C., SCE cols. 403–407; H.L. Vol. 501, cols. 246–249.
Section 101	H.C., SCE cols. 407–411.
Section 102	H.L. Vol. 491, cols. 414, 415; H.L. Vol. 501, cols. 284, 285.
Section 103	H.L. Vol. 491, cols. 415–417; H.L. Vol. 493, cols. 1363–1365.
Section 103(2)	H.L. Vol. 491, cols. 417, 418.
Section 104	H.L. Vol. 491, cols. 418–420; H.L. Vol. 493, cols. 1365–1368; H.L. Vol. 495, cols. 670, 671.

Section 104–106	H.C., SCE cols. 490–500.
Section 105	H.C. Vol. 138, cols. 186–189; H.L. Vol. 501, cols. 286, 287.
Section 107(1)(c)	H.L. Vol. 491, cols. 420, 421.
Section 107(5)	H.L. Vol. 491, cols. 421–423.
Section 107(6)	H.L. Vol. 491, cols. 423, 424.
Section 108	H.L. Vol. 491, cols. 424, 425; H.L. Vol. 501, cols. 246–249.
Section 110	H.L. Vol. 491, col. 425; H.L. Vol. 493, cols. 1369, 1370.
Section 111	H.L. Vol. 491, cols. 425, 426; H.L. Vol. 493, cols. 1370–1373; H.L. Vol. 495, cols. 671–673; H.C., SCE cols., 411–415.
Section 113	H.C., SCE col. 416.
Section 114	H.L. Vol. 501, cols. 246–248; H.C. Vol. 140, cols. 272, 273.
Section 116	H.L. Vol. 491, cols. 486–489; H.L. Vol. 493, cols. 1373, 1374; H.L. Vol. 495, cols. 673–675; H.C., SCE cols. 417–426.
Section 117	H.L. Vol. 491, col. 489; H.C., SCE cols. 426–428; H.C. Vol. 140, cols. 273, 274.
Section 118	H.L. Vol. 491, cols. 489–492; H.L. Vol. 495, cols. 675, 676; H.C. Vol. 138, cols. 190, 191.
Section 119	H.L. Vol. 491, col. 492.
Section 120	H.L. Vol. 491, col. 493.
Section 121	H.L. Vol. 491, cols. 494, 495; H.L. Vol. 493, col. 1375.
Section 122	H.L. Vol. 491, cols. 496, 497.

Section 123(3)   H.L. Vol. 491, cols. 497, 498; H.L. Vol. 501, cols. 291–294.

Section 124   H.L. Vol. 491, cols. 499, 500.

Section 125   H.L. Vol. 493, cols. 1376–1378.

Section 126   H.C., SCE cols. 428–431; H.L. Vol. 501, cols. 298–302.

Section 127   H.L. Vol. 501, cols. 294–298.

Section 128   H.L. Vol. 493, col. 1378.

Section 129   H.L. Vol. 491, cols. 504–512; H.L. Vol. 493, cols. 1378, 1379; H.C., SCE cols. 431–435; H.L. Vol. 501, col. 304.

Section 130   H.L. Vol. 491, cols. 520–522.

Section 131   H.L. Vol. 491, cols. 522–524.

Section 134   H.L. Vol. 491, cols. 524–527.

Section 135   H.L. Vol. 491, cols. 527, 528.

Sections 135A–G   H.C., SCE cols. 444–456; H.C. Vol. 164, col. 49; H.C., SCF cols. 1454–1464; Vol. 172, cols. 345, 346; H.L. Vol. 521, cols. 1657–1695; Vol. 522, cols. 839–848, 1188; H.C. Vol. 178, col. 612.

Section 136   H.L. Vol. 491, cols. 528–531; H.L. Vol. 493, col. 1379.

Section 138   H.C., SCE cols. 435, 436.

Section 139   H.L. Vol. 501, cols. 305, 306.

Section 140   H.L. Vol. 491, cols. 531–533.

Section 141   H.L. Vol. 491, cols. 533, 534; H.L. Vol. 493, cols. 1379–1381.

Section 143(1)(b)   H.C., SCE cols. 436, 437.

Section 143	H.L. Vol. 491, cols. 534, 535.
Section 143(2)(a)	H.L. Vol. 501, cols. 306, 307.
Section 144	H.C., SCE cols. 136–139; H.C., SCE cols. 485–488.
Section 144(3)	H.C. Vol. 138, col. 194.
Section 145	H.L. Vol. 491, cols. 536, 537; H.L. Vol. 493, cols. 1383, 1384.
Section 145(2)	H.C., SCE cols. 437–441.
Section 146	H.L. Vol. 491, cols. 537, 538.
Section 149,150, 152	H.L. Vol. 501, cols. 308–310.
Section 148(2)	H.L. Vol. 493, col. 1385.
Section 150	H.C., SCE col. 441.
Section 151(1)	H.C. Vol. 138, cols. 195–197.
Section 152	H.L. Vol. 491, cols. 538–542; H.C., SCE cols. 441, 442.
Section 152	H.C., SCE cols. 441, 442.
Section 153(3)	H.L. Vol. 491, col. 542.
Section 154(1)	H.L. Vol. 491, cols. 543, 544.
Section 155	H.L. Vol. 491, cols. 544–547; H.C., SCE col. 444–456.
Section 157	H.C. Vol. 138, cols. 198, 199.
Section 157(5)	H.C., SCE cols. 456–458.
Section 160(1)	H.L. Vol. 495, col. 677.
Sections 161, 162	H.L. Vol. 491, cols. 549–553; H.L. Vol. 493, cols. 1387–1398; H.C., SCE cols. 458–461; H.L. Vol. 501, cols. 312, 313.

Section 163	H.L. Vol. 491, cols. 553–562; H.L. Vol. 493, cols. 1389–1396; H.L. Vol. 495, cols. 677, 678; H.L. Vol. 501, cols. 193–197.
Section 163, 165	H.C., SCE cols. 91–107.
Section 164	H.C. Vol. 138, col. 94; H.L. Vol. 501, cols. 193–197.
Section 165	H.L. Vol. 501, cols. 193–197.
Section 168	H.L. Vol. 491, cols. 562, 563; H.L. Vol. 493, col. 1396.
Section 169	H.C., SCE cols. 461–463.
Section 171(1)(e)	H.L. Vol. 491, cols. 563–566.
Section 171(3)	H.L. Vol. 490, cols. 1174–1176 (spare parts exception). H.L. Vol. 491, cols. 75–78; H.L. Vol. 493, cols. 1162–1164; H.L. Vol. 495, cols. 630–635 (public interest defence).
Section 172(2)	H.L. Vol. 491, cols. 568–570.
Section 172(3)	H.L. Vol. 491, cols. 567, 568; H.L. Vol. 501, cols. 315, 316.
Section 174	H.L. Vol. 493, cols. 1396, 1397.
Section 175	H.L. Vol. 491, cols. 570, 571; H.L. Vol. 493, cols. 1397, 1398; H.C. Vol. 138, cols. 199, 200.
Section 176	H.L. Vol. 493, col. 1399.
Section 178	H.L. Vol. 491, cols. 571, 572; H.C., SCE col. 464; H.L. Vol. 501, cols. 208–214 ("electronic"); H.C., SCE col. 465 ("writing"); H.L. Vol. 501, col. 316 ("computer generated", "judicial proceedings").
Section 180	H.C., SCE cols. 503, 504.
Section 182(1)	H.L. Vol. 491, cols. 869–882; H.L. Vol. 493, cols. 1402–1404.

Section 183	H.L. Vol. 491, cols. 882–885; H.L. Vol. 495, col. 679–680.
Section 184(1)	H.L. Vol. 493, col. 1405.
Section 184(2)	H.L. Vol. 491, cols. 885, 886.
Section 185	H.L. Vol. 491, cols. 886, 887.
Section 187	H.L. Vol. 491, cols. 887–889; H.L. Vol. 495, cols. 680, 681; H.C., SCE cols. 504, 505.
Section 189	H.L. Vol. 501, cols. 318, 319.
Section 190	H.C., SCE cols. 510–514; H.L. Vol. 501, cols. 320–322.
Section 191	H.L. Vol. 491, cols. 890, 891.
Section 192	H.L. Vol. 493, cols. 1406, 1407; H.C., SCE col 506.
Section 193	H.L. Vol. 491, cols. 891, 892.
Section 195	H.L. Vol. 491, cols. 892–895.
Section 197	H.L. Vol. 491, col. 900, 901; H.L. Vol. 501, cols. 324, 325.
Section 198	H.C., SCE cols. 506, 507.
Section 198(1)	H.L. Vol. 491, cols. 895, 896.
Section 198(3)	H.L. Vol. 491, cols. 896, 897.
Section 199	H.L. Vol. 491, col. 897.
Section 201(1)	H.L. Vol. 491, cols. 897, 898.
Section 206	H.L. Vol. 491, col. 898.
Section 208	H.L. Vol. 493, cols. 1408, 1409.
Section 209, 210	H.L. Vol. 491, cols. 899, 900.

Section 210	H.L. Vol. 501, cols. 312, 313.
Section 211	H.L. Vol. 495, col. 697.
Section 213	H.L. Vol. 491, cols. 1088–1115; H.L. Vol. 494, cols. 104–111; H.L. Vol. 495, cols. 697–700; H.C., SCE cols. 519–577; H.C. Vol. 138, cols. 36–63; H.L. Vol. 501, cols. 328–332.
Section 213(4)	H.L. Vol. 494, cols. 111, 112; H.C. Vol. 138, cols. 63–72.
Section 215(2)	H.L. Vol. 491, cols. 1115–1118; H.L. Vol. 494, cols. 112–116; H.C., SCE cols. 577–582.
Section 216	H.L. Vol. 491, cols. 1118–1126; H.L. Vol. 494, cols. 116–121; H.L. Vol. 495, cols. 700–702; H.C., SCE cols. 582–590.
Section 217	H.L. Vol. 491, cols. 1127–1129; H.L. Vol. 494, cols. 121, 122.
Section 220(4)	H.L. Vol. 494, cols. 122, 123.
Section 223	H.L. Vol. 491, cols. 1129, 1130.
Section 226	H.L. Vol. 491, cols. 1131–1134; H.L. Vol. 494, cols. 123–127; H.L. Vol. 495, cols. 702–704; H.C., SCE col. 591, 592.
Section 228	H.L. Vol. 494, cols. 127–130.
Section 236	H.L. Vol. 491, cols. 1135–1137.
Section 237	H.L. Vol. 491, cols. 1138–1141; H.L. Vol. 494, cols. 133–135; H.C., SCE cols. 593–560.
Section 238	H.L. Vol. 491, cols. 1153–1154.
Section 239	H.L. Vol. 491, cols. 1154–1157; H.L. Vol. 494, cols. 135, 136.
Sections 240, 243	H.L. Vol. 491, cols. 1157–1161; H.L. Vol. 494, cols. 136–140; H.L. Vol. 495, cols. 706–710; H.C., SCE cols. 600–609; H.C. Vol. 138, cols. 85–93.

Section 240(3)(a)	H.C. Vol. 138, col. 87.
Section 243	H.C. Vol. 138, cols. 86–93; H.L. Vol. 501, cols. 335, 336.
Section 246	H.L. Vol. 494, cols. 140, 141; H.C., SCE cols. 609–611.
Section 247	H.C., SCE cols. 611, 612.
Section 248	H.C., SCE cols. 612–614.
Section 250	H.C., SCE col. 614; H.L. Vol. 501, cols. 337, 338.
Section 252	H.L. Vol. 495, col. 710.
Section 253	H.L. Vol. 501, col. 338.
Section 253(3)	H.L. Vol. 491, col. 1162; H.L. Vol. 494, cols. 142, 143.
Section 255	H.C., SCE cols. 615, 616.
Section 256	H.C., SCE cols. 616, 617.
Section 257	H.C., SCE cols. 617, 618.
Section 296	H.L. Vol. 501, cols. 350, 351.
Sections 297A, 299(2), (5)	H.L. Vol. 521, col. 1695; Vol. 522, col. 1188; H.C. Vol. 178, cols. 612–614.
Sections 298, 299	H.L. Vol. 501, cols. 351–353.
Schedule 1	H.L. Vol. 491, cols. 573–589.
Schedule 1, para. 8(2)	H.L. Vol. 501, col. 357.
Schedule 1, para. 10	H.L. Vol. 501, cols. 357, 358.
Schedule 1, para. 14(6)	H.C., SCE col. 466.
Schedule 1, para. 31(2)	H.L. Vol. 493, cols. 1401, 1402.
Schedule 2	H.L. Vol. 501, cols. 318, 319.
Schedule 2, para. 3(1)	H.L. Vol. 491, cols. 902, 903.
Schedule 2, para. 16	H.L. Vol. 491, col. 904.

Appendix I: Hansard References

Broadcasting Act 1990, Section 176, Schedule 17.

> H.C. Vol. 164, col. 49; H.C., SCF cols. 1345–1362, 1364–1384, 1466, 1499–1501; Vol. 172, cols. 346–348; H.L. Vol. 521, cols. 1700–1710; Vol. 522, cols. 850–853; H.C. Vol. 178, cols. 592–594.

The Copyright (Computer Programs) Regulations 1992.

> H.L. Vol. 541, cols. 514–516.

INDEX

EUROPEAN COMMUNITIES—*cont.*
directives
cable retransmission, on, 1–52,
1–56—1–56B, 4–55, 8–118,
H–44—H–61
computer programs, legal
protection of, on, 1–52,
1–54, 2–2, 2–9, 8–19, 8–46,
8–47, 9–4, H–14—H–25
failure to implement, 14–12
proposed, legal protection of
databases, on,
1–58—1–58B, 8–31
rental rights and lending rights,
on, 1–52, 1–55—1–55A,
8–76, 12–12, 23–3A,
H–25—H43
satellite broadcasting, on, 1–52,
1–56—1–56B, 4–55, 8–118,
H–44—H–61
semi-conductor products,
protection of, 1–52
term of protection of copyright,
harmonisation of, on,
1–51G, 1–52,
1–57—1–57B, 4–55, 6–5A,
6–7, 6–16, 6–17, 6–18,
6–19, 6–21, 7–10, 22–61,
23–50, H–62—H–77
topographies of semiconductor
products, legal protection
of, on H–1—H–13
droit d'auteur system, 1–51A
duration of copyright, Directive
on, 6–5A, 7–10, 22–61
European Union, creation of,
1–51, 14–1A
failure to implement directives,
14–12
Follow-up to the Green Paper, 1–51G,
1–58, 1–59B, 1–60
free movement of goods, 1–51C,
14–24, 14–25
associated territories,
originating in, 14–69,
14–70
conflict with, 14–38
originating outside EEC, 14–67
freedom to provide services,
1–51C

EUROPEAN COMMUNITIES—*cont.*
GATT, Uruguay Round, 1–61
Green Paper on the Legal
Protection of Industrial
Design, 20–64A
harmonisation measures, 14–44,
14–46
Green Paper, 1–51D—1–51F,
1–54
need for, 1–51C
home copying of sound and
audiovisual recordings,
1–59A—1–59C
industrial design, Green Paper on
Legal Protection of, 20–64A
internal market
completion of, 1–51C
definition of, 1–51C
law
present state of, 1–52
proposals for future,
1–59—1–59C
UK law, incorporation into
case law, 14–16
Treaty and implementing
measures, 14–15
Maastricht Treaty, 14–1A, 14–23,
14–25, F–1—F–10A
national laws, harmonisation of,
14–44, 14–46
separate legal order, as, 14–3
Treaty on European Union,
14–1A
Treaty of Rome
interpretation of, 14–10
Maastricht Treaty, amendment
by, 14–1A, 14–23, 14–25,
F–1—F–10A
UK law, incorporation into,
14–15

EUROPEAN ECONOMIC AREA (EEA),
1–51, 1–60, 14–70A

EUROPEAN UNION, 1–51, 14–1A

EXECUTION
choses in action, against, 5–6
copyright not taken in, 5–6

EXHAUSTION OF RIGHTS
common origin of rights,
14–93—14–95

462

UNIVERSITY OF WOLVERHAMPTON
LIBRARY

LIBRARY